The journal *Khamsin* is named after a scorching desert
wind that has its source in Upper Egypt and, according to
popular legend, scalds the Middle East for fifty days a
year. It was founded in 1975 by a group of anti-Zionist
Israelis and Arabs united in their socialist vision and their
opposition to economic exploitation, political domination, and social oppression. Independent of all organized
political tendencies, it is a forum for discussion of all the
crucial issues of Middle Eastern politics.

GW00645377

AL SAQI
BOOKS

Khamsin
An Anthology

Al Saqi Books

Distributed by Zed Press

Forbidden Agendas

Intolerance and Defiance in the Middle East

*Selected and Introduced
by Jon Rothschild*

The articles in this anthology were first published
in the journal *Khamsin* 1976 – 83. BM Khamsin, London WC1N 3XX.

This collection first published 1984.
Al Saqi Books, 26 Westbourne Grove, London W2.
© Al Saqi Books, 1984, for the collection.

Filmset in English Times by
Red Lion Setters, London

Printed in Great Britain by
The Thetford Press Ltd
Thetford, Norfolk

ISBN 0 86356 111 X Hbk
ISBN 0 86356 021 0 Paperback

Contents

*Dedicated to
the memory of
ELI LOBEL*

Presentation

In various places around the world, winds have names. There is the mistral in southern France, the sirocco in Italy, the föhn in the Alps, and the Santa Ana in southern California. In each case, legend and folk wisdom cast the wind as harbinger or bearer of misfortune, as heralding or causing anything from natural disasters to aberrations of human behaviour.

The Middle Eastern equivalent is the *khamsin*, a scorching desert wind that sweeps from Upper Egypt through the eastern Mediterranean. It takes its name from the Arabic word meaning *fifty*, for it is said to blow for fifty days a year, in particular the fifty days between Easter Sunday and Pentecost, a Christian holiday commemorating the day the Holy Spirit is supposed to have descended on the apostles. Of all the world's named winds, the khamsin is perhaps the most evocative of its region, for metaphorically at least, the khamsin has blown relentlessly over the Middle East for decades.

That is why *Khamsin* seemed an apposite title for a journal whose aim was to deal with all the intractable predicaments of the Middle East, from points of view likely to be ill-received by supporters of any of the states, political rulers, or even mass movements of the region. The image may be hackneyed, but one of the reasons for its over-use is its verisimilitude; as long as anyone alive can remember, the countries of this part of the world have been flayed by the destructive gales of religious intolerance, nationalist excess and oppression, economic exploitation, sexual discrimination, colonialism, industrial under-development, brutal civil wars, and debilitating wars between states. The Middle East has been among the most tortured regions of the world in the twentieth century: there is hardly a problem of contemporary society and politics that does not possess a particularly severe form there. Nevertheless, in all the various countries, there have always been people who have challenged the status quo with the vision of a future that, however distant and elusive, nonetheless contains some hope.

The journal *Khamsin* was founded by a small group of such people in Paris, in 1975. The participants were citizens of a number of different countries; they included anti-Zionist Israeli Jews and Arab oppositionists from various states. The originator of the idea for the journal, and its most active editor during the early issues, was Eli Lobel, to whom this volume is dedicated and who died in autumn 1979. (A tribute to him, which appeared in *Khamsin 7*, is reprinted here on pages 13 – 15).

The intention of the founding group was to create a journal which, while committed to the fight for progress and against all species of oppression and exploitation in the Middle East, would avoid alignment with any particular organized political tendency, and would therefore act as a forum for discussion and debate free of the constraints of organizational engagements. Some editors and contributors, of course, have been members of different political groups, but the journal itself has never acted as the mouthpiece of any of them. The members of the editorial group and the editorial collective share a common outlook on certain crucial points, such as their radical socialist outlook, their opposition to nationalism as an ideology, their commitment to the struggle against Zionism, their rejection of foreign domination and of the oppression of women. But there has been—and still is—a pronounced lack of uniformity among the contributors and editors in their views on any number of particular political and ideological issues, small or large.

The first four issues of *Khamsin* were published in French, by Editions François Maspero in Paris. With issue number 5, published in 1978, the journal moved to London and began to be produced in English, primarily so as to reach a larger number of readers in the Middle East itself, and to take advantage of the more widespread use of English among potential contributors, nearly all of whom are from Middle Eastern countries. Since then, each issue has featured a particular theme, on which several of the articles of that issue have been centred. The theme of *Khamsin 5* was Oriental Jewry, of *Khamsin 6* Women in the Arab World, of *Khamsin 7* Communist

Parties of the Middle East, of *Khamsin 8* Politics of Religion in the Middle East. *Khamsin 9* had a continuation of that theme, plus Capitalism in Egypt; the theme of *Khamsin 10*, the latest to be published so far, was Israel and its War in Lebanon. The journal is now published by Ithaca Press, London.

Each issue (normally 128 pages in book format) contains, apart from the articles on the theme, a range of contributions including such items as book reviews, correspondence from the Middle East, debates about conjunctural political questions (such as the strategy and tactics of the Palestinian resistance movement), and essays on historical subjects and contemporary analysis.

The criterion of the present selection of articles has been to choose those dealing with topics the very discussion of which is often proscribed or fettered in the Middle East itself. The choices are also among the least dependent on the particular circumstances that prevailed at the time the pieces were written. To some extent, of course, the division of this book into thematic sections is arbitrary. The nature and practice of the Zionist movement is a repeated theme throughout the collection; the articles dealing with women naturally also treat questions of religion, which also feature prominently in the section on the Oriental Jews in Israel. In fact, one of the hallmarks of *Khamsin* is its idea of the basic interdependence of the region— politically, economically, and socially. Yet it is fair to say that the sections of this anthology accurately reflect both the central concerns of *Khamsin* as a journal and the critical issues of the region.

The preponderant place of the question of Israel and the Palestinians both in this collection and in *Khamsin* generally is a product of the pressures of reality, and not a matter of the preferences of the editorial group. In fact, from the beginning the editors have sought to treat a wide gamut of subjects extending beyond the Arab-Israeli conflict. Some indication of how well they have succeeded may be afforded by a list of some of the articles that were not selected here. They include pieces on the limits of industrialization in the Arab world (focusing on the case of Iraq); the reasons for the decline of Egyptian Jewry; the development of the class struggle in Egypt; the question of national formation in the Arab world, confronting the theories of Samir Amin; the history of the Communist Parties of Lebanon, Palestine, and Jordan and the positions of Arab Communist Parties on the Palestine question in the forties; the insurgent republic in Gilan province in northern Iran in June 1921; the economic and political development of the Arab ruling classes in the 1970s; the role of the Shi'i clergy in modern Iranian politics; the rise of capitalism in Egypt and the character of the Egyptian social formation; the place of tragic heroes and victims in Zionist ideology and Israeli literature.

Since the articles in this collection are arranged by theme, they may be read in any order desired. Within each section, the articles are generally, though not rigidly, presented in chronological order of their appearance in *Khamsin*. The brief introductions to each section are intended merely to set a context for the articles, and in some cases to explain the conditions in which they were written. Authors are also identified in these introductory paragraphs.

No substantive editorial changes have been made, only the correction of a few minor errors, the addition of a number of explanatory remarks and references, and some small stylistic alterations. Otherwise, the articles are printed here as they were first published. It should be superfluous to add that the various authors are responsible only for their own articles, and not for the collection as a whole or for the introductions to their pieces.

Eli Lobel

FROM KHAMSIN 7

Khamsin is bereaved. Eli Lobel, editor and founder of our journal, died tragically on Thursday, 4 October 1979.

The life story of this outstanding revolutionary socialist and great internationalist is, in more than one way, the story of a whole generation.

Born in Berlin in 1926 to a family of Polish-Jewish refugees, Eli spent his early childhood in the Germany of the late Weimar Republic and the first years of Nazi power. Then the family was forced to flee back to Poland. But Poland, too, was unsafe, and in 1939, just in the nick of time, the family managed to leave for Palestine. There Eli soon joined the left Zionist youth movement Hashomer Hatza'ir, and in 1946 was one of the founders of kibbutz Nirim in the northern Negev.

A few years later, he went to Paris as a journalist for the daily paper *'Al-Hamishmar*, organ of Mapam, the political party of Hashomer Hatza'ir. There, in Paris, he studied statistics and economics; one of his teachers was the socialist economist Charles Bettelheim. There too the seeds of his political radicalization germinated.

Hashomer Hatza'ir—like all left Zionist movements—was a living contradiction: it claimed to combine Zionism with Marxism. Throughout the history of that movement there have always been individuals and small groups who took Marxism more seriously than the left Zionist leaders intended and who resolved the contradiction by jettisoning Zionism. Just as, in the years immediately after the Russian revolution, dissidents from the older left Zionist Po'alei Zion founded the Palestinian Communist Party and helped to spread Marxism in the Arab East, so from the 1930s onwards the revolutionary Marxist movement—in Europe and Latin America as well as in Palestine and later in Israel – drew to itself a continual if small stream of dissidents from Hashomer Hatza'ir. (One of the most notable figures among them was Abram Leon, author of the brilliant Marxist analysis of the Jewish question, who was murdered by the Nazis in 1944.)

Back in Israel, Eli joined the left opposition inside Mapam. In 1953 the opposition was expelled and formed the Socialist Left Party, which developed in an anti-Zionist direction. Like other adherents of this new party, Eli was also expelled from his kibbutz, Nirim.

At the end of 1954 the Socialist Left Party joined the Israeli Communist Party. Eli would most probably have done the same, but by that time he had left Israel again: at the invitation of Charles Bettelheim he joined a team of economists in India (including Bettelheim himself and Joan Robinson) who were working on that country's problems of under-development. From then on, Eli was passionately involved in the economic and social problems of the Third World and eventually became an authority on the economics of colonialism and under-development.

Returning to Paris, he devoted much of his energy to supporting the Algerian revolution. Because of this activity, he had to leave France, and he joined a team of economic advisers in Mali, which, under Modibo Keita, was then one of the more progressive states of black Africa. In Mali, Eli fulfilled tasks of great responsibility and represented that country at the World Bank.

During all this time, he kept up his interest in Israeli politics and established contacts with the Socialist Organization in Israel (Matzpen), which had been formed in 1962.

After a brief stay back in France, Eli left for Cuba as a member of a team of left-wing economic experts. Not long after his return from Cuba, the Paris events of May 1968 broke out. Eli was passionately involved in these struggles, which marked the happiest period of his life. At the same time, as a member of Matzpen, he was intensely active in France (as well as in other countries) against Zionism and in support of the rights of the Palestinian people. It is in large measure due to his internationalist activity as a speaker, journalist, and writer that the revolutionary left in France and in many other countries has been able to understand the true nature of Zionism and adopt a revolutionary socialist attitude towards the problems of the Middle East.

Eli was profoundly committed to the struggle against Zionism. But he was not a simplistic anti-Zionist: he did not reject Zionism merely to exchange it for support to some other nationalism, no matter how 'progressive', but in order to transcend all nationalism in the fight for a united socialist Middle East and a socialist world. In particular, while being fully committed to supporting the struggle of the Palestinian people against social and national oppression and for emancipation and self-determination, he was highly critical of, and deeply grieved by, recent regressive developments within the Palestinian movement.

His great and fruitful political activity is widely known to the revolutionary left in many countries. But his personal friends and close comrades also knew his purity of heart, his noble simplicity. Socialism for him was not a mere abstraction or an alienated 'purely political' activity. It was a deeply felt moral commitment of a man who hated all privilege and oppression and identified with the deprived and oppressed.

With his death, the socialist movement in the Middle East and elsewhere has lost an outstanding torch-bearer, and we who knew him have lost a dear and beloved comrade. His memory will illuminate our struggle for the ideals in which he believed.

1

Israel's Oriental Subjects

Not the smallest of the many problems that have afflicted Zionism from its origins as a modern political movement has been the divergence between its conception of world Jewry on the one hand and the reality of the living conditions and cultural identities of the world's Jews on the other. The early theorists of Zionism held—and their intellectual progeny continue to maintain – that all the Jews of the world constitute a single 'nation', or 'people', whose members lived in 'abnormal' conditions exactly because of their geographical dispersal. It was this abnormality, they argued, epitomized in the Jews' lack of a state of their own, that made them unable to defend themselves against anti-Semitism, which was seen as an eternal phenomenon independent of particular social and historical circumstances.

For many decades, Zionism was but one trend among various forms of Jewish nationalism that had arisen in eastern Europe, alongside myriad other nationalisms. As a species of nationalism, it exhibited the exclusivist features that mark any such ideology. But since its putative constituency was scattered in many different countries, and since the Zionist movement claimed to represent *all* the Jews of the world and not merely those who lived in the few countries in which the movement existed as an organized force, Zionist ideology was impelled to place special emphasis on the alleged unity of the 'nation'—even more than nationalism commonly does. The task the Zionist movement had set itself was not merely to defend (or even to champion or aggrandize) a particular existing nation, but to convince potential members of the supposed nation that it actually existed. Later, as the colonization of Palestine began in earnest, disparate elements had to be forged into a genuine nation that would stand as the temporal embodiment of the mythical one.

This emphasis on 'national' unity, already unusually intense, was further aggravated by historical circumstance: the land on which the 'normalized' nation was to establish its state was inhabited by another people, who therefore had to be subdued or displaced if the Zionist project were to have any chance of successful application. Insistence on Jewish unity was therefore complemented by mounting hostility to the Palestinian Arabs, who were seen at best as mere impediments to Jewish freedom and at worst as agents of Jewish destruction.

These components of Zionist ideology, inherent in the very conception of the project of establishing a Jewish state in Palestine, were distilled into increasing purity in the alembic of Middle Eastern politics. By the end of the First World War, once British rule in Palestine was imposed, the Zionists needed the approval and support of Western powers. At the same time, the Arabs of the Middle East had launched a nationalist movement of their own, which had raised the demand for political independence—a goal which, if achieved in Palestine, would abort the Zionist mission. Finally, the way the early Zionist settlers went about establishing what would later become the socio-economic foundations of the state of Israel was to defend and expand an exclusively Jewish economy implanted within Palestinian society, for the Jewish state required Jewish workers, Jewish peasants, Jewish factory owners, Jewish policemen, and even, as one poet of the twenties once put it, Jewish thieves and Jewish prostitutes. Add to this the fact that Zionism was in origin a European political movement imbued with the culture and political attitudes that prevailed in Europe at the time, among which were a general contempt for 'the Orient' and a racist conviction that non-European peoples were congenitally inferior.

The state of Israel was thus founded by a movement whose members, leaders, culture, and ideology were European, a movement that preached Jewish unity and exclusivism and stood in the forefront of a political and military struggle against a non-European people, the Palestinian Arabs.

But when that state declared its independence in 1948, acting in the name of all the world's Jews, the vast majority of its potential citizens stayed put. Even with the influx of tens of thousands of survivors of Nazism, who were denied any choice of destination, the Jewish population of the new country remained dangerously small. The 1950s, however, saw a massive immigration of Jews from Arab countries, in part because of the anti-Jewish outbursts in these countries inflamed by the 1948 war, but also as a result of active efforts by a Zionist leadership hungry for more Israelis. A number of Arab states were nearly emptied of their Jewish inhabitants. Thus it was that nearly half the Jewish population of Israel came to be composed of 'Oriental Jews'.

Since these people were Jews, they were counted among the Jewish nation, and therefore shared in the privileged status all Jews in Palestine enjoy at the expense of the indigenous Arabs. On the other hand, they were also seen as part of the despised Orient: many of them spoke Arabic, were shaped by Arab culture, looked like Arabs, and shared many of the social attitudes and modes of behaviour of the countries in which they had grown up. Although members of the privileged nation, they were brought—in many cases lured—to Palestine to perform the most unenviable tasks, so that while they did benefit from the advantages Zionism conferred upon Jews, they also suffered from the racism endemic to Zionism. The state of Israel was built in struggle against the Orient; but once it had been built, about half its (Jewish) people were offspring of that same Orient. Neither the Zionist movement nor the state of Israel has ever been able to resolve that contradiction.

The Oriental Jewish population of Israel has internalized its position as second-class members of the dominant group in a kind of political split personality. There was a time, in the late sixties and early seventies, when many expected that the Oriental Jews would be a fount of radicalization in Israel, challenging the state apparatus and moving eventually to leftist, perhaps even anti-Zionist, positions. And there were some hesitant steps in this sense. By the late seventies, however, the Oriental Jews had become the largest component of the electoral base of Menachem Begin's Likud government, and today they are widely seen as the mainstay of the right in Israeli politics.

The place of the Oriental Jews in Israel has been treated in various articles published in *Khamsin*. Four of them are reprinted here. In 'Zionism and Its Oriental Subjects' (*Khamsin 5*), Raphael Shapiro, an independent left-wing Israeli intellectual, examines the ideological contradictions that have shaped Zionism's conception of the Oriental Jews. He describes the many different Jewish communities in Israel and recounts both the various shifts in policy by the Zionist leadership before the foundation of the Israeli state and the subsequent manipulation of the Oriental Jews.

In 'Oriental Jews in Israel: Collective Schizophrenia' (*Khamsin 5*), A. Hoder, a leading Israeli civil-rights activist writing under a pseudonym, offers a riveting portrait, based on a conversation overheard in a public-service taxi travelling between Tel Aviv and Jerusalem, of the psychological contortions to which many of Israel's Oriental Jews fall victim. This is followed by a description of some of the more subtle forms of racism that permeate Israeli society.

In 'Class Divisions in Israeli Society' and 'Oriental Support for Begin: a Critique of Farjoun', both published in *Khamsin 10*, two Israeli members of the *Khamsin* editorial group, Emmanuel Farjoun and Avishai Ehrlich, the former a professor of mathematics, the latter a sociologist, debate the reasons why so many Oriental Jews have aligned themselves with the right wing. The two authors agree that the phenomenon is grounded in the socio-economic structure of Israeli society, but disagree sharply about its class implications.

The Oriental Jews, of course, are far from the only victimized group in Israel. Indeed, nearly everyone would agree that their place in the Israeli social structure and their political psychology are strongly affected by the even more deplorable conditions of those Palestinian Arabs who live under Israeli rule. The political and military sides of those conditions have been widely treated in the international press. Less attention has been paid to the critical part played by Palestinians in the Israeli economy. 'Palestinian Workers in Israel' (*Khamsin 7*), also by Emmanuel Farjoun, is a thorough statistical survey of the subject. Although this article was written in the late seventies, the qualitative picture it presents has altered little, despite the inevitable quantitative changes. It was originally written in Hebrew, and published in Jerusalem as a pamphlet by the Socialist Organization in Israel (Matzpen), in 1978.

Zionism and Its Oriental Subjects

Raphael Shapiro

Zionism claims to speak in the name of all Jews, but in fact it is a movement that emerged in the Ashkenazi (central and east European) communities, and it has never embraced any other part of world Jewry. Of course, some form of religious longing for 'Zion' as a symbol of messianic apocalypse and of religious pilgrimage has existed in most Jewish communities; but one should not be misled into identifying this spiritual symbolism with the Ashkenazi movement of political Zionism.

European anti-Semitism has tragically imposed on Europe's Jews successive changes in the bases of their existence, mainly by migration or, when possible, by assimilation. In addition to these two spontaneous processes, modern anti-Semitism has generated two organized Jewish reactions: on the one hand the Jewish Bund, a part of revolutionary Social Democracy, which struggled for the autonomy of East European Jews on the basis of their actual language and culture, in the framework of a future socialist Europe; and on the other hand the Zionist movement, which crystallized under the influence of the general drive towards self-determination, headed by the national bourgeoisies of central and eastern Europe. Thus, Zionists regarded their movement as the perfect embodiment of Jewish political self-determination.

The concept of self-determination applies to situations in which a group struggles to achieve an independent political structure that may enable it to express freely its *existing* character. This is a purposely broad definition, which encompasses legitimate as well as dubious forms of national, linguistic, religious, or racial separatism. However, Zionism has no place even in this loose framework (although the Bund does). The Zionist movement had set itself the aim not of expressing Jewish reality but of totally and radically reshaping it.

This is the very opposite of self-determination: it is a form of transcendental self-definition. The elements of an authentic movement for self-determination are replaced in Zionism by archaeological realities of the 'ancestors', as conveyed by religious texts. The Zionists' fascination with archaeological excavations is well known. The Ashkenazi Zionists have always had profound disdain for their European origin. They scorn 'the diaspora mentality'. The vanguard of Zionism, especially before the compromise urged by Berl Katsnelson in the 1930s, wished to transform the nature of the Jewish community down to the last detail: absolute atheism, Hebrew in place of Yiddish, manual labour instead of trade and the liberal professions.

As opposed to this self-repudiation, the realities of Zionist self-reconstruction were very much in the spirit of nineteenth-century national movements in central Europe and the Balkans, where rival historical claims to territory were vehemently exchanged between virtually any two neighbouring nationalities. However, while the silly 'historical' irredentist claims were an appendage to genuine demands for these national movements, the Zionist 'historical' claim was the indispensable core of the whole enterprise.

This basic contradiction, then, between a claim of self-determination and an actual self-repudiation was followed by a transcending archaeological redefinition of self. This has cast its shadow over all aspects of Zionist existence. Its first implication is this: if the basis of your self-determination is not your actual self but some archaeological 'other self', then you also 'self-determine' all other people who happen to bear the same relation as you to that archaeological entity, even though they may be totally alien to you.

Specifically, since the Zionists defined the Jews as a 'nation' on the basis of their assumed common descent, it followed that *all* descendants of the same ancestors were to be included. To be sure, this did not mean that they rushed to invite representatives of the Oriental communities to take part in their frequent congresses—for the obvious reason that they had little in common with them. But the idea was there. And when the need arose, Zionists did not even consider including Palestinians in their national enterprise, but rather chose to manipulate other Jewish communities, some of whom (such as Indian Jews from Cochin and Jews from the Moroccan Atlas mountains) were much more foreign to them than the Palestinians. It should be understood that religion has played only an indirect role in defining the 'Jewish nation'. The religious definition of a Jew is in effect ethnic: a Jew is anyone—even if an atheist—born to a Jewish mother, or a person officially converted to Judaism. The number of conversions to Judaism throughout history is, supposedly, negligible, which is why religion has been used by atheist Zionists as a test of what really mattered: being a descendant of the ancestors. (There was furious Zionist reaction to a recent book by Koestler[1] which asserted that millions of European Jews are descendants of the massively converted Khazar population of medieval southern Russia.)

To sum up, Israel is dominated by its Ashkenazi population primarily because the Zionist state is a creation of the Zionist movement, a purely Ashkenazi enterprise. By now this fact is realized by the great majority of Oriental Jews in Israel. In a recent interview with a foreign television reporter, an Oriental woman said in a very matter-of-fact tone: 'Of course they treat us as second-rate people; after all, it's their state.'

It should be noted that non-Ashkenazi Jews on the fringes of the Ashkenazi world, in Greece, Serbia, and Bulgaria, did take some part in the Zionist movement. An example is David El'azar, chief of the general staff during the 1973 war, who was a Sephardi from Serbia. His father, on the other hand, was not a Zionist, and refused to leave Yugoslavia.

The Fiction of Jewish Unity

The Jewish state embodies the concept of 'Jewish national unity' which, though fictitious, is a necessary postulate of the Zionist movement. Contrary to common belief, there are not just two Jewish communities, Ashkenazi and Sephardi. These large groups may be sub-divided; but more important, they are but two in a much longer list of communities. From a religious point of view, there are five main groups, corresponding to five variants of Jewish liturgy:

1. Arthur Koestler, *The Thirteenth Tribe: The Khazar Empire and Its Heritage*, New York 1976.

German (Ashkenazi), Spanish (Sephardi), Italian ('Roman'), Iraqi (Bavli), and Yemeni. Of these, the first two had their own languages, Yiddish (a Middle Rhine German dialect) and Ladino (a medieval dialect of Castilian). In addition, there are communities that fall outside these five main groups. Among them are the large Moroccan community (speakers of Arabic or Berber); the Aramaic-speaking Kurdish community; the Persian community (whose language is not modern Persian but a medieval Iranian dialect), and the Jews of Cochin in southern India.

The linguistic cohesion of each community is usually only one of several common characteristics developed under the impact of the surrounding culture, though not in unison with it; among others are folk music, dances, plastic arts, tales, humour, dress, cooking, style of family life, and so on.

In addition to these cultural differences, the physical ethnic differences between the various communities are also striking. All communities were affected by periods of intermarriage with the surrounding population. However, some communities are probably the direct result of organized conversion; on historical evidence this is quite likely in the case of the Yemenis (a Jewish kingdom existed in Yemen in the fourth century), the Falashi Jews of Ethiopia (who seem to be converted Amhiras), and the Jews of Cochin. All these are ethnically indistinguishable from their unconverted compatriots.

Once they had settled in Israel, the many differences among the various Jewish communities led to mutual discord, aggravated by a strong clannish spirit within each group. As they had been subjected to some form of discrimination in each host country, Jews developed strong feelings of kinship with their own kind, and fear and suspicion of others. In many cases, this kinship was highly structured and organized; in regions such as Iran and the remains of the Ottoman Empire, where many nationalities coexisted under a despotic state, the structured community and sub-community (clan, *hamoulah*) were a basic form of social organization.

Roughly speaking, the greater the cultural and ethnic differences between two Jewish communities, the more noticeable was their mutual hostility in Israel. However, violent clashes occurred in the 1950s even between various Oriental communities, when these were placed close to each other. This was a great surprise to the Ashkenazim, who would lump all non-Ashkenazi Jews together under the label 'Sephardim' (since the Sephardi community was the only non-Ashkenazi one known to them from Europe). Following several riots, the different communities were settled separately, in ethnically homogeneous geographical units (rural colonies or urban neighbourhoods). The frequently brandished slogans about 'the melting pot' and 'the merging of the nation' had become mere fictions.

Of course, the greatest hostility existed between the Ashkenazim and the rest. The Ashkenazim were the ideologically and economically dominant half of the Jewish population, which manipulated the other half in a spirit of paternalism mixed with contempt. Being frequently called *schwarze* (black) and *frenk* (pejorative for Sephardi) by Ashkenazim, the Orientals retaliated by calling the Ashkenazim *Vusvus* (from the Yiddish word *vus*, meaning 'what'). Violent outbreaks of hostility were usually confined to individual cases, such as an assault on an Ashkenazi official in his office, or on an Ashkenazi foreman in the workshop, since the geographical separation between Ashkenazim and Orientals was usually sufficient to prevent riots. Nevertheless, the few exceptions are significant. For instance, the Moroccan Jews who were setted in the formerly Arab quarter of Wadi Salib in Haifa rioted in 1959 in the Ashkenazi part of the city.

The 'Jewish state' of the 1950s was a state of distinct cultural and ethnic communities. Since then, the organized and coherent communities have disintegrated under the impact of new socio-economic realities, and the Jewish population has gradually moved towards a clearer dichotomy—Ashkenazi versus Oriental. But the earlier situation has helped to create an atmosphere of ethnic hostility and levels of segregation and discrimination which mark Israeli society up to the present time.

The Basic Class Contradiction

The early Zionists were really concerned about only one contradiction: between the largely middle-class composition of the Jews and the need of Zionism, like any national enterprise, for a working class.

For rather complex historical-economic reasons, Jews had been concentrated in non-productive occupations.[2] True, late in the

---

2. Cf. Abram Leon, *The Jewish Question, a Marxist Interpretation*, New York 1970.

nineteenth century, a part of the Jewish population of eastern Europe, mainly in southern Russia and western Poland, underwent a profound process of proletarianization, while another group settled down as farmers.[3] However, this section was still comparatively small (especially in the Zionist centres of eastern Poland, Lithuania, Galicia, and Bessarabia) and gave its political support to the anti-Zionist Bund movement.

A form of charity Zionism (which preceded political Zionism) did actually base itself on the middle-class composition of the Jews. When, in the second half of the nineteenth century, the small and prosperous Jewish communities of western Europe began to worry about the stream of Jewish immigrants from the East, the French Baron Benjamin Edmond de Rothschild ('the charitable') initiated a project to divert this stream to Palestine. He tried to settle East European Jews on lands he had bought, where they were to become farmers employing native agricultural workers, somewhat like the French colons of Algeria. This project failed: ideologically, it had little national attraction, and in individual terms East European Jews found it much more sound and promising to emigrate to the New World or western Europe than to the Ottoman Empire.

While praising the Rothschild project for pioneering the 'Jewish return to the land', the early Zionist activists criticized its inadequacy as a national programme. Their own response to the class contradiction mentioned above was in the way they rejected their identity as European Jews: they tried to transform themselves into manual workers, and, as a central element in their endeavour, completely to reverse and reshape the form of Jewish existence. The early ideologists of 'left Zionism' set as their main task the 'inversion of the Jewish social pyramid': Jews were 'abnormally' concentrated in the higher and non-productive strata of the social spectrum, and the task of Zionism was to create a 'normal' population with a majority of manual workers.

Consequently, the young Zionist immigrants organized themselves into work brigades which engaged in early collective colonization (in eastern Galilee and the Judean plain) as well as in wage labour for Jewish farmers in the older settlements. It was indeed important not only to form new settlements, but also to integrate the existing Jewish colonies into the Zionist project.

3. Trotsky's father was one such farmer.

This movement was dramatized to mythical proportions. A kind of pseudo-Marxism was combined with romantic Tolstoyan mysticism to create the 'Religion of Labour' of A.D. Gordon, which idealized manual labour, especially in agriculture, as a supreme purification of man. The young idealists, mostly of lower-middle-class origin, regarded themselves as martyrs of the new religion.

However, few of these early idealists could stand the hardships of toil and the inhospitable climate. Of the first wave of pioneers around the turn of the century (the second *'aliyah*) about 90 per cent went back to Europe. Those working for Jewish employers could not compete economically with the Arab workers, who were accustomed to the climate and to manual labour, and were being paid derisory wages. The Zionist project seemed doomed.

At this point, the Ashkenazi Zionists discovered that they could manipulate other Jewish communities into becoming workers in the framework of the Zionist enterprise. The Palestine Office of the Zionist movement commissioned Dr J. Thon, one of its specialists, to prepare a report on ways of making Jewish labour more competitive with Arab labour. The report, submitted in October 1908, began by stating that 'it is hardly in need of proof that the question of employing Jewish instead of Arab agricultural workers is one of the most important problems of the colonization of Palestine'.[4] It went on to suggest that 'the human labour force can and must come from two sources:

'1. From the Zionist youth in the diaspora, especially from Russia.

'2. From among the indigent Oriental Jews, who are still on the same cultural level as the [Arab] fellahin.'[5]

The small Jewish communities—both Ashkenazi and Oriental—living in Palestine before the arrival of the Zionist pioneers were regarded by the pioneers as economically and culturally backward. They had to be 'made productive' in the service of Zionism. However, while the Ashkenazi Jews living in Palestine were considered at best fit for urban crafts, 'the Oriental Jews, on the other hand, especially the Yemenis and Persians, have a role to play also in agriculture. Since they are frugal, these Jews can be compared to the Arabs, and from this point of view they can compete with them.

4. Quoted in Alex Bein, *History of Zionist Colonization*, Masada, 4th edn, 1970 (in Hebrew), p. 97.
5. Ibid., p. 98.

True, their productivity would not be greater than that of the Arabs.'[6]

A few thousand Yemeni Jews, motivated not by Zionism but by 'religious-messianic longings', had arrived in Palestine in the 1880s. Here they found no market for their traditional crafts (especially as goldsmiths and silversmiths) and soon became pauperized. In the first decade of the century, there were some Zionist-sponsored attempts to re-employ the Yemenis in their own traditional crafts and to teach them new ones, more useful from a Zionist point of view. Thus some of them were given special instruction in stonemasonry, a trade that 'had hitherto been monopolized by Arabs'. From 1904 there were also some attempts to use them as seasonal agricultural labourers in the settlements of Judea.[7]

The 1908 Thon report proposed that the hitherto inadequate efforts to turn the Yemenis into agricultural labourers be intensified. 'Even now the Yemenis are employed in considerable numbers during the eight to ten weeks of the grape harvest in the colonies Rishon le-Zion, Rehovot, and Ghedera, and in general the farmers are pleased with their work. If we could cause Yemeni families to settle permanently in the colonies, we would achieve another thing: the [Yemeni] women and girls would work as domestics instead of the Arabs [women and girls], who are now employed as servants by almost every family of colonists for high wages (20 – 25 [French] francs a month). So far, no serious attempt has been made to replace Arab workers by Yemenis. The principal difficulty is that the Yemenis in Jerusalem and Jaffa, while very poor, have dwellings of their own, whereas in the colonies they cannot stay permanently with their families because of lack of accommodation (during the grape harvest they sleep in the open).'[8]

While the Thon report urged that greater efforts be made to convert the Yemeni Jews who were already present in Palestine into regular (rather than seasonal) agricultural workers, the Palestine Office decided to take a more radical approach and to import new immigrants from Yemen for that purpose. In December 1910, Shmuel Yavnieli (formerly Warszawski), member of the 'left' Zionist party Hapo'el Hatza'ir, was sent to Yemen to tour the country

6. Ibid.
7. Ibid., p. 99.
8. Ibid., p. 98.

and spread among its Jews the Gospel of religious Zionism, declaring that the days of the Messiah were at hand and that wealth awaited all Jews in the land of their ancient ancestors. His success 'exceeded all expectations and requirements'. In 1912 alone several hundred Jewish families emigrated from Yemen to Palestine and were employed there in Jewish farms.[9]

However, this was not a genuine solution to the crisis in the colonizing movement. After all, Zionism had been created not to establish Oriental Jews in Palestine, but to provide an answer to the problem of Jewish existence in eastern Europe. In an article published in the spring of 1912, Ahad Ha'am—always a shrewd observer and always sceptical of political Zionism—made this comment: 'Of late, Jews have been arriving in Palestine from Yemen, and have been settling in the colonies and working there as labourers. Talk in the Zionist camp already has it that by them, by these Yemenis, will The Land be built. But this experiment, too, is not yet conclusive in any way. And many [Jews] in Palestine think that most of the Yemenis are physically not sufficiently strong for hard labour, whereas their cultural condition and their entire mentality are so different from ours that the question automatically arises whether by their increase the quality of the whole *yishuv* may not change, and whether this change would be for the better.'[10]

In fact, once the quota of hands immediately needed by Jewish farms had been filled, the Palestine Office decided to stem the influx; Yavnieli had been 'too successful'. Instructions were therefore dispatched to Yemen that no more Jews should be sent to Palestine 'until further notice'[11]—that is, presumably, until Ashkenazi Zionism would need more hands.

The prospects of Zionism were brightened considerably by the British victory over the Ottomans in the Middle East, and by the Balfour declaration. The British organized Palestine as an administrative and military centre of their newly acquired Middle Eastern empire, thus allowing the growth of European-style towns. Jewish immigrants could find occupation in commerce, administration, transportation, and services. By 1936, half of the Jewish labour

9. Ibid., p. 101.
10. Ahad Ha'am, *Collected Works*, Jewish Publishing House, 1947 (in Hebrew), p. 426n.
11. A. Bein, p. 101.

force in Palestine (but only a quarter of the Arab labour force!) was employed in these branches.[12] During the period 1924 – 31 a wave of middle-class and lower-middle-class immigration (the fourth *'aliyah*) arrived from Poland, caused by the growing plight of the Jews in Europe—but no doubt also attracted to Palestine by the prospect of commercial opportunities. Almost all new immigrants settled in the towns, mostly in Tel Aviv. The same pattern was repeated on a much larger scale by the immigration from Poland and Germany (the fifth *'aliyah*) during the 1930s.[13]

The new prospects, coupled with the growing anti-Semitic threat in Europe, made Zionism more popular among Jews in Europe, and the volume of donations increased. This enabled the Jewish Agency (which was, in effect, the Palestine branch of the Zionist movement) to buy large tracts of arable land from Arab landowners, mainly in the fertile valleys and coastal plain. The Palestinian tenants were evicted, often with the aid of British forces, thus freeing the land for Jewish colonization. This was followed by scattered acquisition of land all over the country. The vanguard of Zionism realized that the success of its project depended on an actual occupation of land by agricultural labour. Furthermore, it was important to spread the new settlements all over Palestine, so as to stake out a claim to the entire country. Being better prepared, organized, and financially supported, and having more land per settler, the new colonizers succeeded where their predecessors of the second *'aliyah* had failed.

The ideology of manual labour had by now been severely modified, and became much more pragmatic. Labour ceased to be regarded as an ideal in itself, around which the 'reborn nation' would crystallize. It became an instrument in building up a political enterprise in the midst of a hostile indigenous population. But only certain kinds of labour were useful for this purpose—in agriculture and in the strategic nodes of the country's economy: the ports, the railways, the oil refineries.

Contrary to a widespread belief fostered by propaganda, only a

12. Nadav Halevi and Ruth Klinov-Malul, *The Economic Development of Israel*, Bank of Israel/Praeger, 1968, p. 25.

13. During the period 1924 to 1931, about 82,000 Jewish immigrants arrived in Palestine, and the Jewish population there roughly doubled, reaching 174,000. During the thirties, about 217,000 immigrants arrived, and the Jewish population reached 450,000. See Halevi and Klinov-Malul, pp. 15-17.

small minority of the Jewish population in British-ruled Palestine was rural. In 1948, about 85 per cent lived in the three urban centres. Also, among the urban population only a small proportion was engaged in manual labour, mainly in small-scale manufacture, crafts, and housing construction. But the rural minority, together with a tiny urban labour aristocracy, being the vanguard and driving force of the Zionist enterprise, constituted a highly respected social elite, to which practically all the leaders of the movement belonged.

The fundamental class contradiction remained totally unresolved. While most Jews in Palestine were still engaged—just as in Europe—in commerce, services, and administration, a vanguard elite minority was proudly performing those kinds of manual labour which were necessary for the capture of strategic positions. (The same minority would, in later years, also produce the military leadership of the state.)

Of course, someone had to do the 'dirty jobs' and the more strenuous work in the Jewish towns. An answer to this problem was at hand: the agitation in Yemen was renewed, to provide the necessary labour force for the low-status jobs, such as seasonal agricultural work and personal services. The expression 'my Yemeni', used by Ashkenazi women, was synonymous with 'my housemaid'. To get Jews to perform strenuous stevedore jobs in the strategic port of Haifa, the Zionist movement successfully recruited immigrants among the Sephardi Jews working in the Greek port of Salonika.

When the 1948 war broke out, Zionist propaganda projected the image of a normal, self-sufficient nation, ready for independence. The reality was quite different. Only a small part of food consumption was supplied by the Jewish agricultural settlements, since they occupied only a relatively small proportion of the arable land in the generally arid country, and many of them had mostly strategic rather than agricultural value. There was only a very small industrial working class, since industry was mostly rudimentary.[14] The strategic infrastructure had been only partly damaged, but it served little purpose after the British had left. In short, this was an

14. Even in 1945, at the end of the war boom and at a time when the Jewish economy was protected and enjoyed a broad market (the British army), only 31.8 per cent of the Jewish labour force was employed in industry (mostly as individual artisans or workers in small-scale manufacture). By 1947, the figure had declined to 26.5 per cent. See Halevi and Klinov-Malul, p. 25.

unproductive society, with a highly glorified appendage of a few dozen kibbutzim. The class contradiction in the new-born state of Israel was still to be solved.

True, in view of the huge financial support from the outside, unprecedented and unsurpassed in history in terms of inflow of funds per capita,[15] the economic problem did not seem urgent at first. Ben-Gurion, always a pragmatist, was worried by more immediate strategic needs. The Palestinian population, which was 'encouraged' to flee and was not allowed to return, had left behind vast agricultural lands scattered with hundreds of deserted villages and towns. The policy of fait accompli—of creating facts—required that these areas be populated by Jews, and a large number of occupants was needed. The army, too, required many new conscripts. This situation created, for the first time, a Zionist need for a massive supply of manipulable Jewish immigrants, and it resulted in the organization of a large-scale immigration of Oriental communities to Israel in the period 1949 – 53.[16]

Being busy with grand national designs, Ben-Gurion despised 'economic trivialities'—an attitude that was shared by all Zionist leaders of his generation.[17] Nevertheless, the need to build up a more productive economy became pressing as time went on. And while the politically motivated pseudo-economy was supervised to a great extent by the large political bureaucracy, the development of a more genuinely productive system revealed the capitalist character of the whole Zionist enterprise.[18] In a Knesset speech on 25 November 1957, Finance Minister Levi Eshkol (later prime minister) gave the following definition of Israel's economic regime: 'What is our

15. See Hanegbi, Machover, and Orr, 'The Class Nature of Israel', *New Left Review*, 65, 1971, pp. 7-9.

16. See below. Until the end of 1951, the Jewish Agency paid the expenses of all Jewish immigrants (including their fare to Israel and the costs of improvised shelter, food, and other vital needs during the first few months after arrival). From November 1951, financing of immigrants became more selective. In general, except in 'rescue' cases, the Agency would finance the immigration of a group of Jews only under the following conditions: 'Eighty per cent of immigrants must be between the ages of 15 and 35, or skilled workers, or owners of at least $10,000 worth of capital; unskilled workers are required to agree in writing to work at assigned jobs for two years after immigration.' (Jewish Agency Immigration Papers, no. 20, quoted in Halevi and Klinov-Malul, p. 55.)

17. Cf. Halevi and Klinov-Malul, p. 30.

18. Cf. Hanegbi *et al.* and Moshe Sneh, *The Israeli Economy*, Central Committee of the Israeli Communist Party, 1960 (in Hebrew).

regime? It is a regime of clearing the ground and paving the way for private capital, if only it exists and wants to come here.'[19] Zionism was bound to develop a capitalist system not only because of its middle-class origin, but mainly because it had to be vitally linked with Western imperialism.[20]

The slow development of a capitalist industry proper, begun in 1958 – 59, finally created a need for a genuine industrial proletariat. Most of this class, especially its lower and middle layers, was recruited from the Oriental Jewish population.

Clearly, there is a fundamental difference between the bureaucratic and authoritarian deployment of Orientals for forced colonization from 1949-55, and the proletarianization of these communities since the late 1950s. The social mechanism regulating the latter process is that of a free labour market, in which social discrimination assumes a more mediated, impersonal and diffuse form. This difference may be roughly compared to the difference between the early coercion of blacks into slavery in the US South, and the subsequent discrimination against them in the industrial centres of the North and Midwest.

The Manipulation of Oriental Populations

Immigration

All the factors mentioned above, as well as others, have combined to bring about the cold-blooded manipulation of the Oriental Jewish communities. Obvious though it is, Zionists refuse to admit its existence. From the start, Oriental Jews were a passive entity for Zionism, there to be led to salvation by the Ashkenazi Zionist movement. Culturally as well as ethnically, they were quite distinct from the Ashkenazim.

This has led the Zionist establishment to perceive them not as individuals (as it did the Ashkenazi Jews), but as diffuse generic entities, treated *en bloc*; and their communal social structures encouraged such an attitude. Also, the Orientals were supposed to be

19. Quoted in Sneh, p. 11.
20. See the discussion below.

more inclined to hard work and harsh living conditions, being more similar to the Palestinian workers, whose endurance the Zionist pioneers could not equal. I have already quoted the Zionist historian's dictum: 'Since they are frugal, these [Oriental] Jews can be compared to the Arabs: and from this point of view they can compete with them.' Observation of the Yemenis taught Joseph Shprintzack, one of the top Zionist leaders, that 'the Yemeni is accustomed to hard work and has endurance. . . . In the Yemeni families in the colonies everyone works: father, mother and older children.'[21]

Other factors of importance are the inherently segregationist character of the state of Israel, the state-worship encouraged by Zionism, and the general Zionist contempt for the Orient.[22]

The large-scale manipulation of the Oriental Jews has had two stages: immigration and colonization.

I have already mentioned the cynical messianic propaganda conducted in Yemen by atheist Zionists. However, such methods could work well only when applied to socially archaic communities (Yemen, Bukhara, Soviet Uzbekistan, Kurdistan). A more widely applicable method of propaganda consisted in making the most fantastic material promises about the future awaiting the prospective immigrants in Palestine, including assurances that many brilliant opportunities were in store for all artisans and craftsmen, who constituted the majority of the labour force in some communities. This method was widely used in North Africa, Turkey, Syria, Kurdistan, and Persia.

However, these propaganda methods would have had only partial success but for the fact that the Oriental communities themselves were in crisis. Whatever wishful thinking is expressed by Palestinian spokesmen, Jews, along with other religious, ethnic, and national minorities, were discriminated against in large parts of the Muslim world—though, to be sure, not in the same way and to the same extent as in Europe. The constant rise of Arab nationalism greatly intensified the discrimination against minorities in the Arab world. This was strongly felt, for example, by the Copts in Egypt and the Berbers in the Maghreb.

A severe blow to the welfare of Jews in the Muslim world in

---

21. Quoted in *Mesilla*, Histadrut Publishing House, 1924 (in Hebrew), p. 43.
22. See below.

general, and in the Arab world in particular, was the Zionist enterprise itself. As they developed an anti-imperialist consciousness, the nationalists in the Muslim countries were constantly being told of the organized settlement of European Jews in the very heart of the Arab world and around the second Holy Place of Islam, under the protection of an imperialist mandatory power. The recurrent violent clashes between the Zionist movement and the Palestinians (1922, 1926, 1929, 1936 – 39, 1947 – 49) were perceived as massacres of Palestinians—and Palestinian victims were indeed far more numerous than Jewish ones. Among the Muslims lived the co-religionists of those aggressors, people whom Zionists claimed to be their fellow nationals. Jewish community leaders were repeatedly requested to clarify their stand on the issue of Zionism and to voice opposition to it; but when they did this they were suspected of disingenuousness. The resulting discriminatory pressure was an important factor in increasing the receptiveness of Oriental communities to Zionist calls for emigration. (Thus Syria 1946, North Africa 1950 – 52, Egypt 1956, Algeria 1958.)

Nevertheless, in some cases even this discriminatory pressure, though combined with Zionist religious calls and material promises, was not enough to provoke a large exodus. This was mainly the case with the more educated and integrated communities, like those of Baghdad and the cities of Morocco. In these places, Jews held higher socio-economic positions, while many of them participated in the local left-wing and nationalist movements. The case of the Baghdad community is especially noteworthy. Zionism had never succeeded in becoming a focus of attraction for the Jews of Iraq, even after 1948. While a section of the Baghdad community consisted of wealthy merchants and bankers, a large part of the Jewish youth adhered to the Communist Party. Even many of the party's leaders were Jews. According to a Zionist historiographer,[23] a Zionist meeting organized in 1946 was attended by three dozen people, while the Jewish Communist Anti-Zionist Alliance was publishing a daily paper in Baghdad with a daily print-run of six thousand.

---

23. A. Ben-Ya'akov, *History of the Jews in Iraq*, Jerusalem 1965 (in Hebrew), p. 257. He also writes about Zionist emissaries who were imprisoned, and were astonished and embittered at the refusal of Jewish Communist fellow prisoners to associate with them. Similar information is given by Grodzenski in an article entitled 'Two Cultures', in the Israeli newspaper *Davar*, 4 June 1970.

In these more difficult cases, Zionist agents went so far as to employ methods of provocation and terrorism. Knowing from their own experience that anti-Semitism was the best stimulus to emigration, they tried either to provoke it or to stage acts of anti-Semitic terrorism. For example, there is oral evidence that Zionist agents sent from Israel distributed anti-Semitic leaflets in Casablanca. More solid is the evidence that bomb explosions in Jewish coffee-houses, shops, and synagogues in Baghdad were caused by Zionist provocateurs led by Mourad Qazzaz (alias Mordecai Ben-Porat, later a Member of the Knesset) and Yehudah Tagir, later an Israeli diplomat.[24] It is probably to these and similar provocations that a Zionist writer refers in the following somewhat enigmatic words: 'But does the State of Israel have duties towards the Jews who are able, but do not wish, to come here? Moreover, do we have the right to tell them: We know better than you what is best *for you*—and we shall therefore act to make you come here, and we shall perhaps even try to make your position more severe, so that you will have no choice but to immigrate to Israel? Note that this last question is not imaginary. We have confronted it in some very concrete situations and we may still have to confront it again.'[25]

Colonization

During the period 1949 – 55 the Jewish population of Israel increased by a million, from about 600,000 to about 1,600,000. Only about half of the million new immigrants were homeless survivors of the Nazi holocaust, but even this number already constituted a huge immigrant intake in comparison with the size of the veteran population. Nevertheless, Zionist policy increased the total to a full million with the Oriental immigration. This cannot possibly be explained as a humanitarian rescue operation; it cannot be maintained in good faith that the Oriental Jews, organized into flocks of immigrants, were facing imminent danger throughout the Muslim world. What remained of the Yemeni community, as well as the communities of

24. This is confirmed by many witnesses. A detailed account was published in *Ha'olam Hazeh*, 20 April 1966 and 1 June 1966.
25. Uri Harari, 'Our Responsibility Towards the Jews in the Arab Countries', in *Yedi'ot Aharonot*, 9 February 1969.

Iran, Morocco, and Cochin (to mention but a few) were in no such danger.

This haste in organizing the Oriental immigration caused unnecessary hardship to both Oriental and Ashkenazi immigrants. It is worth adding a few words here about the reason for it.

The Israeli government had a very weak claim over those areas controlled by its army in 1949 which exceeded the territory allocated to the Jewish state in the 1947 UN partition plan—a plan that the Zionist leadership had verbally accepted. The claim was weak both in practice and in international law.[26] Ben-Gurion's policy, aimed at consolidating that claim, consisted of two mutually complementary elements: on the one hand, military stabilization of the armistice lines into de facto international borders; on the other hand, massive colonization of the territories inside these lines.

Here, 'military stabilization of the lines' does not mean sealing them against intrusion of regular enemy units—the danger of such intrusion did not exist in 1949 – 53, and the Israeli army could be greatly reduced by demobilization during that period. The aim was rather to seal the lines against the Palestinian peasants massed in refugee camps just on the other side, who persisted in their attempts to cross over, to return to their homes, or at least to work their fields (usually at night) on the Israeli side. The job of preventing this could largely be performed by the existing structures of the Ashkenazi vanguard.

A chain of armed kibbutzim was established along the armistice lines, manned by the Zionist-socialist youth movements, who, during the 1948 war, had provided the most devoted and socially coherent military units, the Palmach. During the immediate post-1948 period, the ideological pressure on the Ashkenazi youth in the cities was very strong. A youngster who did not join a pioneering youth movement and did not wish to settle in one of the frontier kibbutzim was made to feel a traitor to Zionist ideals.

However, the massive occupation of the new territories was of even greater importance. The UN repeatedly demanded that Israel allow the repatriation of the Palestinian refugees, regardless of any final arrangements of peace and permanent borders.[27] Of course, a massive repatriation of Palestinians was inconsistent with the

26. Cf. Nathan Weinstock, *Le sionisme contre Israël*, Paris 1969, pp. 410-24.
27. Resolution 194 (111) of the United Nations General Assembly, 11 December 1948. This has been reiterated in numerous subsequent UN resolutions.

existence of an exclusive Jewish state within the expanded borders. However, strange as it may sound now, the principle of an exclusive Jewish state had never been accepted by any part of the international community. Thus, according to the 1947 UN partition plan, the Jewish state (whose area was to be 14,000 km² rather than the 20,000 km² that Israel occupied by 1949) was to have 403,000 Palestinian Arabs living in it as equal citizens.

To offset this threat to its policy of fait accompli, the Israeli government needed to amass a large population in all areas previously inhabited by Palestinians. In fact, the numbers of people the Israeli authorities installed in these areas exceeded the needs of normal economic planning, and can only be explained by this political motive. As one of the organizers of this colonization put it, 'we were spurred to occupy all abandoned Arab towns and villages. There were these houses, and someone had to fill them.'[28]

Conceivably, the filling could have been done with the many new Ashkenazi immigrants. But in practice this was not feasible: these immigrants were not easy to manipulate, nor did the Zionist establishment itself show any wish to manipulate them.[29] Most of them had relatives, old acquaintances, and friends, both among the veteran Israeli Ashkenazim and abroad. The establishment saw them as they saw themselves—as individuals. If they were forced to face harsh living conditions without a prospect of rapid improvement, they would re-emigrate to Western Europe, the US, Canada, or Australia—as indeed hundreds of thousands of them have done in any case.

The only really manipulable element were the Oriental Jews, and their precipitate immigration was organized for this, and only for this, reason. Total strangers in the country, unable to return home, waiting to be guided in their next steps into a destiny over which they had lost control, they were gathered in the sparsely populated strategic regions.

Behind the chain of kibbutzim strung along the armistice lines, as many as 214 rural settlements (moshavim) were set up between 1949 and 1955, with a total population of about seventy thousand, of

28. A. Assaf, *The Moshav Ovdim in Israel*, Tel Aviv 1953 (in Hebrew), p. 178.
29. A significant exception were the Jews from the rural parts of Romania, who were not Zionists, did not speak Yiddish, and were treated almost on a par with the Oriental Jews.

whom (in 1960) 78 per cent were Oriental. (The remaining 22 per cent were settled in very different conditions.) The settlers were allocated small plots to farm—about one tenth of the arable area per capita that was allocated to the Ashkenazi settlers in the 1930s.

Yet even this population was not large enough to consolidate the claim of the Israeli government over all the territories under its military control. Therefore these territories were further filled out with about twenty towns, baptized 'development towns', set up in the most strategic regions, often immediately behind the chain of kibbutzim. (Kiryat-Shmoneh, Beit-Shan, Ma'alot, Megido, Shderot, Beit-Shemesh, Kiryat-Gat are some of the latter type.) Into these an even larger population, also predominantly Oriental, was herded. By 1961, the development towns had a total of one hundred and twenty thousand inhabitants, and two years later the figure had reached one hundred and seventy thousand, of whom 71 per cent were Oriental.[30] The motive for establishing these towns was purely political. Thus an official source states, 'The development towns were set up and populated within the framework of the policy of population dispersal; this policy was designed on the one hand to prevent over-concentration of the population in the coastal region, and on the other hand to populate desolate areas.'[31] There was little economic planning, and the development towns were in fact economically unviable. For example, in 1963 the rate of unemployment in the development towns was 22 per cent (as compared to the national average of 4 per cent), and while their population was only 6 per cent of the country's total, they had as much as 32 per cent of Israel's unemployed.[32]

The forced colonization through the Oriental Jews is a story of

30. *Bank of Israel Annual Report for 1963*, Jerusalem 1964 (in Hebrew), p. 15. Strictly speaking, the figure of 71 per cent refers only to the *immigrant* population of these towns. A quarter of the inhabitants were in fact Israeli-born—mostly young children of immigrants. Since the birth-rate among Oriental Jews is far higher than among Ashkenazim, the proportion of Orientals among the *total* population must have been 75 at the very least. The Ashkenazi 25 per cent were largely officials and their families.

31. Ibid. The term 'desolate' here refers not only to areas that were actually depopulated through the expulsion of their Palestinian Arab inhabitants, but also to areas that still had a dense Arab population. The Bank's statistics thus include the 'development town' of Upper Nazareth, set up alongside the crowded Arab town of Nazareth as part of the project of the Judaization of Arab-populated Galilee.

32. Ibid.

years of great suffering, humiliating discrimination, and bleak frustration.

The Jewish State as a Segregating Entity

According to Zionist doctrine, Israel is defined as 'the state of the Jewish people'. This definition is unique—a state that is not the state of its actual citizens but of a group (the Jewish people) of which its citizens are a minority, and to which only part of them (the Jewish citizens) belong. According to the famous Law of Return, any Jew has an automatic right to become an Israeli citizen upon entering the country. For that matter, even this condition may be waived, and on several occasions Israeli citizenship has actually been offered to Soviet Jews while still abroad. Zionist doctrine still demands that a genuine Zionist must emigrate to Israel, but one can well imagine that, should the need arise, the Israeli government would grant Israeli citizenship wholesale to all those Jews abroad willing to accept it. By this means, even if the Palestinian citizens of the state ever came to outnumber its Jewish inhabitants, Zionism could still remain in power as representing the 'democratic majority' of all citizens.

The victims of this particular practice of the Israeli state are not only the Arab citizens, who are constitutionally of lower rank, but also the Oriental Jewish citizens. If Israel is the state of all Jews, then it must be an Ashkenazi state, since the overwhelming majority of *world* Jewry are Ashkenazim, even though Oriental Jews are the majority in Israel itself. Thus the impotence of Oriental Jews in Israel is not just a historical outcome of various socio-economic and ideological factors, but an integral part of Zionist legitimation.

This is not a mere quibble; the point has serious material and psychological implications. The ties with the Zionist section of the Jewish diaspora are vital for the Zionist enterprise politically, economically, and financially. The Israeli establishment makes every effort to charm European and American Jews, to mobilize them, to squeeze them, to organize them, to teach them, and to save them from the horrible fate of assimilation. Contradicting their previous repudiation of their identity and disdain for the diaspora mentality, the Israeli leaders are ready to support the most aggressive form of medieval clericalism, the Habbad Hasidic sect, and they even try to revive Yiddish language and culture—the very language and culture they themselves once spurned. To take one somewhat grotesque example: in Jerusalem a couple of years ago, several hundred Zionist activists from the US gathered for a 'congress of Yiddish writers'—a moribund species. They were addressed by the president, the prime minister, and the minister of education, a triple honour to which congresses of Hebrew writers have not been treated for many a year. The education syllabuses in Israel are changing in the same direction: at all levels, growing emphasis is put on Jewish Ashkenazi culture. Ashkenazi supremacy in Israel is reinforced by the Zionist state's need to present to the influential and wealthy Ashkenazi communities abroad an image with which they can easily identify. From this point of view, Oriental Jews are bound to be considered a minority in Israel; in fact they now slightly outnumber the Ashkenazim, but even if they should outnumber them two to one or ten to one, they will still be a 'minority group' as far as the Zionist leadership is concerned.

The Oriental Jews are victimized not only by the reference to world Jewry as the defining constituency of the state, but also by the exclusion of the non-Jews. This exclusion establishes a constitutional segregation between distinct categories of citizens. But once such exclusion is made, it establishes a norm that affects all aspects of the relations between the state and its citizens. A hierarchy of citizens is established; the Arabs are categorized into sedentary Muslims, Christians, Bedouin, and Druze (in ascending order). For instance, a sedentary Muslim will under no circumstances be conscripted into the Israeli army, even if he wishes to be (there have been such cases); a Christian may be, if he volunteers; Bedouin of certain tribes and all Druze are conscripted. (Druze conscientious objectors have been imprisoned.) Continuing this hierarchy upwards, hardly any Oriental Jew has ever achieved one of the top four military ranks.[33]

To take an example from another sphere: Ashkenazi Jews were settled in the 1960s in 'Arad, a promising new town with independent economic resources; but at about the same time Orientals were being settled in Migdal Ha'emek, a new town without an economic base. Non-Jews are not allowed to create any new village or town;[34]

33. One ostensible exception, General David El'azar, was a European Sephardi (see above).

34. A bizarre episode occurred during the 1950s. Several groups of Arab youth were

however, when the Jewish town of Eilat recently needed hands for some rough service jobs, several dozen Druze were 'brought' there (this term was used by the Israeli press).

The way citizens are stratified into six categories (the four categories of Arabs already mentioned, plus Oriental Jews and Ashkenazim) is evident everywhere in Israel. Recently, one of the Druze notables earnestly begged the Israeli government to treat his community on a par with the *Oriental* Jews; not with 'the Jews', since these do not constitute a single category in the hierarchy; and not with the Ashkenazim, since that would be asking far too much.

Worship of the State[35]

Like many other nationalist movements, Zionism has tended to develop a fetishistic attitude to the state; the state is regarded as an entity for its own sake, whose subjects exist to serve it and contribute to its glory, not to be served by it. This ideology is expressed without reserve by a great number of Israelis. There are a number of factors, peculiar to Zionism, which have particularly encouraged this worship of the state.

First, the organization of the processes of immigration and colonization gave rise to a huge bureaucracy, accustomed to manipulating large population groups. Second, the constant conflict with the Arab world has tremendously boosted the prestige and power of the military; a large and growing part of the social, bureaucratic, and political elite is made up of retired generals. In addition, a kind of collective paranoia has developed among large sections of East European Jewry, as an understandable result of a long history of discrimination and pogroms, culminating in the horrors of Nazi extermination. The state crystallizes their instincts of fear and defence,

recruited by the 'left' Zionist party Mapam, educated in kibbutzim, and indoctrinated in the movement's 'pioneering values'. In 1958, however, when the young Arabs wanted to practise what had been preached to them, and sought to found a new cooperative farm, they discovered that the land was allocated for *Jewish* settlement only. See Y. Netzer and T. Raz, *The Pioneering Youth Movement Initiated by Mapam—a Topic in the History of Israel's Arabs*, Shiloah Institute, *Skirot* series, Tel Aviv, May 1976 (in Hebrew).

35. The subject of this section is dealt with in detail in the article 'Crisis in Israel: The Danger of Fascism', by Avishai Ehrlich, published in *Khamsin 5*.

which have further developed as a result of the continual state of war. Early Zionist leaders were also inclined to a despotic view of the state by their experience in their countries of origin—Tsarist Russia, the Austro-Hungarian Empire, fascist Poland, Romania and Hungary of the inter-war period.

In view of all this, one may wonder why, after all, Israel has shown only partial symptoms of fascist tendencies. The main reason, I believe, has been the great weakness of any genuine ideological opposition to the ruling 'Labour Zionism'. A Jew coming to Palestine was, to the extent that he was politically conscious, a Zionist almost by definition; and while the non-Zionist opposition has always been marginal, the right-wing opposition has offered only a slightly different (and less pragmatic) variant of the same ideology.[36] The opposition between labour and capital has also been considerably blunted, since massive financial support from outside has enabled the working class to receive relatively high material benefits.[37]

Another major obstacle to the development of an openly despotic state has been the Zionist dependence on support from North America and Western Europe. A dictatorial state would dash any hope for a significant immigration from this Zionist diaspora—or so it seemed.[38]

These moderating factors were, nevertheless, only partly effective, and in any case less relevant to the relation of the state to the Oriental communities than to the formal state institutions and their relations to the Ashkenazim. Worship of the state has therefore been one of the major ideological elements facilitating the rough manipulation of the Oriental Jews.

However, state fetishism affects the Oriental subjects on a personal level as well. Whatever aid or service they receive is considered

36. In recent years the situation has changed somewhat. The extent of Israel's eventual withdrawal from the occupied territories is a serious issue on which the Zionist camp is divided, although the present division to a great extent cuts across the old party lines. This seems to be the reason for the recent acceleration of moves towards a 'strong state'. It did not occur earlier precisely because of the ideological uniformity of the system.

37. That is, relative to the low productivity of the economy. See Hanegbi, Machover, and Orr.

38. By now, however, this hope has practically evaporated in any case. The most militant Zionists in the United States are now themselves moving towards support of a 'strong state'.

as charity, not a state obligation, and the Zionist establishment is very proud of itself for it. Also, young Ashkenazim have been repeatedly encouraged and organized to do charity work among Orientals, as a substitute for the sorely needed improvement in the derisory public services and the deficient education system. In this and similar ways, charity and paternalism govern all aspects of the relations of the Zionist establishment to the Oriental Jews.

The same attitude is also expressed in an inverted form in the Ashkenazi grudges against the Oriental Jews (as well as against Israel's Arab citizens, and even the population of the occupied territories). Since public aid and services are felt to be dispensed as charity rather than obligation, any complaint by the recipient is regarded as ingratitude. There is absolutely no feeling of guilt in the Zionist establishment for its cynical manipulation of the Orientals. On the contrary, it is very proud of having raised them slightly above the rest of the despised Orient. This outlook is conveyed in frequently used expressions such as: 'We are the ones who have built up the country, so that they may come and enjoy it'; 'When have they ever had such a high standard of living before?'; 'Whoever would have treated them so well?'.

After her single meeting with Israeli Black Panther activists, Prime Minister Golda Meir had only this to say: 'Once they were nice kids, and I hope that among them there are still some nice kids, but some of them, I'm afraid, will never be nice kids.'[39] These words became, for a number of years, a symbol of Ashkenazi paternalism, which accepts no Oriental grievance as legitimate.

Zionism Versus the Orient

In his programmatic book *The Jewish State* (published in 1896) Theodor Herzl, the founder of political Zionism, made the following promise: 'For Europe we shall serve there [in Palestine] as a bastion against Asia, and be the vanguard of civilization against the barbarians.' This idea, a leitmotif of Zionism since its very beginning, was quite natural. Like any other colonizing movement, Zionism needed the backing and support of an imperialist power.

39. See, for example, *Yedi'ot Aharonot*, weekend supplement, 28 May 1971.

However, whereas most colonial movements were generated in the first place by some specific imperial power as part of a particular colonial venture, and were therefore automatically supported by the sponsoring power, Zionism was created by an independent dynamic and was therefore seeking the sponsorship and support of 'the West' as such, of imperialism in general. Consequently, Zionism's antagonism towards the Orient was more deeply part of its character, and hence more radical and complete.

Of course, the link with imperialism could not remain abstract. It had to be cemented by specific alliances. Herzl started by seeking the patronage of the German Kaiser. Then, from 1915 to 1939, there was a long and fruitful alliance binding Zionism with British imperialism. This partnership was broken by the British when they began to see it as more of a liability than an asset. This also turned out to be in the long-term interest of Zionism, which was then free to forge an alliance with American imperialism, the new master dominating the Middle East,[40] and to obtain vital (albeit short-lived) support from the USSR (which, like the US, was seeking to accelerate the disintegration of Britain's Middle East empire).

The Zionists' conflict with Britain also enabled them to appear as politically independent and indeed as 'anti-imperialist' during a crucial period of history. Thereafter—notwithstanding a flirtation with moribund French imperialism, culminating in the Suez affair of 1956—Zionism has remained attached to its American patron.

Zionist devotion to the West has not abated with time—quite the contrary: Israel has never ceased to proclaim that it is not only 'Western' in character but is actually part of Europe. As a matter of fact, Israel does belong to the European sections of various international organizations, such as sports bodies and UNESCO. Like all colonizers, Zionists have developed deep contempt towards the 'natives'. A whole pattern of prejudice against the 'Arab mentality' has been created, sometimes by projection of anti-Semitic themes: the Arabs are two-faced, cowardly, dirty, lazy, crafty, noisy, and so on. This racism has been extended to apply to the whole Arab world, and to the Orient in general.

40. 'In those very years of struggle [with Britain] there occurred a process of a beginning of a new attachment: America – Zion instead of England – Zion—a process that relied on the fact of US penetration into the Middle East as a decisive world power.' This is an assessment by the veteran Labour Zionist political commentator Michael Assaf, in *Davar*, 2 May 1952.

In addition, a zealous cult of technology has emerged in Zionism, fostered by the capitalist character of the state of Israel, fuelled by the worship of weaponry, and fanned by abstract admiration for the West and its technological culture. The Orient is despised all the more for its inability to master Western technology.

The contempt in which the Israeli Ashkenazi elite holds the Orient is reflected in a very conscious and explicit way in its attitude towards the Oriental Jews. From the very first contacts, Ashkenazi prejudice has despised them for being 'black', 'uncivilized', and, generally speaking, similar to the Arabs. According to a widely told story which is regarded as very witty, Bialik, the Zionist national poet, used to explain that he disliked Arabs—because they were so like Oriental Jews.

This aspect of discrimination against the Orientals is evident especially at the level of the educated elite. Oriental Jews are not entrusted with positions of real power in civil or military bodies. The few high-ranking non-Ashkenazi officials are usually in powerless, ornamental, or representative positions, such as chairman of the Knesset; or they are Sephardim, who are not really Orientals, in the most minor cabinet posts. The better educated an Oriental Jew is, the worse is the discrimination to which he is subjected.

This last assertion is based, among other sources, on the statistical data in the official report of the Horowitz committee, nominated in 1971 by Golda Meir in order to 'investigate' and confirm the official explanation for discrimination against Oriental Jews: their lower level of education. If this explanation were correct, then the gap between Ashkenazim and Orientals in Israel should gradually be narrowing. But in fact, 25 years after the mass immigration, almost 100 years after the arrival of the first Yemeni Jews, and in spite of some efforts at integration by the Zionist establishment, the social, economic, and educational gap is as wide as ever, and remains a central internal contradiction of Israeli Jewish society.

Oriental Jews in Israel: Collective Schizophrenia

A. Hoder

Who are the Oriental Jews, and how do they perceive themselves, the Ashkenazi Jews, the Arabs, and the Palestinians? There are no simple answers—I can only sketch some impressions.

I was travelling the other day in a service taxi from Tel Aviv to Jerusalem. The passengers were all Jews. One of them, a talkative woman in her mid-fifties, and the driver, both Moroccans, were deep in conversation. The other passengers, five Ashkenazim and one Yemeni, spent the hour-long journey listening.

The Moroccan woman's torrent of conversation with the driver covered everything from rising prices to her family situation. We learned in no time that her husband runs a coffee house in Musrara (a poor Jerusalem quarter) and that she has ten children and a few things to say about Ashkenazi Jews, to whom she refers as *Vusvus*.[1] 'They are not like us at all, not our kind.'

Driver: How do you mean?
Woman: Take those Vusvus women. There I was, visiting my daughter and her husband, see, and there is this Vusvus woman, half-empty shopping bag, and she wants her husband to carry it! So I say to her, 'Madam, you are pestering your husband.' And my very own daughter turns on me: 'Mama, that is no way to behave, you embarrass me', she says; and I have to listen to her because she lives among the Vusvus in Givataim.[2]
Driver: Good neighbourhood?
Woman: Excellent! You hardly see any blacks there; but she deserves

---

1. A nickname derived from the Yiddish *vus, vus*, meaning 'what, what'.
2. A township near Tel Aviv.

it, my Rachel. I always used to say, 'You study good and catch a good husband.' And not only did she finish secondary school, she went to university for one year, and caught a big Vusvus, and not any old Vusvus: he is a pilot in the air force. She is the talk of Jerusalem, my Rachel is. At least my grandchildren will not have to grow up among blacks.

Driver: She sure was lucky; but then, that is women's luck. She won't have to carry shopping bags, not with a Vusvus husband.

The conversation is interrupted by the four o'clock radio news: 'Grenades exploded in Jaffa . . . the police are conducting searches among the minorities.'[3]

The taxi reaches the inevitable traffic jam near Beit Dagon. As we inch our way through, we observe the cars and buses carrying Arab labourers stopped at the roadside, and rows of Arabs standing waiting for 'inspection'.

The inspection is accompanied by occasional slapping of faces, and much loud swearing. Some Arabs are singled out for 'further treatment' and herded into 'detainees' buses'. We, of course, do not undergo any such inspection (Arab-owned cars are marked differently from Jewish-owned cars).

The conversation in the car stops as we view this spectacle, but the Moroccan woman soon resumes it.

Woman: That's not enough. Burn some of them, it's the only way they'll learn.

Driver: That's right, the Vusvus don't know how to treat Arabs. We know.

Woman: My Vusvus pilot knows all right. He too says they should be burnt.

Driver: An exceptional Vusvus.

As we leave the scene behind, the conversation continues with a laboured description of the difficulties with the coffee house.

Woman: It wasn't bad before October seventy-three. But now! . . . I have to make a living out of our pimps.[4] And I say to them, 'How can

---

3. A euphemism for Arabs.
4. Moroccan pimps, she means.

you? Don't you people have a god in your hearts? You supply murderers with our daughters.' Not Vusvus women, mind you; only *our* daughters are ready to fuck those murderers. Burn them all. And you know what they say? 'Mama, what do you want? You know as well as we do that we could not make a living if it were not for the Arabs in Jerusalem. Neither could you . . . ' And I have to agree, the kids have to eat. But why do Vusvus women get away with it?
Driver: Vusvus women are independent—they do the same thing but they don't need our pimps . . .

The conversation moves to the inevitable rising prices. Where does it all go? They both agree: It goes to national security.

Driver: . . . but we don't have it as good as we did in Morocco. There, you could make a living, live in peace. Here, they are all thieves and there's no peace.
Woman: The Vusvus are to blame; they don't have a clue, and the worst Vusvus of them all is that Kissinger—he does not know what Arabs are made of. Burn a few, then there will be peace. I still remember, that is how it used to be done in Morocco.

Somehow, as we approached Jerusalem the conversation switched from burning Arabs to Umm Kulthum, the famous Egyptian traditional singer.

Woman: A Vusvus fixed my TV aerial, the way only a Vusvus could: beautiful, you can get Cairo. Paid him 100 pounds[5] extra. Now I can hear Umm Kulthum and Farid al-Atrash[6] to soothe the soul.

At this juncture we arrive in Jerusalem and the passengers scatter.

I have listened in to many conversations like this one. They express the schizophrenic make-up of all those Jews in Israel who originate from Arab countries.

The contradictions kept coming up in references to Ashkenazi Jews—the Vusvus: those supermen who know everything 'better than us', are 'good catches', but at the same time are not 'one of us'

---

5. About £8 at the time.
6. Farid al-Atrash is a popular Egyptian singer.

and 'don't understand anything' when it comes to dealing with Arabs.

As for the Arabs, the same contradictions are apparent. While the Arabs trigger only hatred and aggression, there is an enormous residue of nostalgia about the 'old country', and TV aerials are directed at Cairo.

It is important to stress that when missing the old country, whether it is Morocco, Iraq, or anywhere else, these Jews are not thinking of those countries as they are now. They are remembering the semi-feudal society they left some twenty years ago.

Among members of the Oriental communities, factual knowledge about the contemporary Arab world is limited, and is derived mostly from the secret-service-inspired Israeli press, which usually covers only the negative aspects of the Arab world and omits any mention of development and progress.

I recall how once I tried, after having come back from abroad, to tell some Iraqi Jewish friends of mine about the new medical centre in Baghdad, its size and splendour. They would not believe me. 'The Arabs are not up to it' (some added 'without us'); they 'assured' me, with examples from the days of Nuri Said, that it is all a propaganda trick.

Terms like Oriental Jews, and Sephardi Jews, used to describe all the non-Ashkenazi Jews, are not only misleading but suggest a consciousness of communal unity which does not exist in fact. What does exist is a rigidly strict hierarchy of communities with the Ashkenazi Jews at the summit.[7] The so-called gap between the Ashkenazim and the rest multiplies as you go down the list, and it is not just economic, but also political and cultural.

Sociological research conducted periodically among school-age children in Israel has shown that until about 1969 children generally preferred playmates from their own community. This pattern was repeated in each community, but in recent years the results have changed radically: from 80 to 95 per cent of children in all non-Ashkenazi communities prefer Ashkenazi children as playmates. The results are particularly unambiguous when they are required to

7. The hierarchical order of the other main communities, from the bottom: Kurds, Tripolitanians, Persians, Yemenis, Moroccans (subdivided into those who came from France and those who came from Morocco), Iraqis, Tunisians, Algerians, and Sephardim.

choose from photographs of children of varying skin tones, or of 'European profiles' as opposed to 'Semitic profiles'.[8] It is hardly surprising therefore that the term *black* has become common currency as an epithet in street brawls as well as in schools, and more so in schools that are predominantly non-Ashkenazi.

Ironically, the 'Nordic type' is regarded as the 'representative type' by the Israeli Zionist propaganda machine, not just in the famous post-1967 war photographs (the story is well-known in Israel about how the 'blond parachutist standing at the Wailing Wall' was selected for 'export'), but in all the internal propaganda and all the media. The army is a principal peddler of the image of the fair Ashkenazi 'soldier against a tank', 'pilot against a plane' variety. Even group photographs are selected and arranged so that the blonds are in the foreground and even mere Slavic types are placed 'discreetly' in the background. All this while 72 per cent of army recruits are non-Ashkenazi. The image of the non-Ashkenazi Jew is prominent only in well-defined areas, such as the 'comic Yemenite' tradition in literature and theatre.

A special role is played by the Sephardi community. It is important to understand the historical context; Sephardi Jews were originally those who came out of Spain in the fifteenth century and settled in Holland, England, a few places in Germany (such as Hamburg), Italy, and the Balkans. The 'real' Sephardi Jews are a very small community that, until recent generations, enjoyed economic prosperity far greater than that of the other communities. Its members kept their 'ethnic purity' with great zeal even with regard to other Jews. Some, notably the late Rabbi Toledano, chief rabbi of Tel Aviv, would add to their signatures an abbreviation meaning 'pure Spaniard'—that is to say that their families did not intermarry or assimilate with other Jews.

Whereas in Europe the Sephardi community was the only non-Ashkenazi one, in the Arab world it was just one of the several smaller communities (predominantly in urban centres). The crucial difference between the Sephardi community and the other Jewish communities in the Arab world showed itself in language. The Sephardim spoke Ladino, a fifteenth-century Castilian dialect written in

8. I found out about this from personnel involved in the research. The results are supposed to be a closely guarded secret.

Hebrew letters, and wherever they were, kept a portion of imported culture, tradition, and custom, though not to the same extent as the East European Jews. The other Jewish communities in Arab countries spoke Arabic in the local idiom, even among themselves.

Economically, until the twentieth century, the Sephardim were the richer class, while culturally they lived on credit from the sixteenth and seventeenth centuries, when they had been the vanguard of Jewish culture. It is this community that is 'recognized' and 'accepted' in Israel, primarily because this acceptance does not imply recognition of the Arabic language and Arab culture. It is impossible in present-day Zionist Israel to 'recognize', say, an Iraqi community, even on a level of folklore. After all, the culture is Arabic, the songs are in Arabic, in a dialect not much different from that of the Palestinians. Instead, what is being promoted and revived is the 'Spanish Romansero' (Castilian ballads) that Sephardic women used to sing until as recently as the last generation.

And so the Sephardi has been made the archetype of all the non-Ashkenazi Jews. It is not surprising that the actor Yoram Gaon, a descendant of a notable ancient Jerusalem Sephardi family, was the only actor thought suitable to play the lead in the musical *Kasablan*, about a Moroccan immigrant—the thought of a Moroccan acting the role of a Moroccan is inconceivable in Zionist Israel.

A more pernicious role is played by the Sephardi Jews in intelligence and in policing the Arabs. The present 'adviser to the prime minister on Arab affairs', Shmuel Toledano, is a Sephardi Jew, and his official biography lists his qualifications: his first language was Ladino, his second Arabic. He studied in a Christian college in Nazareth among Christian Palestinians in the 1920s, as was the custom of Sephardi families of the period. In Zionist Israel that kind of background and education is tailor-made for intelligence work. Indeed, it is known that the intelligence high command have been complaining about the destructive effect state education has had on the younger generation of Sephardim, who now speak neither Ladino nor Arabic.

It is apparent that the Sephardi community, with its special skills and privileges, is required primarily to represent the non-Ashkenazim in a way that will continue to maintain Ashkenazi hegemony. There is nothing special or surprising about it all. One could find analogies in other similar colonial situations, but the real question is:

is there a way out? Can a movement of 'Oriental' Jews really challenge Ashkenazi hegemony?

It is doubtful, for various reasons. First, non-Ashkenazi Jews are divided, even in their own consciousness, into separate, numerically insignificant factions, too small to challenge Ashkenazi supremacy. Second, the Ashkenazi community is solid and stable, it has a continuity of social customs that are maintained by each generation with little or no questioning. This kind of stability is absent in the Oriental communities, whose younger generations often despise what little they know of their original culture and traditions, and regard the Ashkenazi customs with ill-concealed admiration. (I recall scenes from military funerals in the aftermath of the October 1973 war. Oriental funerals: noisy, emotional. Ashkenazi funerals: restrained and disciplined. Non-Ashkenazi youths would remark, 'look at ours, like animals; and them—human beings'.)

The Ashkenazi community not only holds, in effect, all real power in the state of Israel, but in addition is backed by the myth it has created—the myth of strength and prestige (a myth hardly dented despite recent setbacks).

Israel, it is worth noting, is not a state with an army but an army with a state apparatus, and this army's hierarchy and structure is the expression of Ashkenazi hegemony: all the high-ranking officers are Ashkenazi. Select units—parachutists, submarine crews, pilots, and so on—are predominantly Ashkenazi, their officers almost exclusively so.

All this leads to only one conclusion: that the solution is to engage in a struggle not restricted to one community or another but directed at the roots of the problem, at the roots of the movement that gave rise to the Ashkenazi hegemony and created the problem of the Oriental communities: the solution is to combat Zionism.

To understand the situation of the oppressed communities and the reasons that brought it about is to understand the essence of Zionism and to realize the need to fight it.

Class Divisions in Israeli Society

Emmanuel Farjoun

In two consecutive general elections—in 1977 and 1981—the lower and middle echelons of the Israeli Jewish working class, consisting mainly of Oriental Jews, gave massive (though by no means unanimous) support to the traditional party of the private bourgeoisie, the Likud, headed by Menachem Begin. To be more precise, the Likud is an electoral bloc whose two main components are the fiercely nationalistic Herut (Freedom) Party and the conservative party of traditional bourgeois Zionism, the Liberal Party.

The second vote of support came during a period of very rapid inflation (about 130 per cent per year), which had taken its toll of the standard of living of the poorer sections of the working class. Only six months before the 1981 election, the economic conditions of wage earners were deteriorating so fast and the popularity of the first Likud government had sunk so low that hardly anyone believed that Begin would be returned to office. In the event, his party greatly increased its power. Inflation was generated deliberately by government policies as a tool for controlling the economy by manipulating prices, taxes, and wages. Just before the elections, the government allowed an artificial but significant reduction in the prices of both foods and durable goods—and it seemed that the electorate had been waiting for just such an excuse to sweep the Likud coalition back to office.

This demonstrated ability of the Likud to retain power even in the face of grave economic difficulties for the mass of their voters raises several questions. In view of the well-known political programme of the Likud (as demonstrated by the war in Lebanon), these questions are of fundamental importance for understanding Israeli society and its future.

It is clear that among Oriental Jews (who form the bulk of the Jewish working class) support for Begin's Likud is greater and more solid than among Ashkenazi Jews. In wide sectors of the Oriental population, commitment to Begin is apparently overwhelming and virtually unconditional: he is seen as Saviour.

What are the reasons for this phenomenon? How does the voting pattern reflect the specific structure of Israeli society?

Obviously, such a clear-cut and powerful sentiment is over-determined: it has several interlinked causes, related to the present social and economic position of the Oriental Jews in Israel, as well as to the painful process of their integration into Ashkenazi-dominated Israeli society, and to their cultural-political background in the Arab countries.

The usual explanation for the voting patterns of Oriental Jews in Israel is that on the whole the nationalist rhetoric and explicit anti-Arab chauvinism of the Likud appeal to them much more than the relatively moderate and cautious tone adopted by the Labour Party.

While this explanation does contain an element of truth, it suffers from several weaknesses.

First, in many cases the actual policies of the first Begin government (1977 – 81) towards the Arab countries, as well as towards the Palestinian Arabs in Israel and the occupied territories, were more open and less harsh than those of former Labour governments. For example, it is now a known fact that when the Labour Party was in office it refused to give up the whole of Sinai in exchange for a comprehensive peace treaty with Egypt; the Egyptians proposed such a deal on several occasions, but were repeatedly rebuffed. Begin's decision to give up the whole of Sinai and to dismantle the Israeli settlements there in exchange for a peace treaty with Egypt was most vehemently opposed by predominantly Ashkenazi extreme right-wing nationalist groups such as the Tehiyyah (Revival) Party and Gush Emunim; it was also opposed, albeit less vigorously, by the Labour Party. On the other hand, the peace treaty was very popular with Israel's Oriental communities.

Thus, while Begin's rhetoric is undeniably more openly chauvinistic than that of the Labour Party, his policies were not invariably so, until well into his second term in office.

Further, the central and most important plank in Israel's anti-Arab policy throughout the post-1967 period has been the massive colonization of the West Bank. But this rapid expansion of the dense network of Israeli settlements has never been popular among the poorer sections of Israel's Oriental communities. They perceived correctly that to accomplish this massive colonization the government must channel considerable resources to the small groups of (mostly Ashkenazi) settlers, and away from the 'development towns' inside the pre-1967 borders, where a large proportion of the Oriental population resides.

Here I would like to consider an entirely different root cause of Begin's popularity—a deep-level class factor that has had and will continue to have a decisive influence on the political structure of Israel. The existence of such a factor is betrayed by the very form of the support that Begin enjoys among wide sectors of the Jewish working class and petty bourgeoisie: *it is an overwhelming and unconditional support, apparently independent of the precise nature of his policies, and often accompanied by strong aversion towards the Labour Party.*

Class Divisions

In fact, a detailed analysis of the public support given to the two major party blocs shows that it is closely related to important divisions in the working class. This division turns out to run parallel to divisions within the Israeli bourgeoisie. Together, they form a striking pattern which has a decisive influence on Israeli society and politics.

Let us examine this pattern. The Israeli economy is divided into two major sectors, roughly equal in size: the bureaucratic-capitalist sector owned by the state or the Histadrut and its affiliated organizations, and the private capitalist sector. Obviously, these two sectors are connected to each other by a multitude of economic (and other) ties; in particular, many firms are owned jointly by capital from both sectors. However, there are important characteristic differences, some of which are summarized in the table. This table is no doubt schematic, but it nonetheless highlights some of the features of each sector.

One crucial point is this: the economic sectoral division of the

Dual structure of Israel's economy

	Bureaucratic sector	*Private sector*
Size and character of firms	Large modern enterprises	Large proportion of small businesses; some medium-size firms
Economic branch	Weapons and other military products, chemicals, energy, oil, cement, large-scale construction, large agri-business, public transport	Consumer goods (metal, wood, textiles, food), small and medium-size construction and services, small-scale agriculture
Market	Strong orientation towards export	Local consumer market; sub-contracting for state enterprises
Work-force	Almost exclusively Jewish (except in construction); very high proportion of Oriental Jews among production workers	Large proportion (about ⅔) of workers are Palestinian Arabs
Pay and conditions	Low pay, but relatively high job security, good working conditions and fringe benefits	Very low pay (less than $200 a month), no job security and negligible fringe benefits (except in electronics and engineering subcontractors for arms industry, where no Arabs are employed)
Ownership and management	Managed by largely Ashkenazi Zionist elite (including kibbutzim); very few Oriental Jews; no Arabs	Large proportion of Oriental Jewish owners, especially in smaller enterprises; a very small proportion of Arabs
Typical political affiliation of owner or manager	Labour Alignment (Labour Party, Mapam)	Likud Bloc (Herut, Liberal Party)

lower echelons of the working class in Israel, between those who work in the bureaucratic and private sectors respectively, corresponds rather closely to the national division of that class, between Israeli Jews and Palestinian Arabs. This is not a mere coincidence; it is rooted in the very nature of Israel as a Zionist settler-state, and its consequences are far-reaching.

From the very outset of the Zionist colonization of Palestine, the Zionist labour movement sought to create a Jewish monopoly in certain key sectors of the economy. This was done by excluding Arab workers from these economic activities. This policy continued after the 1948 war: industries and economic activities that were under the control of the state or the Histadrut (including its affiliated organizations, such as the kibbutzim) were generally closed to Arab workers.

With the rapid development of the economy, especially after the 1967 war, a total ban on Arab labour could no longer be maintained, since there was an acute shortage of labour-power. Thus the public construction industry came to depend on Arab labour. Today the giant Sollel-Boneh construction concern relies almost exclusively on Arab manual labour. This concern belongs to the Histadrut—the peculiarly Zionist bureaucratic structure, which combines in one entity the country's only legally recognized trade union and its largest industrial holding company.

But in most other Histadrut-owned enterprises Arab workers are not to be found. As for state-owned industrial firms, they are almost hermetically closed to Arabs. Thus Arabs are excluded not only from the huge state-owned arms industry, which employs more than a hundred thousand people, but also from the oil and chemical industries, electronics, aviation, ports, the sophisticated parts of the engineering industry, shipping and airlines. It goes without saying that tele-communications, the electricity and gas industries, and the like are also closed to Arabs. All these are considered strategic areas, and a Jewish monopoly is maintained in them not only at management level, but also, with very few exceptions, among the work-force.

The technique of keeping Arabs out is simple: all employees are required to have a record of military service and a security clearance. This automatically rules out all but a very small number of Arabs. The few exceptions—mostly members of the Druze religious sect, who are conscripted to the army—are dealt with individually. Even the Druze are excluded from most 'sensitive' and strategic areas of employment, but their exclusion is not total. Thus, for example, about half of the manual workers in Israel's biggest sea-port, at Haifa, are now Druze Arabs: the shortage in manpower was so acute that they had to be admitted into this former bastion of exclusively Jewish labour.

The policy of keeping Arabs out of the strategic industries has created a shortage of skilled and semi-skilled labour in these industries. Since the mid-1970s, the shortage has been getting progressively sharper, because military-related production has become the fastest growing area of Israel's economy; by now, it employs about one quarter of the country's total labour force.[1] As a result, the Jewish workers in these industries have been able to obtain relatively good working conditions and fringe benefits: higher pay, shorter working week,[2] longer holidays, greater job security. Managements have been forced to grant all this, in order to attract enough Jewish workers. Similar conditions do not generally exist in private industry, except where the work-force is highly skilled and purely Jewish—again for 'security reasons'.

The Arab worker is forced to seek employment in the private sector. The only major exceptions are the large public construction firms, which use mostly Arab labour on the actual construction sites; but here again, only Jews can be found in the office rooms, where design, finance, and other paper-work is done.[3]

Some of these points are well illustrated in the following excerpt from an article in a local Jerusalem newspaper: 'There are types of industrial enterprise where, because of their defence-related character, there is not an Arab worker to be found—such as most of the military industry. In Jerusalem I visited a large enterprise of this kind, employing 500 workers. Jewish workers only. They operate automatic machines of the most modern type. Their starting wage is relatively low, at $250 a month, while the average wage for the

1. For a survey of Israel's arms production and exports and of the militarization of the Israeli economy, see Esther Howard, 'Israel, the Sorcerer's Apprentice', in *MERIP Reports*, 112, February 1983.
2. The normal working week in Israel is six days.
3. For details on the role of Arab labour in the Israeli economy, see E. Farjoun, 'Palestinian Workers in Israel: a Reserve Army of Labour', *Khamsin 7* (reprinted in the present volume).

country is $350 a month. The firm works a five-day-week schedule [instead of the usual six-day week]. Two meals a day are provided free of charge. The neighbouring non-military firms find it difficult to recruit Jewish workers. In Jerusalem there are thousands of industrial firms, mostly tiny, which together employ 17,000 workers, of which 5,500 are Palestinian Arabs. Typically, the proportion of Arab workers is still higher in the newly established factories, built with government support in the occupied territories. There, except for one large factory, most of the 2,800 workers are Palestinian Arabs.'[4]

As a result of this division, firms in the private sector are utterly dependent on Arab workers. From the viewpoint of the private employer, this state of affairs is not an unhappy one: while there are political barriers to the super-exploitation of large sections of the Jewish working class, Arab workers do not enjoy similar political protection. The private employers can therefore go much further in squeezing the utmost out of their workers, while keeping wages and working conditions to the minimum level that the labour market will bear.

These developments in Israel's private sector were given a tremendous boost by the outcome of the 1967 war, which opened a huge new market to the civilian consumer-goods industry. Israeli consumer goods are not only sold in the West Bank and the Gaza Strip, but are also carried (often after being repackaged, to disguise their origin) across the 'open bridges' into the Arab countries. At present, this accounts for about one third of Israel's total exports. At the same time, the territories occupied in 1967 provided Israel's private industry with a large new labour market, more than doubling its reserve of Arab workers. More than one hundred thousand workers from these territories are now employed in various branches of the Israeli economy.

These developments, which matured during the 1970s, have had two important political consequences that concern us here.

First, the ranks of the private Jewish bourgeoisie were swollen and it became considerably more independent of the state bureaucracy. The ability of the private sector to take care of itself economically and politically was greatly enhanced. Its appetite for political power,

4. *Qol Yerushalayim*, 19 February 1982.

to complement and reflect its newly acquired economic muscle, was rapidly whetted—and it now had the financial means to mount a proper, large-scale election campaign.

Second, due to the vast expansion of the public-bureaucratic sector, especially the arms industry, and the resulting shortage of Jewish labour-power, the Jewish working class also became increasingly independent of the state and Histadrut bureaucracy and its political arm, the Labour Party. One no longer had to vote Labour in order to get a proper job.

The division of the working class according to nationality, between the public-bureaucratic and private sectors, is supplemented by an important division of the Jewish wage-workers along the major ethnic cleavage that divides Israeli Jewish society: between Oriental Jews (mostly immigrants from Arab countries, and their Israeli-born descendants) and Ashkenazim (Jews of central and east European origin). The bulk of the Jewish working class—especially in non-managerial, manual jobs, whether skilled or not—is made up of Oriental Jews.

While the formula for separating Arabs from Jews is 'military service' and 'security clearance', the euphemism used for excluding Oriental Jews is 'education'. Most white-collar government jobs are filled by Ashkenazim. Some government departments, such as the Post Office, have no educational requirements, and indeed a very high proportion of workers there, including white-collar employees, are Oriental. However, for most Oriental Jews, especially those who live in 'development towns', far from the central government sites of Tel-Aviv and Jerusalem, the only way to secure a respectable job is to join some firm owned by the state or the Histadrut (including firms owned by organizations affiliated to the Histadrut, such as the big public transport firms and 'regional enterprises' owned jointly by several kibbutzim and employing hired labour). As mentioned above, these firms are dominant in 'strategic' branches of the economy such as arms production, the chemical industry, etc. Competition with Arab workers in the private sector makes that sector very unattractive to Oriental (let alone Ashkenazi) Jewish workers. Of course, this does not mean that no Jewish workers are employed in the private sector; many are. But their preference is to work in the public-bureaucratic sector.

The pattern that has resulted from the operation of these selective forces over the years is that the typical employment of the 'average' Oriental Jewish worker is in a blue-collar job in the public-bureaucratic sector, usually in a 'strategic' industry.

Class Consciousness of Israel's Oriental Jews

Let us now return to our original question and see how the political inclinations of Israel's Oriental Jews are affected by their specific position within the country's economic and cultural life.

As we saw, the vast majority of Oriental Jews are employed in manual jobs, mostly in the public-bureaucratic sector. While their position is superior to that of Arab workers, it is inferior to that of the Ashkenazim, who hold most of the managerial and professional jobs.

Ever since the early 1950s, when large waves of Jewish immigrants arrived from Arab countries, these immigrants were regarded by the Ashkenazi Zionist elite as an inferior group who must somehow be 'raised' to the true cultural level of Jewry, represented by the Ashkenazim. Clearly, some groups of Oriental immigrants had to go through a painful period of adaptation in order to acclimatize themselves to a society fashioned by European, bourgeois-liberal, and mostly secular traditions. But this difficult process of adaptation was aggravated by the attempts at a forced Europeanization of all aspects of their life. Although as a matter of fact many of the new Oriental immigrants had belonged to the middle-class and professional strata in their countries of origin, a stereotype of Oriental Jews was created in the image of the least educated and most backward (from a bourgeois point of view) among them.

The logic of the whole period of development was to mould these Oriental ethnic groups into a hard core of the Israeli Jewish proletariat, working under the supervision of Ashkenazi managers and professionals. The fact that the Oriental immigrants had many cultural traits in common with Arabs made it easier for the Ashkenazi elite to relegate them to an inferior socio-economic position.[5]

When the Oriental Jews were slowly and painfully integrating into Israeli economic life, they always faced the Ashkenazi Jew as a

5. Concerning the attitudes of the Zionist elite to Oriental Jews, see R. Shapiro, 'Zionism and Its Oriental Subjects', *Khamsin 5* (reprinted in the present volume).

contemptuous boss who ordered them about and on whose goodwill their very livelihood depended. Their immediate class enemy—the boss—was most often a Labour-Party bureaucrat put in control of this or that Histadrut or state enterprise. Moreover, their trade-union 'representative' in the Histadrut was again an Ashkenazi, nominated from above or entrenched in this position since the old pre-state days. The government and Histadrut offices in charge of their education, housing, welfare, employment, and health-care were also staffed almost exclusively by Ashkenazim. For many years they were coerced into voting for the party of this state-bourgeoisie and union bosses, the Labour Party. This political coercion was most effective outside the main urban centres, in villages and smaller towns populated almost exclusively by Oriental Jews. There, improvements in employment, housing, and so on could be made conditional on 'favourable' electoral returns. (In the large cities this type of blackmail was less effective, and a large proportion of Oriental Jews living there indeed voted for Herut even in the early days.) Political coercion of this kind was gradually becoming more difficult to enforce, with the general liberalization of Israeli economic and political life, especially after the fall of the first Big Boss, David Ben-Gurion, Israel's first prime minister and for many years leader of the old Labour Party (Mapai).

What routes of upward socio-economic mobility were open to an Oriental Jewish worker? In the public-bureaucratic sector (including the armed forces) such mobility was slow and difficult, if not entirely impossible. Managerial and supervisory positions in this sector were firmly held by Ashkenazim. The educational route upwards was also largely blocked: to this day, the number of Oriental Jews in universities is relatively very small, partly because tertiary education is economically beyond the reach of most working-class families and partly because children of Oriental families are handicapped by the inferior quality of primary and secondary education accessible to them.

On the other hand, there was a route of advancement open to Oriental Jews—that of becoming self-employed or an owner of a small private business. In the free market of the private sector, the way up was much easier than in the public-bureaucratic sphere. As a result, a very substantial number of small independent businesses sprang up owned and run by Oriental Jews.

The typical aspiration of an Oriental Jewish worker—if there is such a thing as 'typical aspiration'—is to rid himself of his dependence on the Ashkenazi bosses and start his own small workshop, where he would employ, say, three, four, or even twenty Arab workers, with whom he has a lot in common culturally but who would be kept in their 'proper place' by the national social barrier. Nor is this mere wishful thinking; thousands of businesses of exactly this type—restaurants, small construction firms, carpentry shops, garages, and the like—have come into existence, and many have prospered.

This complex reality determines class consciousness. The Labour Party is correctly regarded by most Oriental Jews as the party of bureaucratic bosses, hated by workers and small businessmen alike. The Likud is regarded as the party of the class they identify with, the class of small businessmen, to which most Oriental Jews would like to belong and some already do belong. The working-class rhetoric of the Histadrut bosses is seen and despised for what it is: mere rhetoric that attempts to cover up the role of the Histadrut as the biggest employer in the country.

The Labour Alignment (including the Labour Party itself) is also strongly associated with the kibbutz movement, deeply hated by most Oriental Jews. This hatred combines resentment at social discrimination and class hostility towards a powerful collective employer.

A large proportion of Oriental Jews brought to Israel were settled —it felt more like being dumped—in small 'development towns' in remote corners of the country, with a meagre economic base and few resources for real development. In the same localities, heavily subsidized kibbutzim have prospered as small agri-industrial communities. The hundred thousand odd members of kibbutzim form a peculiar layer of Israeli society; it can perhaps be best described as Israel's equivalent of the English landed gentry.

The cultural, social, and political background of the kibbutz is totally alien to the Oriental Jews, who therefore find it virtually impossible to join these oases of prosperity. Even in the rare cases when they try to join, their 'mentality' is usually judged to be 'unsuitable'. On the other hand, the rapidly developing economy of the kibbutzim has become increasingly dependent on the exploitation of wage labour. About half of the labour-power employed by the kibbutzim comes, in the form of wage labour, from the Oriental communities in such 'development towns' as Qiryat Shmonah in the north or Shderot in the south. Some of these workers are hired by individual kibbutzim; many others work in 'regional enterprises' owned and managed jointly by several kibbutzim and relying exclusively on hired manual labour. These Oriental hired workers of the kibbutzim sometimes work alongside Arab workers, but they rarely meet kibbutz members except as bosses, managers, and supervisors.

Here is an excerpt from an Israeli newspaper report on the town of Qiryat Shmonah, where public meetings of the Labour Party, addressed by the party's leader, Shim'on Peres, were broken up by angry Oriental inhabitants. 'Qiryat Shmonah, which from time to time reaches the headlines, is a good model for a close study of the relations between the two sides [namely, the town's Oriental inhabitants and the nearby kibbutzim]. From government publications one can learn that ... about 80 per cent of Qiryat Shmonah's population do hard physical work, with very limited prospects for on-the-job advancement. Half of all the workers are employed by the kibbutzim in regional enterprises such as a bakery, plants for processing agricultural products, hotels, quarries, as well as in various kinds of hired work inside the kibbutzim. Some time ago, when unemployment in the town was high, the government was forced to set up a plant of the arms industry, in which there are higher-level jobs and therefore the feeling of the workers is better. Here wages are also better, and so are the prospects for advancement. When the father of a family comes back home from his job in the kibbutz and talks about his experiences there (wages which are sometimes low, hard physical work, kibbutz snobism), the family absorbs these stories and the pronouncements, so it seems, pass from father to son.'[6]

It is perfectly natural that the relationship between the two communities is one of total estrangement. The kibbutzim are perceived as the darlings of the state, who have got the best land, water, and other resources, such as cheap credit, and who thrive by exploiting the miserable living conditions and political weakness of the Oriental Jewish workers.

This political weakness is what Israel's Oriental Jews are trying to

6. *Ha'aretz*, 4 November 1982.

reverse by voting Likud. The Labour Alignment is closely identified with the kibbutz movement; during election campaigns, kibbutz members go into the development towns to solicit votes for Labour; and a relatively high number of Labour candidates are members or ex-members of kibbutzim. For most Oriental workers, it is unthinkable to vote for such people, and will continue to be so for the foreseeable future. They are seen as arrogant bosses, who should be politically checked, not encouraged.

Conclusions

The political allegiance of Israel's Oriental Jews to the Likud, and their rejection of Labour, are firmly rooted in the history and class structure of Israeli society. It does not depend very much on the position taken by the Likud on this or that national or economic issue. Begin will have their support both in taking chauvinist positions and in adopting more moderate stands. This contrasts sharply with the support that Begin enjoys in the fascist-religious milieu of Gush Emunim or the Tehiyyah (Revival) Party, whose members are mostly Ashkenazim. This latter support is entirely conditional on the Likud's commitment to a Greater Israel, from which Palestinian Arabs are to be expelled.

The political support of the Likud among Israel's Oriental Jewish working class can be expected to continue for quite some time. It may decline slowly, following changes in the ethnic composition of the state-bureaucratic section of the Israeli bourgeoisie. Such changes may come about precisely as a consequence of the Likud's remaining in office long enough, especially if it succeeds in capturing the Histadrut, in addition to the state apparatus, which it already controls.

Oriental Support for Begin: a Critique of Farjoun

Avishai Ehrlich

Careful consideration of the article by E. Farjoun raises a series of questions about several of the 'facts' presented, the conclusions derived from them, and his method of analysis, which consequently appears incomplete. That the Oriental support for Begin is a form of protest against the Labour Party is not a new theory; what Farjoun claims to add is:

1. That this support is not dependent on Begin's national or economic policies, nor is it an indication of agreement with these policies.

2. That the protest is an expression of (working-) class antagonism to the Labour corporate bureaucracy.

The 'Facts' Disputed

To prove the first point, Farjoun argues that: 1. Begin's Oriental supporters voted for him despite his economic policy, which affected them adversely. 2. The return of Sinai was more popular with the Orientals than with the Ashkenazim. 3. The poorer sections of the Oriental community which support Begin are also against his policy of massive colonization of the West Bank.

These arguments are incredible and spurious to say the least, as they fly in the face of known facts.

1. In contradistinction to most right-wing governments in the present world crisis, Begin's government has continued and increased government deficit-spending. This has exacerbated the balance of payments situation and the foreign debt; but, together with a sophisticated system of indexation and other welfare mechanisms, it has

enabled most of the population to retain and even increase their standard of living. Moreover, this high-inflation policy allowed the government to maintain a very low rate of unemployment (about 4 per cent) among Jews. The main attack by Labour on Begin's policy was that it was mortgaging the future for short-term benefits. These benefits, among others, included the satisfaction of the economic interests of his supporters. Farjoun argues that they voted for Begin despite suffering economically under him; but in fact they voted for him because they would have suffered more under Labour.

2. To argue that the Oriental community was more in favour of the return of Sinai, as part of the peace agreement with Egypt, than the Ashkenazi community is also unfounded. It is, however, correct that the extreme right movements that were against the withdrawal (the Revival Party, Gush Emunim, the Jewish Defence League) are mainly Ashkenazi in composition. This fact, nonetheless, is only half the truth, because the other half is that the organized support for the return of Sinai and for the Sadat agreement was also mainly Ashkenazi in composition (the Peace Now movement). There was never a *wide* public movement among Orientals for the withdrawal from Sinai prior to the agreement. The unpleasant truth is that most of Oriental public opinion passively trailed behind the official policy.

3. With regard to Oriental attitudes towards the massive colonization of the West Bank, it is again correct that in the first phases of colonization most of the settlers were supporters of the extreme right, which is in the main Ashkenazi. However, so was, and is, the opposition to the colonization. Zionist pioneer settlement of frontier zones was always carried out by ideological movements which were Ashkenazi. Once the framework was established, Oriental Jews were brought in. This was the case with the newly occupied territories after the 1948 war, when the first to move in were kibbutzim, and only afterwards was the area densely populated by villages and 'development towns' whose inhabitants were mostly Oriental. The pattern recurs at present with one variation. With the exception of the Golan Heights, the kibbutz movements, which are mainly Ashkenazi, were reluctant—for political reasons—to be the vanguard of settlement in the occupied territories. Their pioneering role was taken by new movements of the political 'right', also mainly Ashkenazi.

The Begin-Sharon government has now entered into the second phase of the settlement and absorption of the West Bank. Massive building of urban and semi-urban neighbourhoods is being completed. These apartment blocks are offered to young families at cheap, heavily subsidized prices; and those finding housing a major problem, mainly Orientals, are beginning to flock in. It will not be long before the West Bank (which, with the exception of Jerusalem, has so far been sparsely populated by Jews) has a much larger Oriental Jewish population. In this way the accusation that the settlements divert funds which would otherwise go towards improving the conditions of Oriental Jews is being averted. The government argues that the solution for the Oriental urban poor lies in their settlement in the West Bank. The claim that there is wide Oriental opposition to the settlement of the West Bank is unfounded; only marginal Oriental groups (supporters of the Black Panthers, for instance) have raised their voices against it. An even greater willingness to move to the West Bank is checked only by the lack of employment prospects in the immediate vicinity of the new settlements, which compels the settlers to commute.

Summarizing, I have shown that Farjoun's argument that Oriental support for Begin is economically altruistic is simply wrong. Also unfounded is the implication that the Oriental supporters of Begin have positive attitudes towards withdrawal from the occupied territories and are against their settlement.

The Incomplete Sector Analysis

Farjoun's refusal to acknowledge the positive reasons for the support for Begin and his policies among Orientals is carried into his second argument, which attempts to analyse the distribution of Orientals and Ashkenazim into class positions within the public and private sectors of the Israeli economy. He reaches two conclusions:

1. That in the public sector Orientals and Ashkenazim face each other in antagonistic class relations: semi-skilled and skilled labourers against supervisory, managerial, corporate bosses.

2. That the main path to upward mobility for Orientals was through entrepreneurship in the private sector. These upwardly mobile sections of the Oriental community relate with antagonism to

the public sector, where their mobility was restricted, and thus identify with the party of the private bourgeoisie.

Here too the claim is that support for Begin is due to his being Labour's opponent rather than because of what he actually stands for. Farjoun and I share the view that a class analysis of Israeli society must include both the ethnic and the national divisions. A class analysis of the Israeli social formation must account for the inter-relationship and changes in the triangle: Occidentals-Orientals-Palestinians. Farjoun's conclusions are based on a concentration on just one pair of relationships within the triangle, the Occidental-Oriental couple, and ignore the Oriental-Palestinian, Occidental-Palestinian couples. It is my contention that his conclusions are the result of an incomplete analysis.

In a capitalist economy, a sudden increase in the supply of unskilled labour will tend to have the following effects (other things being equal):

1. The price of unskilled labour-power will tend to decrease.

2. The differential between the prices of skilled and unskilled labour-power will tend to increase.

3. The ratio of cost of labour to cost of capital will decrease, encouraging labour-intensive processes of production.

If, however, as in Israel, the economy has two sectors, one of which does not utilize the increased labour supply, the effects on this sector of the introduction of the new supply of unskilled labour will tend to be:

4. A wider differential of labour prices between the two sectors.

5. A tendency to increase capital-intensive processes of production.

These simple theoretical conclusions are of particular significance in the class analysis of Israel. They account for some of the consequences of the segregation of the Jewish and Arab economies in Palestine in the pre-state period; they are also fruitful for an understanding of the impact of waves of immigration to Israel, in particular the Oriental immigrations. Since 1967, they are important for understanding the impact of the absorption of the Palestinian labour force, and they also help to illuminate the relationship between the kibbutz sector and the rest of the Israeli economy.

Effects of Palestinian Employment on the Jewish Working Class

What were the main consequences for the Jewish working class of the absorption of a large Palestinian labour force? In the private sector the new source of cheap labour made it possible for larger numbers of Jews, Oriental and Occidental, to move from positions of employees to becoming employers. These very small capitalist enterprises stand or fall on the continued supply of cheap Palestinian labour. The 1967 occupation signified for them the opportunity to move out of the working class. At the other end of the labour force, there was a fraction of the Jewish working class, almost entirely Oriental, which was unskilled. The introduction of cheap Palestinian labour threatened to further reduce their wages. To mitigate the effects of this competition, the Histadrut and the Ministry of Labour intervened to enforce basic minimum pay rates, but only where the work-force was mixed. The main trend, however, was towards the division of labour along national lines, which opened channels of upward mobility for Jews within the class.

In the segregated sector of the Israeli economy, where Arabs are not admitted, the effects of the Palestinian work-force were indirect. It made the supply of the Jewish labour force more scarce and thus increased the pay differentials between the *Jewish* and *mixed* sectors. The scarcity of labour and its high price was also a cause for capital-intensification, which itself increases the demand for more skilled labour, thus raising the differentials even further. It is possible to argue that this sector of the Jewish working class also benefited from the incorporation of Palestinian workers into other sectors of the economy.

Although the effects of the incorporation of Palestinians on changes in the Jewish class structure require more research, it is easy to see even from the above sketch that the Jewish working class, and not only the bourgeoisie, benefits from the incorporation of Palestinians into the economy and has an interest in the continuation of this situation. The converse is also true: wide sections of the Jewish working class and new small capitalists have much to fear in terms of personal status, incomes, and mobility from the discontinuation of Palestinian employment. To the extent, therefore, that the Labour Party is perceived as willing to negotiate Israeli withdrawal from occupied territories, this is seen by these sections as a socio-economic threat. On the other hand, Begin's stance—no return of the territories—coupled with actions to make the separation of the West Bank from Israel impossible, is in line with their material interests.

There is no contradiction between the hostility of many Oriental workers to the Labour bureaucracy and their interest in maintaining the Arab labour force. Indeed, some, mainly the new Oriental entrepreneurs, may combine the two sentiments, as they may well imagine that the return of the territories would necessarily mean the stoppage of mass Palestinian employment in the Jewish economy and that this could create a return to the situation of the 1950s, where in the absence of Arabs they themselves were forced into the lower echelons of the working class, subordinated to the Ashkenazim.

The view of many Jewish workers that they do benefit from the incorporation of Palestinians into the economy may lead them to object to the return of the territories, but also to be against massive expulsions of the majority of the Palestinians. Thus, not many workers support the most extreme right, fascist movements who call for the expulsion of Palestinians from 'Greater Israel'. Both extremes of Zionism have in common the aspiration of Israel as purely Jewish. The difference is in the method, and the geographical scope of what is seen as Israel, but not in concept. The interest in permanently retaining the Arab labourers in the Jewish economy as a subordinate stratum presupposes the open and formal institutionalization of an unequal status for Arabs: discriminated against, but tolerated.

I have tried to show that Farjoun's analysis is incomplete, that wide sections of the working class and of new small capitalists support Begin not just against Labour but also positively; they endorse what he stands for. Furthermore, there is no contradiction between a protest against Labour and positive support for Begin's policies.

Is the Oriental Reaction a Particular Class Antagonism?

Farjoun claims that it is so, but this is very much a matter of an operational definition. To reach his conclusion, he conflates the Orientals and the working class; simultaneously, to create the 'class' enemy, he excludes Occidentals from the working class. If we define the working class as those who do not own means of production and make their living by selling their labour power, we still find that a majority of Occidentals are workers, perhaps highly skilled, professionals, perhaps not proletarian, not employed in the productive sectors, but workers nonetheless. At most we could say that Occidentals and Orientals are differentially distributed in various fractions of the working class. This argument echoes a current debate among Marxists, whether to define the working class minimally or maximally, a debate that reflects the complex division of labour in advanced capitalism as well as different political strategies.

One of the effects of the incorporation of the Palestinian labour force into the Israeli economy has been to open up and diversify the class composition of the Oriental communities. It is now less correct to assume a class homogeneity of Oriental Jews than it was at any time since their arrival in Israel. It would be of interest to find out whether the Oriental supporters of Begin, a subset of the Orientals, are concentrated in particular class positions, whether these positions are mainly working-class, and in particular in which fractions of the working class. The concepts 'lower' and 'middle' echelons are inadequate; they mean, presumably, lower and middle income groups—but this is not a particularly Marxist criterion of class determination. I have doubts as to whether the staunchest supporters of Begin among the Orientals are also the most proletarian elements among them, that is, workers in the productive sectors of large industry.

There is a need for more detailed empirical data on various aspects of the composition of the Oriental community before this debate can be taken further. However, it has occurred to me that if Oriental support for Begin is indeed a class protest against the Labour Party, it should have been reflected more in the elections to the Histadrut than in the elections to the state's parliament. A larger percentage of the voters in the Histadrut elections are workers. If, as Farjoun argues, most of them are Oriental and most of them view the Labour Party antagonistically, then there should have been a larger swing towards the Likud in the Histadrut than in the Knesset—in fact the opposite happened (see table, p. 76).

To be precise, I do not argue that the Oriental support for Begin is not a protest against the Labour Party; it probably is. What I question is whether this is a class protest.

Percentage of Vote for Labour and Likud in Histadrut Elections

Year	1969	1973	1977	1981
Labour	62	58	57	63
Likud	22	23	28	27

(Source: D.M. Zohar, *Political Parties in Israel*, 1974, p. 124; and A. Diskin in *The Jerusalem Quarterly*, no. 22, winter 1981, p. 101.)

Other Related Issues

My criticisms have been confined to Farjoun's two main theses, but his article is unclear on wider issues. It is not clear whether it wishes to explain the causes of Begin's ascent to power or whether it means to confine itself to explaining the Oriental vote for Begin. This vote is one, albeit important, reason for Begin's rise, but it is by no means the only one. Begin's first government, of 1977, the watershed point that signified the breakdown of Labour hegemony, was made possible not just by Oriental protest but also by the protest vote of Occidentals for Yadin's Democratic Movement for Change, and by the deep transformation in the ranks of the religious bloc of parties, traditional coalition partners of Labour which deserted it. These shifts, as well as the continuous crisis of Labour, still require proper analysis.

Palestinian Workers in Israel: a Reserve Army of Labour

Emmanuel Farjoun

In Israeli parlance the term 'Arab', which denotes a member of the Arab society of the areas ruled by Israel, has a dual connotation. First, the Arab is a *person* born and bred in Palestinian-Arab society, a non-Jewish resident in the Jewish state. Second, the Arab is a *worker*, who arrives early in the morning from his village to build houses and roads, clean, do the garden, repair cars and fill them with petrol; and who at night usually goes back home—to the West Bank, the Gaza Strip, Galilee or the Triangle.

The Arab as a person is seen as an abomination. His very existence mars the Jewishness of the state of Israel. He belongs to that Arab people with which the Jewish settlers' society has been contending since the very beginning. As the writer A.B. Yehoshua puts it: 'Therefore was this nation severely enjoined to be strictly apart, without the nearby gentile.... There is nothing more dangerous than allowing the gentile back into our midst (and he is very deep in our midst, entirely woven into our economic infrastructure, but penetrating also into other spheres of our life.)'[1]

Israeli society persecutes the Arab person, and therefore hates him. It makes every attempt to conceal his very existence and even to remove him beyond the pale of its dominion. He cannot join a kibbutz or a moshav, the crowning glory of Israeli society. Most Jewish towns and villages in Israel are closed to him by virtue of local or national regulations (in the whole of Israel there are just *six* towns and townships with mixed Arab and Jewish populations). In the evening, after work, he cannot walk about unharassed in the streets of Tel-Aviv, but must huddle in a dark corner behind a locked and

1. *Bitfutzot Hagolah* (In the Diaspora), 1975 – 76, p. 38.

bolted door, or go back home to his village. Even the term 'Arab' does not appear in Israeli official statistics, which recognize 'only one national group in Israel: Jews'. The rest are 'minorities', 'non-Jews', 'Moslems', 'Christians', 'Druze', and so forth.

The Arab as *a worker* is, on the contrary, an acceptable and welcome member of the household in many quarters of Israeli society—and it is precisely this which enrages 'liberals' like A.B. Yehoshua. He is admitted into the kitchens and gardens of the Israeli elite, where he cooks, cleans, and digs; he is welcome on building sites, petrol stations, timber yards, and factories; and he is even allowed into army camps. The gates were opened wide for him in 1966, when structural changes were made in military rule (under which the Arabs in Israel have been living since 1948) and the daily pass system was waived, allowing masses of Arab workers fairly free movement throughout Israel (except the south of the country). The Histadrut (General Federation of Labour), a cornerstone of the Israeli establishment, not only allowed him to join—for the first time since its foundation in 1922—but even changed its name for his sake: it used to be 'The General Federation of *Hebrew* Workers in Eretz Yisrael', but now the word 'Hebrew' was dropped.

As we shall see, the Arab worker has become a decisive factor in major sectors of the Israeli economy: construction, road building, tourism, agriculture, and various branches of industry. He is gradually penetrating typical areas of Israeli industrial production: food processing, textiles, manufacture of building materials, and many other industries.

In this survey I shall try to describe the characteristics of the Arab labour force in Israel. In other words, I will largely ignore the Arab's status as a person, as a citizen, and as a member of the Palestinian Arab people, though this is a vitally important aspect of the national and class structure of the emergent Israeli society. The focus will be on the role of Arab workers in Israel's economy—workers from both within the 'green line' and outside it, that is from the West Bank and the Gaza Strip.

The obvious difficulty in trying to distinguish between the two aspects and to isolate the purely economic side of the story is illustrated in the following frank journalistic account, written by Ya'ir Kottler in an article about the Home Guard and its role as guardian of Jewish purity in Tel-Aviv:

'The time is two hours before midnight. In the back seat of the jeep sit two young volunteers armed with guns and ammunition. The mission—combing through Shuq Hakarmel [Tel-Aviv's main market]. They search for Arabs spending the night in Tel-Aviv—in tiny nooks, on building sites, in warehouses, even under greengrocers' stalls. They are not supposed to stay on in the Jewish city beyond 1.00 a.m. unless they have special permits, which most of the workers from the occupied territories, who flood into Tel-Aviv and the neighbouring towns, do not have.... The Home Guard is helping the police. The frightened Arabs, unaware of the police-like authority of this civil militia, answer questions and show their papers. They are harassed. They are temporarily detained at a base near a large elementary school. Before 1.00 a.m. they cannot be arrested. They can be harassed, though. This is precisely what is done. The district police chief, Commander Moshe Tiomkin, states in an interview that in his district, inhabited by 1.1 million people, there are already 70,000 Arabs from the occupied territories—50 per cent of these in Tel-Aviv proper. This is, by any standard, an astonishing figure. The police cannot cope with the problem. They seek the help of the Home Guard. But the volunteers have not joined the Guard in order to become policemen in disguise, hunting and interrogating Arab workers who seek night shelter from the law in dark holes, in locked poulterers' shops, in back yards and in rented rooms in Jewish homes, always for a few dozen liras per bed per night. "Can we detain thousands? If we do this," says Tiomkin, "we would be screwing ourselves. Next morning the big city would lose its workers. They are building the city." If they were detained, there would be no one to clean the streets .... Somewhere near the beach we stopped three Arabs. One was terrified—he had no papers; he had come to work with a friend from Hebron. The Hebronite, 19 years of age, has been working in Tel-Aviv for the last five years [since he was 14] mostly as a night watchman, earning IL70 a day, sometimes more. He wouldn't give up his work in Tel-Aviv for a state of his own. He simply fell in love with the Hebrew city, with its girls and its sights. Jews don't know how to work, he says, adding that Shuq Hakarmel is full of Arabs from Gaza. Commander Tiomkin is of the opinion that the increase in crime in the district, particularly in Tel-Aviv, is a result, amongst other things, of the presence of tens of thousands of Arabs from the occupied territories. They remind him of a "slave market".'[2] The present survey does not deal with the overall role of Palestinian Arabs in the Israeli economy, but examines their contribution as workers, be it labourers or skilled and self-employed workers, since the Arab labour force in Israel consists mainly of hired or self-employed workers. The capitalist stratum within Arab society in Israel is very small, and there are few Arabs in administrative jobs. Arab society in Israel has a limited economic base: according to official reports,[3] there were only three Arab-owned industrial enterprises in Israel in 1976. In Israel's political economy, a factory can neither be opened nor continue to exist without active government aid, but the state institutions do not permit even the most consistently collaborationist villages to develop Arab-owned industrial zones. Two of the above-mentioned enterprises are small sewing shops and the third is a metal works (200 workers) in the village of Yarka in Galilee. Even if one or two new enterprises have come into existence in the last couple of years, the fact remains that there is no Arab capitalist bourgeoisie in Israel. Moreover, even Jewish-owned enterprises are hardly ever located in Arab villages: according to latest reports, there are some fifty small enterprises, mostly sewing shops and carpentries. The bourgeoisie of the Arab sector is a petty bourgeoisie made up of traders and agricultural producers. More than 70 per cent of the total Arab labour force are hired workers, mostly in production: construction, agriculture, industry; and in private-sector services such as hotels, restaurants, and so forth. Only a small proportion work as clerks or in the public services, in finance or in the professions. Thus the Arabs' almost exclusive contribution to the Israeli economy is as productive workers, from whose labour someone—a contractor, an industrialist, a businessman—profits directly. Only few of them are self-employed: farmers, sub-contractors, and so on.

If one follows the development of this labour force, its composition, the sectors in which it is concentrated, and its socio-economic characteristics, one discovers that there is a *definite regularity* in the development of the Arabs' place and role in the economy.

Throughout the history of Zionist colonization, the Jewish *yishuv* tried, on the whole, to create a society based on purely Jewish labour, at least in some focal areas. But the natural development of a

2. Ya'ir Kottler, *Ha'aretz*, 9 September 1977.
3. H. Harari, *Israeli Arabs, 1976, in Figures*, Giv'at Havivah—Arab Studies, no. 10.

capitalist economy, as well as the recurrent clashes with the Arab world, led to an ever-increasing concentration of Jewish labour in definite 'strategic' sectors of production. At first this meant agricultural production—settling on the land, erecting purely Jewish colonies, moshavim and kibbutzim on every possible site. (The rules of the Jewish National Fund (JNF) were framed towards that very end, forbidding the purchase, lease, or cultivation of its lands by non-Jews.) Other such sectors were the diamond industry and the ports.

With the establishment of the state and the mass deportation of Arabs from hundreds of villages came the expropriation of most of the Arab lands, in order to seize control of the main asset—the soil—and create the pre-condition for Jewish domination of agricultural production. On the other hand, the now largely landless Arab population remaining under Israeli rule increased apace. (More than half of that population was 'acquired' by Israel in 1949 as a result of the Rhodes agreements and the change in the cease-fire line in the area of the Triangle and Wadi 'Ara.) From 160,000 at the end of 1949, the Arab population inside Israel grew to 400,000 in 1967, and reached 550,000 in 1978. This created a heavy pressure of workers willing to work for low wages and in bad conditions.

At the same time, an important change occurred in the Israeli economy with the development of an Israeli armaments industry in the sixties, and particularly with the decisive changes both in the geopolitical map of the country and in the balance of power between Israel and the Arab world as a result of the 1967 war—changes that brought about a huge influx of capital into Israel, and turned it from a privileged *protégé* of the West into an *ally* having the status of a local power. Following these changes, agriculture ceased to fulfil a strategic role and the accelerated economic development in both agriculture and industry created an ever-increasing demand for a cheap, mobile, and under-privileged labour force: *a 'free' labour force in the classical economic sense.*

This demand was met by the Arab workers from the new territories acquired by Israel as well as by 'Israeli' Arab workers, who were just beginning to flow into the market in large numbers.

Because of the need to sustain a settlers' society, living on its sword, in constant and expensive conflict with the world around it, it was necessary to grant the Jews special privileges and to try at all costs to secure for them a relatively high standard of living, in order to prevent Jewish emigration (*yeridah*) and to help maintain maximum political stability. These imperatives imposed political constraints upon the Israeli bourgeoisie's freedom of economic action *vis-à-vis* the Jewish worker. This applies particularly to that part of the bourgeoisie which was then in power, represented by the Labour Party and Mapam, the bureaucratic bourgeoisie of the public sector. Security of employment and income, and a standard of living higher than in the surrounding Arab world, became cornerstones of the Israeli political system. Therefore, while the accelerated economic development after 1967 created the above-mentioned demand for a 'free' labour force—cheap, mobile, without job security, without political representation—this demand could not be met by Jewish workers.

The post-1967 military and political development also created a huge demand for Jewish labour in the armaments industry, in the army, and in the general administration of the extended colony. The inevitable result was that Arab workers began to form a decisive part of the Israeli economy's *free labour force*, in the above-mentioned sense, which until then had consisted mainly of Oriental Jews. Since 1967 the Arab labour force has become (along with the lowest strata of the Jewish proletariat, made up mainly of Oriental Jews) a major and indispensable element. Thus the Israeli civilian economy, particularly in the private sector, is becoming largely dependent on Arab labour. The national division of the population in the territories ruled by Israel is increasingly becoming an economically significant division: on the one hand the privileged group employed in industries and services connected with the state, and army, and strategic production—a protected group enjoying a certain monopoly and virtual security of tenure, and whose working conditions are constantly improving through organized struggles and political pressures (through the Histadrut, the Labour Party, etc.); and on the other hand the *'free'* part of the working class, which gives the private economy its flexibility, its capacity to adjust to crises. It is the latter group that makes the manpower reservoir into a *labour market* in the classical capitalist sense and constitutes the *reserve army of the Israeli economy*.

At the same time, this free labour force gives the private bourgeoisie, in both agriculture and industry, a degree of independence of the Histadrut, the state institutions, and the bureaucracy. This is one of the sources of strength of the private bourgeoisie, as opposed to the state-bureaucratic bourgeoisie (the Histadrut, the kibbutzim, etc.). The Histadrut cannot use strikes to bring pressure on a private businessman employing Arabs, since when it comes to Arabs they are in the same boat; a strike by Arab workers would endanger both sectors. Moreover, due to the relative abundance of Arab workers in the Israeli economy, their manoeuvring room is limited and their bargaining power almost nil. Thus the Arab labour force has contributed to the historical tendency of the strengthening of the private bourgeoisie in Israel in relation to the state-bureaucratic bourgeoisie, a tendency that has gathered momentum since 1967. This sometimes gives rise to apparently absurd situations, when representatives of the state-bureaucratic bourgeoisie, like A.B. Yehoshua, who is a 'left' Zionist, talk and act more dogmatically, in a harsher and more racist way, against the 'Arab presence' in Israel than their counterparts on the right, some of whom would like the two nations to live together —under the iron hand of the Israeli army, to be sure.

This survey is mainly statistical and attempts to sketch the development and present position of the Arab working class in Israel, using mainly official Israeli publications and, to a lesser extent, occasional articles published in the Israeli press. But the figures, though indicating the general picture, tell only a small part of the story of the Arab workers in Israel: in order to tell the whole story a full sociological study would be needed. A short visit to an Israeli town may afford a glimpse of reality no figures could ever express.

Take Beersheba, for example—a town 'cleansed' of its pre-1948 Arab inhabitants, like hundreds of other towns and villages captured by the Israeli army during the 1948 war, and which now has a population of about a hundred thousand. Over the years, it has attracted thousands of Bedouin-Arab workers from the whole Negev. Most of these Arabs were peasants, driven off their lands by the kibbutzim and moshavim, whose aim it was to 'make the desert bloom'. Those workers cannot, of course, live inside Beersheba; the houses they build are destined not for Arabs but for new Jewish immigrants, or for Jewish workers, for example. As a result, Beersheba is now surrounded by a belt of shanties where the Arab workers reside. These shanty towns, from which the workers emerge each morning in order to build Beersheba and work in its factories, have no running water, sewage system, electricity, or roads. Like the black townships in South Africa, the legality of their very existence is doubtful, and with the expansion of the town they will no doubt be bulldozed further away, outside the town's boundaries. Such townships tell more about these workers than cart-loads of figures. They exist round other cities in Israel, like Ramleh and Haderah.

The government and its 'settlements minister', Ariel Sharon, keep reminding us that tens of thousands of Bedouins have 'infiltrated the coastal plain'—into the heart of the Jewish state. Sharon forgets that these very same Bedouin 'infiltrators' fill his car with petrol and work on his large farm, and that without their 'infiltration' many Israeli firms, including most of the agricultural export sector, would grind to a halt.

This survey hardly touches upon any of these social aspects. It has four sections. The first deals with the whole working population and with the reserve force of the Israeli economy. It will be seen that the Jewish industrial reserve force in Israel has been greatly depleted —all skilled and semi-skilled Jewish workers are fully, though not always most efficiently, employed, in spite of five years of deep recession since the 1973 war. The manpower problem is of course related to the general population balance between the two national groups: the Israeli Jews and Palestinian Arabs. In this section we shall see, for instance, that the growth of the Arab labour force is twice as fast as that of the Jewish.

The second section deals with the distribution of the Arab labour force, both from the occupied territories and from Israel, between the various sectors and enterprises. It will be seen that in the main productive industries and occupations, where someone makes a direct profit out of the workers' labour, the Arabs' relative contribution is much greater than their proportion in the population and in the general labour force. I shall also try to estimate their relative contribution to the overall output of workers in Israel.

The third section reviews an important characteristic of the Arab working class—its mobility, which distinguishes it sharply from the Jewish working class. This very mobility makes it a 'free' labour force economically speaking, subject to the fluctuations of the market. The recent recession, which caused no unemployment in the Jewish sector, reduced dramatically the number of Arab workers, particularly from the West Bank, in certain branches of employment.

The fourth section deals with wages and working conditions. This section is on the borderline of statistical research and in order to cover this subject fully one would have to study the social conditions of the Arab working class—which is beyond the scope of this work. We shall see, however, that not only is the average per capita income of the Arab workers half that of the Jewish hired workers, but also that *within each occupation* there is a difference of up to 40 per cent between the wages of Arab and Jewish workers.

The Arab Working-Class Population

Even a cursory glance at the population statistics of the two national groups in Israel—Israeli Jews and Palestinian Arabs—shows that the latter's contribution to the labour force far exceeds its relative size. For the moment, let us confine ourselves to the population of Israel proper, within the 'green line'. Among the Arabs the median age is 15, whereas the median Jewish age is 22; only 3.4 per cent of Israel's Arab population is above retirement age (65 years), whereas among the Jews the proportion is almost three times as high—about 9 per cent. There are in Israel approximately three million Jews and half a million Arabs—a ratio of 6 to 1. But, as a result of the different age structures, the respective *annual increase* of the economically most active age groups (20 – 65) is in the ratio of less than 3 to 1. In fact, during the last few years the Jewish population in this age group increased by about 24,000 annually, while the corresponding figure for the Arab population was about 9,000.[4] This high rate of growth of the potential Arab labour force is less surprising if we remember that despite Jewish immigration, the overall annual rate of increase of the Arab population (4 per cent) is twice that of the Jewish population (2 per cent). Every year there are some 60,000 additional Jews, compared to 20,000 Arabs. Already the number of Arab children (ages 1 to 10) is *one-third* that of Jewish children.[5]

To sum up: whereas the number of Arabs in Israel is *one-sixth* that of Jews, the size of the *potential* Arab labour force (counting Israeli citizens only) is *one-third* that of the potential Jewish labour force: for every three Jews added to the labour-force reservoir, one Arab is also added.

4. *Israel Statistical Annual, 1977.*
5. Ibid.

In addition to these figures, some deeper factors must be considered. For example, the data on youth labour show that among Jewish youth (ages 14 to 17) about 23 per cent belong to the labour force (that is, are working or seeking employment), whereas the corresponding proportion among Arabs is considerably higher—37 per cent.[6] Moreover, the part played by secondary education is incomparably smaller among Arabs than among Jews. This, of course, is a result of a deliberate policy. This policy was expressed, long before the famous 'Koenig report', by the then 'Adviser to the Prime Minister on Arab Affairs', Uri Lubrani, who wrote in *Ha'aretz*: 'It might have been better if there were no Arab students. Had they remained hewers of wood and drawers of water it might have been easier to govern them. But there are things beyond our control. We cannot prevent this, but we should think of ways to localize the problem'.[7] This approach manifests itself in the token government support given to Arab education and Arab local authorities, which is totally out of proportion to their numbers. The disproportion can be measured, for instance, by the number of secondary school teachers: 1,800 in the Arab sector as opposed to 24,500 in Jewish schools; so less than 7 per cent of secondary teachers are working in the Arab sector, although its secondary-school population constitutes 20 per cent of the total.

But Arab workers resident in Israel constitute only about *half* of the Arab workers employed in Israel. The other half come from the occupied territories (the West Bank and the Gaza Strip), and several hundred even come from Lebanon. Then there are also the workers from East Jerusalem, officially annexed to the state of Israel and appearing in most official publications as part of Israeli statistics.

Including East Jerusalem, there were about 540,000 Arabs in Israel in 1978, of whom some 110,000 belonged to the labour force, according to official figures. However, for several reasons these figures must be taken with a grain of salt. They are based on surveys and questionnaires and obviously some people do not report that they are working, in order to avoid income tax. Also, it seems that only a small part of Arab working women are included in those statistics, according to which only 10,000 Arab women resident in Israel belong to the labour force. In fact, thousands of women do agricultural work on domestic

6. *Report on Youth Labour*, Ministry of Labour, 1975.
7. *Ha'aretz*, 4 April 1961.

plots or are employed by labour contractors in small spinning mills in their own villages or in seasonal work such as fruit picking—and many of them certainly do not appear in official statistics. But a similar statistical distortion occurs, perhaps to the same extent, in official data on the Jewish labour force; so by ignoring it we shall probably not distort our estimate of the *numerical proportion* between the two national groups too much. (Note, however, that among the Jews it is mainly the self-employed in commerce and services who belong to the unofficial 'black' economy, whereas in the case of Arabs it is, on the contrary, mostly workers employed by 'black' employers.)

On the other hand, official statistics of workers from the occupied territories employed in Israel are completely unreliable. Here are the official figures for 1977.

Population and labour force in the occupied territories, 1977[8]
(thousands)

	Population over 14	Labour force	Employed in Israel
West Bank	373	125	37
Gaza Strip & Sinai	235	78	25
Total	608	203	62

These figures were derived from questionnaires put to a representative sample of some two thousand extended families in the West Bank and the Gaza Strip. They are not based directly on the situation on the ground, since few employers would report accurately how many workers from the occupied territories they employ. There are many reasons for this: for one thing, these workers are legally forbidden to stay inside Israel overnight; also, the employer wants to avoid paying income tax, insurance for the workers, and so forth.

The official statistician Hanokh Smith, director of the Manpower Planning Authority, has the following to say about workers from the occupied territories employed in the Beersheba region: 'According to official data there are about 5,000 workers from Judea and Samaria, but in reality the number is at least double.'[9] The Tel-Aviv police commander said late in 1977 that in Tel-Aviv alone 70,000 workers arrive every morning from the occupied territories.[10]

8. *Statistical Quarterly for the Occupied Territories*, vol. 7, no. 2, 1977.
9. Hanokh Smith, *Manpower in Israel—Annual Report, 1976.*
10. *Ya'ir Kottler.*

The Ministry of Labour itself reports[11] that it has in its possession a card index of 150,000 workers from the West Bank and the Gaza Strip who have at some time worked in Israel. These workers were of course employed officially, through the labour exchanges. (This figure does not seem to tally with the official overall figure of the labour force in the occupied territories, namely 203,000, even if we take into consideration that these are cumulative records of ten years of occupation.) According to the same report, approximately 60,000 workers from the occupied territories are currently registered and employed through the labour exchanges.[12] The labour exchange for the Gaza Strip and the north of Sinai, for example, has reported a steady decline in the number of workers registering with it. Among the reasons given is the red tape involved in the payment of wages, hence the attraction of getting a job through a private labour contractor *ra'is* who pays on the spot. It also seems that official wages paid through the labour exchanges are *lower* than those paid on the open market. They are also taxed, and subjected to all sorts of other deductions such as pension contributions, which no Gaza Strip worker wants to pay, since there is no guarantee he will get anything in return for them when he reaches retirement age.

The following is a sample of the Gaza Strip labour-exchange records, giving the numbers (in thousands) of registered workers during the last few years:[13]

1969	*1970*	*1971*	*1972*	*1973*	*1974*	*1975*	*1976*
31	25	25	26	23	24	18	20

These figures show a sharp decline, even during the boom years 1969 – 73, when there was actually an enormous increase in the number of workers from the occupied territories working in Israel.

According to the Ministry of Labour report, for every five registered workers, there are four who work unofficially.

In view of all this, there is no doubt that the number of workers from the occupied territories working in Israel averages 100,000 at least—more during the busy seasons in agriculture and construction, less during other seasons. It follows that the total number of Arabs

11. *Report on Activities*, Ministry of Labour, Administered Areas Unit, August 1976.
12. Ibid., p. 13.
13. *Report on Activities, Gaza Strip HQ, 1975 – 6*, Ministry of Labour.

employed by the Israeli economy is about 210,000 men and women, or some 17 per cent of the total labour force.

The importance of this labour force derives also from the fact that in Israel the rate of participation in the civilian labour force (that is, the percentage of the total population employed or seeking employment) is among the lowest in the world, just 33 per cent. By way of comparison: the corresponding figure for England is 46 per cent; Switzerland 48 per cent; Holland 38 per cent; Hong Kong 45 per cent; Japan 48 per cent; and Romania 54 per cent. Israel, in fact, is in the same category as countries like India (33 per cent) and Sudan (29 per cent). Actually, the true figure for Israel must be somewhat higher than the official statistics; but even so, it is quite low for an industrialized country. One reason for this is the size of the standing army, which swallows up huge quantities of manpower. Also, in comparison with other industrialized countries, Israel has relatively few people engaged in agriculture, construction, and industrial production.

Israel's accelerated development, the development of the economic infrastructure, and the large capital investments in the years 1967 – 73 would have been impossible without the Arab labour force, and particularly the workers from the occupied territories.

The Bank of Israel Annual Report for 1976 has the following to say regarding the role of Arab labour from the occupied territories:

'The workers from the [occupied] territories, who entered employment in the Israeli economy on a large scale until 1974, have begun to be ejected from it in the last two years. The economic boom in the Arab countries and in the [occupied] territories themselves has made this ejection easier. [But] in spite of attractions outside the Israeli economy, the determinant cause of their employment or ejection is the volume of the Israeli demand for these workers. This is apparent from the differential development in the various branches: in 1976 about 6,000 workers from the [occupied] territories left the construction industry, which has been contracting rapidly, while in manufacturing industry and the services the number of employees from the [occupied] territories went up, probably in parallel with the growth of exports and tourism.

'These workers, whose wages are lower than those of Israeli workers, and whose real as well as relative wages went down in 1976, have gained an almost exclusive hold on various kinds of labouring jobs in construction, in agriculture, and in services (including hotels, which have benefited this year from an increase in tourism). The slow-down of the Israeli economy has not yet harmed them, except insofar as this was unavoidable due to their concentration in some branches (like construction), since competition on the part of Israelis is diminishing constantly both because of the rise in the level of education within the Israeli labour force and because family allowances to Israeli families reduce the incentive to compete for labouring jobs, the wages for which are low and getting even lower. There is a difference between the inhabitants of Judea and Samaria [the West Bank] and those of the Gaza Strip working in Israel. The former find it easier to get work in the Arab countries and their numbers in the Israeli economy have decreased in the last two years. They are being replaced by workers from the Gaza Strip, whose numbers increased in 1976 in all branches of employment in Israel.'[14]

This report touches—albeit insufficiently—upon the three most important characteristics of the whole Arab labour force: first, its absolute dependence on market forces (I will return to this in the section on the mobility of the Arab labour force); second, its concentration in certain sectors (though, as we shall see, it is not limited to labouring jobs only); third, the low price of Arab labour power, with which I shall deal in the section on the Arab workers' wage structure.

Distribution of the Arab Labour Force by Sector and Occupation

As we have seen, the Arab labour force (including that from the occupied territories) constitutes 17 per cent, or one-sixth, of the total in the Israeli economy. In order to assess the real contribution of this labour force and its role in the economy, we shall examine its distribution, compared with that of the Jewish labour force, according to three criteria:

—*Sector* of employment: agriculture, construction, services, finance, etc.

—*Occupation* within each sector: skilled worker in an industry as against service worker in that same industry, teacher, clerk, scientist, etc.

14. *Annual Report for 1976*, Bank of Israel, p. 219.

—*Place* of employment, by ownership and size: public or private, large plant or small workshop.

An important feature of the development of the Jewish labour force in Israel is its growing concentration in service sectors such as administration, finance and commerce, and its steady decline in the basic production sectors—manufacturing industry, construction, and agriculture—as well as in service occupations within business (cleaning jobs in factories and offices, waiting on tables in restaurants, etc.) This trend towards re-deployment can be measured in two ways. First, in absolute figures: for example, we may determine how the *number* of Jewish industrial workers has evolved over the years. Second, in relative figures: here we ask how the *proportion* of industrial workers in the total Jewish labour force has varied from year to year. It is, of course, the latter that is of greater interest, since in any case the total labour force has grown with the increase in population, and the main question is how the general structure of employment has been evolving.

We shall soon see that there is a very strong long-term trend in the Jewish labour force away from the three key sectors and the occupations mentioned above. This trend exists independent of the economic situation, and is manifest during boom years as well as in times of recession. During the last few years, no doubt because of the economic slow-down, there has even been an absolute decline in the number of Jewish workers in each of these sectors and occupations.

The Arab labour force, on the other hand, has always been concentrated in the three main productive sectors—manufacturing and crafts, construction, and agriculture. About 86 per cent of all workers from the West Bank and the Gaza Strip and some 70 per cent of the Arabs resident in Israel—or, taken together, 78 per cent of all Arabs employed in the Israeli economy—work in these three main sectors of production. This is roughly double the corresponding figure for Jews in 1976, which was 36 per cent.

Moreover, the Arabs employed in services tend to concentrate in 'productive services'—business services from which a private businessman profits directly. The Jews, on the other hand, tend to concentrate in government services, which are non-profit making and are part of the institutions of power, or services supplied by the state in order to ensure continuous and smooth economic and social activity. This includes clerks, policemen, teachers, and so on.

The next table, taken from manpower surveys, sums up the development of the occupational distribution of the two nationalities in Israel between 1969 and 1976. The occupations are divided into two categories: *A* represents material production, including industrial workers, craftsmen, agricultural and construction workers, both skilled and unskilled. *B* represents professional and technical services, including academics, clerks, service workers, salesmen, managers, and engineers. The second category also includes important production workers, like engineers, though their number is relatively small. In other words, we may say that category *A* comprises the 'blue-collar' workers, though this is not entirely accurate, since cleaners, who are 'blue-collar' workers, are included in category *B*.

Occupational distribution of Jews and Arabs resident in Israel
(Selected years between 1969 and 1976; all figures are percentages of the labour force of each nationality)[15]

	Jews		*Arabs*	
	A	B	A	B
1969	45.2	54.8	74	26
1970	44.4	55.6	71	29
1971	43	57	73	27
1973	40.5	59.5	65.7	34.3
1975	37	63	72	29
1976	36	64	67.7	32.3

A: 'blue-collar' workers—production.
B: 'white-collar' workers—services.

The next table, included here for the sake of completeness, gives (in absolute figures) the distribution of the Jewish and Arab labour force according to nine occupational categories. (Here the category *academic-scientific* includes researchers, pharmacists, lawyers, chartered engineers; *professional-technical* includes teachers, accountants, social workers, nurses, technicians, draughtsmen; *services* include cooks, waiters, domestics, cleaners, hairdressers, policemen, janitors.)[16]

15. H. Harari, p. 21.
16. *Uniform Job Classification, 1972*, Central Bureau of Statistics.

Occupational distribution of Jews and Arabs
employed and resident in Israel[17]
(thousands)

	Jews				Arabs			
	1971	*1973*	*1975*	*1976*	*1971*	*1973*	*1975*	*1976*
Total	902.5	981	995.2	1018	94.6	107	107.8	109
Academic-scientific		61	72	75.8		0.8	1.4	1.3
	151.7				6.6			
Professional-technical		115	131.7	135.8		8.2	7.7	7.8
Managerial		34.5	34.3	43.4		0.8	0.5	0.4
	171.9				3.3			
Clerical		168	184.8	187.9		5	4.1	4.5
Tradesmen, agents, salesmen	68.5	78	79.6	82.4	2.5	7.5	6.7	7.5
Services	110.8	122.5	117.4	117	10.3	11.5	9.6	10.2
Agricultural	65.1	60	51.6	54.3	22	15.6	17.4	17.1
Construction and industry – skilled		279	262.6	258.2		38	43.4	44.2
	327.4				45			
Construction and industry – unskilled		55	51.8	55		16.7	13.6	12.5
Unknown					4.9	4	3.4	3.5

These tables show that the Jewish labour force indeed tends to concentrate mainly in 'white-collar' and service occupations—in 1976 these category *B* occupations accounted for 64 per cent of the total, following a steady increase from 54.8 in 1969. On the other hand, the Arab labour force tends to concentrate in the 'blue-collar' productive occupations of category *A*—in 1976 this category comprised nearly 68 per cent of the total. True, here there was a slow decline, but it did not amount to a steady trend; rather, it seems to have fluctuated with the state of the economy.

A more detailed analysis of the data shows that whereas in the Jewish labour force there has been a steady decline in the relative weight of each of the productive occupations (for example, skilled

17. *Israel Statistical Annuals*, table XII-1.

workers in industry and construction made up 28, 26, and 25 per cent of the total in 1973, 1975, and 1976 respectively), the decline of category *A* among the Arabs derives from a steady downward trend in one occupation only, namely *agriculture*, while in other skilled and unskilled occupations, in industry and construction, the trend is consistently *upwards*.

There are two reasons for the decline in the agricultural Arab labour force. First, *lack of land:* most of the arable land best suited for modern methods of cultivation has been expropriated and given over to Jewish kibbutzim and moshavim. Three-quarters of the land possessed by Arab villages in 1948 has by now been expropriated, and this process is still going on. In his book *The Arabs in Israel*, Sabri Jiryis shows that the government practises systematic discrimination against Arab agricultural production and favours Jewish agricultural production. The second reason is more general: in every economy undergoing industrialization and transition to mass production, the weight of agriculture in the labour force tends to decline, while that of industry tends to go up. However, while in the Jewish labour force the proportion of workers in agriculture has also tended to decline, this has not been accompanied by a corresponding increase in the proportion of industrial workers, but rather in that of employees in clerical-managerial jobs, in finance and the professions.

Where does the Arab labour force released from agriculture go? According to our tables, the answer is clear: it goes to other productive occupations, as well as to business services. This latter category includes, according to the official *uniform job classification*, cleaners, janitors, watchmen, and the like. And these are the only category *B* occupations whose relative weight in the Arab labour force is constantly rising.

We can sum up this part of our analysis with the broad statement that among the Arabs the proportion of blue-collar occupations is rising at the expense of agriculture (whose relative weight is declining in the Israeli labour force as a whole), whereas among the Jews this proportion is constantly declining and the proportion of white-collar workers is steadily going up.

But there is yet another interesting development discernible in the last few years (the relevant data for previous years are unavailable): the ratio of skilled to unskilled Arab workers in manufacturing industry and construction has increased rapidly despite the severe recession in Israeli industry. The following table gives this ratio (computed by dividing the number of skilled workers by that of unskilled workers) for both national groups.

Number of skilled workers per one unskilled worker in industry and construction[18]

	Jews	Arabs (resident in Israel)
1973	5.1	2.3
1975	5.1	3.2
1976	4.7	3.5

(We have no data on the ratio among workers from the occupied territories, but it seems that a similar trend exists to some extent also in their case.)

This shows that Israel's manufacturing and construction industries are increasingly dependent on Arab labour not only for unskilled jobs. Obviously, as Arabs resident in Israel move into skilled occupations, they are replaced in unskilled jobs by workers from the occupied territories, about whom I shall have something to say later.

The dynamic of growing concentration of Arab workers in skilled jobs in production encounters some well-known political and social obstacles. A very considerable part of Israel's industry is directly or indirectly engaged in the production of arms, ammunition, and components for weapon systems. But engineering and electronics plants connected to the military industry, such as the huge Tadiran complex, are virtually out of bounds to Arab workers. Likewise, there are very few Arab workers in the large enterprises of the public (state and Histadrut) sector, such as the Dead Sea Works, the Kur steel corporation, the ports, and even the agri-business firm Tnuvah. Every day the Israeli papers carry advertisements by firms seeking to recruit skilled workers which specify that only 'ex-servicemen' need apply. The term 'ex-serviceman' has become a euphemism for 'Jew', just as 'member of the minorities' is a euphemism for 'Arab'. Large companies in the services sector, for example in insurance, also advertise jobs for secretaries or switchboard operators who 'have

18. *Israel Statistical Annuals*, 1975 – 77, tables IX, XII – 1.

completed their national military service'.[19]

The worst discrimination in the labour market is exercised by the large corporations, which mostly belong to the state or the Histadrut and are virtually closed to Arab workers. They are based on a fairly stable work-force and are not acutely affected by market fluctuations. The military and aviation industries, of course, also exclude Arab workers. (According to some estimates, these industries, with their various ramifications, employ about half of all Jewish industrial workers.) There are also some branches of private business that traditionally exclude Arabs. One example is the diamond industry, although a very small number of Arab workers have recently been admitted into it.

Broadly speaking, therefore, the Arab industrial labour force is to be found mainly in small to medium-sized private firms. Such firms pay low wages (about half of the wages paid in the public sector) and are vulnerable to market pressures. They work for the civilian market and produce consumer goods such as food, building materials, wood and rubber goods, and textiles. It is doubtful whether such enterprises could develop and thrive without Arab labour. Sometimes they suffer such an acute manpower shortage that they are forced to farm out work on a contractual basis to small workshops in the West Bank and the Gaza Strip, since it is easier to employ women and girls there. This practice is particularly widespread in the fashion industry:

'The fashion industry suffers from a shortage of skilled manpower, particularly cutters and sample makers. . . . The factories have to compete for manpower by offering better wages. . . . The supply of skilled workers is low. . . . A large fashion manufacturer complained to me of the excessive reliance on sewing workshops beyond the green line. He said that if there was a political change the fashion industry might be harmed and would probably be unable to meet its orders.'[20]

Small sewing workshops have also been set up recently in some Arab villages inside Israel, for instance in Umm el-Fahm. Their owners pay the women half the current wages paid in Tel-Aviv, but, because of the social conditions and the Arab family structure, many women and young girls prefer to work for half the wage near home than for the full wage in Tel-Aviv.

19. *Yedi'ot Aharonot*, 17 February 1978.
20. *Ibid.*, 29 August 1977.

With the growing importance of private industry, however, many of the obstacles facing the Arab worker trying to get a skilled job are being removed. The decisive factor here—as always with these workers—is the market. The Israeli economy is still suffering a chronic shortage of manpower in all productive sectors. This shortage is particularly evident in private industry, where the average wage is about half that in the public sector. The shift of Jewish labour from production to services necessarily causes an increasing flow of Arab manpower, which is the only reserve force at the disposal of private industry.

Detailed occupational distribution

The foregoing analysis described the general picture. Let us now examine the distribution of Arab workers by occupation in some detail. (According to the 1972 *uniform job classification*, there are ten major occupational groups, each of which is further sub-divided into eight to ten occupations.) The data we have quoted so far were based on surveys of samples of a few thousand families. However, the most reliable data can be obtained from the population census.

The following table is based on the last census, taken in 1972. To explain how it should be read, let us take, for example, the third row, *Primary school teachers*. The table shows that, of the total number of employed Israeli Jews, 4.2 per cent were primary school teachers; and the corresponding figure for Arabs resident in Israel was 5.5 per cent. Jewish primary school teachers earned on the average IL7.1 per hour, whereas their Arab colleagues earned only IL5.8. Thus, the hourly earning of a Jewish primary school teacher was 1.2 times as much as (or, in other words, 20 per cent more than) that of an Arab colleague. To avoid needless clutter, I have omitted figures that represent less than one per cent of either national group; and occupations that account for less than one per cent in *both* national groups have been omitted altogether.

From our table, and from the full table[21] (of which ours is a shortened version), the following important conclusions can be drawn.

1. In virtually all occupations, a Jew earns more than an Arab.

21. *Statistical Monthly*, 1976, Appendix, p. 92; also Appendix 8.

(This is also the case in the full table.) In fact, the only significant exception is unskilled agricultural work. The typical difference varies around 20 per cent, but since the Arabs are concentrated in lower-paid occupations, the average *overall* difference (see bottom line of the table) is 40 per cent. I shall discuss this in the final section of the present article.

2. The full table comprises about one hundred detailed occupations. But nearly 60 per cent of all Arab employees in Israel (in 1972) were concentrated in sixteen typical occupations. Even more striking: about 46 per cent—nearly one half—were concentrated in only seven occupations: self-employed farmers, skilled agricultural workers, tinsmiths and welders, carpenters, builders, drivers, and unskilled workers in manufacturing and construction.

3. Jews, on the other hand, are much more evenly distributed among the various occupations: there are only three occupations in which their concentration is 4 per cent or more (bookkeepers, general service workers, and tinsmiths/welders). In the case of Arabs, there are eight such high-concentration occupations.

4. The full table shows that there are several industries in which there are virtually no Arabs (less than 0.1 per cent). One example is the diamond industry, in which 0.8 per cent of all Jewish employees (about 7,000 in all) are concentrated.

5. Service occupations in which Arabs are concentrated are usually those that are productive in the economic sense: waiters, hotel workers, and so on. Many of these serve Israel's tourist industry.

6. There is a very high concentration of Arab workers in occupations that tend to be pursued in small businesses.

Using this table, we can estimate the total number of workers of either nationality within each occupation, since we know how many people were employed in 1972. This calculation shows that in some occupations Arab workers (including those from the occupied territories) constitute a majority. We shall come back to this point soon.

Workers from the West Bank and the Gaza Strip

Employment in Israel accounts for about 32 per cent of the total employment of the inhabitants of the West Bank and the Gaza

Employed persons resident in Israel,
by detailed occupation, hourly earnings, and nationality, 1972
(figures under one per cent omitted)

	Percentage of total		Hourly earning (IL)		Ratio of earnings
	Jews	Arabs	Jews	Arabs	
Engineers (chartered)	1.3	—	7.9	—	—
Secondary school teachers	1.7	—	8.4	—	—
Primary school teachers	4.2	5.5	7.1	5.8	1.2
Writers, artists	1.1	—	5.8	—	—
Nurses	2.3	1.2	4.5	3.0	1.5
Engineering technicians	2.5	—	5.4	—	—
Production managers	2.3	—	8.4	—	—
Bookkeepers	5.3	—	4.9	—	—
Secretaries	3.6	—	3.9	—	—
Storekeepers	2.1	—	4.4	—	—
Office clerks	1.2	—	4.1	—	—
General clerks	2.3	—	4.2	—	—
Self-employed in commerce	3.2	3.5	5.1	3.9	1.3
Salesmen, shop assistants	2.7	2.2	3.4	2.3	1.5
Waiters	—	1.1	—	2.5	—
Household help (domestic)	2.4	—	2.7	—	—
Policemen	1.3	2.5	3.9	3.5	1.1
General services (cleaners, janitors)	4.1	2.8	2.8	2.5	1.1
Self-employed in agriculture	1.7	5.1	5.3	3.5	1.5
Skilled agricultural workers	2.8	5.5	2.9	2.7	1.1
Unskilled agricultural workers	1.8	2.1	2.6	2.8	0.9
Tinsmiths, welders	4.2	4.1	4.1	3.2	1.3
Mechanics	2.1	2.8	4.2	3.0	1.4
Plumbers	—	1.4	—	3.3	—
Electricians	2.4	1.3	4.3	2.8	1.5
Skilled workers in food industry	—	1.3	—	2.3	—
Carpenters	2.6	8.8	3.7	3.3	1.1
Spinners	1.6	1.7	3.3	2.4	1.3
Tailors	2.7	1.9	2.7	2.0	1.3
Builders	2.2	6.9	4.7	3.5	1.3
Drivers	3.9	5.7	4.2	3.3	1.3
Porters and stevedores	1.1	1.0	3.6	3.1	1.2
Workers in mineral industry	—	1.0	—	3.1	—
Unclassified building workers	—	1.7	—	2.9	—
Unskilled workers in manufacturing and construction	1.4	8.3	3.4	3.0	1.1
Total	100.0	100.0	4.6	3.3	1.4

Note: The occupation descriptions on the left are incomplete and are meant only as an approximate guide.

Source: *Statistical Monthly*, 1976, Appendix 7, p. 92; also Appendix 8.

Strip.[22] Among employees (that is, excluding the self-employed), the proportion employed in Israel is obviously higher: even official estimates put it at about 50 per cent. This figure has been increasing steadily since the occupation began in 1967, because there is a shortage of jobs in these territories. According to Bank of Israel and Ministry of Labour estimates,[23] about 15,000 industrial workers are employed there—a number that has been stagnant since 1967.

Although the proportion of workers from the occupied territories in the total labour force of Israel is not particularly high—7 to 10 per cent—there are certain industries and occupations, such as construction, carpentry, and general labouring jobs, where they make up 40 or 50 per cent of all employees. Moreover, they are the most elastic and 'free' section of the work-force. For example, in 1970 – 73, during the great boom in construction, 60 per cent of the *newly recruited* manpower in this sector came from the occupied territories,[24] and another 20 per cent from among Arabs residing in Israel. The importance of this elasticity is often stressed in Bank of Israel reports. For example, in its 1976 report the Bank says:

'Despite the recession, manpower surveys show outstanding stability in the number of men employed, and a continued increase in the number of women employed in services. The data indicate that the supply of labour has adjusted to the various components of demand, a phenomenon which existed also in the boom years. A change in migration patterns, an adaptation of the propensity to work among the marginal age-groups, *elasticity of the depth of employment and mobility of the employed persons from the occupied territories who move in and out of the Israeli economy*—all these provide an explanation for the unusual phenomenon of slow-down and even stagnation in production without a significant rise in unemployment.'[25] (Emphasis added)

The word 'men' in the first sentence of this quotation evidently does not refer to Arab men from the occupied territories. What the Bank is saying is that in times of depression, when workers must be

22. *Statistical Quarterly for the Occupied Territories*, vol. 7, no. 1, 1977; *Israel Statistical Annual*, table XXVII – 23; A. Bergman, *Economic Development in the Occupied Territories 1968 – 73*, Bank of Israel Research Department, 1975.

23. *Report on Activities*, Ministry of Labour, Administered Areas Unit, August 1976; also Bergman.

24. B.V. Arkadie, *Benefits and Burdens*, Carnegie Endowment, 1977.

25. *Bank of Israel Report, Abstracts*, 1976, p. 29.

made redundant, the Israeli economy can avoid the political dangers of mass unemployment by dismissing only the elastic part of the work-force: marginal age-groups (the young and the old) and marginal people, workers from the occupied territories.

In a system totally dominated by Israeli Jews, there are obviously very few openings in the public services for Arabs with higher education. In a Bank of Israel publication, Bergman writes: 'Analysis of the rate of employment in relation to the level of education shows that, contrary to the position among Israel's Jewish population, the rate of employment in the administered [that is, occupied] territories decreases as the level of education . . . increases. This is probably caused by a shortage of work suitable for educated workers. A similar problem exists also in the case of educated non-Jewish workers in Israel, among whom the level of unemployment is relatively high.'[26]

The sectoral distribution of Palestinian workers from the occupied territories is also very clear-cut: a high concentration in basic production sectors. In particular, there is a movement into manufacturing industry, where these workers fill vacancies created in unskilled jobs.

The next table refers only to workers who are hired through official channels.

Workers from the occupied territories, by sector of employment selected years, 1970 – 76

	Total (thousands)	Agriculture (per cent)	Industry (per cent)	Construction (per cent)	Other (per cent)
1970	20	24	11	54	10
1972	52	23	17	50	10
1975	66	14	18	54	13
1976	65	15	20	49	15
Trend	up	down	up	stable	up

It is perhaps reasonable to assume that among the tens of thousands of workers hired through unofficial labour contractors a higher proportion are employed in agriculture and construction, and relatively fewer in industry.

In the services sector the proportion of workers from the occupied

26. Bergman.

territories is increasing steadily. Many local authorities depend on them for street cleaning, refuse collection, and the like. (One notorious case is that of the municipal council of Holon; in October 1977 it transpired that the council had hired, through a labour contractor, 12-year-old boys as sweepers in Holon's industrial zones, commercial centres, and streets.) They are also employed as maintenance and sanitation workers in private institutions of all sizes. The Hadassah hospital in Jerusalem employs dozens of cleaners from the West Bank in its laboratories and wards; in this case the foremen and supervisors are still veteran Jewish cleaners.

It is well known that agricultural production in many moshavim and kibbutzim depends on Arab labour. During the fighting in Lebanon [in 1978], when hundreds of Lebanese workers were unable to turn up for fruit-picking in the kibbutzim of the Hula valley, an acute manpower crisis developed in this area. Israeli agriculture, which is increasingly export-oriented—about half of the produce is currently exported—could make the transition to labour-intensive crops, such as vegetables, flowers, and strawberries, only thanks to the abundance of cheap labour from the occupied territories. During the busy season, scores of workers from the territories arrive each morning at every moshav, and it is they who do the various agricultural labouring jobs. The Jewish moshavniks have for the most part become capitalist farmers who organize the production process, occasionally operate the heavy agricultural machinery, and do the necessary paperwork. A considerable number of these Arab workers are not registered with any official agency, and neither they nor their employers have any reason to declare the fact of their employment in the surveys upon which official statistics are based.

Age distribution of workers in manufacturing and construction

The consistent trend towards the concentration of Israeli Jews in white-collar occupations and in the services sector comes about in two ways.

First, Jewish workers actually move from blue-collar to white-collar occupations, or from jobs in the manufacturing and construction sectors to the services. This occurs particularly in times of economic recession, when there is little new investment, factories are closed down, and workers are laid off. In some cases production workers, instead of being laid off, are transferred to white-collar jobs (such as marketing or administration) within the same firm. This happened, for example, in the Jerusalem firm of Friedman, which closed down its production lines of heaters and refrigerators and became an importer and distributor of similar goods.

Second, young Jewish workers, entering the labour market for the first time, tend to go to white-collar occupations and to the services sector. This is reflected in the age distribution of workers in the various sectors. For example, while in the total Jewish labour force 42 per cent are under 35 years old, the proportion of this age-group among Jews employed in the construction industry is only 36 per cent. This indicates that young Jews in this sector tend to be veterans who have by now established themselves and have won job security, seniority pay, and various other benefits which make it worth their while to stay there. Thus, while it is true that there are tens of thousands of Jews in this sector, many of them belong to the permanent staff and are employed as clerks and administrators in construction firms; and this number also includes about four thousand contractors. But the younger manpower of this industry—that employed on building sites and engaged in actual construction—is for the most part Arab.

For example, it is known that the permanent staff of the giant Histadrut-owned Sollel-Boneh, which is basically a construction firm, is made up mainly of Jews. This staff is engaged in maintenance and administration, away from the building sites, in jobs that depend only slightly on the seasonal and economic fluctuations of the construction industry. On the other hand, the temporary workers of Sollel-Boneh, often hired on a daily basis, are for the most part Arabs who work on the actual building sites; and by now these even include foremen. Since Sollel-Boneh is a Histadrut firm, which regards itself as having a 'mission' beyond mere profit-making, it considers this situation abnormal, even a crisis. The firm believes that Jews must work in actual building, and if new Jewish hands do not go into construction, this spells a crisis—a big headache for the Council of the Union of Construction Workers, which is of course totally dominated by Jews, although more than half of all construction workers are Arabs. The council's secretary, Mr Amster, has warned that 'many skilled Jewish workers are leaving the industry [due to the recession] and will not come back even if there is a recovery. The young generation is not going into the industry, and the [Jewish] reserves are dwindling yearly.'[27]

Let us therefore examine the age distribution in the various sectors; we shall see that Mr Amster's worry is well-founded. The data are summarized in the following table.

The figures in each column (for either nationality) do not add up to 100 per cent, because I have omitted the older age-groups (50 +), which are irrelevant to the trend of the last twenty years.

Age structure of Israeli labour force in 1975, by nationality and sector[28]

	Total	Agri-culture	Industry	Con-struction	Business services	Public services	Personal services
			(per cent)				
Arabs							
15-24	30	26	40	30	20	19	34
25-34	30	26	30	34	27	32	29
35-49	28	30	22	26	31	30	25
Jews							
15-24	20	23	22	15	26	17	13
25-34	22	20	23	21	26	26	10
35-49	30	25	27	34	24	30	10

The first column, which gives the age structure of the *total* labour force of both nationalities, shows clearly that the Arab labour force is considerably younger than the Jewish, as we have already noted in the beginning of the first section (on the Arab working population). But to get an idea of the *differential* rates at which younger workers are absorbed by the various sectors, the figures for each sector should be compared with those in the first column. Thus we find, for example, that the age structure of the Jewish labour force in industry is roughly the same as that of the whole Jewish labour force; but the Arab industrial labour force is 'young' even in comparison with the total Arab labour force. This indicates a differential trend of young Arabs towards industry.

27. *Yedi'ot Aharonot*, 15 September 1977.
28. *Israel Statistical Annual*, 1975, p. 332.

Social scientists J. Matras and D. Weentroub of the Brookdale Institute in Jerusalem base the following statement on research completed in 1976 that included wide-ranging surveys:

'The most basic and evident gap in Israel between patterns of occupational and educational advancement is that between Jews and non-Jews . . . . For Jewish men, the patterns of occupational changes as between father and son reflect a process of spreading and penetration into a wide range of occupations in a modern economy, starting from a situation of relatively high concentration in the parents' occupations. This process includes a strong and comprehensive upward mobility—into academic, professional, and managerial occupations, as well as lower "white-collar" occupations. There is also a downward mobility into skilled and semi-skilled occupations.

'For non-Jews, the patterns of occupational changes as between father and son reflect an almost exclusive move from agriculture to "blue-collar" occupations, be they skilled, semi-skilled, or unskilled, with a very restricted mobility into "white-collar" occupations.'[29]

Overall contribution to Israeli production

Because of the high concentration of Arab workers in the production of goods and services and because of their relatively low wages, their overall contribution to the total value of commodities and to surplus-value is particularly high; in fact, it is not very much less than that of the Jewish workers, although the latter outnumber the Arab workers in the ratio of five to one.

In trying to estimate the Arab workers' share in the production of value, it is convenient to confine one's attention to material production—that is, to agriculture, manufacture, and construction. It is true that this excludes transport, catering, and other productive services, but that does not greatly affect the general picture, since the Arab workers' share in these productive services is at least as high as in the production of material goods. In any case, only a crude estimate can be made, for several reasons. One is the existence of the 'black' economy, which does not appear in reports and surveys, except perhaps in the Shimron report on organized crime and in a

29. J. Matras and D. Weentroub, *Ethnic Differences in Intergenerational Mobility*, Brookdale Institute, Jerusalem 1977.

book by the journalist B. Nadel.[30] But again, there is no reason to suppose that owners of 'black' businesses are particularly reluctant to employ Arab workers. Quite the contrary, there is no doubt that many 'underground' enterprises rely on the labour of Arab workers without rights, without a union, and, in the case of workers from the occupied territories, without work permits. Hence the true contribution of the Arab workers must be greater than any estimate based on official statistics.

Moreover, for political reasons big firms tend not to dismiss their Jewish workers even during prolonged recessions. In some cases, for example, the whole economy of a development town depends on one firm. Whenever such a firm announces its intention to make a few hundred workers redundant, public and political pressure is soon mobilized to prevent the dismissals; very often a grant or subsidy is made available to the firm to enable it to keep its Jewish workers. Firms engaged in military production keep their skilled Jewish workers on the payroll even when business is slack and there is nothing for them to do; for such workers are generally in short supply, and the firm may not be able to replace them when business picks up again. (In firms working wholly or partly for military production, Arab skilled workers cannot be used as substitutes.)

On the other hand, an Arab worker will not normally be left on the payroll of a private or public firm unless he or she is actually needed for current production. These workers have no political defence; the Israeli press does not kick up a fuss when, say, Friedman sacks a hundred workers from the West Bank; and they can always be re-hired when required. This applies particularly to unskilled workers —the great majority of the workers from the West Bank and the Gaza Strip.

Comparing the total number of Jewish workers employed in production in manufacturing, construction, agriculture, and mining with the total number of Arab workers in the same occupations, we find that while the former is declining both absolutely and relatively, the latter is constantly increasing, and the two are rapidly converging. This tendency has been particularly evident during the last few years of recession.

The following table shows the number of workers of each nation-

30. Barukh Nadel, *The Nadel Report*, Tel Aviv.

ality in the above-mentioned productive occupations in selected years.[31]

	1971	*1973*	*1975*	*1976*
Total number of Jewish workers in material production (thousands)	392	394	365	364
Total number of Arab workers in material production (thousands)	117	135	144	159
Proportion of Arab workers out of the total (per cent)	23	25	28	30

These figures show that in the basic productive occupations there are nearly half as many Arab as Jewish workers; moreover, this proportion is increasing steadily, and will no doubt increase still further, given the younger age structure of the Arab population and the greater differential tendency of young Arab workers towards productive occupations.

This proportion, of nearly one Arab worker to two Jewish workers, pertains to material production in the aggregate. But the detailed figures for each separate occupation show a great deal of variation because, as we have already noted, there is a high concentration of Arab workers in a few very specific occupations. As a matter of fact, there are already some occupations in which Arab workers are the majority.

Fairly accurate figures can be obtained for 1972, using the census results. The following table gives the number of workers of either national group, for three occupations in which there is a particularly high concentration of Arabs. The data given in this table are the most reliable for 1972, being based on the census of that year rather than on statistical estimates. But since, as we have seen, the proportion of Arabs in the basic productive occupations has been steadily increasing, their present contribution to the production of value and surplus-value in Israel is greater, both absolutely and relatively, than is reflected in the last two tables.

31. This table is derived from tables given above and from *Statistical Quarterly of the Occupied Territories*, vol. 7, no. 2, 1977; *Israel Statistical Annual*, 1976, table XXVII – 22; and *Israel Statistical Annual*, 1975, table XIV – 1.

Workers in selected occupations, by nationality; 1972 census[32]
(thousands)

	Arabs resident in Israel	Arabs from occupied territories	Arabs (total)	Jews
Unskilled workers in industry and construction	10	26	36	16
Skilled builders and construction workers	6.2	20	26.2	20
Agricultural workers	5.5	18.5	24	32.5

Mobility

One of the most important characteristics of the Arab labour force is its high mobility, which has several components and is connected to the whole mode of existence of these workers in Israel.

Most Jewish workers in Israel have security of tenure, and cannot be dismissed without receiving considerable severance pay. They are also normally protected against dismissal by the Histadrut and by a whole system of political pressures. Arab workers, in contrast, rarely have job security, and are normally employed on a daily basis. They also lack political muscle, and possess scant trade-union and political defence against redundancy. Most Arab workers, who can so easily be dismissed, are employed in the private sector, which is therefore able to adjust to changing market conditions, to recessions and rapid upturns in trade.

One component of mobility is geographical, and relates to the distance between the worker's home and work-place. As is well known, most workers work far from their villages. Even in Arab towns there are hardly any factories, and in most Arab villages there are no workshops employing more than two or three workers, not to mention factories. Because of the massive expropriation of Arab lands in the 1950s, young Arab villagers can find little agricultural employment in their own villages. In fact, it is estimated that about 50 per cent of all Arab workers resident in Israel work away from their own

32. See note 21.

villages or towns,[33] and this proportion is likely to increase as more young people join the labour force. If we include also workers from the West Bank and the Gaza Strip, it follows that about 75 per cent of all Arab workers employed in Israel work far from their homes —a remarkably high proportion.

I shall not go into a detailed analysis of the causes of this phenomenon. Let it simply be noted that in addition to the lack of employment opportunities in Arab villages and towns, there are also great obstacles preventing Arabs from moving house nearer their workplaces. Most Jewish villages and many towns, such as Safad, Karmi'el and 'Arad, are hermetically sealed against Arabs, who are simply not allowed to reside there permanently. In places like Tel-Aviv or even Haifa, where Arabs can in principle live, it is in practice difficult for them to find a flat in most quarters, since Jewish residents show great resistance to an Arab moving in. Of course, the Arab worker himself is usually not highly motivated to move house nearer his work place: since he lacks job security, he may in any case need to look for another job before long.

Whatever the reasons, this geographical mobility enables the Israeli economy to exploit Arab labour exactly where it is needed. If a large construction project is started in Jerusalem or, say, in Qiryat Shmonah, Jewish workers cannot be attracted away from their homes and secure jobs; so the temporary but urgent demand for manpower is satisfied by Arab workers from villages in the Triangle and Galilee, the West Bank and the Gaza Strip.

Another component of mobility relates to the frequency with which workers change their jobs or places of employment. (The two components are clearly inter-connected: a worker having a steady job is more highly motivated to move house near his or her work place; equally, a person working near home is somewhat less likely to seek another job.)

Since 1967 there has been, as far as we know, only one survey dealing with the frequency with which employees (that is, wage or salary earners) change their place of employment. In this survey, conducted in 1971, data were collected on the number of times employees had changed jobs during the preceding five-year period

33. H. Harari, p. 22.

(1966 – 70). The results are summarized in the following table.

Employees resident in Israel, by number of changes of place of employment during the five years 1966 – 70[34]
(per cent)

| | All age groups | | Age group 20 – 34 | |
Number of changes	Arabs	Jews	Arabs	Jews
0	59	72.5	53	62
1	13.5	19.5	13.5	27
2	6	4.5	6.5	6
3 +	20.5	3.5	25	5
Total	100	100	100	100

From this table we can deduce two important facts. First, Arab employees change their jobs much more frequently than their Jewish colleagues. Thus, for example, about 20 per cent of all Arab workers made three or more changes during the five-year period in question, as compared to only 3.5 per cent of Jewish workers. And in the 20 – 34 age-group one quarter of the Arab workers made three or more changes, as compared to only 5 per cent of the Jewish workers.

Second, it seems that Jewish workers tend to settle down to a steady job as they grow older, whereas Arab workers remain mobile even when they are no longer young, so the difference in mobility between the whole population of Arab workers and its 20 – 34 age-group is smaller than for Jews.

The mobility of Arab workers and the ease with which they can be dismissed lend great flexibility to the Israeli economy. This is particularly true of the private sector, but the public-bureaucratic sector of Israeli capital benefits as well. This is well illustrated by the following newspaper story:

'Sollel-Boneh has announced the dismissal of 150 workers in the 'Afulah and Valley district, because of a sharp decline in activities. ... It was promised that every effort would be made to keep a "skilled nucleus" of workers in the region. Senior sources told me that the responsibility for employment in the region has virtually been handed over to the Housing Ministry, which will have to find

34. *Statistical Monthly*, Appendix 2, 1971, p. 22.

employment for the Jewish construction workers in the region of the Valley of Jezreel.'[35]

It is well known that the permanent skilled nucleus of Sollel-Boneh, including administrative workers, engineers, and technicians, consists almost exclusively of Jews.

A story published in the same newspaper exactly one month earlier contained another example, referring to the Herut lift factory: 'Due to the recession in construction, there will be a controlled reduction in the number of employees. The first to be dismissed will be workers from the [occupied] territories. As for engineers and technicians, an effort will be made to transfer them to jobs abroad.'[36]

The difference in mobility between Jewish and Arab workers is also reflected in the following fact. In the fiscal year 1976 – 77 there was a sharp decline in construction, as a result of which thousands of workers were made redundant. In fact, about 1,500 Jewish workers and 10,000 Arab workers lost their jobs—a ratio of one to six or seven.[37]

A worker in a factory owned jointly by several kibbutzim put it all very succinctly: 'The permanent work-force [in our factory] are [Jewish] *hired* workers. The seasonal workers are *Arabs*, and the managers are *kibbutz members*.'[38]

Mobility of workers from the occupied territories

Above I have quoted some data on the frequency of work-place changes among Arab workers resident in Israel. As for workers coming from the occupied territories, A. Bergman reports that only about one-third of these workers have been working for their present employer for two years or more, and only about one-sixth for more than four years.[39] These figures indicate, on the one hand, a high degree of mobility; but on the other hand, they also reveal a growing dependence of many businesses and farms on labour from these territories. The Ministry of Labour reports that out of 600 workers from the Gaza Strip employed in 27 enterprises in the Erez district,

35. *Yedi'ot Aharonot*, 14 December 1977.
36. *Ibid.*, 14 November 1977.
37. *Ibid.*, 15 September 1977.
38. Quoted in *Hashavu'a Bakibbutz Ha'artzi*, no. 1219, August 1977.
39. Bergman.

about 430 left their jobs during the first three years of their employment.[40]

Although workers from the West Bank and the Gaza Strip make up only 7 to 10 per cent of the labour force employed in Israel, their contribution to the immediate supply of labour (that is, to filling current vacancies), particularly in certain key sectors, is extremely high. This is reflected even in the statistics of the official labour exchanges, although only a little over half of the workers from the occupied territories go through them. The following table gives, for the years 1973 – 75, the monthly average of workers who obtained employment through the labour exchanges, and the proportion of Arabs from the occupied territories among them.

Manpower supplied through labour exchanges; monthly average[41]

	Total number of orders supplied	Of these, supplied by occupied territories	Percentage supplied by occupied territories
	All occupations		
1973	23,500	5,500	23
1974	19,000	4,600	24
1975	17,500	4,000	23
	Construction workers		
1973	1,200	650	54
1974	900	570	63
1975	1,000	600	60
	Unskilled workers		
1973	17,500	4,800	27
1974	13,600	4,000	29
1975	12,600	3,800	30

These figures show that workers from the occupied territories make an important, and apparently growing, contribution to supplying the immediate demands of the Israeli labour market; and in the construction industry their contribution is decisive. Moreover, it is safe to assume that most workers who are hired without the

40. *Report on Activities, Gaza Strip*, Ministry of Labour.
41. *Statistical Monthly*, no. 7, 1976, p. 59.

mediation of the labour exchange are also Arabs, either from the occupied territories or from Israel.

Mobility and unemployment

Arab workers, along with 25,000 Jewish workers from the 'development townships', are virtually the only ones to be hired for certain jobs which by their nature are seasonal and require mobility, such as fruit-picking, weeding, and similar agricultural work, as well as citrus-packing and food-canning. Such workers hardly ever attain job security or a monthly wage. According to Histadrut regulations, an agricultural worker is entitled to job tenure only after twelve years' continuous employment for the same employer. Of course, employers prefer to lay off workers, even if they have to be re-hired after a short time, precisely in order to prevent them achieving tenure. This trick can be played more easily on Arab workers, and for this reason many employers prefer to have Arab rather than Jewish workers. When the above-mentioned dismissals occurred in the 'Afulah branch of Sollel-Boneh, the redundant Jewish workers appealed to the seventy kibbutzim and moshavim of the district not to use Arab labour for their domestic construction work, and to hire Jewish workers instead. But the kibbutzim and moshavim refused to do so, knowing full well the heavy obligations involved in employing a Jewish worker: fringe benefits, the demand for job security, the difficulty of dismissal. When an Arab worker has finished doing the job he was hired for, he can be sacked; but with a Jewish worker, it is a different matter.

Thus, precisely because Arab workers can be dismissed more easily, employers often prefer to hire them, rather than Jewish workers, *for certain kinds of work*. Moreover, the difference in occupational structure between the Arab and Jewish labour force occasionally results in a firm's wanting to trim down its work-force, sacking its less essential Jewish service workers rather than Arab workers who do vital production jobs. This happened, for example, in the Kittan-Dimonah textile mill in October 1977, when 200 Jewish men and women workers were dismissed. This was bitterly opposed, since hundreds of families were reduced to the bread-line because of temporary difficulties in the factory on which their livelihood depended. But the owners, the Klal firm, were adamant and got their own way. Throughout the period of negotiations, the owners offered to sack Arab production workers instead of the redundant Jewish service workers, provided the latter agreed to replace the former at the machines, in conditions of tremendous noise and mental tension. According to press reports, 'Mr Steingrad, the general manager of Kittan-Dimonah, which employs about 400 workers from the [occupied] territories (one-third of the total workforce!), because there are not enough Jewish workers suitable for work at the looms, spinning, and finishing machines, etc., said that any Jewish worker prepared to work at these machines would be allowed to do so.' This no one agreed to do—certainly not at the going wage rates, which were in the region of IL70 – 80 per day for Jews. Arab workers were being paid about IL50 per day.

But despite such occasional and almost paradoxical situations, in which Arab workers are saved from unemployment precisely because of their greater vulnerability and exploitability, it is they who generally bear the brunt of economic recession.[42] This can be seen from the trend in the employment figures during the crisis of 1973 – 78. Unlike the 1965 – 66 crisis, when there was significant unemployment among Jewish workers, the present crisis has had no such effect, and was reflected only in a lack of new investment and a decline in *Arab* employment.

Number of persons employed in Israel, 1973 – 77
(thousands)

	Total number of employed persons	Of these, Arabs resident in Israel	Of these, men
1973	1094	107	94
1974	1096	101	90.5
1975	1112	105	94.8
1976	1126	108	97.3

The last table shows that whereas the total number of employed persons continued to rise steadily, albeit slowly, during the period 1973 – 76, there was no rise in the employment of Arabs resident in Israel, and in the worst years of the crisis their employment actually declined.

42. Gideon Kessler, *Dynamics of a Minority Community*, Ph.D. thesis, The Hebrew University, Jerusalem, 1972.

This confirms once again that Arab workers serve as Israel's reserve army of labour. Being politically defenceless, this labour force is employed for purely economic reasons; that is, only in so far as employers can derive immediate financial profit from it.

Wages

The growth in consumption, and in particular in the construction of houses, in Arab villages both within the 'green line' and in the occupied territories has created the impression that the Arab worker is well paid, sometimes even better paid than the Israeli Jewish worker. In fact, the huge increase in the employment of Arabs in the Israeli economy since 1967 has led to a rise in the overall income of Arab workers. But an examination of the daily or monthly wage and the working conditions of the average Arab worker reveals a far less rosy picture.

Wages of workers from the occupied territories

In analysing the level of wages, certain basic facts must be borne in mind. *Virtually all workers from the occupied territories are employed temporarily, on a daily basis.* Therefore they have no secure monthly wage, and their income depends on the number of days actually worked. For workers from the occupied territories, it is estimated that the average number of working days—allowing for Saturdays and religious holidays, rainy days, days of sickness, and so forth—is twenty-one per month.[43]

From the gross pay one has to subtract income tax as well as other deductions such as national insurance and pension contributions, which the worker never gets back in any form, since the present administrative machine is hardly able and even less willing to keep track of the sums that accrue to the credit of a worker who is hired by the day and changes his or her place of work about twice a year. In addition, we have to deduct travel expenses, which are very high —about IL20 per working day in 1977—for workers who generally work very far from home. As to the size of these deductions,

---

43. *Statistical Quarterly for the Occupied Territories*, vol. 7, no. 2, 1977.

we quote the following report from G. Kessler's Ph.D. thesis, *Dynamics of a Minority Community.*

'In one case I examined in 1971, a labour contractor from Juraish ...received from an employer IL23.40 per day for a worker employed in pruning orange groves. The contractor in turn transmitted IL21.60 to the labour exchange, which, after making deductions, paid the wage through the Gaza branch of Bank Le'umi, where the worker collected his wage to the tune of IL11.35.'[44]

Thus the *ra'is* and the labour exchange between them deducted about half the worker's wage. This rate of deduction, 50 per cent, is very common. The worker, of course, gets nothing in return for the huge tax he is made to pay.

The following table, published by the Ministry of Labour, lists wages and salaries paid by some Israeli employers in and around the Gaza Strip to Arab employees from the Strip.

Gross pay of employees from the Gaza Strip, 1975[45]
(IL)

Employer	Daily pay	Monthly pay
Banks (Le'umi and Hapo'alim)	50	1000
Moshav Sadot	20	420
Ben-Bassat Carpentry	20	420
Pioneer (cement)	40	840
Avi Erez (metal)	30	630

According to data published by the Central Statistics Office (see notes 8 and 43), the average gross monthly wage of workers from the occupied territories employed in Israel was IL924 in 1975 and IL1134 in 1976—an increase of less than 25 per cent; in the same year, prices, as well as the average wage of Jewish workers, rose by more than 40 per cent. (Indeed, during the period 1970 – 75 the real average wage of Gaza workers fell by 17 per cent.[46]) By way of comparison: the average gross monthly pay of all employees in Israel was IL2920 in 1976.[47] After deducting taxes and so on, as well as travel expenses,

44. Kessler, p. 107.
45. *Report on Activities, Gaza Strip HQ, 1975 – 6*, Ministry of Labour.
46. Ministry of Labour, Administered Areas Unit.
47. *Israel Statistical Annual*, 1977, p. 337.

the worker from the occupied territories is left with a truly minimal wage, for which no Jewish worker would be prepared to work. Indeed, as pointed out in the Bank of Israel report quoted above (see note 14), the various welfare benefits and other allowances received by 'ex-servicemen' (that is, by Jews) add up to more than the net wage of an Arab worker from the occupied territories.

Workers employed *inside* the occupied territories are on the whole better off: their average gross monthly wage was IL1050 in 1976. This is slightly less than the corresponding figure for those who travel to work in Israel (IL1134); but then, they do not pay nearly as much in tax and travel expenses. On the other hand, workers from the occupied territories employed in Israeli *industry* are much worse off: their gross monthly wage was IL840.

All the figures quoted so far are official averages, relating to workers employed through the labour exchanges. Of course, there are many thousands of workers who are employed unofficially, and some of these earn more than the figures quoted above. But it must be borne in mind that they do not enjoy even the few fringe benefits given to those who go through the labour exchanges, such as compensation for industrial accidents. Also, they are mostly hired for agricultural and other seasonal work, which implies a higher risk of unemployment during part of the year. In this free labour market, a daily wage of IL100 is considered (in 1978) to be on the high side. These wages are often paid in 'black money' so that no taxes are deducted. To determine the net wage, we therefore have only to subtract travel expenses, say IL20. This leaves a net daily wage of about IL80 (or about £2.70 at the 1978 rate of exchange), which works out at IL1680 for an average month of 21 working days.

How does this compare with the wage of an Israeli worker? In most branches of the Israeli economy, fringe benefits add up to something like 40 per cent of the basic wage. These fringe benefits, which are part and parcel of the effective wage in every modern economy, and particularly in Israel, include payment for holidays and sick leave, production bonuses, presents, a 'thirteenth month' and even 'fourteenth month' in salary. The vast majority of Arab workers do not enjoy such extras; from a Ministry of Labour report,[48] which contains data on holidays, sick-benefits, and compensation, it

48. Ministry of Labour, Administered Areas Unit.

is evident that an Arab worker from the West Bank or the Gaza Strip receives virtually nothing beyond his or her bare wage. Thus, the average wage of an Israeli worker (which was IL3500 per month in 1977) adds up, together with fringe benefits, to earnings twice or three times those of an Arab worker from the occupied territories.

Arab workers resident in Israel

The wages of Arab workers resident inside the 'green line', while normally higher than those of workers from the West Bank and the Gaza Strip, are much lower than those of Jewish workers. At the bottom end of the scale are women working locally in small village sewing workshops or in agriculture, whose wages are very low indeed —as low as the average wage of workers from the occupied territories. On the other hand, skilled workers in construction and other industries earn as much as they are able to get on the free market; here too a daily wage of IL100 to 120 (that is IL2100 to 2520 per month) is considered (in 1978) to be on the high side. Most of these workers also are hired by the day, and therefore do not enjoy the benefits and extras that are given to regular monthly workers. And they too must spend considerable sums in travel expenses.

There is fairly detailed and reliable statistical information on the wages of Arab workers resident in Israel. The most reliable data on Israeli society in general are those derived from the last census, conducted in 1972. So far, only a small part of the census results have been published, but fortunately these include data on the earnings of both national groups in Israel.

First, let us look at the distribution of employees (wage and salary earners) by income.

The difference is quite striking. The under-IL800 income bracket contained less than half of all Jewish employees, but nearly three-quarters of all Arab employees.

This huge difference in wages cannot be explained merely by the high concentration of Arabs in unskilled jobs. In the second section, dealing with the occupational distribution of the Arab labour force, I presented a long table showing the distribution of Jewish and Arab employed persons by detailed occupation, based on the 1972 census. Turning back to the table, we find that *in every detailed occupation (with one single exception) in which a significant proportion (at least*

**Distribution of employees
(Jews and Arabs resident in Israel) by income, 1972[49]**
(per cent)

	Annual income (IL)				
	Less than 4000	*4000 – 7999*	*8000 – 11999*	*12000+*	*Total*
Jews	20	28.5	24	27.5	100
Arabs	32	40	18.2	9.8	100

*1 per cent) of the total labour force of both nationalities is repre-
sented, the Arab worker is paid less than the Jewish worker.* Thus,
an elementary school teacher earned IL5.80 an hour if he or she
happened to be Arab, but IL7.10 if he or she was fortunate enough
to belong to the Jewish people. And if this is the case for government
employees, so much the more so in the private sector: an Arab tinsmith IL3.20, a Jewish tinsmith IL4.10; an Arab builder IL3.50, a
Jewish builder IL4.70; and, of course, an Arab unskilled worker
IL3.00 and his Jewish mate IL3.40. From the same table we see that
the average hourly earnings of an employed Jew were (in 1972) about
IL4.60, while an Arab earned only IL3.30.

*Therefore, the average earnings of a Jew were 40 per cent higher
than those of an Arab, while the mean difference within the same
occupation is about 20 or 25 per cent.*

As for the total *per capita* income, including child allowances,
which are paid to Jewish families at double the rate given to Arabs
(the excuse being that they are 'ex-servicemen's relatives'—in reality
this is merely a euphemism for Jews), we find that in 1972 the
average per capita income of a Jewish employee's family was 130 per
cent higher (more than double!) that of an Arab employee's family.
A similar result is obtained if other components of effective earnings
are also taken into consideration.

For more recent years it is difficult to find equally reliable figures.
Some less reliable surveys indicate a significant erosion in the
Jewish-Arab wage differential in the last few years. This may have
been caused by two facts. First, the general decline in real wages
during the crisis years may have hit Jews relatively harder than
Arabs. Another, possibly less important reason is the tendency of

49. See note 21.

Arab workers to move into more skilled occupations. The erosion of the wage differential is reflected in the next table.

Average gross annual income from wages and salaries
(IL thousands)

	1967	1970	1972	1974
Jews	9.4	11.9	15.5	17.6
Arabs	7.0	8.1	11.2	14.9
Differential (per cent)	34	47	38	18

According to these figures, the Jewish-Arab wage differential, which in the early 1970s fluctuated around 40 per cent, has been reduced to 18 per cent. However, it must be pointed out that these data, even if correct, refer to the gross wage, without fringe benefits.

The differential in net income (that is, after deducting taxes and so on and adding fringe benefits and welfare allowances) is greater, for two reasons. First, as I have already noted, most Arab workers are hired by the day and are employed by small firms, and therefore do not receive many fringe benefits. Neither do they receive the special welfare allowance granted to Jews under the euphemism 'ex-service-men's family allowance'. Second, Jewish employees in many places —the south, the north, development townships—pay taxes at a reduced rate.

The wage differential between Jewish and Arab workers apparently results from two factors. First, in each occupation Jews are paid something like 20 or 25 per cent more, simply because they are Jews. Second, Arab workers are concentrated in the less well-paid occupations: as *production workers* and unskilled labourers, 'hewers of wood and drawers of water'. But this second part of the explanation really begs the question, because there is no economic law that production workers must be particularly badly paid. For example, in the United States production workers in many factories, as well as construction workers, are on the whole better paid than clerks. It seems that one of the reasons why wages in 'Arab' occupations are so low is precisely that they have a high concentration of Arabs. In occupations from which Arab workers from Israel and the occupied territories are not excluded for social or political reasons, a larger supply of labour is created, an influx of unorganized and politically defenceless workers who do not constitute a significant pressure group in Israeli society. This, together with competition between workers over jobs, enables the employers to keep wages low. Thus wages in these occupations decline both absolutely (in real terms) and relative to wages in other occupations; this is also confirmed by the 1976 Bank of Israel report from which we have already quoted (see note 14). As the level of wages declines, more Jewish workers leave these occupations, because they would be better off on the welfare allowances that are given to Jews. In this way, an increasing concentration of Arab workers is created. We have seen above that about 50 per cent of all Arab workers resident in Israel are concentrated in seven occupations, five of which (agricultural workers, tinsmiths, carpenters, unskilled workers in construction and manufacturing) are particularly badly paid.

We have also remarked that Arab workers tend to be employed not only in specific occupations but also by a specific kind of employer. There are very few Arab workers in firms employing more than a hundred workers. Such firms, which make up only 2 per cent of all Israeli enterprises but which employ about 50 per cent of the total industrial labour force, are owned by the state (the Chemical Industries, Dead Sea Works, Aviation Industry) or by the Histadrut (such as Kur), or else they are private firms intimately connected to the arms industry, such as Tadiran and other electronics firms.

Arab workers are concentrated in smaller firms which produce mainly for the local Israeli market in branches such as food processing, leather, wood, rubber, textiles, or in private sewing or metal workshops. Most of them—indeed, most workers in this kind of firm, including Jews—are employed on a daily basis. Both wages and fringe benefits are considerably lower than in the bigger firms. The following table shows how big is the difference in wages between small and big firms.

Here we see another reason for the low wages of Arab workers: they tend to be concentrated in firms employing fewer than twenty workers, where the *average* wage is 40 per cent lower than in the big firms. Similarly, privately owned firms pay less well than public (state or Histadrut) enterprises: IL2500 per month as against IL4500.

The large wage differential is also reflected in differences in the standard of living between the Arab and Jewish populations in Israel.

Distribution of wages (1976), by size of firm[50]

Number of employees	1-4	5-19	20-49	50-99	100+
Mean gross monthly wage (IL)	1800	2200	2500	2600	3300

For example, although Arabs make up 17 per cent of Israel's population, they own only 5 per cent of all private cars; this is no doubt partly due to other reasons, such as the size of Arab families, but is certainly also connected with their lower level of income. Apart from the wage differential, there are other economic benefits enjoyed exclusively by Jews, which thus contribute to widening the gap between Jewish and Arab standards of living. We have already mentioned the special allowances paid by the government to relatives of 'ex-servicemen', and the reduced rates of taxation enjoyed by Jews living in border areas and development regions. No Arab village has ever been designated a development or border area for tax purposes. All Jews, especially young couples, are entitled to various housing grants and interest-free loans. Arabs, on the other hand, hardly ever receive any housing subsidies, except when the authorities wish to remove them from existing Arab quarters. Jewish local authorities receive from the central government annual grants which average IL120 per inhabitant, whereas Arab local authorities receive only IL7 per inhabitant.

In conclusion, it can be said that the wages paid to Arab workers, particularly those from the West Bank and the Gaza Strip, are on the average much lower than those paid to Jewish workers, especially in the food-processing, textile, and packing industries, as well as in agriculture and mining. However, in times of economic boom the Israeli economy is hungry for labour, and this sometimes creates conjunctures in which a skilled Arab worker can get a better return for his labour power. All Arab workers depend far more than their Jewish colleagues on the state of the labour market. Thus, for example, an Arab skilled builder could find a relatively well-paid job in 1972 – 74 without great difficulty; but in 1977 this became much more difficult.

50. *Statistical Monthly*, 1977, Appendix 5.

2

Women

To consider the position of women in any society is to consider nearly all aspects of that society's structure: its politics, economics, culture, religion. In the Middle East, there are further complications as well. Women in the Arab countries not only face all the problems generally associated with underdeveloped social formations, but must also confront the difficulties posed by the application, more or less strictly in the various states, of the tenets of Islam regarding family life. In Israel, the lives of women, like just about everything else, are affected directly and indirectly by the peculiar character of the Israeli state, which is simultaneously a product of Zionism and an instrument for its further advancement.

Articles about women in the Middle East will therefore inevitably touch on many facets of social, political, and economic life in the countries concerned, and will tell us as much about the nature of Zionism and the Arab societies as they do about women themselves. Most of those collected here were first published in *Khamsin 6*, whose theme was 'Women in the Arab World'. The aim of that issue was to open a discussion of women in the region that would not confine itself to 'women's problems', but would begin to correct the often unintentionally fostered impression that all the social struggles of the Middle East are waged by 'men who happen to have mothers, sisters, wives, and daughters in tow'. The contributions in that issue covered a range of subjects, and others have appeared in various numbers of *Khamsin* since then.

'Arab Women' (*Khamsin 6*), by Magida Salman, a Lebanese member of the *Khamsin* editorial group, is a synoptic survey of the influence of Islam on the position of women in Arab countries. It was written at a time, in the late seventies, when many people denied that the ideology and institutions of Islam were decisive in sustaining the oppression of women. Although that misconception has lost a good deal of its currency in recent years, especially since the Iranian revolution, another notion has meanwhile arisen: that although in practice women suffer oppression in Islamic societies, Islam itself manifests deep concern for the rights of women, who collectively would have much to gain from an 'enlightened' application of Islamic practices. This article lays both these illusions to rest. It demonstrates, on the one hand, that under Islam the social position of women is inferior to that of men as a matter of principle, and on the other that those portions of Islamic ideology relating to women are exactly the ones on which the contemporary rulers of Arab society have been most unyielding, even when they have updated and adapted other aspects of Islamic theory that conflict with modern conditions. Since Islam in the Arab world increasingly came to be fused with Arab nationalism, even militant social struggles against foreign domination have often sanctified the inferior social position of women.

'The Rise of Islam: What Happened to Women?' (*Khamsin 10*) is an examination of the changes introduced in the Arabian peninsula by the early Muslim state, which succeeded, for the first time, in overcoming tribal rule and preparing the world-wide expansion of Islam. It is widely accepted, by Muslims and opponents of Islam alike, that however retrograde towards women Islam may be in the societies in which it now holds sway, it originally represented a major improvement of their status, abolishing barbaric practices like the murder of female infants and guaranteeing women certain rights previously denied them. Azar Tabari, an Iranian journalist and member of the *Khamsin* editorial group, argues that the reality was more complex. In some respects, the early Muslim state merely countenanced practices that were already becoming prevalent and are nowadays regarded as specifically Islamic innovations. In others, the undermining of the tribe, while it entailed some advantages for women, actually eroded rights they had formerly enjoyed.

The other articles collected here deal with more contemporary themes. In 'Women and Politics in Lebanon' *(Khamsin 6)* Yolla Polity Sharara offers a personal account of the experiences of a generation of Lebanese women activists. They came to political consciousness under the influence of the new feminist movement of

Western Europe, during the post-1968 ferment that saw so many facets of social relations challenged. The country in which they were active had special historical and intellectual ties with Europe, especially with France, but was also Arab, and dominated by other issues and concerns. How was the problem of the emancipation of women viewed in such a context—by women themselves, and by political organizations—and what was the effect of the civil war? These are the questions Sharara treats.

'Changes in Palestinian Society' (*Khamsin 6*) looks at the traditional social structures of the Palestinian Arabs and examines how they have been warped and inflected by the Israeli state. The authors, members of the Socialist Organization in Israel (Matzpen), in whose Hebrew journal the article was originally published, describe the connection between the traditionalism of indigenous Palestinian social relations and the success of the state apparatus in abridging the rights of all Palestinians.

'Ideology Without Revolution: Jewish Women in Israel' (*Khamsin 6*) dismantles the myth of the liberated Israeli woman, soldier and pioneer. The authors—Dina Hecht is a writer, Nira Yuval-Davis a sociologist; both are Israelis and members of the *Khamsin* editorial group—argue that, on the contrary, the Zionist colonization of Palestine actually forced women into the most traditional subordinate positions as the helpers of men, keeping the home fires burning while the men set out to build the brave new world. That status has remained more or less unchanged since the establishment of the Israeli state, and the requisites of the survival of Zionism actually place Israeli women under burdens more onerous than those faced by women in Western Europe or North America.

In 'Zionism, Demography, and Women's Work' (*Khamsin 7*), Avishai Ehrlich, an Israeli sociologist and member of the *Khamsin* editorial group, concentrates more specifically on the way Zionism's demographic needs have affected both the sexual division of labour and the structure of the Israeli work-force. He considers not only the pre-1948 period of colonization of Palestine, but also the development of the labour force since statehood, and concludes that women are still adversely affected by the vicissitudes of Jewish immigration to Israel and by the continuing Zionist mission of the state.

Arab Women

Magida Salman

Is it a lapse into impressionism to 'lend great importance to the weight of Islam' in considering the roots of the oppression of Arab women? Despite all the social transformations that have occurred in the Arab world since the era of the caliphs, secularization has yet to take hold in nearly all the Arab countries. Legislation dealing with marriage, divorce, and the status of women (inferior in all cases) is still based on, or directly inspired by, Koranic law in all the Arab-Islamic states. What role is played by Islam, what is its influence, and how is it used? This article will deal with some of these questions.

Islam, a State Religion

The administration of society under Islam is regulated by the sacred texts as elaborated in the Koran. The moral system preached by the prophet Muhammad is itself law. The Muslim religion has found expression in a code of practical laws to be observed not only with respect to Allah but also with respect to the Muslim state. Indeed, the Koran, the *shari'a*, and the *hadith*, subjects of polemics among legislators even today, were themselves shaped by the experience of the prophet as the ruler of a state.

Koranic law explicitly stipulates the superiority of men over women. To begin with, the Koran itself is addressed exclusively to men, and not to women: 'Men have authority over women because Allah has made the one superior to the other.... As for those from whom you fear disobedience, admonish them and send them to beds apart and beat them' (*The Koran*, translated by N.J. Dawood,

Penguin Classics, sura 4, 'women', pp. 360 – 61). Countless other quotations of similar character could be adduced. Some defenders of the Islamic position on women have made the claim that Islam represents an advance over other monotheistic religions in that it introduces sexual equality, by expunging from sexual pleasure any notion of sin or guilt. This lack of guilt, however, is not synonymous with freedom, for it profits only men and in fact consecrates woman's role as sexual object. For example: 'Women are your fields; go then into your fields as you please' (sura 2, 'the cow', p. 347).

As has been pointed out: 'Thus, "love" exists not as a human relation but as a sexual relation, as servitude. In reality, there are no women, only females. For the Arab man, women exist in various personifications: virgin girl, wife, mother. There is no room for the woman friend or lover. . . . The woman in the Koran is not a lover but a wife. There is no love, only sexuality. . . . Marriage is a sexual pleasure on the one hand and a means of procreation on the other; the image of the wife is thus identified with that of the mother.'[1]

It is not my purpose here, however, to enter into a long discussion of the sacred texts. The important thing is that since Islam is a state religion nearly everywhere in the Arab world, the Koran and the shari'a form the foundation of judicial law, or even inspire it directly. Nonetheless, in many areas attachment to the teachings of the prophet has given way to adaptation to the conditions of the modern world. Usury, for example, is a great sin in Islam. But even the 'most Muslim' ruling classes do not forswear the interest generated by their bank accounts. Profits, you see, can no longer be regulated by the norms that prevailed during the seventh century. No, it is only when it comes to all the norms regulating the lives of women— marriage, divorce, polygamy, the care of children, the imposition of male guardians for women—that adherence to the teachings of the prophet is complete. In other words, although Islam, like all other ideologies, has made adjustments to the social changes imposed by history, it has displayed a remarkable rigidity on all subjects involving the role of women in society.

Indeed, so strong has this conservatism been that it has incorpora-

---

1. A. Khalili, *al-Turath al-Falastini wa'l-Tabaqat* (The Palestinian Tradition and Classes), Dar al-Kitab, Beirut (in Arabic).

ted many laws and traditions that were generally assumed to be Islamic and were thus preserved over the centuries, even though they were actually products of reactions to Islam and its effect on pre-Islamic society, or of purely conjunctural necessities that arose at certain points in the evolution of this or that society. One striking example may illustrate the point: the wearing of the veil.

This practice seems to have developed as a reaction to the Koranic reform that guaranteed women the right to inherit property; it became general as the nomadic tribes were settled during the early years of the expansion of Islam. 'In making inheritance by women obligatory, the Holy Book ... struck a terrible blow at the tribe: a blow that tribal societies, even as with more or less good grace they converted to Islam, have bent their energies to evading ever since. . . . We can see today that the geographical distribution of the veil, and of female seclusion, corresponds roughly to respect for the Koran on the question of inheritance by women.'[2]

' . . . we are dealing with a causal sequence which I have observed personally: 1. religious fervour imposes female inheritance; 2. female inheritance destroys the tribe; 3. the destroyed tribe accepts outsiders; 4. fathers then veil their daughters *to preserve them for the boys of the family notwithstanding.*'[3]

In *The Social Structure of Islam*, Reuben Levy presents details concerning the appearance of the veil among Muslim women: 'Closely bound up with the subject of marriage in Islam is that of the veiling and seclusion of women. In ancient Arabia, custom appears to have varied, the women of the desert-dwellers going unveiled and associating freely with men, while women in the cities were veiled.'[4] Levy points out that women were not required to wear veils during the reign of the caliph 'Umar (634 – 44).

The exact date of the generalization of the veil and the definitive reasons for it remain to be determined in many cases. What is certain, however, is that the custom pre-dates Islam to some extent and was not specifically stipulated by the prophet Muhammad. Nonetheless, once it became identified as 'Islamic', it was raised to the level of custom, and often even law.

2. Germaine Tillion, *The Republic of Cousins*, Al Saqi Books, London 1983, p. 150.
3. Ibid., p. 30.
4. Reuben Levy, *The Social Structure of Islam*, Cambridge 1969, p. 124.

The confounding of religious structures and state structures, of law and sacred texts, is a general characteristic of the societies in which Islam emerged and triumphed. This characteristic has prevailed, with differences in form, from the epoch of the Muslim conquests and the first caliphs through the Ottoman empire and even into the epoch of capitalism.

Nevertheless, this phenomenon has been most striking in everything that relates to the position of women in society. The impact of Islam in this matter may be grasped more clearly by taking a look at the argument of the great reformers of the late nineteenth and early twentieth centuries (the era of the *Nahda Arabia*, or Arab renaissance). Most of these reformers had attended French universities and, upon returning to their countries, issued appeals for the modernization of the state (men such as Salamah Musa and Qasim Amin[5]). Amin, one of the greatest of the reformers, is considered a pioneer in the domain of the emancipation of women. Of Turkish origin, he studied law at the University of Montpellier in France and later served as a legislator in Egypt at the end of the nineteenth century. He was the author of several works on the status of women. In his book *The Liberation of Woman*, Amin called for equality for women in the realm of social life and insisted on the need for the education of women. At the same time, he strove ceaselessly to fuel his argument with quotations from the Koran. For him, correspondence with the Koran was the very proof that he was on the right path, that he stood within the legitimacy of 'our society'. This led him into long religious digressions, which are interlaced in bizarre fashion through his otherwise rational thought. For instance, after citing the passage in the Koran instructing believers to 'enjoin believing women . . . to cover their adornments (except such as are normally displayed); to draw their veils over their bosoms and not to reveal their finery except to their husbands, their fathers, their husbands' fathers, their sons' (sura 24, 'light', p. 212), Amin writes pages attempting to demonstrate that 'adornments' (in other words, 'private parts') do not include the face or the hands.

This was at the beginning of the twentieth century. And today? Not more than three years ago an 'emancipated and enlightened'

5. Salamah Musa, *al-Mar'a Laysat Li'bat al-Rajul* (Woman Is Not the Plaything of Man), Cairo; Qasim Amin, *Tahrir al-Mar'a* (The Liberation of Woman) and *al-Mar'a al-Jadida* (The New Woman), Cairo.

shaikh came to a round table discussion organized by feminists at Dar al-Fann in Beirut to convince the audience that Islam has liberated women and that the Koran must be followed to the letter in all matters of personal status. He simply repeated the official positions on which the 'partisans of equality of the Muslim woman' have been harping for decades. And of course, he defended the legitimacy of the theocratic state.

Bourgeois Ideology in the Arab World: an Arab-Islamic Ideology?

'Our bourgeoisies seem to find the drafting of a secular personal code more dangerous than nationalizations.'

In some non-Arab Muslim countries secularization was achieved by a bourgeoisie struggling to modernize and strengthen indigenous capitalism. This demonstrates that the explanation for the humiliating position of Arab women (and the sources of the unhealthy obsession with virility among Arab men) are not to be sought merely in the content of the Koran. They lie, rather, in the necessity felt by the ruling classes—and the local bourgeoisies now in power—to 'respect' Islamic tradition and to administer Islamic states (except in the special case of Lebanon, where secularization does not exist in any event, and Tunisia, which must be examined separately).

After the revolution led by Kemal Atatürk in Turkey, the state was secularized and many changes were introduced in the status of women, especially in the towns. Why weren't Nasser's attempts to establish an independent and modern Egypt strengthened by the proclamation of a secular state? Why didn't the Algerian National Liberation Front resort to this weapon against the reactionaries and against the demagogy of 'forward-looking' imperialists, even at the peak of the anti-imperialist struggle? Why has the Ba'th Party felt compelled to identify the struggle for Arab unity with Islamic identity and, once in power, why has it hurried to declare Islam the state religion, in both Iraq and Syria? (The intellectual founder of the Ba'th, Michel Aflaq, who is of Christian background, converted to Islam about a year ago, claiming that Arabism and Islam could not be separated.) And one could add the caricatures of such phenomena: Qadhafi's 'Jamahiria' or Saudi Arabia, where the ridiculous in no way alleviates the atrocious oppression that denies women any choices whatever, even women of the ruling classes.

One of the reasons for this apparent anomaly is that the reaction to colonial and imperialist oppression in the Arab world took the form of attachment to local traditions and beliefs as a response to the cultural pressure of the settlers. 'When the French landed in Algeria in 1830, the society they attacked was, regardless of their own prejudices and ignorance, part of an old civilization which had long competed with their own, Arab-Islamic civilization. . . . The Koranic prohibition of Muslim women marrying non-Muslims . . . protected Muslim women from delivering their bodies to the oppressor. . . . But this refusal, on the other hand, placed the women of North Africa even further under the grip of the men of their own society, for the women, along with everything connected to private life, became a symbol for the men, a concrete refuge from the colonial indignity to which they were subjected. That is why the women were forced to live in narrow confines, jealously overprotected, their lack of public appearance and their very intangibility serving now as the ultimate guarantee of masculine dignity, now as an excuse for those who were compromised by collaboration with the occupier.'[6]

The authors of the article from which this quotation is taken explain the varying influence of colonialism on the status of women in North Africa and in Mexico on the basis of this differing precolonial reality. (Spanish colonialism in Mexico during the sixteenth century confronted a tribal society; this led to cultural and 'racial' blending, which was not the case in North Africa.)

This sort of reaction was to assume a broader, although more contradictory, dimension during the epoch of imperialism. The division of the Arab world by the European imperialist powers led to the development of nationalist consciousness, an important element of which was the desire to reassert the Arab unity that had been destroyed by the 'Westerners'. This consciousness found expression in an attachment to the unifying elements that had preceded the division: language, customs, and religion experienced as a cultural tradition. Islam thus became a component of bourgeois nationalist consciousness. The Arab woman has suffered from this reaction, which

6. C. Souriau, resumé of the article of C. Souriau and R. Thierleci, 'Tradition, Modernism, and Revolution: A Comparative Study of Mexico and the Maghreb', University of Aix-en-Provence, p. 8.

has acted to circumscribe the upheavals in her status that could have been introduced both by contact with European society and by the mass struggles for liberation from the domination of European imperialism.

The reaction to imperialism, however, was contradictory, precisely because of the influence of imperialism on the pre-capitalist socio-economic structures of the Arab world. The needs of imperialism and of the new, imposed mode of production required that young girls be sent to school (especially in the cities) and that a layer of women employees in the tertiary sector be developed. In some cases there was also a need for cheap female labour power. Indeed, the changes wrought by the entry of capitalism and by the imbalances through which it developed gave rise to the first struggles of Arab women.

The ensuing contradiction may be summarized in this way: On the one hand, the oppression and social changes imposed by imperialism created the objective basis both for the development of women's struggles and for the integration of women into the more general national liberation struggle against colonialism; on the other hand, the form in which bourgeois nationalist consciousness took root among the masses entailed a strengthening of Islam and even a tendency towards the assimilation of Islam into that consciousness itself. This latter factor militated against the rise of women's struggles and even against the active participation of women in the national liberation struggle. Later, bourgeois nationalist consciousness in the Arab world, fully identified with Islamic ideology, was to become a weapon in the hands of the indigenous ruling classes which assumed state power in place of the European colonialists. In other words, the Islamic position on women, along with the Islamic position on other social questions, became an instrument for the perpetuation of general domination by the Arab ruling classes.

'Arab Socialism': an 'Islamic' Socialism

'We favour neither communism nor capitalism, but an Arab socialism, an Islamic socialism.'

For reasons I will not go into here, the national liberation struggle in the Arab countries, which reached its peak during the 1950s, was led by nationalist movements. These movements came to power either through coups organized by young army officers or through the action of political parties whose base was essentially petty bourgeois. The bourgeois regimes established by the anti-imperialist struggles and movements in the Arab world were often impelled to take radical measures against imperialist intransigence. They were thus compelled to rely not only on the urban petty bourgeoisie, but also on the peasantry and the working class, and even to mobilize the workers and peasants to some extent. But it was also necessary to ensure that radicalization and popular mobilization would not sharpen the class struggle, that the upsurge of mass action could be contained within limits compatible with the perpetuation of the capitalist mode of production. The formula by which this delicate equilibrium was assured was well chosen: Islamic socialism. Or to put it another way: socialism for popular consumption, Islam for the survival of capitalism.

All that women gained from this was a number of political rights (such as the right to vote) and the right to work whenever the new, independent state was short of labour power. The religious authorities were always on hand to declare either that Islam permitted women to participate in social activities or that Islam required the seclusion of women, depending on the needs of the moment. (The latter sort of declaration, of course, was of special value during periods of social unrest, sharpened class struggle, or rising unemployment.) The pronouncements of the shaikhs of al-Azhar mosque in Egypt, guardians of the Koran and the shari'a, are striking in their contradictions.

In the countryside, the only perceptible change in the status of women was the intensification of poverty, especially since the various agrarian reforms all ended in failure.

In all these independent states, secularization was regarded as an excessively disruptive element in an already precarious stability. In all these states, personal status is based on Koranic law and the lives of women are regulated by 'the traditions of our Muslim culture'.

Let us take one example. What has 'Islamic socialism' meant for women in independent Algeria, a country whose liberation movement, the National Liberation Front, has been held up as having radically transformed the conditions of women?

Since 1967 the official government newspaper, *el-Moujahid*, has ceaselessly issued advice for the right-thinking, such as: 'Our socialism rests on the pillars of Islam and not on the emancipation of women with their make-up, hairdressers and cosmetics, from which arise unchained passions harmful to humanity.'

In the chapter entitled 'Hypocrisy' in her book *Les Algériennes* ('Algerian Women'), F. M'Rabet quotes from an article published in the magazine *el-Jaish* in 1965: 'What would become of Algerian virility and glory, of the Arab-Islamic national character of our vigorous youth, into what state would our young men fall, if they saw their sisters in the arms of foreigners, who are their enemies and the enemies of the whole Arab nation?'[7]

In the countries in which Islam is the state religion there is generally only one political party, the ruling party, and the organizations of the various sectors of the masses are tightly controlled by this party. Thus, the National Union of Algerian Women declared during its first congress, in 1966: 'The congress must ... entirely devote itself to the protection of the family unit ... through the establishment of structures that conform to the Algerian personality and to Arab-Islamic culture.'[8]

In 1972 the initial draft of the family code made this stipulation in regard to marriage: 'Error in person or violence entails the annulment of the marriage.'[9] Yes, the veil plays tricks. The prospective husband (who has paid a price for his chosen bride) can be deceived and find himself married to someone else, for the 'error in person' can be discovered only after the marriage, when the veil falls.

Although the proposed family code rested on Islamic law, it had, of course, to be adapted to some modern necessities and thus divested of a few excessively embarrassing rules. The 'sacred texts' were consequently juggled about. Article 49 of the draft stipulated:

'The requirement of monogamy has its foundation in the Koran and the shari'a.... Averroës taught that monogamy was obligatory.... This was also the view of the caliph 'Umar Ibn Abi al-Khattab, 'Umar Abdel Aziz, Mu'awiya. In addition, this custom has long been common in our country. A *fetwa* (religious ruling) rendered by Abu Zakariya al-Moghali in the ninth century illustrates this clearly

7. Fadela M'Rabet, *La Femme Algérienne, suivi de Les Algériennes*, Paris 1969, p. 108.

8. Ibid., p. 113.

9. Ministry of Justice, initial draft of the family code, Algiers, p. 2. Not published officially.

and precisely. The commission has thus considered it its duty to consecrate this custom in the present article.'[10]

Was it really necessary to seek justification from all these celebrated Muslim personalities simply to propose the establishment of monogamy, especially since, *pace* the legislators concerned, monogamy in no way 'has its foundation' in the Koran?

The Muslim Brotherhood: an Arab Version of Fascism

Since the Arab bourgeoisie is an Arab-Islamic bourgeoisie, it is only logical that local fascism has taken the form of an exaggerated version of this religious identity. Created in 1919, the Muslim Brotherhood was to remain numerically modest until the late 1940s, a period of great social and popular agitation in the Middle East. The principles of the movement then became increasingly popular, primarily among the petty bourgeoisie (especially in Egypt and Syria). Indeed, the Muslim Brotherhood waged a campaign against 'big capital', for the defence of private property, against the 'Occident' and its imported values (although they refused to use the word 'imperialist'), against the communists (the main enemy), and above all against any reform of religion and against secularization. The Muslim Brotherhood has waged a constant and determined struggle against the liberation of women. They mobilized according to the watch-word 'communism = atheism = liberation of women'. The recent reappearance of the Muslim Brotherhood in Egypt is a result not merely of de-Nasserization (the organization had suffered great repression during the Nasser period) but also of the exacerbation of the social crisis in the country and of their desire to counter an unorganized but quite militant workers' movement.

While fascism in Europe strove to confine women to children, church and the kitchen, the Muslim Brotherhood demands the reveiling of women, the rejection of any reform of the family code, the stoning to death of adulterous women, etc. The Brotherhood's activity in Cairo after the workers' rebellion of January 1977 testifies to this.

In Lebanon in 1970, during a period of rising class struggle, the

10. Ibid., p. 52.

Hizb al-Tahrir (Party of Liberation), an instrument of the Muslim Brotherhood, distributed a long leaflet in the Sunni Muslim petty-bourgeois neighbourhoods of Beirut, explaining that Islam prohibits the mixing of men and women in public places, that schools are public places, and that girls should therefore be withdrawn from co-educational schools. But the danger is that the Muslim Brotherhood is not content with merely handing out leaflets; it uses violence, sometimes with the implicit agreement of official authorities and with generous material aid from the Saudi Arabian and Libyan regimes. In Algeria for the past two years, Muslim Brothers, sometimes aided by the police, have been attacking women who walk alone at night, repressing them physically.

Given this overall situation, it is difficult not to stress the weight of Islam when considering the struggle for the liberation of Arab women. It is difficult not to take account of the direct physical oppression Arab women suffer because of attachment to Arab-Islamic traditions. It is no accident that the demands of the Union of Egyptian Women, founded in 1923 in the wake of the revolution of 1919, concerning the reform of the personal status code are still on the agenda even today. The especially intense oppression suffered by Arab women and the direct guardianship of the males of the family, whose honour and virility are determined according to the behaviour of their wives, do not result in a higher level of consciousness among Arab women; just the opposite. This persistent weight is always present, ready to be used to serve stagnation and counter-revolution. Although its elimination can be the result only of a social revolution that eradicates all forms of exploitation and enables women to put an end to the humiliation they have suffered for centuries, the present and future influences of this oppression must on no account be minimized.

The Rise of Islam: What Happened to Women?

Azar Tabari

This article was written several years ago, as a discussion paper. Since then, a lot more literature on the same topic has come to my attention and new works have been published. I am nevertheless submitting it for publication without any updating, because I believe that some of what it contains may still serve as a starting point for further discussion and clarification.

Introduction

The recent emergence of Islamic movements in the Middle East, particularly in Iran, has led to new interest in historical investigations into Islam. Such investigations are long overdue, but are particularly important now, when prevailing mystifications and falsifications regarding the history of Islam serve to consolidate the ideological grip of a very reactionary political movement. Of no other social issue is this more true than the situation of women under Islam. Not only do the present-day proponents of Islamic governments propose a most reactionary and retrogressive set of norms, values, and rules of human behaviour as the sole salvation of women, but they also claim that Islam has already proved its emancipating mission by liberating Arab women from the oppressive circumstances prevalent in pre-Islamic Arabia, in the dark period of so-called *Jahiliya* (ignorance). To be sure, the proponents of Islam do not claim that women were granted equal rights; neither do they propose to do so today. They argue that equality of rights, as understood and interpreted by Western thinkers and their followers in the Muslim world, is but a diversion from a real emancipation of women, because in this context equality has come to mean *identity* of rights. This, they argue, is both unnatural and unjust. Islam has offered the proper solution by assigning suitable responsibilities and rights to the two sexes. And in the recognition of these rights and responsibilities lies the only road to the emancipation of women.[1]

Even on the Marxist left, although most agree on the reactionary character of Islamic codes for women today, there is often an unspoken acceptance that perhaps Islam did carry some positive gains for women *as women* when it arose almost fourteen centuries ago. As a universalist religion, Islam provided the basis for the emergence and consolidation of a centralized state that, no matter how one may judge its role today, served to propel Arabia forwards from its tribal pre-state conditions to a world empire.

How valid are such claims concerning the liberating role of Islam for women, either as argued by proponents of Islam, or as accepted almost as an article of a faith in historical progress by many on the Marxist left? What was the real status of women in pre-Islamic Arabia and how did it change as the Islamic community took shape? Did pre-Islamic Arabs really bury their female infants alive? Were pre-Islamic Arab women deprived of property rights? What were the rights of fathers, brothers and husbands over women and how did Islam modify these traditional norms and customs?

In attempting to answer some of these questions and open a discussion on others, two caveats are required. First, it is not the task of this essay to give an analysis of Islam in general. Therefore, statements related to this general question, the conditions of the rise of Islam and its subsequent impact and development, will be asserted rather than demonstrated. One justification for this choice is the already existing literature on this topic.[2]

The second caveat is more problematic: I am referring to the problem of sources and documentation. As Maxime Rodinson has summarized the problem, 'There is nothing [in Muslim literature and sources] of which we can say for certain that it incontestably dates

1. Exhaustive coverage of these arguments is given in Murteza Mutahhari's book, *Nizam-e Huquq-e Zan dar Islam* (The System of Women's Rights in Islam), Qum 1974 (in Persian), particularly in chapter 5, entitled 'The Human Status of Women in the Koran', pp. 107-42.

2. Among such works, to mention only a few contemporary sources, are: Marshal Hodgson, *The Venture of Islam*, three volumes, Chicago 1974; Bernard Lewis, *The Arabs in History*, London 1950; and Maxime Rodinson, *Mohammed*, London 1971.

back to the time of the Prophet.'[3] The Koran itself, the only text over which there is almost general agreement amongst all Muslim schools and sects, was not committed to writing during Muhammad's lifetime. It is said to have been collated during 'Uthman's caliphate, some twenty years after Muhammad's death. Being accepted as the word of God, it remains to this very day closed to scrutiny and not in any need of documentation and historiography as far as Muslims are concerned. The *hadith*, the body of oral tradition that is supposed to go back to the time of Muhammad himself, was collected in the second and third centuries of Islam, and the Shi'i version only in the fourth century. The Abbasids in particular, in their attempt to run a vast empire on Islamic precepts, needed a thorough codification of laws, social and political guidelines to run the state. This had to be developed through formulations of precedents and interpretations of the Koran set by the Prophet himself, since in Islam the legislative powers belong solely to God, and His laws were conveyed only through the Prophet.[4] The *hadith*, therefore, cannot be depended upon for factual and historical documentation. As Goldziher has aptly noted, the common formula that opens each *hadith*, 'the Prophet said', simply means that the matter as explained further is correct from a religious point of view, or more often that the matter as explained by the *hadith* is the right way of handling the given problem, and perhaps the Prophet would have also agreed to this.[5] Nonetheless, the *hadith* are not without historical value of a different kind. Apart from facts that can be extracted from the stories told, they reflect what the emerging Muslim community and state legislated, thought, and attributed to a previous period. Here I tend to agree with W. Robertson Smith's evaluation of the *hadith* and other such literary sources: the stories could be purely fictitious, but the hypothetical social settings could not be invented arbitrarily.[6]

The anthropological data on the period under discussion are also meagre and uncertain. Despite these difficulties, one can attempt to project certain logical and historical hypotheses, which—due to the

3. See Rodinson, pp. x-xii.

4. See Ignaz Goldziher, *Darsha'i dar baray Islam* (Studies on Islam), Tehran 1979 (in Persian), pp. 90-102. This, in fact, is a Persian translation of Goldziher's *Vorlesungen über den Islam*, Heidelberg 1910.

5. Goldziher, p. 89.

6. W. Robertson Smith, *Kinship and Marriage in Early Arabia*, Cambridge 1885 (Beirut edition 1973), p. 86.

difficulties just mentioned—must remain open to further documentation and challenge, and serve only to initiate a long-overdue historical investigation.

The Historical Setting

The emergence of Islam as a universalist religion and a centralizing political movement led to and necessitated three inter-related social developments in early Islamic society (as compared to pre-Islamic Arabian society), which are relevant to our discussion of the situation of women.

First, the emergence of a centralized state, demanding total loyalty from all its subjects instead of the old traditional tribal loyalties, required the universalization of all norms throughout the Islamic community. One unified code had to replace the multiplicity of norms, customs, and arrangements that varied from one tribe to the next.

Second, this disintegration of the tribal system and the emergence of the larger community, while dissolving the tribal networks, responsibilities, and mutual contracts, consolidated the smaller patriarchal family unit (composed of husband, wife, and children). As against the larger and much looser kinship network, the individual family was now defined, delineated, and consolidated through a whole series of regulations. This probably affected the lot of women more than any other part of Islamic legislation.

Third, the individual was emphasized as against the tribe or other kinship networks. It was the individual that was responsible for his own salvation through conversion to the faith. It was the individual, and not the tribe, as was the custom of pre-Islamic Arabia, that was to be punished for any contravention of the social code.[7]

It was this combination of the emergence of the larger community of Muslims, coupled with the consolidation of the smaller family unit and the emphasis on individuality, all against the background of a disintegrating tribal system and the break-up of the larger kinship networks, that explains the changes that occurred in the situation of

7. For a fuller discussion of these points, see I. Goldziher, pp. 14-19; M. Rodinson, pp. 25-37, 140-52; and M. Hodgson, vol. 1, pp. 130-35.

women. To examine these changes, let us start from a discussion of the family and the legislation and codification surrounding it. This will cover most of the points related to women. Other issues, such as female infanticide, will be dealt with at the end.

Tribe, Family and Individual

There has been a long-standing discussion about the existence or otherwise of a matriarchal period in Arabia. W. Robertson Smith, whose book *Kinship and Marriage in Early Arabia* remains to this day the single most valuable source on the topic, makes a strong case for the predominance of the matriarchal family in Arabia. However, much of the evidence marshalled in support of the matriarchal theory could be explained even more convincingly in other and simpler ways. For example, one need not adhere to a matriarchal theory to explain the factually established pattern of women staying with their own tribe (rather than moving to the husband's tribe) after marriage. One only has to remember that a very large number of young and middle-aged men spent prolonged periods (measured in years) away from their place of residence with trade caravans. Under these circumstances, it would seem quite natural for the woman to stay with her own tribe to enjoy their protection and help, rather than move into an alien tribe. It seems more likely that at the time of the emergence of Islam, the Arabian peninsula was not going through a transition from matriarchal to patriarchal family. Rather, it was going through a period of consolidation of the family unit (which *was* patriarchal, to be sure) at the expense of the larger kinship networks and tribal fluidity.[8] The earlier, tribal norms were in some ways more favourable to women, accepting a more lax attitude to sexual and marital relations. In certain cases they gave women *de facto* rights to divorce, and even allowed polyandrous practices. (This may have been connected with the long periods during which men were away from home, making it acceptable for a woman to take another husband.) Let us look more closely at some of these pre-Islamic customs.

There seems to be ample evidence that in pre-Islamic Arabia there

8. For this discussion, see also Hodgson, vol. 1, p. 181 and Rodinson, pp. 229-32.

existed three types of marriage, which differed from each other in the arrangements for the residence of the wife and children. (It should be pointed out that, in the eyes of contemporary society, the main issue was the eventual tribal affiliation of the children rather than the location of the wife.)

First, the woman could leave her own tribe and join the husband's, in which case all the children would automatically belong to the husband's tribe, unless the wife's tribe had stipulated conditions to the contrary.

Second, the wife could stay with her own tribe and the husband would pay her occasional visits. In this case the children would belong to their mother's tribe, or join their father's tribe after the first few years of infancy. It is apparently this mode of marriage that provided the basis for the later Islamic legislation, according to which the mother has guardianship of her sons and daughters up to the ages of two and six respectively.

Third, the woman could stay with her tribe and the husband would join her. Here the children would belong to the mother's tribe.[9] W. Robertson Smith cites many examples from different sources to illustrate these different types of marriage. Here is one such story:

'An illustration of this kind of union as it was practised before Islam is given in the story of Salma bint 'Amr, one of the Najjar clan at Medina (Ibn Hisham, p. 88). Salma, we are told, on account of her noble birth (the reason given by Moslem historians in other cases also for a privilege they did not comprehend), would not marry any one except on condition that she should be her own mistress and separate from him when she pleased. She was for a time the wife of Hashim the Meccan, during a sojourn he made at Medina, and bore him a son, afterwards famous as 'Abd al-Mottalib, who remained with his mother's people. The story goes on to tell how the father's kin ultimately prevailed on the mother to give up the boy to them. But even after this, according to a tradition in Tabari, 1:1086, the lad had to appeal to his mother's kin against injustice he had suffered from his father's people. . . . The same conditions underlie other legends of ancient Arabia, e.g., the story of Omm Kharija, who contracted marriages in more than twenty tribes, and is represented as living among her sons, who, therefore, had not followed their respective fathers.'[10]

9. See Robertson Smith, pp. 76-79; Rodinson, p. 230.
10. Robertson Smith, pp. 85-86.

Amina, Muhammad's mother, is said to have stayed with her tribe, and 'Abdullah, Muhammad's father, paid her a visit. Muhammad himself is said to have lived with his mother until her death, at which time his father's kin took charge of him.

More interestingly, it seems that it was acceptable for a woman to ask for sexual intercourse (outside any formal union), or to reject her husband's demand for sexual intercourse, without incurring any shame or guilt. Again the stories implying such norms are post-Islamic; but regardless of their factual value—which is often not very great—they show that even several centuries after Islam, Muslim historians did not find it necessary to associate shame or guilt or scorn with these pre-Islamic customs. Robertson Smith quotes from Aghani (16:106) a story related to the marriage of Hatim and Mawiya: 'The women in the Jahiliya, or some of them, had the right to dismiss their husbands, and the form of dismissal was this. If they lived in a tent they turned it round, so that if the door faced east it now faced west, and when the man saw this he knew that he was dismissed and did not enter.' He later summarizes the three features characteristic of the marriage of Mawiya as follows: 'She was free to choose her husband, received him in her own tent, and dismissed him at pleasure.'[11] We must add parenthetically that the same story and many similar ones also show that the later Muslim theologians' boast that in Islam women cannot be married off against their wishes, unlike the Jahiliya period when women are supposed to have been treated like cattle, is unfounded. At least in some parts of Arabia, a woman would only marry the man she chose. It is likely that Muhammad, as in many other cases that will be discussed later, selected among the existing customs those that were most suited to the general development of a universalist religion with emphasis on the individual.

The story associated with the conception of Muhammad himself contains a case of rejection as well as demand on the part of a woman of nobility:

'Taking 'Abdullah by the hand 'Abdu'l-Muttalib went away and they passed—so it is alleged—. . . the sister of Waraqa b. Naufal. . . . When she looked at him she asked, "Where are you going, 'Abdullah?" He replied, "With my father." She said, "If

11. Ibid., pp. 80-81.

you will take me you can have as many camels as were sacrificed in your stead." "I am with my father and I cannot act against his wishes and leave him," he replied.

'Abdul-Muttalib brought him to Wahb . . . and he married him to his daughter Amina. . . .

'It is alleged that 'Abdullah consummated his marriage immediately and his wife conceived the apostle of God. Then he left her presence and met the woman who had proposed to him. He asked her why she did not make the proposal that she made to him the day before; to which she replied that the light that was with him the day before had left him. . . .

'My father Ishaq b. Yasar told me that he was told that 'Abdullah went in to a woman that he had beside Amina b. Wahb when he had been working in clay and the marks of the clay were on him. She put him off when he made a suggestion to her because of the dirt that was on him. He then left her and washed and bathed himself, and as he made his way to Amina he passed her and she invited him to come to her. He refused and went to Amina who conceived Muhammad.'[12]

Note, by the way, that according to the story Waraqa's sister was not only very rich (she offered to give 'Abdullah 100 camels for his sexual favours) but also had the power to dispose of her property as she wished.

Marriage and Sexual Codes Under Islam

Muhammad, in his attempts to ban all forms of marriage except those regarded as proper in Islam and to strengthen the family headed by the husband, had to impose very severe punishments for *zina'* (sexual intercourse outside marriage or concubinage): 100 lashes to each partner if the woman was unmarried, death if the woman was married. And the husband of a disobedient wife is *recommended* to resort to a whole range of punishments, from cutting off her allowance to beating. It seems unlikely that such strict punishments would have been necessary if extra-marital sexual relations and rejection by the wife of her husband's sexual advances were very

12. A. Guillaume, trans., *The Life of Muhammad* (English translation of Ibn Ishaq's *Sira* as edited by Ibn Hisham), Oxford 1955, pp. 68-69.

unusual or were already stigmatized as socially unacceptable and subject to scorn and contempt.

Numerous Koranic verses (I have located fifteen at one count) describe in amusing detail what sexual relations are permitted, which ones are prohibited, and whom one can or cannot marry. In pre-Islamic Arabia, a whole range of marriages existed and were acceptable. Some, such as the *musha'* marriage, where several men shared a common wife, were acceptable and existed only amongst the poorer members of the tribes, those who could not afford a bride-price each. Other marriages, such as *istibdha'*, where a husband would send his wife to a strong man in order to get strong offspring, were short-term and had a specific goal. Many marriages, particularly among the heads of tribes, were political acts. One source lists ten different types of marriage, most of which were later explicitly banned under Islam.[13] Apart from *musha'* and *istibdha'*, he cites the following: *istibdal*, where two men would temporarily swap wives—banned in the Koran (4:20-21); *maqt*, the automatic right of a son to inherit his father's wives—banned in the Koran (4:19); *mut'a*, temporary marriages that are automatically annulled at the end of the specified period—still prevalent amongst Shi'is and Malikis, but banned in all other Islamic sects; *shighar*, an arrangement between two families where each marriage would count as the *mahr* (the bride-price) for the other, so that no bride-price would be paid—banned under Islam by the ruling that the bride-price must be paid to the woman herself; *sifah*, basically amounting to prostitution—banned in many Koranic verses (along with *khiddan*, taking free lovers), for instance 4:25, 5:5. There seems to have also existed a custom of offering one's wife's sexual services to another man in exchange for certain favours. Several verses in the Koran forbid husbands to prostitute their wives. One's female slaves were also not to be forced into prostitution against their wishes, though otherwise it was not banned.

A word must also be said here about polygamy. Muslim apologists have offered various justifications and interpretations of this practice. Some hail it as the proper solution for correcting the supposed arithmetical imbalance between men and women. There

13. Hesam Noqaba'i, *Sayr-e Takamol-e Huquq-e Zan dar Tarikh va Sharaye'* (The Development of Women's Rights in History and Religions), Tehran 1963 (in Persian), pp. 47-48.

are always, they argue, more women than men—especially in times of war, and Arabia at the time of Muhammad was certainly a war-ridden zone. Others claim that the famous Koranic verse (4:3) that commands men to be just to all their wives practically outlaws polygamy, as it is impossible for a man to practice such justice. More pragmatic theoreticians accept that Islam neither invented nor banned polygamy. But they claim that by restricting the number of wives to four and by commanding the practice of fairness towards all wives, Islam improved the status of wives. Mutahhari devotes almost a quarter of his aforementioned book to the discussion of polygamy and insists that Muhammad strictly enforced the 'four wives only' law to the extent that if men with more than four wives were converted to Islam, he would force them to abandon their extra wives.[14] He cites several *hadith* in support of his argument—which does not stop him from also recognizing without the slightest hint of moral or religious qualm that Muhammad himself in the last ten years of his life had ten wives and many more concubines.[15] Shari'ati, on the other hand, who does not like portraying a Muhammad who does not practice what he preaches, dates the revelation of verse 3 of *sura* 4 to the eighth year after *hijra*, that is, when Muhammad already had all his ten wives and it would have been unfair and inhuman to abandon any of them.[16] The generally accepted date of the marriage legislations in *sura* 4 is shortly after the battle of Uhud, in the third year after *hijra*.

But there are several problems with this whole line of justification and interpretation of *sura* 4, verse 3.

First, as Rodinson has noted, 'It is, in fact, by no means certain that polygamy was so widespread in pre-Islamic Arabia. It is hard to see how an encouragement to take concubines if one is afraid of not acting fairly towards a number of wives can be a move in the direction of the supposedly more moral ideal of monogamy. Moreover, the Koranic text is clearly not a restriction but an exhortation, somewhat vaguely (for us) connected with fairness to orphans. Probably, as a result of battles and other factors, the community of Medina included more women than men. Those who

14. M. Mutahhari, pp. 413-14.
15. Ibid., p. 416.
16. Shari'ati, *Zan dar Chashm-o Del-e Muhammad* (Women in Muhammad's Eyes and Heart), in Persian, p. 32.

had lost their fathers, and women especially, were not always well treated by their guardians, who took advantage of their position to rob them. Muslim widows and orphans had to be married off as soon as possible. Once again, in order to understand a phenomenon, it is necessary to set it in its historical context before allocating praise or blame in the name of supposedly eternal moral, religious or political dogmas.'[17]

Second, the verse in question is not only highly exhortative; it is by no means restrictive. The numbers two, three, four, are used in the verse merely as numerical examples and in no way can one take the verse to mean *no more* than four. Other verses in the Koran, like 4:24, encourage men to take as many wives as they can afford. What does in fact call for a historical explanation—something that has never been offered, and which I am also unable to provide—is why the later Muslim theologians took *sura* 4, verse 3 to be a restrictive clause at all.

As already mentioned, Islam banned some of the previously practised forms of marriage in an attempt to universalize norms and customs across the Muslim community and to supersede varying tribal practices. Some legislation clearly aimed at eliminating what were considered spurious sexual relations and at consolidating the family unit (banning *sifah, khiddan*, and *istibdha'*). Other prohibitions would both strengthen the family and establish the primacy of individual over tribal and kinship rights—an important element in all universalist religions, which call for individual conversions and responsibilities, and promise individual salvation (as opposed to group rights and responsibilities). The ban on *shighar* and *maqt* would seem to emphasize the importance of women as individuals. The same observation goes for the insistence on paying the bride-price to the woman herself rather than to her father. This practice, however, was already becoming dominant before the emergence of Islam.[18]

Closely related to the consolidation of the family and the new emphasis on individualism was Islam's insistence on the determination of fatherhood, clearly a problem with practices such as *musha'*,

17. Rodinson, p. 232.
18. See *Shorter Encyclopaedia of Islam*, 1961, p. 447: 'But even before Islam it had already become generally usual for the bridal gift to be given to the woman herself and not to the guardian.'

istibdal, or offering one's wife's sexual services in exchange for favours. Strict observation of a waiting period for a woman prior to a new marriage was also imposed to the same end (three menstrual periods after a divorce—Koran, 2:228—and four months and ten days after the death of the husband—2:234—the extra forty days are presumed to be for respect of the dead man).

Correspondingly, divorce became more restricted and was regarded unfavourably. In pre-Islamic Arabia, at least in those parts where women stayed with their own tribes and retained their own tents, it seems that they had the right to discontinue the marriage at any time; so had the men, of course. The only constraint seems to have been that the woman's tribe would have to pay back the bride-price to the man's tribe. Moreover, if a man divorced his wife but did not claim back the *mahr* he had paid, he would retain the right to go back and claim the wife again.[19] Islam outlawed this practice by discouraging men from keeping women 'suspended', as it was called; it limited the time within which a man could go back and seek reconciliation to the three-period waiting time of the divorced wife; and it prohibited remarriage with the same woman after three consecutive divorces, unless the woman was first married to another man (Koran 2:230).

In *mut'a* marriage, the contract was automatically terminated after a prescribed period. This was a very common practice, considering the 'mobile' life style of many men. Rodinson quotes Ammianus Marcellinus saying of the Arabs in the fourth century: 'Their life is always on the move, and they have mercenary wives, hired under a temporary contract. But in order that there may be some semblance of matrimony, the future wife, by way of dower, offers her husband a spear and a tent, with the right to leave him after a stipulated time, if she so elects.'[20]

Robertson Smith considers the *mut'a* already a restriction on the previous rights of women, when they could divorce their husbands at any time.[21]

Apart from *mut'a*, Islam further restricted women's divorce rights by leaving it to the husband alone to decide on divorce. Although the practice of forgoing one's *mahr* for a divorce

19. Robertson Smith, p. 87, pp. 112-13.
20. Rodinson, p. 15.
21. Robertson Smith, p. 83.

continues to exist in Muslim countries even now, it no longer guarantees the wife a divorce: the husband has the right to refuse a divorce even if the wife is prepared to forgo her *mahr*. Only very limited circumstances (such as disappearance of a husband for four years, or extreme physical deformities leading to sexual impotence) entitle a wife to ask an Islamic judge for a divorce. The final decision is left to the judge, however.

Honour, Shame, and the Veil

Along with these elaborate and restrictive rules of marriage and divorce, new concepts of honour, chastity, and modesty for women began to emerge. We have already noted that in many stories about pre-Islamic Arabia, in poetry and in *hadith* (related to the circumstances of Muhammad's conception)—regardless of the factual value of such stories—no concept of shame or dishonour comes through regarding women's lax sexual relations and frequent marriages. I have argued that the severe punishment against *zina'* was aimed at uprooting these practices. The question of the veil itself also makes sense in this context of trying to create a new image of modesty in women. The origin of the veil (the large scarves that women wore in Arabia) remains in dispute. What is clear, however, is that, regardless of its pre-Islamic functions, in the Koran women are urged to cover their bosoms, to conceal their ornaments, and to avoid making noises with their ankle ornament (*khalkhal*) *as a sign of modesty* and to show these only to their husband or to those with whom they could or should not have sexual relations. Here is the full text of *sura* 24, verse 31:[22]

'And say to the believing women, that they cast down their eyes and guard their private parts, and reveal not their adornment save such as is outward; and let them cast their veils over their bosoms, and not reveal their adornment save to their husbands, or their fathers, or their husbands' fathers, or their sons, or their husbands' sons, or their brothers, or their brothers' sons, or their sisters' sons, or their women, or what their right hand owns, or such men as attend

22. English translation from A.J. Arberry's version, New York 1955, vol. 2, pp. 49-50.

them, not having sexual desire, or children who have not yet attained knowledge of women's private parts; nor let them stamp their feet, so that their hidden ornament may be known. And turn all together to God, O you believers; haply so you will prosper.'

Women are commanded not simply to cover themselves, but to cover themselves for a specific purpose: to keep men's eyes off them, not to try to attract men through physical display and sensuous games.

Muhammad's wives are subject to even more severe restrictions—these are presumed commendable for all Muslim women:

'Wives of the Prophet, you are not as other women. If you are god-fearing, be not abject in your speech, so that he in whose heart is sickness may be lustful; but speak honourable words. Remain in your houses; and display not your finery, as did the pagans of old.' (33: 33-34) And further in the same *sura*: 'O believers, enter not the houses of the Prophet, except leave is given you for a meal, without watching for its hour. But when you are invited, then enter; and when you have had the meal, disperse, neither lingering for idle talk; that is hurtful to the Prophet, and he is ashamed before you; but God is not ashamed before the truth. And when you ask his wives for any object, ask them from behind a curtain; that is cleaner for your hearts and theirs. It is not for you to hurt God's Messenger, neither to marry his wives after him, ever; surely that would be, in God's sight, a monstrous thing.' (33:53)

To this day, any physical contact between a man and a woman who may be sexually attracted to each other is forbidden in Islam. Mutahhari recommends that women working in modern offices or going to universities wear gloves at all times to avoid possible accidental touch. Even touching through gloves or other clothes is permissible only if there is no intention of enjoyment or games.[23]

The last two issues to be discussed are inheritance and female infanticide. Muslim writers on the subject of inheritance often state that Islam instituted inheritance and property rights for women, something that they were presumably deprived of in pre-Islamic Arabia.[24] This is simply false and in contradiction to many statements in the Muslim *hadith* itself. For example, if women had

23. Mutahhari, *Mas'alay Hijab* (The Problem of the Veil), Qum (in Persian), pp. 243-44.
24. See, for example, Mutahhari, *Nizam*, p. 247.

no property rights, it is inexplicable how a woman such as Khadija (Muhammad's future wife) is supposed to have had large fortunes and sent off sizeable trade caravans, several of which were led by Muhammad. Presumably she had inherited the wealth either from her father or from a previous husband. The story of Waraqa's sister, cited before, is also testimony to the existence of women with considerable property and complete right over its disposal. There are numerous examples to the same effect.

What the historical evidence points to is that in some cities, such as Medina, where an established patriarchal culture had taken root (possibly under the influence of Judaism, from which Islam took over a vast number of its civil codes and religious practices), women do not seem to have had a share in inheritance; while in other cities, in particular Muhammad's own town of Mecca, they did have a traditional share, half that of a man.[25] Similar provisions existed concerning blood-money (at the time of Muhammad, one hundred camels for an adult male and fifty for an adult female) and in witnessing procedure (where the testimony of two women could replace that of one man).[26] These Meccan customs Muhammad institutionalized across the Muslim community.

The practice of female infanticide seems to have existed in some areas, but not at all to the extent that has been generally alleged later. Robertson Smith refers to one source indicating 'that the practice had once been general, but before the time of the Prophet had nearly gone out, except among the Tamim.'[27] He, along with most other writers, tends to attribute the occasional practice to poverty. He cites several examples where it seems that the practice of infanticide had appeared again only after long periods of severe drought. The practice seems to have affected both male and female children, but more the latter. As men were more mobile and more vital to the continuing of the traditional trade and possibly pastoral life and defence of the tribe, sons were taken care of, while female infants were seen as useless burdens upon already meagre resources.[28]

The Koranic verses concerning infanticide refer to general

25. See Rodinson, p. 232; Robertson Smith, pp. 116-17.
26. W. Montgomery Watt, *Islamic Political Thought*, Edinburgh 1968, p. 7.
27. Robertson Smith, p. 292.
28. Ibid., pp. 292-94.

infanticide in three places (6:141, 152; 17:33) and to female infanticide only once (81:8).

Conclusion

What can we conclude from this survey? I think the most general observation that can be made today remains roughly the same as was made about a century ago by Robertson Smith regarding the Islamic system of marriage:

'Though Islam softened some of the harshest features of the old law, it yet has set a permanent seal of subjugation on the female sex by stereotyping a system of marriage which at bottom is nothing else than the old marriage of dominion.

'It is very remarkable that in spite of Mohammed's humane ordinances the place of woman in the family and in society has steadily declined under his law. In ancient Arabia we find, side by side with such instances of oppression as are recorded at Medina, many proofs that women moved more freely and asserted themselves more strongly than in the modern East.'[29]

Remarkable though this verdict may be, it is nevertheless not surprising or illogical. No matter what the impact of Islam may have been in other aspects of social life in Arabia and elsewhere as it spread through countries and continents, it invariably had the effect of institutionalizing the subjugation of women. The disintegration of tribal ties and the emergence of the community of Muslims may have given the general community new strength in the face of outsiders, but it lost women a source of protection they had enjoyed, that of their tribal solidarity. This, along with the consolidation and rigid institutionalization of the patriarchal family, put women in a weaker position within the family. In the face of undesirable marriages they could no longer ask for a divorce or enjoy the support of their tribe in such a dispute, and had to abide by newly instituted norms of modesty and be more and more secluded 'behind a curtain', as Muhammad's wives were advised. That Islam became, from its inception, a state religion *par excellence*—in the words of Rodinson, Muhammad combined Jesus Christ and Charlemagne in

29. Ibid., pp. 121-22.

a single person—has contributed to the consolidation of this subjugation in a particular way: throughout the centuries the forces backing the perpetuation of this subjugation were not limited to economic and social factors, customs and cultural pressures, families, and so on.[30] It was directly the state itself, its laws, its ideology, and the culture it regenerated, that at every level reproduced and enforced the subjugation of women in Muslim societies. To this day this remains the distinguishing feature of the subjugation of Muslim women.

30. Rodinson, p. 293.

Women and Politics in Lebanon

Yolla Polity Sharara

Mothers build homes and sons build countries.

The mother who rocks her new-born son with her right hand does not shake the world with her left hand.

ARAB SAYINGS

I think I experienced my relationship with politics as the transgression of a taboo. Of course, in the 1960s we were no longer living in the era of the veil. Lebanese society, despite its reputation for Westernization and modernism, was nonetheless still carefully partitioned: boys' schools and girls' schools, girls' games and boys' games, motherhood and homemaking for women, professional work for men. This division of roles and behaviour, seldom transgressed in practice, was instilled very early on within the family. Boys were openly preferred to girls, and girls were intensively prepared for their role as wives and mothers. Housekeeping skills and docility were the qualities most appreciated in a marriageable young girl. Women and politics were two opposite poles, or two spheres which never intersected. Politics was 'public', 'outside activity', 'history'. A woman was everything that was most private, most eternal and 'ahistoric'; the 'within', the 'at-home' that everyone, boy or girl, found in the home; the mother.

Politics was the preserve of men. We had obtained equal civic and political rights in 1953; we could vote and we could be elected. But it was good form not to make too much use of these rights. We would go and vote with our fathers or husbands, and we would vote the same way they did. Was it worth stirring up trouble in the family to vote for or against people we did not know from Adam or Eve, men foreign to our family? Was it worth the ridicule to stand as a candidate, as two women had done just after we had obtained the right to vote? Political questions were settled for us at the level of what is 'done' and 'not done', of what was or was not suitable for a woman. Although legally citizens, we continued to be ruled by our families and we had few, if any, official relations with the state.

To engage in politics, or to 'enter politics' as we put it, was not the thing to do for young women. We entered despite the opposition of our frightened parents. We joined as though we were joining a religion, eager to learn, to catch up on secular backwardness, serious and hardworking, obeying all the bizarre rules that governed meetings and demonstrations. The world of politics had the taste of forbidden fruit. We were proud to have been admitted, proud to meet celebrated leaders in the corridors, and especially proud finally to be taken seriously. Men, our comrades, listened carefully and with respect, and we were at ease discussing economic, historical or international problems with them. We were flying high, far from the kitchens of our mothers, and far from the embroidery work destined for our trousseaus.

It is necessary to have lived in these closed societies, where roles are rigidly defined from infancy, to understand our euphoria and also our blindness. We thought we had escaped the usual fate of women. We had slipped through a breach into the world of men. We tried to acclimatize ourselves to that world, always thinking our setbacks were due to our own ignorance. We were not yet ready to bring men and their values into question, and still less to question 'politics'.

Our elders who, like us, could not bear their situation, did not have the same opportunities as we did. In their time, political parties did not admit women, and no woman dared publicly to meet men who were not known to her family. So they founded women's charitable and social associations. For a long time they denied that they were involved in politics. When they took a position on a political or national problem, they took great care to show why, as mothers, they could not accept this and why, as wives, they demanded that. They led a campaign for political rights, and from 1953, they tried vainly to bring women into political life.

These women's organizations saw the problem as lying solely at the level of national power. Politics was the world of deputies and ministers. Women were excluded, and that was unfair. Several unsuccessful attempts to get themselves elected to the legislature were occasions for diatribes by members of these organizations against backward voters, and against women who did not understand their own interests, were traitors to their own sex, and lacked confidence in the ability of women to represent them. There were diatribes also, and especially, against the power of money, electoral fraud, and the manoeuvres of politicians whose victims were women candidates. Pure and innocent women mounting an assault on a corrupt electoral system were defeated by *Male*volent forces and corruption. All of which said to the most indulgent, 'They can't make the grade' and to others, 'It's a good thing; they shouldn't mix in matters which don't concern them.'

Although disgusted by these defeats, the women did not abandon their project. During a meeting before the last legislative elections, one woman speaker made an apologia for the Syrian and Egyptian regimes, which had allowed women into the body of deputies. Conceding that these women had not been elected but designated on the lists of single parties or simply nominated by the executive, this speaker, warmly applauded by the audience, demanded that in Lebanon as well, a certain number of seats be reserved *ex officio* for women nominated by the *Conseil Général des Femmes* and the president of the republic. This support for a system of nomination was astonishing on the part of women who otherwise swore by democracy in Lebanon, and criticized the absence of democratic rights in neighbouring Arab countries. But the advantages they saw in this system led them to gloss over everything that accompanied it.

Thus, they said, a woman 'would remain dignified, would not have to have her photo on the walls of the town, nor be confronted with the base material considerations of an election campaign. She would not lose her femininity, nor run the risk of a humiliating defeat, but would gain power.' Alas, all this required an amendment of the constitution and the electoral law, a difficult process in Lebanon.

Perhaps the dream of gaining power could be achieved more easily and more quickly at the level of ministerial posts? Every time there was a change of cabinet (which was frequent during these troubled years) we saw these same women's organizations rushing to the newly nominated head of the government during his consultations:

'women are under-represented, you must give us a portfolio.' The same thing happened every time: the prime minister received them courteously while they were served titbits to eat, and the press, in ironic mood, noted the visit; meanwhile, everyone waited for the women to finish their activities so that serious matters could be dealt with.

In fact it was pathetic. These women assumed that their sex alone was the reason for their exclusion from power, and presented themselves as women, without any consideration of political tendencies, religions, parties, programmes, international or Arab affiliations—the essence of the political game. It was also pathetic because it took the authorities, who presented themselves as democratic, at their word: representative of all citizens, without distinction of sex, class, or religion, a just and egalitarian regime. It was as though the right to something was sufficient to obtain it; as though the exclusion of women resulted from an oversight, which would be rectified on the spot once it was realized.

The women who joined political parties were less naive. They regarded politics as something requiring time and work. They had transferred their ambitions for power to the party. The majority thought that the conditions of women would change if they joined political parties. They expected that political and social transformations would make reforms possible. According to which party they belonged to, they struggled for Arab unity, the Lebanese nation, or socialism, but very little for the cause of women. It was very important for them to be recognized as full members of the party. They disliked being assigned to the women's section and wanted to prove that they were as capable as men at dealing with any problem. Thus they avoided talking about women, a minor subject, in order not to be put down. Within the many parties which, while admitting women, kept them in separate groups, the women met among themselves, waited for instructions from a party leader, and were mobilized particularly when the party had to show its strength in demonstrations and especially in electoral campaigns. In these situations, women were suddenly necessary and even indispensable.

In 1975, as part of the activities of International Women's Year, the Democratic Party invited representatives of Lebanese political parties to a meeting to draw up a balance sheet of the participation of women in political parties and to consider the possibility of agreeing on a platform of demands and common action. Women from the Phalangist Party, the National Bloc, the Progressive Socialist Party, the Ba'th Party, the Communist Party, as well as other women belonging to small groups, all met together; distrustful, rivals, convinced in advance that no agreement was possible.

However, agreement was possible. It was sufficient to point to the one or more paragraphs in each party's programme devoted to women to realize that all the parties—at least in principle— favoured equality between men and women, optional civil marriage, the application of the law on equal pay, the generalization of education for girls, better professional training for girls, an extension of creches, and so on. Officially, it was because of the war that this preparatory meeting was not followed by others: the leftist parties ordered a boycott of the Phalangist Party, so women from the left-wing parties could not sit at the same table with Phalangists. In fact, it was because of the anguish provoked by the agenda.

The first question was strictly political: 'What is the position of your party on women's questions?' Everybody, on the left and the right alike, was doubtful whether they would agree. How would a communist look if she had nothing either to criticize in, or add to, what was proposed by a Phalangist? How was it possible to end up with no more than differences of detail in demands over women, starting from so many different and antagonistic ideologies representing the whole organized Lebanese political spectrum? Was it sufficient to attribute the agreement to the demagogy of the right, which in its programmes made promises to women that it had no intention of keeping? This was not a serious approach, and one felt that it revealed a grave problem, that of an inadequate analysis of the exploitation and oppression experienced by women in Lebanese society.

The second question, although also political, was of a more existential nature: 'In your party, what is the number of women members, and the number of women who are in leading positions? What problems do they have because they are women?' Of all those present, only the Democratic Party could point to women in its politburo. No representative would agree to give figures or even a rough estimate of the proportion of women members in relation to the total membership of the party. There was great reticence in admitting there were problems at all. Thus, if there were few women in the party, this was because women lacked consciousness; if they did not hold responsible positions, this was because they were not sufficiently competent—the party itself did not discriminate. Women found themselves using standard male modes of thought in regard to other women: they talked like men. The same mechanism that makes women loath to complain of their lot in front of women they do not know, especially if they are rivals, was at work there. These women militants, when they were conscious of the discrimination of which they and their comrades were victims, when they were not themselves token women in the party, preferred to wash their dirty linen at home. They refused to question publicly the men from their own party, to recognize that their party, their men, were not the most advanced, the most egalitarian, or the most revolutionary. Alienated, and preferring their hard-won identity as members of the party to the less prestigious identity of committed women, they left without having really met, without having talked or listened.

The possibility of politicizing the women's question, of applying the same criteria as were applied to any other question, analysing it in terms of relations of power, of positions through which one group of people (in this case men) control another group (women) seemed to be a long way off for at least the majority of Lebanese women. But some women began to do this. They had been militants for several years in the left parties. They had lived with and undergone subtle or brutal discrimination from society, from militants of other parties— but especially from their own comrades. They had been confronted with the disastrous consequences of the etiquette of principal and secondary contradictions, the contradiction between the sexes being, of course, always secondary. They had realized the futility of any revolution that kept intact the basic unity of exploitation and oppression, that of one sex over the other, of masculine over feminine. They had also lived through the laceration of the war, in which, although perhaps in different forms according to the side, the male order had been the sole victor.

It is this reflection, still embryonic, that I want to account for. To try to see in the present political situation in Lebanon an antagonism of class and of religious communities, but also an antagonism between the sexes, to try to see the war through, and starting from, the feminine universe.

It is hardly astonishing that in Lebanon more than in other places women experience politics as something foreign to their daily lives, since their lives are ruled by community and not national laws. The principal moments of their lives are punctuated by the intervention of men from their communities and religious authorities, rarely from the state. It is essential to understand that in Lebanon all matters relating to personal status depend on confessional laws and tribunals. There is no civil marriage. There are as many different laws for women as there are religions. Marriage, divorce or separation, relationships, guardianship of minors, inheritance, all these problems have different solutions according to whether one is a Maronite Christian, a Greek Orthodox, a Greek Catholic, or a Sunni or Shi'i Muslim. Of course, the state also intervenes: education policy, employment policy, wages, prices. But these problems are secondary, or rather experienced as secondary by most women, with the exception of politicized women who are interested in them.

In 1975 the women's organizations held a congress to discuss the laws relating to personal status, and demanded optional and non-compulsory civil marriage. A law forbidding discrimination against women in the family was presented by women from the Democratic Party and adopted by the congress. All the parties that declare themselves opposed to confessionalism talk about the necessity of having unified and secular laws in all spheres of life, especially that of personal status. The left parties add that this reform is all the more necessary because the present laws are disadvantageous to women, but their declarations remain at the level of principles, and everyone carefully avoids entering into details.

However, at the moment of civil war, the question of women became the central point of negotiations between the right and the left, and it is not irrelevant that it also became the point of rupture. The 'Committee for National Dialogue', laboriously created during one of the many cease-fires that punctuated the war, attempted to list points of disagreement and bring together different points of view. It broke down over the question of secularization. The left demanded total secularization, as did the Christian right. The Muslims wanted political and administrative secularization, but refused secularization of personal status, considering it a matter of private and non-political problems. Since the beginning of the war the left had been a prisoner of its Muslim allies. Its leader, Kamal Jumblatt, known for his misogyny and political opportunism, declared that since the 'Muslim and national side' was not ready for such a reform, they could put the question of civil marriage to one side. One could not open a breach in the alliance over such secondary problems! The important thing was to remain united in the face of the enemy and to deal with 'political' and military problems. It should be noted that this abandonment by the left of the women's cause went almost totally unnoticed.

The Christian right affirmed that for its part it wanted civil marriage. Assured of a Muslim rejection, it could indulge in all sorts of proposals to project a modern and Western image. In a recent interview with *Le Monde*, Bashir Gemayel stated: 'Alone, we achieved secularization a long time ago.' Describing the federal structure he supported, he said: 'Each community should rule itself according to its own laws, and no one should impose their views on others.' But isn't this precisely what happened before the war? As for secularization, that is a trap-word for women. For the Napoleonic code was a secular code, as was the Rocco Code, drawn up by Mussolini in fascist Italy. What sort of code, then, are the Phalangists and the Guardians of the Cedar, allied to the Lebanese monks, preparing for us?

Here we touch on a very important aspect of intercommunal relations. We are dealing with two communities struggling for power, for leadership. Within each community, masculine domination over women takes place under different conditions and according to different laws, but it is nonetheless implacable. It is a matter of keeping the women for the men of the community. Muslim men, however, have legal access to Christian women; the reverse is not true. A Muslim woman cannot marry a non-Muslim without at least converting, and in that case losing her inheritance. Marriages are very common between Lebanese Christians and foreign Christians. Mixed marriages are very rare between Christian men and Muslim women, and often in these cases the man converts to Islam.

When civil marriage is discussed, traditionalist Muslim men immediately imagine a cohort of young women, their daughters and sisters, rushing into the arms of Christian men the minute the law is passed. This threat is absolutely intolerable. One exasperated Muslim said to me: 'When we discuss secularization with Christians they ask me: will you give us your daughter in marriage? Would that they would leave our women alone!'

For centuries, these communities have lived side by side concocting myths about the women of the other community. In the Muslims, the Christians see the East with all its seduction, its sensuality, and its docility, in short—the harem. The Muslims imagine Christian women as being more advanced, more educated, and more modern than their women. To join them is a promotion. But since intercommunal relations remained relatively rare, because of the fear of reprisals from jealous fathers and brothers (sometimes leading to murders, qualified as 'crimes of honour'), negative myths grew up, helping to make frustration tolerable: 'Bunch of whores', said Muslims of Christians who rejected them; 'stupid and ignorant women', said Christians of Muslim women they lusted after, but who were inaccessible.

A kind of rule operated in peace time, an implicit understanding between the males of the two communities, recognizing the mutual right of each over the women of their respective communities. This entente, based mainly on fear of reprisals, protected women of the two camps in the first stages of the war. Few women were kidnapped, and if they were arrested they were quickly released. They could move around more easily than men; militiamen on barricades did not ask them for identity papers. One got the impression that if one side broke this agreement and started to seize women, it would be terrible. If the walls that held back repressed and aggressive desires suddenly broke, the consequences would be uncontrollable.

These walls were effectively breached at times, when the war reached extremes of violence: Qarantina, Damour, Clemenceau, Tel al-Za'tar. These were points of no return, where through the association of sexuality with power, through the rape of women and young girls, the aggressors signified their absolute (but momentary) domination over the other camp. In all the random shelling, houses in flames, banks looted, hotels destroyed, factories sacked, some elements of the patriarchal order—religious, political, and military leaders and women's property—were spared. This 'gentlemen's agreement', based on a cult of authority and hierarchy, and on an extraordinary respect for force and violence, as much in their own camp as within the enemy camp, led to some aberrations: Hawi, military leader of the Phalangist militias, was captured by the

Palestinian resistance and released several hours later. When people wanted to hit Chamoun, they executed his nephew; and as a reprisal, it was Jumblatt's sister that was assassinated.

If certain of the leaderships were hit during this war, those who survived emerged even more ingrained with authoritarianism and violence. Both sides attributed their previous 'defeats' to the softness of their leaders; they wanted the strongest leaders, the best armed militias, the most organized—that is, the most easily controllable—population. Any questioning of authority had to be fought, any criticism or reservations were put down to laxity; politics was no longer a citizen's right, only guns talked. These were phallic values *par excellence*.

The people had to be mobilized to accept the infernal life that gripped the combat areas, Beirut in particular: scarcity and sometimes total lack of water, electricity, bread, vegetables and meat; children without schools; workers without jobs; stealing and looting; destruction and death. Those responsible for the war were aware that it was the women who bore most of the burden of everyday life. They attempted to gain their support. Radio programmes were specifically directed at women from both sides. Despite references to the 'Cedars of Lebanon' or to the Arab destiny of the same Lebanon, these programmes were very similar. They talked about 'the necessary contribution of women to the national cause', and of 'the price to be paid'. They exalted the spirit of sacrifice of the mothers who had borne the heroes. Heroes, yes, but how to acknowledge their deaths, and the death of so many victims of random shelling and the bullets of snipers? 'Umm-al-shahid', the mother of the martyr, became the object of endless glorification. The violence of the apparatus and ritual of funerals was useful as a means of making death unreal, and silencing the women's grievances: the profusion of guns, shots in the air, the bodies removed to the wailing of the women, and the men accompanying the hero-martyr to his final resting place.

Pathetic as always, women from the women's organizations, corroded like everybody by the confessional evil, completely bypassed by events and not knowing what to do, took up a position against the war. One day they tried to remove the barricades of the militias, and this led to kidnappings. Going from east Beirut to west Beirut, from Phalangist barricade to progressive barricade, they spoke in the name of wives, mothers, and sisters. They wanted an end to the killing. They had built homes and now, contrary to the saying, the sons were destroying the country. Of course, their campaign had no success, although it reflected the feelings of many people.

Women belonging to parties, and many others who joined in during the war, organized assistance and food for both camps. Not having been able to leave the area controlled by the progressive forces and the Palestinian resistance during the whole of the war, I don't know in detail what happened in the Christian camp. However, everything leads me to believe that women from both sides ran into the same problems.

On the progressive side the disorganization would have reached unmanageable proportions without the participation of the women. They formed aid teams, provided help for the injured, welcomed refugee families, gave food for the fighters, sewed sheets and linen for the hospitals. An incredible amount of energy was and continues to be expended. Very few male militants took part in this work unless they were overseeing it. This was considered to be women's work, and regarded with contempt; men who participated in it felt themselves diminished, and were mocked by their comrades. Everything was just the same as in the family. For women, the servile jobs, for men, the noble jobs; in war the noble jobs were carrying arms and fighting.

Women did take part in the fighting—and their presence was considered to be neither natural nor obvious. On the surface, men were proud to have women fighting in their ranks. This conformed to the scheme of 'people's war'. In actual fact, the presence of women was felt to be an intolerable blow to their virility. They defended themselves by attacking: sexual and verbal aggression or attempts to put the women down. The attitude of the military instructors was full of condescension, as though they were saying: 'I'm too important to waste my time with women.' The military commanders were no better. Women fighters were always given the least prestigious arms on the excuse they had not had enough training, and the worst places on the pretext of 'protecting' them. To be treated as equals, the women had to be more courageous and more competent than the men, and at that point they became the token women, heroines. Each party and each militia had a few of them.

In addition, the women fighters had to defend themselves against the ever-present accusation of being whores. 'In the trenches, it's an orgy', was a fantasy often expressed by male fighters talking about the enemy camp or rival militias. Women had no right to be there; they were a nuisance. Every pretext was good.

And why were we there?

Why, even by taking up arms, did we fill precisely that role given to us for all (patriarchal) eternity: that of the beautiful woman fighter, or the avenging mother defending her little ones? Why were we involved in a struggle from which we would gain nothing?

Why did we let ourselves into this sinister adventure?

Changes in Palestinian Society

Ehud Ein-Gil and Aryeh Finkelstein

The Zionist settler society has been built upon the ruins of Palestinian society, destroyed by Zionist colonization. That part of the Palestinian people which after 1948 remained inside the state of Israel, under direct Zionist rule, has undergone deep social changes over the years. For example, the confiscation of their lands forced the Palestinian peasants out of agriculture and into wage labour. In this article, we consider the significance of these changes and their effects on the structure of Palestinian village society inside Israel, and in particular on the position of women.

The Hamoulah[1]

The institutions of Palestinian village society drew their strength from specific economic conditions. The growth of the main village institution—the *hamoulah*—was based on land ownership, an agrarian economy, and a relative weakness of contacts with urban centres; and it was reinforced by Arab culture, tradition, and religion. Even in the nineteenth century, with the intrusion of the imperialist powers into the region, contacts with Western civilization and its values were mainly confined to the small urban population of Palestine; the village remained largely isolated from European influence until Zionist colonizing activity became intensive.

After the defeat of the Arab states in the 1948 – 49 war, the Zionist movement subjected the Palestinians who remained inside Israel to

1. A *hamoulah* (pl.: *hama'il*) is a unit of social organization smaller than a clan and consisting of several extended families that have (or believe themselves to have) a common ancestor in the male line.

its policy. But Zionist policy towards Israel's Palestinian subjects has been a combination of two mutually contradictory tendencies. On the one hand, it has aimed to preserve the traditional *hamoulah* structure of village society, in order to make it easier to keep the Palestinians under control. But on the other hand, by expropriating the Palestinians' lands, it has destroyed the economic basis of the very traditional structure that Zionism has sought to preserve. Without its lands, the *hamoulah* has lost its economic foundation: its members are dispersed as wage labourers in the Israeli economy, and the ties that had bound them together are severed. But despite all this, the *hamoulah* has not collapsed.

In countries like England, which had undergone an industrial revolution, the expropriation of the peasants' lands destroyed the old rural society; the peasants migrated to the towns in search of new sources of livelihood, were transformed into an industrial proletariat, and created new social frameworks appropriate to their new class. But in England both dispossessors and dispossessed were English. It was a process rooted in the intrinsic economic development of England.

In Palestine, on the contrary, the process through which the peasants were dispossessed of their land was caused by a clash between a colonizing movement of immigrants and the indigenous population; it was not a process resulting from the intrinsic economic development of the country. Although in this country, just as in England, the dispossessed peasants were proletarianized, the traditional framework of the Palestinian village society was not broken. For the new Palestinian proletarians did not migrate to the towns: legal restrictions (military rule, to which Arabs inside Israel were subjected and which operated a pass system, was lifted only about ten years ago[2]) and racist discrimination on the part of the authorities and the 'man in the street' prevented them from moving into the Jewish city near their place of work. The villages became working-class dormitories. But the old *hamoulah* structure of these villages was preserved.

Why?

The 1948 defeat left the Palestinian population inside Israel

---

2. This refers only to Israel itself, in its pre-1967 borders. The Arabs in the territories occupied in 1967 are still under military rule.

beaten and broken. Most of the urban population, as well as the inhabitants of more than three hundred and fifty villages, had been driven out of the Zionist state. The only remaining social institution was the *hamoulah*, which now became a kind of kernel around which Palestinian identity inside Israel would be recreated and preserved. The Zionist attempt to obliterate and deny the existence of Palestinian national identity brought about a response characteristic of oppressed minorities—the strengthening of traditional structures.

But the traditional social structures could not serve as a framework for resistance and struggle against oppression, and were therefore turned into instruments of the authorities. In order to dominate and control the great majority of the members of a *hamoulah*, it was enough for the authorities to harness the headman to their wagon. A party that could bribe the headman would get most of the votes of his *hamoulah*. In this way the *hamoulah* structure was turned from a stronghold of resistance to Zionist policy into the institutional framework through which Zionist domination over Palestinian society is mediated. Even in those cases in which the headman did not sell out to the authorities, the *hamoulah* could not serve as a basis for broad struggle; for the ties of solidarity it fosters are exclusive to its own members, and do not bind the broad mass of the people together.

The *hamoulah* preserved its prestige and influence, and with it were preserved values and conventions that had characterized traditional Arab society. More than anyone else, it is Palestinian women who have got the worst of this state of affairs: they not only belong to an oppressed people suffering from discrimination, but also have an inferior and underprivileged status within that people.

Women in Palestinian Society

'The family honour' is the concept in whose name most of the restrictions upon Palestinian women's freedom of movement are imposed. In particular, women's individual liberty continues to be violated by the segregation of unmarried people of opposite sexes, a segregation based upon religious and traditional values as well as social conventions. Thus the unmarried woman is prevented from participating in socio-cultural activities in which men take part; this includes not only going to the cinema or to the coffee-house, but sometimes even sitting together with guests in her own house. The married woman's freedom of movement is also restricted: she too is not allowed to participate in socio-cultural activities at which men are present, unless she is accompanied by her husband.

Betrothal and marriage arrangements in Palestinian society make it difficult for a woman (and indeed also for a man) to marry a person of her (or his) own choice. At the same time, these arrangements are an important means of preserving social differentiation. In general, marriage is an economic transaction; a rich family will make sure that its sons and daughters marry brides and bridegrooms belonging to rich families. This is ensured by the bride-price: a man who cannot afford the high bride-price demanded by a rich family cannot marry a daughter of that family.

Incidentally, a similar phenomenon also exists among Israeli Jews. Israeli-Jewish society is more 'open', and in it marriage is theoretically a matter of free choice for both partners. But before the wedding there is usually a meeting of the families of both 'parties', in which they finalize the commercial transaction—how much money is to be paid to the young couple by each side in order to ensure its economic status. Not infrequently, weddings are called off before that stage is reached; the parents' opposition overcomes love and 'free choice'.

But in Palestinian society the situation is, if anything, worse. A father's prestige and authority over his family are much greater, and only very few young people would dare to defy the 'family' and marry a person of their own choice. The imposed segregation between unmarried men and women makes it difficult for love relationships to develop, and enhances the power of the head of the family: in the absence of love ties, the resistance of his sons and daughters is weaker than it might have been, and it is that much easier for him to impose his own will in the matter of marriage.

But in this, as in other social matters, the situation is gradually improving. For the time being, change is rather slow, but it is gathering momentum. Of course, it all depends on the young people themselves, both men and women. Both share an interest in liberating themselves from the authority of the *hamoulah* tradition, in order to facilitate a freer contact between the sexes, before and after marriage, and to win the right to choose their own spouses. A struggle to abolish the institution of bride-price will be an important first step along this road.

Historically, the concept of the 'family honour' was used to dictate a restriction of women's participation in the social process of production. But the Zionist expropriation of land has worsened the situation of Palestinian women in Israel. In the past, women used to take part in the family's production process, in agriculture. But when there was no longer any land, the men went out to work in the city, while social conventions tethered the women to their village homes.

However, the harsh economic realities of the last few years—rapid price inflation accompanied by a meagre rise in nominal wages—have forced the Palestinians to allow women to go out to work as wage labourers in order to supplement the family income. The Israeli economy, particularly the food and textile industries, was crying out for cheap manpower—or womanpower: Palestinian women fulfilled the demand of the labour market. Between 1967 and 1972, some seven thousand Palestinian women entered work in industry.[3] Thousands of women are employed in agriculture on Jewish farms. Thus the 'sanctity' of the concept of 'family honour' was exposed; its role was clearly seen: to preserve relations of authority based on a socio-economic situation belonging to the past. When economic and social conditions had changed, family honour was no longer capable of keeping the woman at home.

Under capitalism, women workers generally constitute a reserve army of cheap labour, deployed according to the needs of the economy. A working woman is not considered to be the family's main breadwinner, and this is used by employers as a justification for not paying her the same wage as a man doing the same job. But in Israel, in addition to this discrimination in wages between men and women, there is also national discrimination in wages between Jews and Arabs. Thus Palestinian women constitute the most exploited section of the labour force in the Israeli economy.

The inferior status of women in the patriarchal family is a circumstance shared by all Palestinian women workers and sets them apart from the other part of their class, the Palestinian male workers. Although they are super-exploited at work, Palestinian women

3. *Davar*, 10 March 1972.

workers find it very difficult to fight against their exploitation. If the very fact of their going out to work is regarded by traditional village society as something unusual and undesirable, how much greater will be the social resistance to any attempt by women to organize and struggle independently! 'Family honour' prevents women from organizing politically, and even stands in the way of their participation in political activity alongside men. And if this applies to their participation in organizing for struggle against national oppression, which afflicts both men and women, it applies all the more to women's organizing for struggle for their own rights.

The *hamoulah*, as guardian of family honour, is therefore the main source of weakness of the Palestinian woman, and especially the Palestinian woman worker, in Israel.

Changing Reality and Stubborn Conservatism

Economic reality imposes changes even upon conservative village society. Palestinian society in Israel still disapproves of women working in industry together with men. In fact, most Palestinian women workers still work in segregation. But women's work is gradually becoming more accepted, and at the same time the family's power over the woman's earnings is growing weaker. More and more women, especially unmarried women, keep some of their wages and do not hand them all to the head of the family. Their participation in the process of production and their growing, if relative, economic independence constitute preconditions for the success of the women's struggle against the bonds of *hamoulah* conservatism.

Other factors, too, contribute to weakening the *hamoulah*'s conservative grip. One of these is the influence of Western social values.

Palestinian society tended to regard the Western bourgeois values imported into this country by the Zionist colonizers as corrupt. In fact, these bourgeois values represented a historically progressive stage of development compared to the old religious-feudal values; but many Palestinians tended to identify these values with Zionist oppression. Moreover, this was used by Palestinian reaction in order to persuade the masses that democracy and socialism also are 'Zionist values' which have to be opposed. As a result, adherence to the traditional social values hindered the development of

Palestinian society and handicapped it in the struggle against Zionism.

The view of woman as an inferior being, unfit to participate in social and political struggle, who must be tethered to the home, impaired the resistance of Palestinian society against Zionist oppression, because half of the population was thereby prevented from contributing its effort and energy to the struggle.

(There was a similar phenomenon in other Arab countries. But wherever the struggle for national and social liberation struck at the forces of reaction and conservatism, women took an active part in the struggle. This was the case during a certain phase in Algeria as well as in South Yemen. Also, in the occupied territories of the West Bank and the Gaza Strip, women play an important and useful part in the struggle against occupation.)

Now, in the course of time it is becoming clear that more and more Palestinians no longer identify democratic and socialist values with Zionism (this refers both to political principles and to socio-cultural values). And accordingly, resistance to the adoption of these values is declining.

For example, among the laws imposed by British rule in Palestine, and later by the Zionist power, there was a law prohibiting polygamy, whereas Islam permits it. But today, the ban on polygamy is no longer regarded as a Zionist value that must be opposed. (We do not claim that this law has solved the problems of the institution of marriage; there is certainly much that should be changed in the arrangements and content of this institution. But the abolition of polygamy constitutes an advance in the status of women.) Accordingly, we do not know of any Palestinian who would seriously advocate the inclusion of the legalization of polygamy in the programme of Palestinian national liberation.

Attitudes to the high birth-rate are likewise changing. The high birth-rate has been used—sometimes consciously and sometimes unconsciously—as a weapon against Zionism. If the Zionists wanted less Arab children to be born, then having more children became a 'patriotic duty'. The relative rise in living standards, which normally has a downward effect on the birth-rate, has not had this effect among the Palestinians in Israel. Their birth-rate, 4.6 per cent per annum, is still among the world's highest. Although this seems to be a policy of struggle, a reaction against Zionist oppression, it tends to maintain the oppression of women. The burden is particularly heavy in villages without electricity, child care and health services.

A family with many children finds it more difficult to provide for them materially and spiritually. This has an adverse effect not only on the women, who are tethered to their homes, but also on the children. However, the use of contraceptives is gradually spreading, and a growing number of women are becoming aware of their right to control their own bodies. Here, too, the *hamoulah*, religion, and tradition have arrayed themselves against change. Village conservatism regards any attempt at change as a Zionist-inspired plot.

From all this it can be seen how difficult it is going to be for Palestinian women in Israel to struggle for their own liberation. It seems as though everything and everyone have joined forces to prevent their liberation and to make it harder for them to organize for struggle.

The obstacles to Palestinian women's liberation are formidable indeed. In addition to those we have already mentioned—religion, tradition, the *hamoulah*—one of the greatest obstacles is subjective: the immense difficulty in becoming fully conscious of their state of oppression, isolation, and lack of organization. In the present situation, any 'rebellious' woman who refuses to surrender to the bondage of convention remains isolated and ostracized. Her first aim is therefore to seek an alliance with other women in her struggle.

The experience of the women's liberation movement in Israel has shown it to be characterized by a particular feature, which is not shared by similar movements in other capitalist countries. For, in the Zionist state of Israel, an Israeli-Jewish woman cannot support free abortion on demand without falling foul of the Zionist attitude to the 'demographic question'; she cannot repudiate the rabbinate's authority in matters of marriage and divorce[4] without taking a stand on their authority to determine 'who is a Jew' (and therefore entitled to a privileged status in Israel) and who is not; she cannot demand equality for women without confronting the counter-argument that 'the duties of men and women are also unequal, because the men

4. The fact that the ecclesiastical authorities in Israel have such wide powers (including monopoly of jurisdiction in matters of marriage and divorce) is also injurious to others besides non-religious Jews, who are placed, against their will, at the mercy of the clerics. Arabs of the Catholic faith, for example, cannot be divorced in Israel, whereas in Rome, under the very nose of the pope, Catholics can obtain a civil divorce.

have to shoulder a heavier military burden'; she cannot demand equality between men and women without also demanding equality between Israeli-Jewish and Palestinian-Arab women. In short, one cannot consistently demand equal rights for women without questioning the most fundamental Zionist principles.

This is a possible meeting point for Jewish and Arab women, for a joint struggle for women's liberation. The development of a Palestinian women's liberation force can intensify the contradictions within the women's liberation movement in Israel and lead to the creation of an internationalist and anti-Zionist women's liberation movement.

Like every colonial power, Zionism divides in order to rule. On the national level, it divides all Jews from all Arabs; on the confessional level, it divides Muslim, Druze, Christian, and Jew from one another; it divides men from women; and among the Palestinians it divides one *hamoulah* from another.

The masses of this country—Arabs and Jews, men and women—can liberate themselves from the national oppression and racist discrimination of Zionism only through an implacable struggle that will expose the lie upon which these divisions are based and will prove the community of interests of all the exploited, members of both peoples, of both sexes, of all religions and all *hamoulahs*, against their oppressors and exploiters: Zionism and Arab reaction, both of which serve imperialism.

A struggle against the oppressive strait-jacket of the traditional institutions of Palestinian society is necessary for the liberation not only of Palestinian women, but also of Palestinian men. Although men are, relatively speaking, socially privileged, the restrictions and prohibitions imposed upon the liberty of women are also restrictions and prohibitions upon the liberty of men.

The *hamoulah*, religion, tradition, and conservative customs are enemies of the Palestinian masses struggling for liberation. They are instruments for the oppression of women, but they also serve the oppression of the Palestinian people as a whole. Therefore it is the duty of all Palestinians, both men and women, to struggle against them.

The liberation of women cannot come about without the liberation of society as a whole; and society as a whole cannot be liberated without the liberation of women. The struggle against all forms of oppression and exploitation, for national and social liberation, is the struggle of all. Women must take part in this struggle. If they take a stand equally with men, in the broader front, it will help their own struggle for social equality.

Ideology Without Revolution: Jewish Women in Israel[1]

Dina Hecht and Nira Yuval-Davis

'In the State of Israel almost every woman is a working woman.

'You meet the working woman on your way to Israel—steward-esses aboard planes and on the ground (the supervisor in the air-port's control tower is also likely to be a woman). Often a police-woman will be the one to stamp your passport, and a pert young woman will greet you at the reception desk of your hotel....

'[Women] are the most dextrous in packing orange crates or strawberry baskets, and they are most expeditious in packaging colourful flowers... and they take part in growing them....

'True, only one out of every three adult women works outside her own household and is designated statistically as "belongs to the work-force", but those who stay at home work at their daily chores, taking care of their family and rearing their children... none will deny that the work they do is vital and that they are contributing directly both to the welfare of their family and to the image of Israel's society.'[2]

A state that relies to the extent that Israel does on outside financial and human resources has to produce a comprehensive public relations policy which is conducted abroad even more vigorously than at home. The brazenness of this venture determines the constant high pitch at which Zionist propaganda is maintained.

1. The authors would like to acknowledge fruitful discussions with Avishai Ehrlich, and are grateful to him for allowing them to make use of some material contained in an article of his to be published in a forthcoming issue of *Khamsin*. (See the present volume, 'Zionism, Demography, and Women's Work'.)
2. 'The Working Woman in Israel', in *Features of Israel*, Israel Information Centre, n.d.

With the resurgence of Western feminism, Israeli propaganda has found not only a new market abroad but also many enthusiastic mouthpieces to further laud the so-called advances and achievements of Israeli women. Indeed, women play a considerable role in the export image of Israel: women conscripts, women in the kibbutz, a former woman prime minister, and 'dextrous orange-crate packers'—all have become successful propaganda currency, and the myth of the equal, liberated or emancipated Israeli woman, although weakening in Israel, is still potent abroad.

In an article 'Revolution Without Ideology: the Changing Place of Women in America', C.N. Delger laments: 'in America the soil is thin and the climate uncongenial for the growth of any seedlings of ideology . . . and so long as [American working women] do not advance such an ideology, American society surely will not do so, though other societies, like Israel's and the Soviet Union's, which are more ideological than ours, obviously have.'[3] Perhaps. But the myth of the liberation and equality of Israeli women, while perhaps gratifying a deep-seated need for feminists in search of identity, cajoles most Israeli women into a state of spirited resignation—content with a public image that bears little or no resemblance to their actual situation.

The dextrous [female] orange-crate packer today is likely to earn 40 per cent less than her male counterpart, despite the equal-pay law of 1964.

During the premiership of Golda Meir, there were only 9 women among the 120 members of the Knesset; at present there are 8. There is not a single woman city mayor, and in the civil service—the largest employer of the female labour force—40 per cent of employees are women, but only 4 per cent in the highest grade.[4]

Some women are indeed conscripted into the army, but in recent years about half of those reaching conscription age have been exempted—a far higher proportion than in the case of men. Of those taken into the army, 60 per cent are employed in clerical occupations; only 30 per cent of army job classifications are open to women.

3. C.N. Degler, 'Revolution Without Ideology', in R.J. Lifton, ed., *Woman in America*, Boston 1964.
4. Committee for the Status of Women – Recommendations, Prime Minister's Office, Jerusalem, February 1978 (in Hebrew).

'*Chen*, the Hebrew acronym for Women's Corps means (as a word) "Charm". And indeed *chen* adds to the IDF [Israel Defence Forces] the grace and charm which makes it also a medium for humanitarian and social activities.

'Today, of course, the goals of *chen* have changed and *chen* girls play purely non-combatant—though thoroughly essential—roles within the IDF framework.

'The *raison d'être* for women's present-day service in the IDF is threefold:

'1. Indirect reinforcement of the IDF's combat forces by fulfilling a variety of administrative, professional and service duties, *thus releasing a larger number of male soldiers for fighting missions.*

'2. Preparing women to defend themselves, their families and homes, due to the unique security circumstances of Israel.

'3. Assisting in the IDF's educational and social enterprises . . . and participating in the national extra-military missions of the IDF as an *absorbent of immigration,* tutor and *rehabilitator* of *socially disadvantaged youth*, etc.'[5]

The verbiage of the official propaganda deserves to be quoted extensively, not only to contrast the myth which it propagates about women in Israel with their actual situation, but also to expose the underlying Zionist ideology and overt political priorities.

The recent change of leadership implies no qualitative change in the Zionist character of Israel. The new government's first year in office was marked by an intensification of the old policies of territorial expansion, perpetuating the traditional Zionist conflict with the Arab world and the indigenous Palestinians. The added *Lebensraum* reinforces Israel's dependence on the immigration of new settlers.

There has clearly been an increase in the degree of fanatic militancy with which the same Zionist aims are pursued. But more important is the further crystallization of the innate structural and ideological relationship between Zionism and the Jewish religion. The role of religion in Israel is, on the one hand, to confirm and reinforce the hegemony of the Zionist state over all the Jews in the world, and on the other to legitimize the Zionist claim on 'the Land of Israel',

5. '*Chen*'—*The Women's Corps,* IDF spokesman, Israel Defence Forces, 30 May 1977 (emphasis added).

that is, Palestine, as the homeland of the Jews and their exclusive estate. Under the patronage of the coalition of the Likud and the National Religious Party, the aims of Zionism are given not merely a religious endorsement but also the fresh impetus of literal biblical justification.

It is only against this background that a coherent exposition and analysis of women's lot in Israel is possible.

Women's Role in the Early Colonization Period

The distinguishing features of Israel as a Zionist state are reflected in the distinctive situation of Israeli women compared to that of women elsewhere in the capitalist world.

It is true that the issue of the role of women in the Zionist enterprise was and still is a prominent one. The pressure to bolster the position of women started in the early years of this century with women settlers for whom 'the commandment of settling the land was sacred'.[6] Throughout the history of Jewish settlement in Palestine, the Zionist movement has undertaken tasks for which it was undermanned; the 'conquest of labour' and the 'conquest of the land' (euphemisms in Hebrew for agricultural colonization and the eviction and displacement of Arab peasants and workers in order to provide jobs for Jewish workers) required the active participation and backing of women. Indeed, these were the first 'lucky breaks' for those women settlers whose Zionist ideology was tinged with feminist notions: some did *men's* jobs. The rest were duly dispatched to the communal kitchen or laundry. However, both received their proper plaudits as each in turn fulfilled her designated role: to release more men for frontier duty.

The frontiers of Israel can hardly be described as fixed, either physically or metaphorically. Within their ever-expanding domain, Zionist objectives may vary and the words used to describe them may change, but the role of women remains the same: to man the rear.

From the beginning, in order to create a socio-economic base from which Zionism could expand, a rapid increase of the Jewish population was required. The Jewish communities abroad furnished the

6. 'The Working Woman in Israel'.

enterprise with both economic and human resources, which in turn enabled Zionism to expand territorially, absorb more immigrants, and command further financial support. This process inevitably escalated the economic conflict with the indigenous population into a political-military one, which in turn has required further resources from abroad and has thus tied Zionism irrevocably to the production and reproduction potential of the Jewish world outside. The embryonic Jewish society in Palestine has suspended, it appears, the tasks of generational reproduction and rearing, and relegated them to the diaspora, the rear.

Palestine was the frontier outpost; this defined the demographic characteristics of the early waves of Jewish immigration — *'aliyot* — especially the second wave (1904 – 14) and the third (1919 – 23). Scarcity of women — not an unusual feature of a colonial process — was but one aspect of it. Most of the immigrants were young and single, or childless couples; the proportion of children under 14 was exceptionally low. In other words, there was a very low ratio of dependants to economically active adults. In effect, the Zionist settler population in Palestine was almost entirely a combatant labour force. These characteristics were even more accentuated in the kibbutzim and work brigades (*plugot 'avodah*) which were, so to speak, the spearhead of the Zionist effort to establish exclusively Jewish agricultural structures. There, men outnumbered women by four or five to one.

Such disparities in the sex ratio might have created a favourable attitude towards women, maybe even a feminist bias. But in Palestine this was not the case. In her book *Fifty Years of the Working Women's Movement* Ada Maimon cites many instances of discrimination and of ridicule of women, especially those for whom 'The New Socialism', 'Proletarianization', and 'Productive Jewish Labour' were values inextricably connected with equality between the sexes.

Sexist attitudes prevalent among the settlers in the collectives were reinforced by the Zionist form of colonization. Kibbutzim and other collectives, where the majority of members were men, refused persistently to accept more than a limited number of women — just enough to maintain the necessary services. In some collectives women were not full members but only hired help. The women in Degania — in the early years before this collective became a kibbutz—were not considered members with equal rights. They were not registered in the annual contract which the collective made with the Palestine Office of the Zionist movement, as the male members were, and did not receive the monthly salary the Office paid to the men both in Degania and in neighbouring Kineret. When the women demanded to be included in the contract, the retort was that 'women work for the men, not for the Palestine Office of the Zionist movement'.[7]

A brief 'History of Working Women in Israel' published by the Women Workers' Council provides a partial picture and numerous rationalizations of the state of affairs. 'These were women of strong character and marvellous emotional powers, and they knew how to translate faith and enthusiasm into deeds. This is the sole explanation of their ability to go out daily and do "a man's job" when they were really delicate damsels only recently separated from their parents' loving care and from their university desks. Their hope was that the formation of the pioneers into specific settlement units, in an independent but co-operative frame-work . . . would also solve the problems of the working woman . . . it soon became apparent that even in the new life context which she had helped form the woman was put into her traditional place. Most of the women worked in the kitchen, in the laundry and in the children's quarters.

'The situation of the women who arrived with the third wave of immigration (after the First World War) was much the same. These belonged to the "labour brigades" and the co-operative groups engaged in public works—road-building and construction. They fought for their right to break up gravel, to hew stones, to work on scaffolding and to *take part in literally building the country. However, since there wasn't enough work to go round, it was first given to the males in the group.*

'Many reasons for this were offered: these jobs were not for a woman; her productivity was doubtful, since soon she would give birth and would be out of the work circle; the *woman's wage was lower than the man's*, so that her contribution to the commune was smaller; and to begin with, why should she work on construction when she could earn money doing other, more *feminine*, things. . . .

7. A. Maimon, *Fifty Years of the Working Woman's Movement*, Ayanot Publication of Am Oved.

Some of the agriculture groups decided to open laundries or restaurants in the cities, as a means of providing their women with employment; they would also serve the group members working in the cities. In other groups, the women went out to do paid housework, so as to be able to add their share to the common till.'[8] (Our italics.)

The missing pieces in this picture puzzle are those depicting the indigenous population; unlike other immigrant-settler forms of colonization, Zionism sought not to exploit the local inhabitants but to displace them. Thus Jewish settlers found themselves in direct economic competition with the Arab labouring classes in the productive sector. In the mode of production that existed in Palestine in the 1920s and 1930s, the Arab wage labourer was often a seasonal migrant or part-time worker, who earned wages only to supplement his family produce and who could rely in return on the supportive service and maintenance functions that the extended family provided.

Compared to these Arab workers, Jewish members of collectives, co-operatives, work brigades, or kibbutzim were at a considerable disadvantage; not only were they novices who lacked any experience in manual labour, but in addition they had no comparable servicing and maintenance support, and were completely dependent on the higher-cost market economy for consumption.

It is in this economic context that the collectivized forms of Jewish settlements evolved and that the division of labour within them, as well as the socialization of domestic labour, can be explained. The status of individuals within the group was directly correlated with their earning ability; their earning ability was measured against the productivity of the Arab male wage labourer.[9] The arbiters were employers such as the mandatory authorities in public works and the Jewish farmers (early settlers and land owners) in agricultural work who had little or no stake either in the successes of the Zionist enterprise or in the achievement of the equality of women. The collective fear that 'women's work will cause a deficit', induced by the Palestine Office of the Zionist movement, which provided financial support, and shared by women members of the collectives, was

8. 'The Working Woman in Israel'.
9. This point is discussed from a different perspective in the article by A. Ehrlich mentioned in note 1 above.

reinforced by the plain fact that at the time women's wages in the labour market were lower than men's. In consequence, the sexual division of labour found its use in the economic battle against the local population. The combatant forces at the front were the all-male Jewish collectives, contending with the Arab wage labourers. The women formed auxiliary forces in the rear to meet the challenge of the Arab extended family.

Surrogate Emancipation

The token few who crossed the sexual divide did so obsessed with the need to live down their femininity, or as Golda Meir put it, 'rights they had in abundance; [they struggled] for equality in duties ... road construction, hoeing in the fields, house building or guard duties ... and not to be condemned to kitchen work. ... I for one continued to be more concerned with the quality of our food than with women's liberation'.[10]

In 1921, a year after the establishment of the Histadrut (Zionist trade-union federation), the first conference of working women resolved—not surprisingly—that: 'the *Women Workers' Council* is mandatory in order to arouse the members to action, and to stimulate and move the various factors to *find work for the working woman....* We have come to the Land of Israel to work, to devote all our energy and dedication to labour, and this pioneering work is *not to be measured by the worker's output*; everything according to capability, and we are to have equal rights in life and at work.'[11] (Our italics.)

Equal rights in life and at work they have not achieved to this day, but the Women Workers' Council (*Mo'etzet Hapo'alot*) took the lead, with other women's organizations following suit, and became on the one hand a centre of surrogate emancipation and on the other one of the principal agents of Zionism in the development of an alternative to the real emancipation of Jewish women.

The scope, structure, activities, and power of those women's organizations are outside the scope of this article. It will suffice to

10. Golda Meir, *My Life*, Ma'ariv Publications, 1975 (in Hebrew).
11. 'The Working Woman in Israel'.

say that they offered a wide enough framework within Zionism to a large number of suitably-disposed women to train, improve, help, advise, absorb, educate, propagandize, and plan for other women, thus not eliminating women from public life but rather confining them to what is broadly known as 'women's affairs'. In the early stages of Zionism such activities meant channelling and controlling the growing number of disillusioned or unemployed women into 'teaching farms' and other training courses and sharing the burden of *qlita* (absorption) of single female immigrants.[12]

Then as now, their ideological role was to reconcile the inherent conflict between Zionism and the accomplishment of women's emancipation. By addressing themselves to the very reasons for women's discontent and glorifying their sacrifices as contributions to national unity and other Zionist expediencies, these organizations and their women leaders have succeeded time and again in taming the militancy of their members. The same Zionist expediencies provided Israeli women and their organizations with new challenges which could be misconstrued as real feminist opportunities.

The Challenge of Military Needs

If women were deprived of their 'rightful' share in the 'conquest of labour' and 'the conquest of the land', the escalation of the conflict with the Palestinian population and the neighbouring Arab countries into war appeared to spell a 'real chance' for aspiring feminist-Zionist women—for once, they were needed.

The early Jewish settler women, it was alleged, had to masquerade as Arab women, veil and all, whenever they walked in the streets, so great was their fear of the Arab population. Not until 1907, when a defence organization 'Bar Giora' was founded by Y. Ben Tzvi (later the second Israeli president), did Jewish women unveil and walk about 'with a whip or a stick in hand'. Regional 'defence' organs like 'Bar Giora' sprang up across the country as Arab opposition to

---

12. On these farms, unemployed women were engaged in growing vegetables. The produce was sold mainly to the British army. On no account, even at the price of failure of the enterprise, was the produce sold to Arab town merchants. (*Isha Va'em Beyisrael*, Women and Mother in Israel, Masada Publications (in Hebrew), p. 353.)

Zionism grew. These organs later fused into what was known as the Haganah (=defence), the embryonic IDF. The skills of Jewish women in disguising themselves came in handy when the Haganah sent Oriental, Arabic-speaking Jewish women, dressed in Arab garb, into Arab neighbourhoods to obtain information, while 'elegant ladies transported arms in their cars'. Apart from such daring pursuits, women were allotted essentially auxiliary tasks: quartermasters, nurses, drivers, signallers, messengers, and guards.

By 1942, when the women in the Haganah numbered ten thousand, the men fifty thousand, a special department for women was set up and a principle enacted that women should 'be part of the defence force, also in the [military] posts, so that a considerable number of men in defence duties could be released for field forces and Palmah' (Hebrew acronym for *plugot mahatz* = shock troops).[13]

Here too, as on the economic battleground, *some* women did cross the sexual divide, but this was the exception, not the rule. The exception was blown out of all proportion in a myth prevalent both inside Israel and outside. The rule, not the exception, was reinforced in 1943, when Jewish volunteers formed the 'Jewish Brigade' in the British army; Jewish women were urged to volunteer for the ATS. Four thousand did just that and slotted neatly into the British army structure and its idea of a women's corps, in addition to which 'they excelled . . . especially in their concern for the Jewish soldier, cut off from his family . . . among strangers. They organized clubs for cultural activities and instilled the atmosphere of the land of Israel in the camps; they celebrated Jewish festivals, produced a Hebrew leaflet, and made pleasant the life of the Jewish soldier.'[14]

During the early stages of colonization, Zionism almost failed in the efficient utilization of Jewish women's enthusiasm and willingness to take part in the enterprise. The long period of enforced unemployment to which Jewish women had been subjected reached its peak, at the height of the economic crisis of 1940 − 41, with the Histadrut directive that no Jewish family should have more than one breadwinner (the head of the family). As the war progressed, this trend came to an end. *Mo'etzet Hapo'alot* was beside itself to find women who would work in the labour camps set up to provide for

13. See *Isha Va'em Beyisrael.*
14. Ibid. From a report by Hana Levine, a Jewish woman officer.

the war effort. One thousand eight hundred worked in those camps; 'they worked for the war effort and infiltrated new occupations'.[15]

At the end of the war, the participation of women rose. Jewish women were sent from Palestine to Europe as *shlihot* (emissaries). How many were sent is obscure, but their tasks were clear; nurses, social workers, nannies, domestic science instructors, and teachers were sent to refugee camps in Sweden and Italy and in the American, British, and French zones in Germany. They 'opened Hebrew schools in the camps...organized public life...administered health education and youth training, and bore the responsibility for running the camps', but most importantly they were entrusted with carrying out tasks that required a real commitment to Zionism: 'the selection of candidates for *ha'apalah'* (= upwards struggle, a Hebrew euphemism for illegal Jewish immigration to Palestine). They trained, equipped, and transported those candidates to ports where others took over.[16] The processing and absorption of displaced Jewish immigrants occupied women before and during the so-called war of independence.

The British mandate's policy of restricting the admission of Jews into Palestine, in order to appease the growing opposition of the indigenous and neighbouring Arabs, triggered bitter anti-British violence. Despite its illegality, Jewish immigration assumed the scale of a powerful national movement. The British intercepted thousands of displaced Jews en route to Palestine and sent them to camps in Cyprus, where again the internal operation was organized by *shlihot* who, as in the European camps, prepared the immigrants for the tasks awaiting them in Palestine.[17]

The Dual Role of Women in Israel

After the establishment of the state of Israel, Jewish immigration was finally under Zionist control, a control that asserted itself through one of the first laws to be enacted in Israel, the Law of Return. This provided the legal basis for the demographic objectives of the Zionist leadership: to achieve a high Jewish population growth

15. *Isha Va'em Beyisrael.*
16. Ibid.
17. Ibid.

in Israel through mass immigration of Jews, and so enable them to 'survive' in the heart of the Arab world, whose population numbered well over 70 million, and to contain a 14 per cent Arab minority having a high rate of natural increase. Hundreds of thousands of Jews arrived between 1948 and 1951, during which time Israel's population more than doubled.

It was then that the principal duality of Israeli women's role was crystallized and found its expression. It mirrored the duality in the attitude of the Zionist leadership towards demographic issues, epitomized in the official euphemistic terminology *'aliyah pnimit* or *'aliyah hitzonit* (internal or external ascent[18]) used in the ongoing debate about the respective roles of natural growth and immigration in securing Zionist demographic aims.

The military service law, which was passed in 1949, exempted from conscription married women, pregnant women, and mothers (as well as women who for conscientious or religious reasons did not wish to be conscripted), thus in effect categorizing Israeli women into mothers who carry out their 'demographic duty to the nation'— *'aliyah pnimit*—and surrogate mothers who carry out their duty to the nation by mothering Jewish immigration— *'alihay hitzonit*. In the self-image of the IDF as a 'melting pot', women soldiers are the stirring spoon. Men soldiers from 'backward countries' (Oriental Jews) receive a fairly comprehensive training programme in the army, where they acquire a knowledge of Hebrew and basic education and skills. The trainers are almost exclusively women, while women who do not possess these skills, possibly arriving from similar 'backward countries', are not even recruited, for reasons of 'low quality'. Throughout the fifties, women soldiers often 'volunteered' to work in transit camps for immigrants, 'pitching tents, digging drainage ditches, . . . [providing] medical care, general instruction, [and] education of children—humane activities that carry a blessing for the State as a whole.'[19] The accent on the absorption of immigrants shifted as the waves of emigration ebbed;

18. The Hebrew words *hagirah* ('migration') and *mehagrim* ('migrants') are used by Zionists to describe all migratory movements of non-Jews, as well as those of Jews who go to and from places other than Palestine. The words *'aliyah* and *ha'apalah* ('ascent' and 'upward struggle') are used to describe Jewish immigration to Palestine. Conversely, the Hebrew word *yeridah*, used by Zionists to describe the emigration of Jews *from* Palestine, means descent.

19. *Isha Va'em Beyisrael.*

this did not change the essence of women's role in the army, but merely redirected it.

Surrogate motherhood, of course, is not confined to immigrants but is the underlying theme of a woman's life in the army irrespective of her occupation, be it regimental quartermaster or radar operator, and is a consequence of the manifest need for 'normalization' that is evident in the wake of every war, the more so in Israel where war and the eventuality of war recur periodically.

Yet the army is no mere melting pot, and its main function is still to further Israel's territorial expansion by military means. Women are not left out, and as well as staffing the traditional rear—clerical, administrative, and light technical occupations—some are required to do even more.

In September 1977, '. . . on one historic evening . . . the Israeli navy commissioned nine girls as seawomen, the first in the navy, the first perhaps in any navy in the world. . . . The original idea', said the (male) commander of the training base, 'was to train girls for these duties in order to release boys for sea duties, all this in the framework of the general utilization of manpower.' He went on: 'Dear (female) officers, the work is not behind you but in front of you. . . . You are not designated for warfare duties, but the duty you will carry out from tomorrow was carried out until yesterday by a (male) commander.'[20] Other women in yet another first course 'were qualified as tank drivers, gunners, and tank commanders'.[21]

This in no way implies that sexual divisions in the army have finally disappeared, but rather that the rearrangement of the map of Israel has taxed the already stretched manpower at the front to the extent that a reappraisal of what constitutes the rear is urgently required. Neither seawomen nor women tank commanders will see combat. The female sailors will patrol the home shores, as no doubt they did during the recent invasion, while the navy was bombarding targets in Lebanon from the sea. Similarly, the female tank unit will be engaged only as instructors, 'thus releasing [male] soldiers for combat duties'.

In the same vein, but in other words, an interim report presented by the 'Committee for Woman's Status in Israel', headed by Knesset

20. *Yedi'ot Aharonot*, 15 September 1977.
21. *Ibid*., 18 May 1978.

Member Orah Namir, states that 'conscription and regular [army] services do not exhaust the possible contribution of women, especially not in technological areas. Women are capable of carrying out more duties and thus alleviating the [current] manpower shortage.'

Internal and External Growth: Reproduction and Immigration

That women both work and produce children is regarded as necessary to the survival of the Jewish state; and for those who might have lost sight of the future shortage of cannon fodder, the Koenig report provides a reminder. This secret memorandum, 'Handling the Arabs of Israel', submitted to Prime Minister Rabin in 1976, was leaked in the newspaper *'Al-Hamishmar* on 7 September 1976. Its author, Israel Koenig, northern district commissioner for the Ministry of the Interior, and as such in charge of Arab affairs in Galilee, points out that 'the rate of natural growth of the Arab population is 5.9 per cent per annum, in comparison with 1.5 per cent for the Jewish population. . . . On this basis, by 1978 the Arabs will constitute over 51 per cent of the population in the [northern] district. . . . The growth in Galilee is dangerous to our very control over the district.' The report purports to evaluate, and suggests ways to counteract, the so-called threat implied in such a ratio. One telling proposal is that 'the government should find a way to neutralize the granting of allowances to Arab families with many children, which could be done either by linking it to economic status or by taking [the administration of] these allowances away from the national insurance and transferring them to the Jewish Agency . . . for Jews only'.

The double bind is that while in Zionist theory the *raison d'être* of the state of Israel is asserted to be the provision of a haven for all the Jews of the world, in Zionist practice the *raison d'être* of Jews is to maintain the state of Israel. In other words, the very existence of the Zionist state supersedes the supposed values of its ideology, chiefly the well-being of Jews.

As early as 1943, at a Mapai (Labour) Party conference on the 'labour force', Ben-Gurion expressed his concern that the Jewish population in Palestine was in a state of demographic and moral decline. He suggested that the majority of Jews in Palestine did not fulfil their reproductive commitments to the nation, that the average of 2.2 per family was not enough, especially when there is no immigration (there was very little immigration at the time) and if this went on, the Jewish community would extinguish itself.[22] In the school of 'Jewish demographic decay', Ben-Gurion was but one pupil. Attention was called to the question by Roberto Bachi, a professor of statistics, who, in a series of articles published between 1939 and 1944, pointed out the threatening implications of the difference between Arab and Jewish rates of natural increase, and called for the formulation of a population policy to curb the fertility decline among Jews in Palestine that would be in keeping with the political objectives of the Jewish community. His was the 'liberal' suggestion that families should have, ideally, three, four, or even more children and that financial inducements should be offered in the form of family allowances and easy credit facilities for big families.[23]

The overtly reactionary voice in this school was that of the late Abraham Adolf Fraenkel, a professor of mathematics at the Hebrew University who, in a number of articles published between 1942 and 1944, translated the mathematics of the indefinite continuation of differential demographic patterns between Jews and Arabs into Hebrew journalistic terrorism. That Jewish families should be urged to have children was not enough; definite policies to achieve this objective should be implemented. 'Total war' should be waged against gynaecologists who performed abortions. Abortion, according to Fraenkel, was not only immoral, a terrible crime tantamount to murder, but also a major reason for the low Jewish birth-rate. To substantiate his assertion that controlling the number of abortions would effectively increase the dwindling birth-rate he argued, 'Among the many means by which Hitler attempted in 1933 to increase the German birth-rate the one effective measure was the war against abortions.' In this vein he proposed that persons involved in the illegal act of induced abortion be liable to severe punitive measures.[24]

22. See D. Friedlander, 'Israel', in B. Berelson, ed., *Population Policy in Developed Countries*, New York 1974. See also D. Ben-Gurion, 'Three Issues', *Hapo'el Hatza'ir* (in Hebrew), vol. 27, quoted by Friedlander.
23. R. Balachi, 'The Decline in Fertility: a National Danger', *Ha'aretz* (in Hebrew), 5 August 1940, quoted by Friedlander.
24. A.A. Fraenkel, *Fertility in the Jewish Community in Palestine*, Aharonson Publications, 1944 (in Hebrew), quoted in Friedlander.

The same reasons underlying those discussions of the early 1940s also underlie the recent concern over population growth in Israel. After the establishment of the state, developments in population policy were generally shaped according to the relatively liberal view, but it was the nationalist-religious camp that kept the issue alive and brought pressure to bear at all levels, especially and most effectively in the administrative machine, where the religious parties had considerable power (as partners in most government coalitions). They fought systematically against the establishment of public family planning services, and campaigned against existing abortion regulations and against women's service in the armed forces.

A 'natality committee', headed by Bachi, was appointed on 1 April 1962 by the then Prime Minister Ben-Gurion. The committee was to undertake research and advise the government on matters concerning natality policies and consider means by which large families could be assisted. Of all the recommendations that the committee submitted in April 1966, only one was implemented: the establishment of the 'Demographic Centre' in 1968 to act as an administrative unit in the Prime Minister's Office. The aim of the centre is 'to act systematically in carrying out a natality policy intended to create a psychologically favourable climate, such that natality will be encouraged and stimulated, an increase in natality in Israel being crucial for the whole future of the Jewish people.'[25]

According to Zina Harman, its first director, the centre is now undergoing 'a period of reappraisal and reorganization of its aims'.[26] This is hardly surprising; until now the activities of the centre have not gone beyond 'research, publicity, and experimentation'. 'Research' means inquiry into Israeli attitudes towards having a third and fourth child. 'Publicity' means promoting the image of large families through the media; and 'experimentation' is merely a small-scale programme whereby couples intending to have another child may, under certain conditions, apply for a low-interest loan for the purpose of acquiring a larger apartment.[27]

What transpires is that Israel cannot afford the investment in a 'demographic revival of the nation' which, according to calculations

25. Friedlander.
26. L. Hazleton, *Israeli Women, the Reality Behind the Myth*, Idanim Publications, 1978 (in Hebrew).
27. Friedlander.

made for the natality committee, would cost about 12 per cent of the gross national product (1969 figures). What remains are the cheap solutions: to continue the orchestrated ideological onslaught on small families; to publicize the large ones; to hope for a renewed flow of immigration; and perhaps to declare 'total war' on abortions.[28]

'Fetal Wastage'

The relative 'ideological pluralism' that was tolerated in the first thirty years of the state brought about a situation where family planning services were absent in an otherwise extensive public health service, and expertly performed abortion could be obtained for a fee that was easily within the means of the well-to-do. Thus despite severe legal penalties, abortion became a common method of family planning—more so after 1952, when the Attorney General recommended that a blind eye should be turned to abortions, and abortionists not prosecuted, provided that the abortion was expertly performed. This practice went on with only one exception.[29] In 1963 the Attorney General's 'recommendations were cancelled as a result of their dubious legality but in practice the same principles apply'.[30]

In 1972, unofficial 'committees for pregnancy termination' were set up in some Qupat Holim hospitals. Their function was to consider cases in which abortion was demanded by a patient. These committees and the criteria they followed in deciding for or against abortion were not endorsed by law.[31]

The voice of the Zionist demographic warriors was subdued, but not silenced. Thus in 1974 Professor Y. Helbrecht of Hasharon Hospital wrote, expressing a 'professional' opinion, that 'the future of the state of Israel depends on the number of its Jewish inhabitants

28. Ibid.
29. The exception was the indictment of two doctors in 1971. Their offence, however, was not having performed an abortion, but having made use of the facilities of Qupat Holim (the Histadrut health service). The double standard came under fire. The establishment reacted in the only way it could: by doing nothing. The case remained open for nine months. One of the accused died, and the case against the other was dropped.
30. Report submitted to the minister of health by the committee appointed to examine the restrictions on inducing abortions, in *Public Health*, vol. 17, no. 4, November 1974, published by the Ministry of Health, Jerusalem.
31. Ibid.

and on their quality. . . . Immigration and natural growth are the basis of our existence in this country and should supplement one another. . . . Even if we succeed in gathering in the remnants of our diasporas, we shall remain few in number in the great sea of the neighbours surrounding us, and it is therefore imperative that we direct all our attention to the maximal reduction of what is called "fetal wastage".[32]

This state of affairs, riddled with contradictions, continued until February 1977, when the Knesset passed the Abortion Law amendment, which permits abortion on the following grounds:

'1. That continuation of pregnancy constitutes danger to the woman's life.

'2. That a danger exists that the continuation of the pregnancy will cause physical or mental damage.

'3. That a danger exists that the child will be a physical or mental cripple.

'4. That the pregnancy is the result of rape or incest.

'5. That the woman is under marriageable age or over 45.

'6. That severe damage might be caused to the woman or her children as a result of difficult social conditions of the woman's environment, for example that a great number of children reside with her.'[33]

This amendment—a temporary victory for the pro-abortion lobby—was due to come into effect in February 1978, but four months after it was passed, the right-wing Likud-NRP coalition came to power. One of the main points in the coalition pact was a pledge to repeal the amendment. At a press conference held in February 1978, it was announced that the coalition was preparing a counter-amendment that would allow abortion only on grounds permitted by Jewish religious law; social and economic grounds will not be taken into consideration.[34] This might appear as merely another exaction of a price by a religious party for its participation in a coalition, again at the expense of women; but in fact it is a tightening up of Zionist demographic policy.

---

32. Ibid.
33. *Ha'aretz*, 29 February 1978.
34. *Ibid.*

Convergence of Zionism and Religion

In Israel the religious parties get only 12.5 per cent of the vote, and only 22 per cent of all Israelis regard themselves as religious.[35] Moreover, it is often officially declared that 'Israel is a state of [temporal] law, not of religious law'. In fact, the body of laws in Israel is derived from as diverse and non-religious origins as British statute and common law and relics of Ottoman legislation; there is also a considerable volume of laws that have been passed since the state was established.

But these are not the only binding laws. 'Like the British regime that preceded it [the state of Israel] has maintained . . . the rule of the autonomy of religious communities in all [matters] concerning family law, and although laws passed by the Knesset have reduced the application of this rule, it is still firm and established in matters of marriage and divorce.'[36] 'In these matters the biblical law applies to Jews and their own religious laws apply to Muslims and to Chrisians',[37] and to this day, according to the law of Israel, everyone is born into some religious community and is subject in issues of personal status to the religious establishment of his or her community and to its traditional laws. On identity cards there is no mention of citizenship, only of religious-ethnic grouping.

In other words, 'The legislature conceded almost complete non-interference in the existing state of affairs. . . . In these matters [marriage, divorce, and most aspects of marital relations], not only is the rule which is applied not a law passed by the Knesset, but the civil courts have no jurisdiction . . . disputing parties have to address their pleas to the rabbinical courts.'[38] One of the published 'basic principles' of the last (Rabin) government asserts that 'the Government will safeguard the *status quo* in the State as regards religious matters.'[39]

The fact is that many aspects of the lives of *all* citizens are governed by religious dogma. The nationalist quest for identity

---

35. Ministry of Religious Affairs survey, published in *Yedi'ot Aharonot*, 8 July 1975.
36. *Israeli Government Yearbook*, 1976 (in Hebrew).
37. Ibid.
38. Ibid.
39. Ibid.

coerces the non-religious population into submission and explains the recurring tactical coalitions between ruling parties and religious parties.

In 1970 the Knesset passed an amendment to the Law of Return that turned this collusion into a permanent covenant. The amendment concluded another chapter in the debate about 'Who is a Jew?'. The answer was couched in terms of religious dogma: a Jew is either a person whose *mother* is Jewish, or a convert to Judaism. This had come about, despite the secular origin of the Zionist movement, when it became clear that any attempt to define 'Jewishness' for all Jews, wherever they were, in different places and diverse cultures, without resorting to religion, or any attempt to found a secular state, would necessarily have caused a rift between the movement and a considerable number of Jewish communities, thus weakening Zionism and reducing its appeal. For this reason, the new Jewish state had to define 'Who is a Jew?' within religious constraints and guarantee Jewish religious culture, legislation, and traditional values in all matters in which these are not in direct conflict with Zionist aims, and especially where they reinforce them.

Conversely, the religious sector, and more specifically the NRP, see the state as an instrument best suited to impose biblical law on the Jewish nation. Their intentions were clearly formulated by Chief Rabbi Goren, who in the anthology *Religion and the State* (NRP publication, 1964) wrote: 'When it comes to determining the quality of life for the whole nation, we are bound by the Torah [= religious law] and the teaching of the prophets [to use] state compulsion.... We are bound therefore by [religious] dogma and common sense to use the machinery of the state in order to maintain the laws and values of the Torah.'[40]

Women in Israel carry the brunt of the pact between religion and Zionism. This may be inferred from the substantial body of law, mainly but not exclusively concerning family, marriage, and divorce, which discriminates explicitly against them. According to Jewish religious law, women have an inferior status. Thus, for example, women are not even allowed as witnesses in rabbinical courts, which have jurisdiction on all matters of personal law.

40. Rabbi Goren, *Religion and the State*, a publication (in Hebrew) of the National Religious Party, 1964, quoted in S. Aloni, *Nashim Kivnei Adam* (Women as Humans), Mabat Publications, 1976, pp. 9 and 47.

Yet Israeli women are not merely pawns in a callous political game. Nor does Israel's order of priorities, in which women come far down, result from paternalistic oversight or neglect. It is, on the contrary, a reflection of the convergence of religious and Zionist aims.

The principle that 'a woman is her husband's property', coupled with the imperative to 'be fruitful and multiply', expresses the Jewish religious attitude towards women as instruments for ensuring generational reproduction of the husband individually and of the race collectively. That 'a woman is her husband's property' is stated in the binding law of the state of Israel.[41] That, and the promise of the then Prime Minister, Y. Rabin, to the Minister of Religious Affairs, Y. Raphael, in July 1975, that 'the [proposed] basic law concerning women's rights shall never be allowed to pass'[42] exemplify the two principal parameters determining the present mode of oppression of women.

The guiding Mishnaic principle of the law, which dates from the end of the second century, states that a woman becomes her husband's property in marriage—in one of three ways: by a payment, by contract, or by coition. From then on she is forbidden to all except her husband and cannot sever the tie until he dies or divorces her. Although she may ask for it, she can only be the passive recipient of the divorce (the term in Hebrew is 'banishment'). The principle that a woman is her husband's property does not extend merely to the husband. If a man dies leaving his wife childless, she cannot remarry until her husband's brother has had an opportunity to claim her.

The consequences range from the tragic to the obscene. Although in modern Israel it is seldom carried to its logical conclusion, in 1967 a case occurred in which both the brother and the widow were deaf mutes. The ancient ceremony called *halitza*, whereby the brother and the widow exchange prescribed phrases and a spit for a shoe, which releases the brother from the obligation, could not therefore be carried out, and the couple were required instead to perform *yibum* (levirate marriage). But the brother was already married, so in order to avoid intercourse that was mere fornication, the Rabbinical Court, armed with permission from both the chief rabbis as protection

41. S. Aloni.
42. Ibid.

against bigamy, sanctified a marriage for a night. A hotel room was hired by the court, intercourse took place in front of male witnesses, and divorce was granted the following morning, leaving the woman free to marry whom she pleased.[43]

The religious concern with the reproduction of the race will even allow polygamy in 'modern' Israel: if the marriage fails to produce children, if the wife is committed to an institution for the insane, or if she is declared 'rebellious', which means that she leaves her husband against his express wish.[44] The same concern marks the persistent opposition of the religious sector, headed by the National Religious Party, to women's conscription into the army. As early as 1959 the NRP protested that conscription was a major reason for the decline of the Jewish birth-rate.[45] The protest paid off; one of the points in the coalition agreement between the ruling Likud and the NRP is the relaxation of the procedures according to which women are exempted from army service. The exemption of women on religious grounds is currently automatic.[46]

Preservation of ethnic purity is just as important to the religious sector as it is in keeping with Zionist aims. In Israel various kinds of marriage are prohibited. In the first place, marriage of a Jew to a non-Jew is not possible. (If a mixed marriage takes place abroad, it is not valid according to the binding religious law.) Within the Jewish community, there are a number of complicated prohibitions. The offspring of certain categories of prohibited unions are condemned to be labelled as bastards, down to the tenth generation. This label in turn carries with it its own marital restrictions. The penalty of bastardy is one to which the majority of the conformist population is vulnerable.

A vast network of self-appointed informers ensures that the rabbinical authorities have up-to-date lists of culprits and potential culprits. These lists, known as 'the blacklists', are computerized and distributed by the Ministry for Religious Affairs. In 1975, through a press leak, the existence of 144 such lists became public knowledge. They include names of bastards, suspected bastards, divorcees and their lovers, suspect converts, and persons whose Jewishness is

43. Ibid.
44. Hazleton, *Israeli Women.*
45. Friedlander.
46. *Ha'aretz*, 18 June 1978.

'doubtful'—all are *psulei-hitun* (unfit for marriage).[47]

The instances in which the religious minority has succeeded in affecting the situation of women in Israel adversely are too many to enumerate; to the detriment of women and the alarm of secular Zionists, this influence is growing, especially since the inception of Gush Emunim, a vociferous nationalistic-religious movement whose supporters are to be found in most Zionist parties. For such people Israel is none but the 'Greater Israel' promised by the Scripture. For them, religion is an endorsement of racist and nationalist demagogy, and women are tools for the preservation of ethnic purity.

Against this background, the non-religious majority tries in private life to regard the religious aspects of the law as an extension of the bureaucracy, everyone hoping that his or her own case is routine, not one of the horror-story exceptions. In recent years, immigration of Russian Jews of 'suspicious' marital circumstances and the increasing number of war widows have made the exceptions increasingly common, and one can observe growing discontent among the non-religious sections of the population, expressed by various movements and platforms calling for liberalization of the law.

The Zionist Feminists

Recent years have seen the budding of an Israeli feminist movement. Realizing the gap between the myth of their supposed liberation and the reality of their imprisonment, Israeli feminists have set out to challenge the status quo.

Emigrées from English-speaking countries have provided the impetus to the Israeli women's movement, as well as the model on which it operates. The movement concentrates its activities in large cities, where consciousness-raising groups operate in Hebrew *and in English*—a telling fact about the class nature and national composition of these groups.

The 1973 war, too, provided Israeli feminism with a considerable boost, judging by repeated references to it as the occasion when Israeli women realized that they had been cheated, so to speak, of their fair share in the national burden. Shulamit Aloni, campaigner

47. Hazleton, *Israeli Women.*

for human rights, champion of 'groups which are discriminated against', describes in her book *Women as Humans* how 'the shock came after the Yom Kippur war; only then did it become apparent how far Israeli society had regressed in all that concerns the inclusion of women in responsible roles in the economy, in the community, in national security, and in the alleviation of the burden in a time of national emergency. The consequences of this shock continued to be felt well into the elections to the eighth Knesset in December 1973.'[48]

This kind of feminist writing is essentially at odds not with the ethos of the regime but with the way it functions. It contends with the regime not over its policy of territorial expansion and military aggression, but over how best to carry out this policy with women's aid. This is not a new school but a variation of the old feminist-Zionist theme: the desire to 'share the duties required by the Zionist enterprise'.

When Bar-Lev, minister for commerce and industry, declared (19 November 1973) that 'more workers will be required in the economy; they will come from among the *'olim* (Jewish immigrants) and volunteers from abroad',[49] he incurred the wrath of the feminist movement and of one Pnina Kreindle in particular. She responded in the feminist movement's organ, *Nilahem* (Hebrew acronym for 'Women for a Renewed Society', which also means 'we shall fight'): 'Is this possible? How has the great work potential of women in Israel been forgotten?'[50]

In Ms Kreindle's opinion the answer is illustrated by the news (*Yom-Yom*, an economic magazine, 20 November 1973) that Cabinet Minister Sapir established an emergency economic committee composed of forty-eight men 'and not a single woman!' 'It is clear, therefore, that with such "balanced" composition the existence of women could easily have been forgotten.'[51]

Kreindle is no pessimist. True, she is furious that 'during the war and after it, "Africa" was a closed club for "men only". Women were kept in "cotton wool" and their wings were clipped'. And she doubts 'whether an appropriate justification exists for the brushing

48. S. Aloni, *Nashim Kivnei Adam.*
49. P. Kreindle, 'What Happened to Israeli Women in the War?', in *Nilahem* (in Hebrew), organ of the Feminist Movement in Israel, no. 4, September 1974.
50. Ibid.
51. Ibid.

aside of women in the army especially at a time of acute shortage of good manpower'.[52] Yet she thinks that 'something is "moving" in Israeli society' and cites the example of another feminist, Dr Dorit Padan-Eisenshtark (head of the Department of Behavioural Sciences in Ben-Gurion University), who leads a team planning a 'women's reserve service'. 'The team is charged with inserting women into "masculine" professional domains, so that during emergencies the economy can [go on] functioning in a normal fashion.' She and other feminists congratulate the Ministry of Labour on its intention to further implement its policy of encouraging women's work by 'training sixty thousand housewives . . . especially in technical jobs, so that in an emergency they can be integrated into the manpower structure, and re-activate the economy as a whole, not just the vital plants'.[53]

This brand of feminism lends its unqualified support and gives its uncritical consent to a regime whose own policies induce an accumulation of internal socio-economic and political strains, a regime that is in the process of losing control over the economy to an extent that could very well impede its future expansion and retard its war abilities. The sterner face that Zionism has acquired as a result of the May 1977 elections may, if nothing else, help the women's movement to shed this particular contingent of feminists.

Others in the movement, most prominently Knesset members Shulamit Aloni and Marcia Freedman, set out to charge at the religious flank of Zionism, proposing liberal laws and amendments that would make possible civil marriage, abortion, and 'equal rights for women', the latter by a new basic law. This light brigade sets out to wrench from the legislature a host of reforms in women's status at work, in welfare, tax, and other domains in which women come under the repressive thumb of the religious authorities.

Although they succeeded in inserting such women's issues as clauses in various party political programmes, they have been defeated time and again in the Knesset and its committees, where strategically situated National Religious Party politicians blocked every proposal, while other politicians clamoured for 'national unity'.

52. Ibid.
53. Ibid.

National unity, in this context, is no empty phrase, but an expression of the need, shared by both 'left' and 'right' wings of Zionism, for a cohesive ideological framework that will prop it up and provide it with the righteous posture required for the accomplishment of its policies. The Jewish religion is such a framework; its imperatives and prohibitions—especially but not exclusively in matters concerning women—are in keeping with 'demographic-national needs'. To 'be fruitful and multiply', as well as the penalties (bastardy) designed to prevent 'racial impurity', are in harmony with the Zionist exclusivist claim over Palestine.

Some feminists are misguided enough to think that a trade-off is possible, that Zionism will exchange 'liberal' laws for women's political consent and for their active economic support, at the price of giving up the benefits that collusion with the religious sector provides. The mainstream of the movement and its front runners in particular have no qualms about the aims of Zionism, only concern for the best ways of achieving those aims.

In the most thorough critique to date, Lesley Hazleton's *Israeli Women—the Reality Behind the Myth*, the author provides a comprehensive exposition of just what the title promises, but stops short of carrying it to its logical anti-Zionist conclusion. In the concluding chapter, 'The Political Challenge', she plays her very own Zionist card: she complains that Y. Yadin—deputy prime minister and leader of the new Democratic Movement—is reluctant to come out against the 'superficial symbolism of Judaism' when he could, in his capacity as archaeologist and leader of the Masada dig, . . . 'erect an alternative to religiousness in the form of a strong and concrete historical bond [that will link] the Jews to their political and cultural heritage in their own country'. In tune with the rest of the Zionist doves she coos: 'Security is a central problem. . . . it is involved with the existential security of the state in all its aspects: Security in its Jewishness, security in its existence and continued survival . . . '[54]

On similar lines, Israeli feminist Joan Yaron, addressing the International Tribunal on Crimes against Women in Brussels in March 1976, enumerated a list of Jewish women's grievances, describing their inferior position in the economy and their subordinate social status. 'The question could be asked', she said, 'how is it that

54. Hazleton, *Israeli Women*.

in a modern democratic state based on socialist [*sic*] principles, such anomalies could be possible?'[55] In the rest of her testimony, she proceeded to put the blame squarely on religious law, but even her thorough exposition of the malpractices that take place in Israel, with religious blessing, does not disguise the fact that Ms Yaron, like the rest of the feminist movement, is in the end no threat to Zionist Israel, and that she accepts the self-portrait of the state in the fashion of early 1976: 'modern, democratic, and socialist'.

55. Reproduced in *Toda'ah*, organ of the Feminist Movement, Jerusalem branch, June 1976 (in Hebrew).

Zionism, Demography and Women's Work[1]

Avishai Ehrlich

Some form of sexual division of labour exists in all known social formations. However, its particular forms and the degree of biological influence are socially determined. Each mode of production, indeed each society, has its own mode of sexual division of labour, which can be understood only through a study of that specific society. Of the many aspects of the sexual division of labour, two are pivotal. The roles of the sexes in *reproduction* and the socialization of the young; and their roles in the *production* process.

Although male domination exists across several modes of production, the meaning of contemporary struggles for women's equality is inseparably linked to changes in the sexual division of labour brought about by capitalism—particularly after the industrial revolution. Capitalism transformed the nature of work, taking production out of the private realm of the household and into the public realm of the factory. It separated the hitherto combined functions of production and consumption in the household. Production became production for the market, production of exchange-values. Labour power became a commodity which has its price in wages. Labour came to stand in a direct cash relation to capital. Concomitantly, capitalism created the separate category of domestic labour. Domestic labour power is not involved in the production of commodities, it has no price in wages and does not stand in a direct economic relation to capital. Its relation to capital is indirect, albeit indispensable, and mediated through personal relationships in the

---

1. This article is a result of work done with D. Hecht and N. Yuval-Davis, whose views were expressed in *Khamsin 6* ('Ideology Without Revolution': see the present volume). Although some of our ideas were developed together, I alone am responsible for the views expressed in this article.

family. Under capitalism domestic labour is predominantly concerned with the reproduction and socialization of the next generation and with the preparation of consumption, which is necessary for the regeneration of spent labour power.[2] This separation of labour into public and domestic, and the relegation of women to the domestic, is one of the revolutions brought about by capitalism; it did not exist in other modes. The main demands raised by women for equality are not ahistorical but specific to these changes created by capitalism: the struggle for the participation of women in all aspects of public labour; the struggle for equal remuneration for equal work; the struggle to control effectively their reproduction; the transfer of domestic labour from private to public agencies (education, family services); and the participation of both sexes in domestic labour. All these demands would make little sense before the emergence of capitalism. They stem from conditions brought about by capitalism and can be satisfied by new avenues opened by capitalism.

The position of women in Israel and the nature of the sexual division of labour there cannot be discussed in isolation from the Zionist characteristics of the society. The colonization process, its requirements, its constraints, its internal contradictions, and the political conflicts to which it gave birth are reflected in every aspect of life of Israeli society—including the position of women.

In the following pages an attempt is made to outline some of the links between immigration, a central feature of Zionist colonization, and the roles women are required to play in the areas of work and reproduction. I hope to show the particular forms that women's work takes, specific to Zionist society, and the particular considerations that determine the possibilities of development of women's situation in Israel. The article confines itself to Jewish women, although Arab women are no doubt influenced by the transformation of Palestine from an Arab society into a Zionist society and their position is but the other side of the same coin. Space does not permit it to be discussed here. Second, this article is not intended as

2. On this see, for example, R. Hamilton, *The Liberation of Women*; E. Zaretsky, *Capitalism, The Family and Personal Life*, 1976; W. Seccombe, 'The Housewife and Her Labour Under Capitalism', in *New Left Review*, 89, 1975; W. Seccombe, 'Domestic Labour: Reply to Critics', in *New Left Review*, 94, 1975; Himmelweit and Mohun, 'Domestic Labour and Capital', in *Cambridge Journal of Economics*, 1, 1977; P. Smith, 'Domestic Labour and Marx's Theory of Value', in A. Kuhn and A. Wolpe, eds, *Feminism and Materialism*, 1978.

a historical piece: that is why, although it starts with the early Zionist period, it soon turns to the present. I analyse two situations of immigration: when the rate of immigration is high and when it declines. The historical data are used to illuminate structural problems and not to write a chronology of events.

Early Immigration and its Character

It was not the productive capability the Jewish settlers created in Palestine that provided the economic means for the Zionist expansion, but the mobilization of funds from Jewish supporters abroad. In a similar manner, it was not the reproductive fertility of the Jewish population in Palestine that was the cause of the constant increase of the proportion of Jews during the mandate period, but the recruitment of immigrants from abroad. Zionism was uniquely dependent, as it still is, both on the production and reproduction of external Jewish communities and on its own ability to draw from these external sources.

Percentage of Jews in the total population of Palestine, 1922 – 1948

1922	*1925*	*1930*	*1935*	*1940*	*1945*	*1948*
12.9	16.1	17.9	26.9	31.2	31.7	34.5

(Source: D. Friedlander, in B. Berelson, *Population Policy in Developed Countries*, New York 1974, p. 47.)

Immigration as a percentage of the growth of the Jewish population of Palestine, 1919 – 1948

1919 – 23	*1924 – 31*	*1932 – 38*	*1939 – 45*	*1946 – 48*
81.9	68.7	82.1	59.2	64.5

(Source: J. Matras, *Social Change in Israel*, 1965, pp. 27 – 34.)

The patterns of Zionist colonization were pioneered by the immigrants of the second and third *'aliyot* (1904 – 14, 1919 – 23). The economic and political organizations they founded were the embryonic models for the future Zionist project in Palestine—the *yishuv*. It was also in that period that the new images of the pioneer man and woman emerged, images that influenced subsequent waves of immigration from Europe. It is in the particular demographic characteristics of these two early waves of immigration and in the conditions with which they were faced that the new Zionist sexual division of labour was rooted.

The demographic characteristics of the early waves of immigration were rather special.[3] To start with, the ratio of men to women was more than two to one. The scarcity of women was even greater in the early kibbutzim and work brigades which spearheaded the Zionist effort. In those groups the ratio of men to women was as high as four or five to one. Furthermore, most of the immigrants in those years were young, single or childless couples. The percentage of children under 15 was low and the percentage of old people above the retirement age minimal. What therefore characterized the early Zionist population in Palestine is that it was virtually a 'pure labour force'. That is, its sex and age structure minimized the ratio of dependents to economically active. The relative scarcity of married couples with young children meant that for the time being this embryonic society was relatively unburdened with families. Necessary domestic labour was minimal and the reproductive function was left to those who stayed behind in the diaspora. There existed, not in any planned way, an international division of labour: the most able-bodied vanguard was in the front zone of the Zionist struggle in Palestine, while the auxiliary forces and supply lines were left in the rear, abroad.

Competition With Arab Male Labour

These demographic advantages of the Zionist immigrants were of special importance for the ability of the Zionists to compete successfully against the indigenous Arab labour force. The pioneers could dedicate themselves to their colonization tasks. Productivization and work were to become the highest values in this strongly

3. See B. Gil, *Dapei 'aliyah – Thirty Years of Immigration Into Palestine, 1919 – 1949*, Jewish Agency Immigration Department, 1950 (in Hebrew); Y. Gorni, 'Changes in the Social Structure of the Second 'Aliyah', in Carpi and Yogev, eds, *Studies in the History of the Zionist Movement and of the Jewish Community in Palestine*, Masada, 1975, p. 57; Z. Even-Shoshan, *Toldot Tnu'at Hapo'alim be'eretz Yisrael*, Am Oved, 1963 (in Hebrew), pp. 399-400.

ideological society. Work was elevated to a religion, and the status and worth of the individual in the group were measured by his or her work ability.

Unlike other colonial societies in which the colons became an exploiting class living off the surplus-value produced by an indigenous labouring class, Zionism aimed at the displacement of the indigenous population. As this could not be done by force under the mandatory government, it had to be done by means of the market mechanism—slowly gaining control over the means of production by buying up land and replacing Arab labour with Jewish labour. This meant cut-throat competition with the Arabs. The Arab labourer had certain advantages over the European middle-class Jewish immigrant. First, he was used to the difficult working conditions and to the climate. But personal adaptability was not his only plus. In the conditions that prevailed in Palestine in the 1920s and 1930s, many of the Arab labourers were only part-time seasonal workers and part-time peasants or share-croppers. The Arab worker could fall back on the natural village economy, and thus had an edge over the Jewish worker, who depended completely on the higher market prices. Furthermore, the extended family structure of Arab society provided the worker with a degree of social security and the benefits of a larger division of labour than the Western-type nuclear family. It is in these conditions of economic competition that the collectivist forms of Jewish settlement evolved.

The collective form of settlement, which was based on horti-culture, reduced the dependence of the Jewish settlers on the Arab market for food products. More important to our topic of the sexual division of labour, however, is the socialization of most tasks of domestic labour. This arrangement minimized the tasks which under capitalism are normally performed in the private realm of the family. Personal services, which hitherto were provided separately within each family, were now handled by centralized agencies. The creation of a domestic service sector made possible economies of scale, specialization and mechanization that resulted in a more rational utilization of the labour force.

But this reorganization of domestic labour does not explain why it was mainly women who were employed in the socialized services, while men were employed in production for the market. The usual explanation for women's involvement in domestic labour is their relative immobility due to childbirth and rearing. However, this could not be the main reason in the early period of Zionism, when there were few children. The sexual division of labour in the early period of Zionist colonization was determined by the need to compete in the productive sector with the Arab *male* worker and the belief that women could not successfully out-perform men in physically arduous occupations such as agriculture and construction. The vital need to prove the economic practicability of employing Jewish labour to those Jewish farmers who employed Arabs, to the mandatory authorities responsible for public works and road building, and to the Zionist funding institutions who doubted the viability of collective experiments, was the main cause for the sexual division of labour. The economic competition between Jewish and Arab labour was the first form of 'war' between the colons and the indigenous population. As we have seen with reproduction, here too a division of roles evolved between 'front' and 'rear': the 'combat forces'— males directly involved in competition with the Arabs, the women taking over the rear duties and thereby freeing men for the 'front'.

Of course, there were women who objected to their status as a socialized domestic labour force; but, as most of them shared the Zionist ideas of 'conquest of labour', they could only argue, and try to prove, that women were as productive as male workers in the jobs performed by males. As the main argument for relegating women to services was the fear that 'women's work will cause a deficit', it is no wonder that women working alongside men were always obsessed with the need to prove that 'they do not fall behind the men in productivity'.[4]

Recent feminist writers in Israel (like Hazleton) have accused these pioneer women of having tried to deny their femininity and of having identified with the males, or alternatively of relinquishing their dreams of equality.[5] What they fail to see is that there really was no Zionist alternative to this sexual division of labour, which was determined by the conditions under which the struggle was conducted.

This argument does not exonerate the male and female pioneers from sexist attitudes, which they had. The point is that the subordination of women in socialized domestic labour was not *in the main*

4. Even-Shoshan, vol. 1, pp. 402-03.
5. L. Hazleton, *Israeli Women, the Reality Behind the Myth*, Idanim Publications, 1978 (in Hebrew), p. 16.

due to ideological reasons of sexism but had an economic-political basis. Feminists who flinch from questioning Zionism and its effects on the social structure of Israeli society wish to imagine another historical possibility, a Zionism that would have had 'equality for women'. It is in order to avoid looking at the conditions under which the 'conquest of labour' took place that sexism is elevated to the main reason for inequality. This idealized line of argument is characteristic of many left Zionists who refuse to confront the hard reality and instead conjure up hypothetical ideological alternatives: 'if only other values prevailed in Zionism.'

The sexual division of labour that evolved in the early *yishuv* was based on the fact that during this period reproduction by immigration largely replaced reproduction by natality. Under these conditions of low family formation there was a high rate of participation of pioneer women in the labour force. This high rate refers only to a certain section of the Jewish population in Palestine—while the rest, the more traditional community, continued its traditional Jewish way of life. However, even within the pioneer community, women's work was concentrated in a very narrow range of occupations, mainly in services. The available survey on the topic from that period (1922) included 2,500 women workers of whom 1,600 were in towns and only 900 in agricultural settlements. The main work places of women were: as cooks, in laundries, in kindergartens, in schools, as nurses, as office clerks and as domestic help. This distribution shows a remarkable similarity to the present occupational distribution among Jewish women in Israel. Only 447 women in the 1922 survey worked in the productive sector, and of those only 53 worked in construction.[6]

Mandatory Restrictions on Immigration

The struggle against the Arab labourer was the main reason for the employment of women in a narrow spectrum of occupations, mainly in services. Another major influence on women's work was the mandatory restrictions on immigration.

The British government soon became aware of the impact of Jewish

6. Even-Shoshan, vol. 11, pp. 197-200.

immigration on the economic and political situation in Palestine. In 1922 (with the Churchill White Paper) the government decided to restrict Jewish immigration in accordance with the economic capacity of the country to absorb newcomers. Immigrants had to prove that they were bringing capital with them or that they had places of employment. The restrictions were further tightened after the economic crisis in 1926, which created a major problem of Jewish unemployment. The regulations discriminated against women: immigration certificates were more easily obtainable by men, and men with certificates could bring their dependent wives with them.[7] As the Zionist organizations were eager to maximize the number of immigrants, pressure was applied on potential female immigrants to attach themselves by fictitious marriages to male certificate holders. As men were not seen as 'dependents', this regulation caused an asymmetric situation, such that to give a woman an independent certificate was to 'waste' a certificate. The need to show that new immigrants were economically necessary and that there were places of employment for them militated against women's employment. Women workers could be replaced by newly arrived men who in any case brought dependent women with them. It was not just unemployment that caused the pressure for men to have priority over women in employment, but unemployment coupled with the Zionist aim of bringing in as many immigrants as possible and as quickly as possible. In a situation of scarcity of available jobs, which were a condition for obtaining immigration certificates, women's work was indeed an obstacle to maximizing Jewish immigration. Pressure mounted on women to become dependents, and men replaced women in all jobs in which the work was acceptable to men. The report of the fourth conference of women workers (1931), the last before the Second World War, complained that although there was a big expansion in the economy and in the absolute numbers of employed women, there was a negative development in the number of occupations in which they were employed. The report also criticized the fact that women were eased out of all jobs that could be done by men.[8]

It is therefore in the needs and constraints of Zionism that the key

7. *Ibid.*, p. 197.
8. *Ibid.*, pp. 165-75.

to the sexual division of labour that evolved in Israeli society is to be found.

The Consequence of a Decline in Immigration

What would be the repercussions on the Zionist venture if its main source of population growth, immigration, declined? This question forced itself on the Zionist leadership for the first time in the late 1930s, because of the declining rate of reproduction of Jews in Palestine,[9] the British White Paper of 1939 (which threatened to stop immigration), the outbreak of the Second World War and later the realization of the scale of the holocaust, which combined to bring about a sharp decline in the rate of growth of the Jewish population in Palestine. Grave doubts were raised as to whether Zionism could still fulfil its aims.

Palestine as a Jewish state required a Jewish majority. In view of the size of the then Arab majority and the much higher rate of reproduction among Arabs, a halt to Jewish immigration could only have one of three consequences:

1. Postponement of the creation of a Jewish state for an indefinite period—an outcome totally unacceptable to the Zionists.

2. A Jewish minority state, which, like South Africa and Rhodesia, would be based on the denial of an equal vote to Arabs. (This was considered by Arlozoroff in the early 1930s.)

3. Partition—a partial postponement of the Zionist aim of securing a Jewish state in all of Palestine and acceptance instead of a Jewish state in a part of the country where a Jewish majority already existed or could be created.

These options were in the background of the developments in Palestine in the 1940s.

A similar problem, a declining rate of immigration, has been facing the Zionist state since the mid-1960s. In the last few years the decline of immigration has been more acute and seems to have become a more permanent feature.

9. See K.P. Gabriel, 'The Fertility of Jews in Palestine', in *Population Studies*, 3, 1953.

Immigration as a percentage of Israel's Jewish population growth, 1948 – 76

1948 – 51	88.3
1952 – 54	16.6
1955 – 57	57.5
1958 – 60	31.6
1961 – 64	59.1
1965 – 71	34.4
1972	50.6
1973	52.1
1974	20.4
1975	1.2
1976	11.5
1948 – 71	60.1
1972 – 76	31.9

(Source: *Statistical Abstract of Israel*, 1977, p. 20.)

The decline in Jewish immigration has had repercussions in various spheres.

1. *Democracy*. With an Arab rate of reproduction more than double the Jewish rate (and the gap is likely to persist for a considerable period), the proportion of Arab citizens of Israel will grow from the present 15 per cent to 20 or even 25 per cent towards the end of the century.[10] This may make a free vote and parliamentary democracy incompatible with continued Jewish supremacy.

2. *Colonization*. In view of the present distribution of the Jewish and Arab populations in territories under Israel's control (including the areas occupied in 1967), the 'Judaization' of regions in which Arabs are now a majority will become less practicable. This, in turn, is likely to lead to increased pressure for the secession of these regions.

3. *Military superiority*. Assuming the continuation, in one form or another, of a conflict between Israel and the Arab countries, and of the disparity in birth-rates, the ratio between Israeli and Arab young people of military age will decline. If Israel is therefore to avoid an eclipse in its military superiority, it will have to compensate

10. See *Statistical Abstract of Israel, 1977*. See also the article by G. Eshet in *Yedi'ot Aharonot*, 25 May 1978.

for the relative decrease in population by longer periods of conscription, at the expense of the civilian labour force. Alternatively, a higher rate of military modernization and labour-saving capitalization will be needed, which would greatly increase the proportion of military expenditure at the expense of productive utilization of available resources.

4. *Economic growth.* Immigration has always been an important catalyst of economic growth in Israel, creating a demand for investment and consumption and thus expanding the market for products and labour. There is a secular positive correlation between the rate of immigration and the rate of economic growth. A decline in immigration presages a slackening in economic expansion.

5. *From a nation to a class.* Since growth of the labour force due to immigration will decline, and since existing Jewish manpower will be increasingly occupied in unproductive activities, a shortage of labour is bound to persist, increasing the dependence of the Israeli economy on Arab labour. This will be a reversal of the Zionist aim of building a Jewish society and will instead create a classical colonial situation of a colon class exploiting an indigenous (Arab) labouring class. This in turn will lead to a convergence of national and class conflicts.

The only possibilities open to Israel for countering some of these implications of a decline in immigration are directly related to the role of women. They are to encourage Jewish women in Israel to increase both the rate of reproduction and their rate of participation in the labour force. It is to these prospects that I will now turn.

A Natality Policy: Not Likely

The most obvious way to compensate for declining immigration is by an increase in internal natality. However, to make up for an annual loss of twenty to forty thousand immigrants would require a total transformation of the existing natality patterns in Israel, which—as in most developed countres—show a secular downward trend.

Such a transformation would in turn require a concerned and comprehensive natality policy. Although in the past several attempts were made to formulate a policy intended to stimulate the birth-rate,

Average size of household (including singles) by place of birth of head of household

	Jews				*Arabs*
Birthplace:	*Europe/America*	*Asia/Africa*	*Israel*	*Total*	*Total*
1960	3.2	4.9	3.3	3.8	5.6
1965	3.1	4.8	3.3	3.8	5.6
1970	2.9	4.6	3.4	3.5	6.0
1974	2.8	4.6	3.5	3.6	6.2

(Source: *Hahevra beyisrael, mivhar netunim statistiyim*, 1976, p. 47.)

none was ever seriously applied.[11] The reasons for this failure are complex. First, a comprehensive policy of incentives and support for larger families is very expensive. As was calculated by Friedlander, a programme like the French incentives scheme would cost Israel 12 per cent of its GNP (in 1969). Besides, as the French case showed, there is no certainty that any such plan will prove a success, despite the heavy investments. A natality policy, even if successful, is only a long-term cure whose effects may be felt in a generation's time. It cannot solve immediate shortages in the military and labour forces; on the contrary, by increasing the number of dependents and by tying down otherwise available labour power it tends to *aggravate* the shortage. A Zionist policy to encourage natality cannot be applied equally to all Israel's citizens, Jews as well as Arabs, as it may backfire and encourage Arab natality. It therefore has to be administered through non-government organizations that can more overtly discriminate against Arabs. As was already shown, encouragement of immigration is a much cheaper, quicker, and more certain solution to Zionism's shortage of human resources.

While recognizing the impracticability of a comprehensive natality policy, the government is aware that the rate of immigration is hardly under its control, and whatever can be done to increase natality without incurring much costs should be attempted. The fear of a decline of the Jewish population is reflected in some piecemeal and inconsistent measures taken by the government. For example, though a comprehensive health service does exist, there are no family

11. The best article in English on Israeli natality policy is D. Friedlander, 'Israel', in B. Berelson, *Population Policy in Developed Countries*, 1974.

planning clinics and there is no comprehensive sex education. This absence, which was related by experts to a government wish to increase the Jewish population, keeps a large proportion of the Jewish working class in ignorance of effective contraception, resulting in many otherwise unnecessary abortions.[12]

Since an easy and certain policy of increased reproduction is not practicable, the only short-term answer to labour-force shortages is an increased participation of hitherto under-utilized sections of the population. Since 1965, the annual rate of growth of the Israeli Jewish labour force has been in decline.[13] The causes of the decline are the falling rate of immigration and the lower participation of men, particularly in the military (18 – 34) age-groups. The decline in the participation of young men was quite substantial, from 80 per cent in 1960 to 63 per cent in 1974. This drop is partly explained by longer education, but mainly by the higher rate and longer period of military mobilization. The two declining tendencies (immigration and young males) were somewhat offset by a higher participation of Arabs in the labour force. The second compensating effect, more important in our context, is the steadily growing participation of women of all ages. The declining and compensating tendencies can be seen as a substitution: *Women enter the labour force so as to enable men to be out of the labour force.* If military service is viewed as a 'front' task, then the model of the sexual division of labour that evolved in the early *yishuv* period is still applicable in the present. Men are released for the front (army) when women take over the 'rear' economic activity.

Percentage of women in the civilian labour force

1955	1960	1965	1970	1974	1978
24.5	25.7	27.7	29.7	32.4	34.7

(Sources: *Statistical Abstract of Israel, 1975,* pp. 290 – 292; *Monthly Bulletin of Statistics (supplement)*, May 1979, p. 21.)

12. This view is held by Friedlander, 'Family Planning in Israel—Irrationality and Ignorance', in *Journal of Marriage and the Family*, February 1973.
13. On this, see R. Klinov, 'Human Resources in Israel 1965 – 74', in *Riv'on Lekalkala*, no. 88 – 89, pp. 46-57 (in Hebrew).

It must be made clear that this model of divisions between 'rear' and 'front' is not a 'national plan' or 'government conspiracy' with which the citizens comply. People enter the labour force for their own reasons. The 'rear' and 'front' division is the objective effect, is an outcome of many indirect and subjective determinations.

Women Replace Men in the Army

The sector of Israeli society in which this sexual division of labour is most obvious is the Israeli army. In this sector the conception of 'men to the front and women to the rear' is a conscious policy and not just a side effect. The army has made it clear that *women are used in order to substitute for men who can thus be released for direct combat duties.* The definition of rear and front means that women are restricted to a narrow range of occupations in the army. Until last year women were to be found in only 210 out of about 700 occupations in the army.[14] Jobs unsuitable for women were defined as: 'combat roles, roles which demand particular physical strength or roles which are conducted under *conditions unsuitable for women*'. Another factor that militates against the diversification of women's jobs in the army is that most women (unlike men) are not called up after their conscription period to do annual reserve duty until old age. This results in the army's reluctance to invest in expensive training schemes which, because of the short period of their service, could not pay for themselves.

The rigidity of this attitude toward women's occupations led to a situation in which the army did not know what to do with many of the recruitable women and had no use for them, while at the same time there was an acute shortage of men. The army has never openly admitted that it has no use for so many women, but its attitude is revealed by the statistics of exempted women. In 1976 – 77 almost half of the women of conscription age were exempted from service: 19 per cent were released due to insufficient education (no men are released for this reason); 18.5 per cent were exempted by declaring themselves religious (this category also has to do with coalition

14. L. Hazleton, *Israeli Women*, p. 114, quotes only 150 occupations. Our figures are quoted from the *Namir Report*, March 1978.

agreements with the religious parties, but the fact that it became easier to be exempted on religious grounds shows that the army did not take a strong stand on the issue on national security grounds); 8 per cent were exempted due to marriage.[15]

Women exempted from the army usually become part of the labour force; or, more likely, they soon become mothers. The substitution model can be applied here too. The better educated women serve in the army, releasing men for the front. The economy draws the exempted women who have some qualifications. Motherhood without participation in the labour force is the fate of the least qualified. There is a three-tier hierarchy of women here: those good enough to complement and replace men in the army; those not good enough for this task but good enough to replace men in the economy (see below); those who cannot replace men in any sector and are of value as breeders and domestic labourers.

The acute shortage of manpower has recently caused the army to reconsider its definitions of 'front' and 'rear', or to apply them less rigidly. Some new avenues were opened for women in the navy and tank corps. Although the declared aim is still to release more men for combat activities, the somewhat greater flexibility is an indication that a growing manpower shortage may be the main reason for an increased participation of women in the army and for the widening of the range of their jobs.

Women Replace Men in the Economy

As in the army, women in the civilian labour force are concentrated in a very small number of occupations.[16] The ten most frequent jobs for women are: secretary-typist, elementary-school teacher, cleaning worker, saleswoman, nursemaid, bookkeeper, domestic help, seamstress and needleworker, unregistered nurse, registered nurse.

15. Hazleton, *Israeli Women*, p. 117, and also *Namir Report*. The remainder are exempted for health reasons.
16. See J. Buber-Agassi, 'The Unequal Occupational Distribution of Women in Israel', in *Signs—Journal of Women in Culture and Society*, vol. 2, no. 4, 1977; also D. Padan-Eisenstark, 'Are Israeli Women Really Equal? Trends and Patterns of Israeli Women's Labour-Force Participation: A Comparative Analysis', in *Journal of Marriage and the Family*, August 1973.

Jewish women are under-represented in the productive sector: less than a quarter of working women, against about a half of working men. Most women, as in the past, work in the services sector. *Arab men*, on the other hand, are over-represented, as compared with Jewish men, in the productive sectors—agriculture, industry, and construction. These facts provide another example of the substitution that characterizes the sexual division of labour in Israel. *The staffing of the services sector in Israel by Jewish women releases Jewish men for the productive sector, where they can replace Arab men.* As in the early *yishuv*, without this sexual division of labour there would be even more Arabs employed in the Israeli productive sector, with severe strategic and structural implications both in terms of security and of the class nature of the Zionist state. As in the army, so in the economy there is an implicit concept in Israel of 'front' and 'rear'. As in the army, where women soldiers release men soldiers for combat duties, so in the economy Jewish female workers in services release Jewish male workers for production sectors.

This sexual division of labour between the services and production, however, also has its drawbacks. Some of these became apparent during the 1973 war. The prolonged mobilization of most of the male population brought the economy to a standstill, which was further aggravated by the inability of the unmobilized women to take over temporarily many of the 'male' occupations, due to lack of skills.[17] Since 1973 there has been a growing demand that concerted efforts be made by the state to diversify women's occupations so that they can better substitute for men during emergencies. As was shown regarding the army, the growing strain on human resources may bring about a less sexually stereotyped division of labour and a redefinition of 'rear' and 'front' in the economy.

Wars have been a major factor in the participation of women in the labour force in the twentieth century.[18] In the United Kingdom 80 per cent of the total addition to the labour force between 1939 and 1943 consisted of women who had previously not been employed or had been housewives. The proportion of women over fourteen employed in Britain rose from 27 per cent in 1939 to 37 per cent in

17. See Buber-Agassi; also R. Bar Yosef and D. Padan-Eisenstark, 'Women and Men in War: Change of the Role System Under Pressure Situations—the Yom Kippur War', in *Megamot*, November 1975 (in Hebrew).

18. See A.S. Milward, *War, Economy, and Society, 1939 – 1945*, 1977, pp. 218-21.

1943. A comparative study shows that the increased participation by women is negatively correlated with the availability of other unutilized sectors of the population: the unemployed, the young, the old, foreigners, etc. Women's participation increased more in places where there were no other labour reserves. In the US women accounted for only half the addition to the labour force during the war: as Milward observes, 'compared to the UK the US had greater available numbers of unemployed people and a far larger population at school and college which could be drawn on.'

The war effort also broadened the range of occupations into which women entered. In the USSR, where women's participation in the labour force was high before the war—38 per cent in 1940—it continued to grow, to 53 per cent in 1942. 'Everywhere women were successfully trained to meet the sudden increase in demand for welders, but in the Soviet Union almost a third of the welders were female in 1942, as well as a third of the lathe operators and 40 per cent of the stevedores. Women tractor drivers, rare in 1940, accounted for almost half of the drivers in the communal tractor stations in 1942.'

The need to change the traditional sexual division of labour in a society during war also depends on the nature of the war. In short 'blitz' wars it is possible to stock the military and civilian provisions in advance. If the war is indeed as short as planned, there is no need to overhaul the existing division of labour. A long war, or a war that becomes prolonged, calls for production and distribution of provisions under radically altered labour-force conditions. Unless provisions can be procured, shipped, or flown in from abroad, (UK, Second World War; Israel, 1973), the whole economic system requires reorganization. The scarcity of men calls for a restructuring of the economically active population by the incorporation of women.

Israel is an interesting case to compare with some other countries in this respect. Although officially Israel has been at war since its foundation in 1948, the periods of actual 'all out' fighting that it was involved in were short and separated by long intervals. This enabled the Israelis to carry on most of the time with the normality of quasi-peace. Even the 1969 attrition war and the 1973 relatively prolonged war were not total or long enough to necessitate a long-term restructuring. The problems faced by the Israeli planners were not so much the recruitment of a hitherto unutilized section of the population, but had more to do with the rigid and restricted sexual division of occupations. The war caused a redefinition of priorities in society between front, in this case the actual war front, and rear, the economy. This required a redeployment of the *available* work-force according to new priorities. The concentration of women in a few occupations and their lack of skills in alternative occupations became a bottleneck in the redeployment scheme. It was not so much that there was an absolute shortage of workers, but that the women in the work-force were immobile, could not be swiftly substituted in other jobs. The suggestions put forward since then intend to rectify this immobility by training women during peacetime to do 'war economy' jobs. This is a beginning of the idea of women doing 'reserve' duty in the economy. More radical suggestions combine this security need with the demand for the equality of women by calling for the opening up of the sexually restricted occupational structure. It is argued that this could help in an emergency by having more women in what now are 'male' occupations, so that the mobilization of men would not paralyse whole sectors. Neither idea has yet been implemented. This suggests either that Israeli planners do not see a need for preparation for a long war, as they do not anticipate one, or that broader participation of women in the economy raises too many other problems.

Strong opposition to the recruitment of women into the labour-force during the war was voiced by the Conservatives in Britain. Churchill believed that this would be bad for the morale of the men at the front. He was, however, overruled by Minister of Labour E. Bevin.[19] Nazi Germany is the best example of a state that objected to the recruitment of women to the war effort. As Hitler put it in Nuremberg in September 1934, it was nice for the men to return from the brutal struggle for survival ... to the enclosed warmth of the supportive family: ' ... the big world rests upon the small world: the big world cannot survive if the small world is not secure ... '. German women had the task of increasing the numbers of the Aryan race; so work, especially in men's occupations, could harm their reproductive potential. Domesticity was the role of German

19. A discussion of this problem may be found in T. Mason, 'Women in Germany 1925 – 1940: Family, Welfare, and Work', Part II, in *History Workshop Journal*, no. 2, autumn 1976, p. 22.

women.[20] The result was that the participation of women in the German labour force in 1943 – 44 was scarcely higher than in 1939. This had detrimental effects on the productive capacity of Nazi Germany.

It is highly likely that Israeli planners have studied the case of Germany, and it is therefore reasonable to believe that despite strong religious and conservative opposition, Israel will not resist the mass participation of women in the labour force should the situation require it. The Zionist view of women, in contrast with Nazi ideology, perpetuates the double image of the pioneer woman: the girl-soldier, a woman also able to do a man's job. It is immaterial whether or not these images are myths. It is precisely the myths that can make it easier to turn women from domestic roles to national duties.

Women Replace Women in the Economy

From a Zionist point of view, the falling rate of immigration requires a higher rate of internal reproduction and a higher rate of participation of Jewish women in the labour force. However, in most modern societies these two demands—higher birth-rate and higher participation—are, *ceteris paribus*, contradictory. The only way they can be reconciled is by a comprehensive programme to ease the yokes of housework and child rearing, traditionally borne by women, by a concerted effort to change the existing sexual division of labour. It requires huge investments in a national network of nurseries and child-care institutions. It calls for a radical change in domestic patterns, which at present still revolve around the private household as a unit of consumption, preparation for consumption and supply of personal services, and its replacement by socialized household services on a mass national scale. Furthermore, it calls for legislation that does not discriminate in terms of a sexual division of labour and for a concerted campaign to change deep-rooted sexist attitudes towards the division of labour. Besides the willingness to undertake such a programme, it requires investment on a vast scale and over a long time. It is abundantly clear that, under Israel's current war

20. T. Mason.

conditions, there is no way, let alone the will, to embark on such a plan. It is for these reasons that comparisons between Israel and some affluent European countries, such as Sweden, where some attempts in this direction are being made, are misguided and misleading.[21]

A glance at the labour and natality statistics of Israel reveals that the main share of Jewish natality falls on one particular section of women, the 'Orientals', while the main share of women's participation in the labour force falls on 'Occidental' women. The rate of reproduction of Jewish women of Oriental origin is double the rate of those of Occidental origin, while the rate of participation of Occidental women in the labour force is almost double that of the Oriental. What seems to have evolved in Israel is a division of labour between women that is reminiscent of the beehive: the worker women and the breeder women. The key determinant of this division of labour is the level of education. The higher the level of education, the higher too is the rate of participation in the labour force and the lower is the rate of reproduction. Occidental women tend to have a higher level of education than Oriental women.

All working women in Israel suffer from sex discrimination. Research shows that the median number of years of schooling of working women in Israel is higher than men's (11.1 years compared to men's 9.8).[22] Education is the key variable in women's employability and earnings. Surveys show that the main factor in women's decision to work is their ability to earn. However, despite legislation and the claim that there is no discrimination, official statistics show that women's pay is substantially lower in all sectors of the economy. Furthermore, there is a positive correlation between occupations in terms of pay and their being sex-typed as 'male' or 'female'. In 'male' occupations the pay differential is as high as 40 to 50 per cent.[23] Another factor in the decision of women to go to work is their domestic tasks, mainly those to do with child-rearing. Women's work varies according to the number of children, the children's ages

21. This is a comment on an article by Buber-Agassi, 'The Swedish Policy for the Improvement of the Status of Women', in *Toda'a*, no. 1, June 1976 (in Hebrew).
22. A. Afeq, ed., *Women in Israel*, Work and Welfare Research Institute, 1976, p. 46 (in Hebrew).
23. Buber-Agassi, in *Signs*, p. 892.

and the age of the youngest child. Education is again, via family planning, a key factor in determining the total number of children as well as their age grouping. Inasmuch as education is connected to higher earnings, it also enables working mothers to get their housework done by hired domestic help.

Domestic help is one of the most frequent occupations of those Oriental women in Israel who participate in the labour force. It is one of the very few occupations open to uneducated women who lack qualifications. Domestic help is also a more temporary job suitable for women whose participation in the labour force is marginal, that is fluctuating according to their marital status, their pressing short-term financial hardship, their children's ages, and their ability to find other jobs. In the present society, domestic help is in its very nature a *substitutive female occupation:* one woman replaces another, for wages, in doing the latter's domestic labour. If the employing woman participates in the labour force, then she buys her freedom from some domestic duties by substituting another woman for herself. Domestic help is also a *class occupation*. It depends on the availability of peasant women, immigrant labour, or natives in a colonial society. In Israel it was particularly widespread in the late 1950s and 1960s, when the large immigration of Oriental Jews brought into the labour market a whole generation of unqualified, uneducated women who had no alternative employment. It was the differential between what they paid for domestic help and what they could earn that enticed many Occidental women to participate in the labour force. In the face of the Zionist need for a higher birth-rate and a higher rate of participation of women in the labour force, what actually evolved in Israel is a division of these tasks between two sections of the Jewish female population. The higher birth-rate is supplied by the Oriental women, while Occidental women fulfil the need for participation in the labour force. However, in order to participate in the labour force, the Occidental women have to be replaced in their domestic tasks, a role that falls to Oriental women.

The fact that the participation rate of Occidental women is almost double that of Oriental women has serious social implications. Research has shown that in Israel the wife's work accounts for 35 per cent of the differences in the incomes of wage-earners' families.[24]

24. P. Ginor, 'The Working Woman and Family Income', in *Riv'on Lekalkal*, no. 77, April 1973 (in Hebrew), p. 85.

This means that where a married woman is not able to work, this is a main cause of the family's poverty. Moreover, the poverty is much greater if the size of the family is taken into consideration, as women who do not work also have more children. The net result is a self-perpetuating cycle of poverty: educated women marry educated men, whose income is on the whole higher; their birth-rate is lower, so their income per capita is, again, higher. They educate their off-spring better, so their children have higher incomes, marry better educated partners, and so on. Another obstacle, apart from inadequate education, to women's participation in the labour force is the lack of nurseries. Until 1973 there were a tiny number of nurseries. In 1977 only some twenty-five thousand children were in day nurseries.[25] Kindergartens for children aged 3 to 4 are available in the big urban centres, but are inadequate in smaller development towns, where most of the population is Oriental. Moreover, the prohibitive fees that parents have to pay prevent many poor families from using available facilities. Here too the hardest hit are Oriental children. Most children between the ages 3 and 4 who are not in kindergartens are of Oriental origin.[26] This is yet again an example of the poverty trap, which perpetuates the division among women between those who work and those who do not work.

The problem of domestic labour is one of the major factors preventing women from participating in the labour force. In Israel two distinct solutions evolved to this problem; neither is satisfactory from the point of view of the equality of women. The kibbutz socialized many tasks of domestic labour (although the present trend in the kibbutz is to reverse this and to return to more private consumption and services); however, the socialized domestic services sector remained almost entirely women's work. This means that, instead of individual household domestic labour, there is in the kibbutz a collectivized domestic-labour sector, where some services are given to the men not by their own spouses but by other women. The majority of working women in towns have another arrangement –

25. See H. Bar and J. Markus, *A Social Service to the Mother and Her Children—A Day Nursery*, The Israel Institute of Applied Social Research, August 1977 (in Hebrew). See also: *Monthly Bulletin of Statistics (supplement)*, June 1979 (Hebrew and English).
26. *Hahevra beyisrael—Mivhar Netunim Statistiyim*, 1976 (in Hebrew), pp. 134–35.

domestic help: a woman avoids her domestic work by buying the domestic services of another woman. This is a class solution which is based on the availability of a cheap, unqualified, and otherwise unemployable labour force of women. In Israel this was possible after the large waves of Oriental immigration, but there is now greater difficulty in finding domestic help. The second generation of Oriental women, having some qualifications, prefer other jobs to domestic services, which are viewed as having low status. Despite the increase in wages for domestic labour, there is a growing shortage; oddly enough, the higher fees have attracted into the domestic-help market older Occidental women and students, whose status is determined elsewhere. Problems of security and traditional values preclude the replacement of Oriental women by Arab women on a large scale. In the absence of widely available child-care and other facilities which reduce domestic labour, the rate of reproduction and the rate of participation of women in the labour force are soon bound to conflict with one another. This illuminates from yet another perspective the dilemma that Israel faces with the decline of immigration.

Conclusion

Marx pointed out that the changing organic composition of capital in its accumulation tends to create a surplus population. This surplus population is the 'industrial reserve army' for capital's spasmodic growth. 'Periods of average activity, production at high pressure, crisis and stagnation depend on the constant formation, the greater or less absorption and the re-formation of the industrial reserve army or surplus population. In their turn the varying phases of the industrial cycle recruit the surplus population and become one of the most energetic agencies for its reproduction.'[27]

Zionism, like capitalism, also developed in a spasmodic way, with periods of rapid expansion followed by periods of stagnation and crisis. The Zionist project in Palestine has always depended on the emergence of political conjunctures favourable to it and on which it had only partial if not minimal influence. The utilization of the favourable conjuncture depended on the Zionist leadership's ability

27. Karl Marx, *Capital* Volume 1, Harmondsworth 1976, p. 785.

to anticipate it correctly and on the availability of reserve resources, financial and human, which could be rapidly mobilized and thrown into battle—military or colonizatory-economic. Jewish communities outside Palestine have provided the Zionists with these reserves. However, there were periods in Zionist history when immigration was not sufficient; and under such conditions of scarcity of manpower, women were used in a limited way and for short periods as alternative reserves. That they were used as reserves is shown by the fact that they were eased out of 'men's jobs' once there were more men. The significance of early Zionist history is that it provides us with a case when the logic of Zionism could not permit the use of Arab labour. Under these conditions and when immigration was insufficient, women were allowed more equality in job choice.

The period of expansion after the foundation of the state was marked by the large immigration of Oriental Jews who provided the additional labour-power necessary for the colonization of the newly acquired territories. During that period the participation of Arab labour in the Jewish economy was low. The participation of women in the labour force also grew very slowly. The need for reserves was supplied by immigrant *manpower*. This phase lasted until the mid-1960s. The second wave of expansion, which resulted from the 1967 war, was not coupled with mass immigration. It is since the early 1970s that the participation of Arabs and women has grown at a much higher pace. Both Arabs and Jewish women are the labour reserve army of Israel; but there are some differences between their roles. First, the Jewishness of the latter force makes it usable in sectors not open to Arab employment. This frees Jewish men to be out of the labour force (in the army), or alternatively to reduce the dependence on Arab labour. The second difference is that since future prospects of mass Jewish immigration are uncertain, Jewish women in Israel are the main Zionist hope for any Jewish demographic increase. This puts pressure on women for both high participation in the labour force *and* high natality—an unlikely combination without major changes in the infrastructure of child-rearing and in social attitudes. Either the rate of reproduction will continue to decrease or the growth in participation will not continue. The latter will increase the proportion of the Arab labour force in the *short* term, while the former, *ceteris paribus*, will increase Arab participation in the labour force in the *long* term.

A major recession and contraction of Israel's economy would change the need for reserves, impelling parts of the Palestinian labour force to look for jobs outside Israel and driving many women back to domestic labour.

3

Civil War in Lebanon

The war in Lebanon will be nine years old in the spring of 1984. Over the years, the carnage in that country has received varying amounts of coverage in the press, radio, and television on all continents, the volume of words committed to newsprint or the air-waves depending on the impact of competing catastrophes elsewhere and on the degree of foreign intervention and therefore of international political interest. Public awareness of the war has tended to be shaped by a number of propositions that have been repeated so often that they have come to be regarded as self-evident: the Palestinian problem lies at the root of the war; the war is but a part of a broader sociopolitical conflict in the Middle East, and its solution must await settlement of the issues of that conflict; the fight is not between Christian and Muslim, but between rich and poor, have and have-not; the root of the problem is Muslim opposition to the domination of the country by the Christian minority; the warring parties in Lebanon are mere cat's-paws in an international, or at least inter-Arab, struggle for supremacy.

Some of these statements undoubtedly contain a modicum of truth; others are almost completely false. But in the spate of geopolitical commentaries, two themes have been widely neglected throughout most of the war: the ideology and popular sentiment that have produced what is, after all, a Lebanese civil war, with the emphasis on the two adjectives; and the thoroughly despicable behaviour of all parties to the conflict. In the autumn of 1982 the massacre of defenceless Palestinians in the camps of Sabra and Chatila by Phalangist fanatics (while the Israeli army, having loosed the assassins in the first place, sat quietly by) received massive international publicity —and quite rightly so. But as many were quick to point out (often out of dubious motives), that massacre was merely the latest in a long sequence. Earlier, equally brutal slaughters were ignored, as were yet other subsequent ones. The conflict in Lebanon—to paraphrase Joan Didion's comment about El Salvador—resists heroic interpretation. In fact, from its very outset, this war has been marked by a savagery born of a most deadly combination: abundant sophisticated military equipment and deeply rooted, religiously based ideologies whose most salient feature is their view of 'the enemy', 'the others', as less than fully human. The armies of the Israeli and Syrian states, of course, have felt at home with such an admixture, and have made their own contributions to it. But all the ingredients were at hand well before their arrival.

The two articles in this section—written by different authors and nearly seven years apart in time—share common concerns. Both seek, though in divergent styles, to call attention to the *Lebanese*, as opposed to international or inter-Arab, components of the crisis and the war, and both refuse to endorse any of the warring sides, or to countenance their behaviour.

'In the Maelstrom of Confessionalism', written by a Lebanese militant who was one of the founders of *Khamsin*, appeared in *Khamsin 3*. It was written in spring 1976, during a lull in the fighting, which had erupted, as the article explains, in April 1975. (The 'confessionalism' of the title refers to the institutionalized system whereby the posts of the Lebanese state apparatus are divided among the various religious sects, or confessions, and more broadly, to the schism that cleaves the entire society along the lines of identification with religious communities.) In early 1976 the Syrian army invaded Lebanon (and has remained there ever since), ostensibly to impose an end to the conflict and to re-establish order. A cease-fire was announced, followed by the first of many declarations of reconciliation and national reconstruction. The level of fighting abated for several months. During the summer, however, there was a fresh explosion. The pessimistic undertone of 'In the Maelstrom of Confessionalism' was more than confirmed by subsequent events; the few optimistic notes of the conclusion were not.

'The Lebanese Communities and Their Little Wars', by Magida Salman, also Lebanese and a member of the *Khamsin* editorial board, was written in early spring 1983 and published in *Khamsin 10*. It, too, was drafted during a period of relative calm. In the late winter of 1982 – 83 and the spring of 1983, expectations of peace were higher in Lebanon than they had been in years. The country was beginning to recover from the shock and devastation of the Israeli invasion and the siege of Beirut; multinational 'peace-keeping' forces were on the scene, with the apparent support of all parties (although for varying reasons); the Palestinian armed organizations, whose presence was widely alleged to have been one of the main causes of the war, had been forced out of Beirut. Amin Gemayel had succeeded his brother Bashir as president with considerable Muslim support, and the Lebanese population, Christian and Muslim alike, thirsted for an end to the torture of unceasing warfare. Once again, however, the guarded pessimism of the author proved sadly accurate, even understated. The eruption of fighting in the autumn of 1983, some of the fiercest and bloodiest in the war's history, not only occurred even before the withdrawal of 'peace-keeping' troops from Beirut, but soon turned these troops into combatants instead of arbiters.

The ultimate causes of the Lebanese civil war have never been fully explained. Nor has the war's gruesome conduct ever been fully recounted. But both these articles were and remain important contributions to guiding the search for answers.

In the Maelstrom of Confessionalism

Nada Kadir

It would take a book, much more than a magazine article, to retrace and analyse the war in Lebanon, which has lasted for a year now and whose roots reach down into innumerable sources. I would like to avoid unwarranted over-simplification of the sort that reduces everything to a few key facts and thereby helps to swell the already extensive distortion of information about the subject. I will therefore use a somewhat unusual method. This article will be no more than a kind of barely developed outline, hopefully a prelude to other studies and analyses of greater depth. Many passages may seem too laconic. Some parts will be even less developed than others, for they require concentration on facts that are quite elementary. Nevertheless, even at this cost, a comprehensive overview of the war is surely necessary if we are to arrive at a picture that approximates reality.

I. The Forces in Conflict

The warring parties, foreign observers, and more especially the local news media, linked as they are to varying interest groups or torn between them, have all been guided by *a priori* assumptions taken for profound truths. A serious reading of the press is therefore quite difficult, for it requires a constant struggle against the news, an effort to untangle facts from sheer politics, and to follow the thread of what is left unsaid.

It is therefore necessary to start with a simple list of the forces in conflict, within Lebanon itself, in the Arab world, and internationally.

A. Inside Lebanon

1. The Lebanese

I will distinguish the Lebanese from the Palestinians, even though the cogwheels of the Lebanese political system on the one hand and of the Palestinian resistance on the other have certainly meshed, and some characteristics of the former have infected the latter, which has itself affected the balance of forces in Lebanon.

a. The Traditional Leaders

Many of the 'ruling' families of independent Lebanon have been the descendants of the *muqata'jis*, who were responsible for levying taxes for the sultan during the Ottoman epoch. Others owe their political status to their role in the state apparatus, more particularly during the period of the French mandate. All of them have maintained a patronage system, exchanging the votes of families or villages for posts 'granted' one or more of their members. Such were the foundations of Lebanese parliamentary democracy. This caste has been a hardy one indeed: despite the reform of Shehab,[1] who instituted a merit system for the selection of civil-service employees, it managed to sustain its patronage system by bringing pressure to bear on the executive branch, and in the end succeeded completely in breaking with twelve years of Shehabism after the election of the present president of the republic, Sulaiman Franjieh.

Among the pillars of the civil war we find Franjieh; Camille Chamoun, a former president; Pierre Gemayel, the head of the Phalangist Party; and Kemal Jumblatt. The latter, hailed as a marvel by a good part of the Lebanese left ('chief and spokesman of the left, socialist and humanist philosopher'), is in reality one of the rare leaders who still maintains, virtually intact, a sort of feudal relation with the masses of his region, Druze and Maronite alike.

b. The Religious Communities

Lebanon is the only Arab country in which the various religious

---

1. Fu'ad Shehab, a former commander in chief of the army, became president of the republic after the bloody clashes of 1958, as the country emerged from a near civil war. He had considerable contempt for the country's politicians, whom he referred to as 'the pocket-liners'.

communities have been strong enough to gain ascendancy over the state.

The Maronite patriarch acquired a certain degree of political power from the Ottoman system of *millas*, which distinguished among the various religious communities in its law on citizenship.[2] With independence, this power was consecrated. Since then it has been extended to the heads of the other religious communities. The Sunni mufti, for example, acquired an enhanced political role soon after the bloody events of 1958. With the internal migrations of the Shi'is and the Israeli attacks on southern Lebanon, it was the turn of Imam Musa Sadr, leader of the Shi'is. During the 1975 – 76 civil war, stardom has also been attained by the Druze Shaikh Akl, the Greek Orthodox and Greek Catholic patriarchs, the Roman Cardinal, and so on.

These communities have very powerful institutions of their own, which are entirely responsible for all legislation and jurisdiction concerning the personal status of their members (marriage, divorce, family laws, and so on). They are also responsible for the greater part of education and health services. Finally, they own immense properties, a good part of which are exploited with modern capitalist methods.

The really aggravating circumstance of the power of these communities, however, is the confessional distribution, dictated by custom and once again enshrined in the new national pact, of the three principal posts in the state apparatus. The president must be a member of the (Christian) Maronite community, the prime minister a member of the Sunni (Muslim) community, the head of parliament a member of the Shi'i (Muslim) community. The National Assembly (parliament) is likewise partitioned according to religion, six-elevenths of the seats being allotted to Christians, five-elevenths to Muslims. This confessional structure—described as a 'unique and marvellous state form' by the choristers of 'the inspired Lebanese formula'—has in fact warped democracy and politics in Lebanon,

2. All non-Muslims living under the Ottoman Empire were organized into groups, each of which was called a *millet* in Turkish (*milla* in Arabic). P.M. Holt, in his *Egypt and the Fertile Crescent 1516 – 1922* (London 1966), has described these (p. 32) as 'in effect corporations with their own officers, their own systems of domestic law, and a large degree of internal autonomy'. As a concurrent part of this status, however, non-Muslims were also 'excluded . . . from the body politic and placed . . . at a fiscal disadvantage'.

helping to imbue the members of the two large communities with a sense of identification with those of their coreligionists who hold power. The president of the republic has thus become the president of the Christians, the prime minister the prime minister of the Muslims, each seeking to gain ground against the other, with the backing of supporters divided among the two major confessions.

It is this 'unique formula' that has sustained the power of the traditional leaders, any threatened change mobilizing the masses into a bloody confessional schism. Indeed, one of Shehab's major mistakes was to have generalized the so-called confessional balance through all the public services. Although he was determined to combat the traditional leaders, Shehab accorded the heads of the communities an even more important role, in exchange for their acquiescence in his plans. In so doing, he afforded even greater scope for the old game of confessional patronage, and thus indirectly bolstered the power of the traditional leaders.

Thus it was that little by little the confessional cancer came to devour all political life in Lebanon, infecting even the parties of the left, as we shall see.

c. The Political Parties

My intention here is not to offer a detailed study of the various parties, but simply to highlight their essential features, the extent of their base among the masses, and their confessional polarization.

Because of the patronage system, most of the parties played a minor role in political life. Before the war, no more than about 2 per cent of the population were members of any party. During the war, affiliation fluctuated widely: membership levels were most often related primarily to the financing of the war, with little ideological content. It seems quite unlikely that any real quantitative change occurred.

1) Right-Wing Parties (or parties of religious ideology).

The right-wing, or religious, parties include the large Christian parties and some of the Muslim groups.

* The Kata'ib, or Phalangists, constitute Lebanon's largest party in both numbers and influence; the majority of the Phalangist Party members are Maronites.

The party has been part of nearly every government over the past seventeen years. In the absence of any genuine popular base, it managed to identify itself with Maronite, and more generally with Christian, confessional sentiment. Moreover, of all the Lebanese parties, it comes closest to being a political party in the modern sense, since it is genuinely guided by a group policy, determined by a political bureau, and not by a purely personal policy. Because of its close alliance with the Church, it approximates the fascist parties of the Iberian peninsula. Populist in the manner of fascist parties, it has been able to attract fresh layers of members or armed sympathizers during periods of crisis. According to some estimates, this party, which had twelve thousand members before the war, has assembled as many as seventy thousand armed sympathizers on the waiting list for combat.

    * The National Liberal Party. Although less numerous than the Phalangists, the National Liberals boast a significant number of adherents. This party is dominated by the personal policy of its chief, Camille Chamoun, and therefore by the alliances he chooses to cement. This explains why certain party notables are Shi'i Muslims or Druze, despite the organization's Maronite majority. It is due essentially to the alliances and electoral patronage of Chamoun. 'Lebanese' nationalists as opposed to the 'Arab' nationalists and their allies, the Phalangists and National Liberals command more or less the same reservoir of sympathizers, with the Phalangists holding a slight edge. Sympathizers of the two parties move readily from one to the other.

    * The other right-wing parties have few members and are rather ill-organized. Little is known about some of the extremist Christian groupings, like the Front of the Guardians of the Cedar or the Zghortiot Liberation Army, the latter based in the village of Zghorta; indeed, they surround themselves in a deliberate air of mystery. Some small Muslim parties of religious bent, like the Najjadés or al-Tahrir, are of similar type. Two other regional Christian confessional groupings, the Zghortiot Assembly and the Zahliot Assembly, both hatched during the war, played a significant role in the fighting.

    2) The 'Front of National Progressive Parties and Forces'.
This front, formed in the mid-sixties under the leadership of Kemal Jumblatt, went through some hard times after the Arab defeat in the 1967 war, actually suspending its activities at the behest of its leader.

And it was again Jumblatt who presided over the rebirth of the Front two years later. Composed of parties, groupings, and small organizations ranging from right to left (including the Communist Party and the Communist Action Organization of Lebanon), from Syrian nationalism (Greater Syria) to Nasserism, Arab nationalism, and internationalism, this Front is marked by many a contradiction and no few weaknesses. Although it lacks a well-defined form, it does have a few characteristic features:

* A 'mushroom' appearance. Despite the large number of participating organizations—there are more than fifteen of them—all the components actually arose in the wake of just two main currents, Nasserism and the Palestinian resistance, and they remain intimately dependent upon them. The Lebanese Communist Party, for instance, which is more than fifty years old and therefore contemporary with the Chinese Communist Party, has nonetheless never managed to work out a policy of its own or to mobilize masses behind it.

* The many parties and organizations still compete among themselves and have few actual members relative to the size of the population on the one hand and to the number of groups on the other.

* They have not succeeded in breaching the wall of confessionalism, even among their own adherents. Among the Muslim population—or at least in the areas these groups have been able to penetrate—attachment to the Front remains vague, often linked to confessional interests. An aggravating circumstance in this has been their failure even to attempt to gain a foothold among the Maronite masses, the poorest and most numerous of the Christian population. The rare places in which the left had won some support, in the early decades of the twentieth century (such as Bikfaya or Hadeth), were entirely lost, not as a result of fighting, but because of the policy of the Communist Party; the Maronites there thus threw themselves into the arms of the Phalangists and National Liberals. Nevertheless, the few instances in which independent leftists have made the attempt indicate that political activity among Maronites can be particularly fruitful.

* The Front soon abandoned any national policy—in the sense of striving to become an independent organization on a national scale—in favour of the personal policy of Jumblatt, its leader. During

the war, the Front therefore appeared as in solidarity with the Muslim confessional group, and distinguished itself from the line of Muslim confessionalism only in a programme of reforms that thoroughly avoided the most acute problem of the Lebanese political crisis, namely confessionalism itself. The Front, like the Muslim leaders, was content to demand a policy of de-confessionalization that would have affected neither education nor the laws on personal status. Here Christian confessionalists went further, at least in words, also demanding de-confessionalization of personal status laws. In reality, however, the Christian confessionalists linked their willingness to accept secularization of the public services to the establishment of secularism in the personal code as well, which they knew very well the Muslims would not accept; they were thus also acting for confessional reasons.

All these characteristics can be traced back to two essential roots. First, in their great majority, the ideological parties are groupings of managers, teachers, journalists, and students, who have often spottily assimilated liberal and Marxist Western culture and who, in addition, are isolated from the popular sources of local culture. Second, they are often the local pendants of larger parties of the Eastern bloc or of the Arab regimes.

d. The Army

The Lebanese army, with its eighteen thousand men, found itself far less well equipped and also less numerous than the various armed groups taken together. A victim of its politicians—both Christian confessionalists, who never tired of insisting that 'Lebanon's strength is in its very weakness', and Muslim confessionalists, who had 'no confidence in the army, which is a threat to the Palestinian resistance'—Lebanon found itself with a ludicrous army despite its location along the Israeli and Syrian borders, in the heart of one of the world's most inflammable regions, its security threatened from without and within alike. Confessionalism contributed to the disappearance of the state in the vital sector of defence.

The Lebanese army is characterized by three main features.

First, the middle- and lower-ranking officers are imbued with a caste spirit and feel repugnance for politicians, as was shown by the members of the military government constituted for a few weeks during the war.

Second, the military spirit has been devoured by the spirit of bureaucratism in this army that has never fought a war, scorned by politicians and exploited by them whenever it suits their purpose.

Third, the army's ideology floats in an uneasy twilight zone between patriotism and confessionalism. The 'confessional balance' enshrined as political law recurs in the army as well, with an accent on the Christian leadership. Tradition and 'balance' have it that the army commander is always a Maronite, and Christian confessionalists have never failed to exploit this state of affairs, picking the commander in chief from among their own clientele. Thus it was that sharp tensions emerged both between the army and the politicians and within the army itself. Those tensions were reflected in violations of military discipline by the army's Christian and Muslim confessionalists, not only in the fighting, but also in desertion, collaboration between politicians and officers, and so on.

All the political forces of the country lined up along the two sides of the confessional schism, which split the country vertically without regard to class affiliation.

Lebanese Muslims and Christians belong from birth to a confessional group. Each has its own legal registries, its own schools, hospitals, and political parties. Although the latter had once promised a different future, in the end they were tamed. Political institutions and even living quarters are confessionally divided. Mixed regions or neighbourhoods are rare.[3]

The only ones to escape this cleavage are the caste of traditional politicians, whose interests have hardly been threatened, as we shall see.

The elements that upset the balance were grafted onto this precarious confessional equilibrium, this absence of national identification. We will see this in the second part of this article, in the section dealing with what set the tinderbox alight.

2. The Palestinians

The Palestinians constitute the second grouping of forces within

3. In many of these regions and neighbourhoods, the majority assaulted the minority in the course of the war, in a deliberate effort to drive them out.

Lebanon, whose territory includes the most powerful Palestinian concentration of any Arab country—demographically, militarily, and ideologically.[4]

a. The Palestinian People in Lebanon

Having arrived in the country in two great waves (the first in 1948, after the establishment of the Zionist state, the second in 1970, after Black September in Jordan), the Palestinians in Lebanon now number some three hundred and fifty thousand. Except for a tiny number of exceptions (generally Christians who were granted Lebanese citizenship and have been integrated into normal national life), they have retained their status as refugees, living in camps administered by international organizations, in particular the United Nations Relief and Works Agency (UNRWA). Uprooted, deprived of any identity other than 'refugee', and lacking any firm link to the soil, the Palestinians constituted a pool of cheap labour available for exploitation; to a large extent, it was their presence that permitted the prosperity of some of the agricultural and industrial installations of Lebanon.

They exert powerful social pressure, a result of their economic role and their numbers (the total Lebanese population is only about 2.5 million).

b. The Palestinian Organizations

The profound injustice of the fate of the Palestinians, the proximity of the usurped homeland, and inter-Arab politics all lay at the origin of the creation of the Palestinian resistance. The latter, born in its present form in the countries of the Gulf and subsequently financed essentially by them, soared into prominence after the Arab defeat of 1967, raising the call for a war of national liberation. Open to the Arab masses, it recruited Arabs of various nationalities, especially Lebanese. It likewise promoted the formation of satellites in the Front of National Progressive Parties and Forces. Linked to the Arab regimes either directly (as are some of the Palestinian organizations, like Sa'iqa, the Arab Liberation Front, and so on) or indirectly through its sources of finance and its political commitments, the

---

4. With the exception of Jordan. Figures on the Palestinian presence—in particular in Lebanon, where the last census was taken in 1932—are notoriously vague and subject to wide fluctuations in time.

Palestinian resistance is subdivided into various organizations whose interests or objectives differ and sometimes run at cross-purposes. For this reason, its struggle wavers between overt subordination and awkward independence, between dependence on and autonomy of the Arab regimes. Likewise, the various Palestinian fronts and groupings have an ill-developed popular organizational structure and remain dominated by the traditional structures of alignment by tribes or villages.

c. Palestinian Ideology

Palestinian popular ideology, like its Lebanese counterpart, remains essentially tribal, although with a somewhat more prominent national dimension (I will return to this question of tribalism later). The spread of Marxism has been superficial, or worse, Marxism has been deformed into neo-religious dogmas. Indeed, this tends to be the case even with the average Arab intellectual.

Nevertheless, the various centres of Palestinian studies—whose objective is twofold: on the one hand, to investigate questions directly related to Palestinian, Arab, and Israeli affairs, and on the other to influence world public opinion, misled as it is by Zionist propaganda—do approach some Palestinian problems scientifically. But the Palestinian organizations themselves rarely feel the need to avail themselves of this ideological weapon, for they have taken too readily to political manoeuvres. The slogan of a democratic secular Palestine, for instance, has been used as an international slogan for quite a while, without affecting the Palestinian masses themselves.

The resistance is a virtual state without a country, dealing with military and international affairs, information, finance, and so on. In Lebanon, where the state in the national sense has been forsaken by politicans more interested in their own personal quarrels and alliances, the Palestinian resistance was sorely tempted to fill the vacuum, and in practice succumbed to the temptation, with the encouragement of the Muslim masses. The latter were painfully aware of this default of the state, and came to identify it with default of the state's national mission. They therefore turned increasingly to Arab nationalism, embodied, in the event, by the Palestinian resistance.

For its part, the 'ruling' caste manipulated the Palestinians by exploiting what might be called the 'Jordan complex'. Fear of being liquidated in Lebanon as they had been in Jordan fuelled the Palestinian desire for a popular 'security belt'. Muslim confessionalists offered them internal alliances tailored to fit the needs of their own political engagements, while Christian confessionalists eulogized the 'justice and sanctity of the Palestinian cause' while shunning any actual solidarity with the Palestinians.

In the Lebanese cauldron, the great majority of the Palestinians cast their lot with a confessional policy, the Muslim confessional policy, and fell into the trap of the powers that sought to exploit the 'Lebanese contradiction'.

B. Forces of the Arab World in Lebanon

The Arab nationalist movement, born under Ottoman occupation, sought to unite all the Arab countries and emphasized their cultural links, rising up (especially among Christians) against the religious link represented by the Ottoman Empire. But the movement soon found itself facing a multiplicity of countries divided up more or less arbitrarily by the mandatory and colonial powers that took control of the Arab East after the First World War. Later, the state of Israel was created on the ashes of Palestine and at the expense of the Palestinian people. Apart from the intrinsic injustice it represented, the state of Israel was a powerful slap in the face to Arab civilization delivered by the West. It defied the Arabs despite their numerical superiority, humiliated them with its advanced technology, and aroused a sentiment of cultural self-defence of wounded Islam and Arab national identification. The process that had hitherto tended to unravel the bond connecting Arab nationalism to Islam was thus halted. At the same time, when the regimes that had presided over the defeat of 1948 fell, it was not under the blows of popular revolt, but through a sequence of military coups d'état carried out under the dual slogans of 'national honour' and the Palestinian cause, now dubbed the 'Arab cause'. The ideological foundations of these coups, however, were gradually whittled down, thanks in part to the flow of oil money. Arab unity was henceforward a chimera.

As a result, the Arab regimes and the masses that they are able to manipulate are mobilized by two essential themes: first, the

Palestinian cause, the state of Israel, and the question of recognition or non-recognition of that state; second, the pole of religion or its opposite, atheism, which is itself understood in a quasi-religious manner.

It was thus 'natural' that as a negotiated solution of the Palestinian problem drew near, both the 'Rejection Front' (which opposes any such solution) and the group supporting negotiations (and here the official attitudes are slightly disingenuous) sought to bring pressure to bear on the freest, most numerous, and most influential Palestinians of the Arab world, the Palestinians of Lebanon. Many of the ruling regimes owe their stability to the silence or violent reaction of the Palestinians of Lebanon, since their own masses feel strong solidarity with them. This applies most particularly to the countries on Israel's eastern front. At the same time, the Arab regimes were also able to fan the flames of civil war in Lebanon by fuelling the sentiment that the Muslims of Lebanon were being 'despoiled'. The conditions of confessional turmoil offered each of these regimes broader possibilities of political manoeuvre. Even if this turmoil did not fully account for the war—as would be shown by later studies—it did provide the essential part of the fuel. Some of the new militias were entirely financed by the various Arab states.

The irony is—but it is irony with some logic, after all—that the most religiously inclined of the Muslim Arab states encouraged Christian fanaticism and lined the pockets of the combatants of both sides. One of the essential reasons for the precarious nature of the current 'peace' in Lebanon is the uncertainty of the solution of the Arab-Israeli conflict. As was the case in the war in Spain, the various states of the region are fighting one another in Lebanon, using Lebanese and Palestinian cannon fodder.

C. Super-Power Détente and Lebanon

The détente between the super-powers, which in no way excludes struggles by each to expand its influence in various parts of the world, has had its effects on the Lebanese war. Hard information on this subject is still hazy, and the accusations hurled by both sides compel the analyst to behave as a detective. Nevertheless, it is incontestable that the Lebanese situation was one of the factors in this détente. The figures on the cost of arms and ammunition used in the war suggest that the total may exceed the country's gross national product by a factor of seven, which means that there has been international financing. Accusations have been made in the US Congress against Godley, the American ambassador to Lebanon and a specialist in anti-guerrilla struggle. In the context of the campaign against the CIA, Godley has been accused of training militia officers and of having pulled some of the strings in the war. The role played by American and European mercenaries in the training of the militias and in directing some of the fighting is also well known.

The East bloc has likewise financed resistance groups, as well as the militias of left parties. Aid from the East has gone well beyond the military uniforms delivered in great numbers to the combatants, especially those of the Lebanese Communist Party, whose financial situation flourished throughout the period of the war. And probably still does.

There has been no lack of ideological justifications: in the West, the struggle against the 'international left', an expression often used by the right in Lebanon; in the East, the struggle against reaction, against religious and ethnic minorities in the predominantly Muslim Arab world, these minorities regarded as necessarily swimming against the stream of history and therefore doomed to submission or extermination in the long run.

In any event, the country that harbours the strongest concentration of Palestinians could not escape the manoeuvres of the patrons of the Middle East peace negotiations. Nevertheless, it seems that the specific calculations have turned around one main alternative:

* Either the partition of Lebanon and the establishment of a Maronite state whose dependence on the United States would be almost complete. Soviet influence would then be dominant in the remaining part of the country, the USSR gaining, through the left and the Palestinians, compensation for the losses recently suffered in Egypt, Syria, and Iraq.

*Or the reconstruction of the present Lebanese state with an international balance of forces, the parties engaged in the fighting emerging victorious internally. The Phalangists and their allies would be strengthened, the parties of the left represented in the government by a member of the 'Front', and Soviet influence thereby augmented among the Lebanese and the Palestinian resistance; this might at least ensure that the billions were not invested in vain.

This second solution now seems to have priority, although there is no reason to rule out ultimate resort to the first.

II. The War

The passages dealing with the war itself will be less developed, for two main reasons. To begin with, the profusion of phenomena that emerged during the war and the changes they brought about are so important that they alone merit a detailed study going well beyond the possibilities of a mere article. Moreover, foreign readers are perhaps more familiar with this aspect of the war, for it was covered extensively, within certain limits at least, by the news media.

I hope that the emphasis of the first part of this article on the political forces will allow for a better understanding of the ins and outs of the war itself. Before proceeding to that subject, however, let me recall the explosive situation that prevailed at the beginning of 1975 and say something about the spark that detonated the explosion.

A. An Explosive Situation

1. Economic Problems

The year 1974 in Lebanon was tougher for consumers than it was in Western Europe and the United States. Indeed, in a country in which nearly everything is imported, international inflation was compounded by powerful groups that enjoy a *de facto* monopoly on imports, and by merchants more generally. The real rate of inflation exceeded 30 per cent, although official figures underestimated it by about a third. The mask of the Lebanese 'miracle' was slipping, increasingly revealing a less alluring reality:

* Impoverishment of the rural areas and the gradual abandonment of agriculture. In southern Lebanon, in the North (the 'Akkar), and in the East (the Beqaa), the impoverishment of farmers was aggravated by the monopoly on fertilizers, insecticides, and the commercial channels of agricultural products.

* The foreign grip on the circulation of capital. Influxes of

capital, for the most part from the Gulf, were protected by 'banking secrecy', which encourages uncontrolled transfers. Although banks in Lebanon are Lebanese corporations, for the most part they actually act as foreign companies pumping the capital of the region around. Speculation on the Lebanese pound was one of the main reasons for the currency's loss of buying power.

* The complete absence of any policy of national development. The postponement of irrigation projects for more than twenty years (as a result of corruption) limited the annual per capita income to \$150 in some regions. Popular housing and planned cooperatives were similarly delayed, while income tax was levied exclusively on wage-earners.

2. Social Problems

a. The Rural Exodus

With the impoverishment of the countryside and the insecurity prevailing in southern Lebanon, labour-power was attracted to industry in the suburbs of Beirut. The city was ringed by a belt of poverty comprising some four hundred thousand inhabitants. A good number of them, uprooted and frequently unemployed, lived in or alongside Palestinian camps.

b. Confessional Spoliation

Basing himself on the poor of southern Lebanon and the migrants to the city of Beirut, Imam Musa Sadr became the spokesman of 'Shi'i discontent'. His movement polarized social discontent on a confessional basis—and succeeded far better than the 'progressive' parties into the bargain. On this subject, it might be appropriate to say a word about the legitimacy of the claim that it is a matter of 'poor Muslims against rich Christians'. Actually, about 45 per cent of the working-class population of the Beirut suburbs is Christian, and more than half of these are Maronites (27 per cent of the work-force in all). These figures, when compared to the demographic distribution of the communities in the country as a whole, show that there is no notable social differentiation between the confessions. The Maronite villages far from Beirut are among Lebanon's poorest. The irony is that very rich Sunni and Shi'i Muslims were assimilated to the disinherited, and played the card of confessional spoliation.

c. Confessional Ideology

The power of the religious communities described earlier has had its most pernicious effects in education.

Two ideologies, apparently contradictory but actually similar in essence, have arisen in the schools and in the neighbourhoods that surround them. The Christians—all of them 'oriental' by the way, not converted to Christianity by colonizers—consider themselves superior to the Muslims, especially Christians of the middle and lower classes. Monogamous, they scorn the polygamy of the Muslims, as well as their lack of concern for the education of their children. They also believe themselves more 'developed', because of their religious links to the West, and refer to France as their *tendre mère*.

The Muslims, meanwhile, scorn the Westernization of the Christians and their frequent use of French expressions in daily conversation, words like *au revoir* and *merci*. They also resent them for the ruthlessness of their quest for diplomas and for their hankering after 'positions above their station'. In reality, on both sides the prevalent ideology is no more than a fundamentally identical feeling of belonging to a clan, in this case extended to the confession as a whole, the sort of sentiment that for centuries has distinguished between 'us' and 'them'.

3. The Press

The Lebanese press, financed by Arab and other regimes (of which each newspaper or magazine is a quasi-official mouthpiece), was quite active in the social turmoil, each organ attempting to act in the interest of the state it represented, and secondarily in the interest of the editorial board and the cliques of journalists that have grown up around them.

4. The Personality of the Lebanese

The real tragedies were played out on the individual level, in particular among individuals who have been urbanized for a generation or less. The peasants, on the contrary, are generally still governed by coherent and fairly harmonious social structures.

Exploited by his family (who in the absence of any social security system regard him as an investment for the future), stifled by a highly authoritarian educational system and employer, having hastily assimilated some 'cultural' notions thought to be of some potential mercantile use, and scorned by the press and the other mass media, the average Lebanese often has an unfavourable self-image. Indeed, it is among the middle-class and poor masses that the latest fads are most rapidly adopted, and exaggerated to absurd lengths. Granted, this description is over-simplified, but it is above all this social group that saw its salvation in the war, a sudden chance to display heroism, to 'redeem' their 'honour'. Honour in this case, however, is not personal, for personal growth has been stunted: it is the honour of the clan extended to the confession that is at issue. And it was in the hastily urbanized suburbs that the fighting was fiercest, and the acts of barbarism committed with the greatest gusto.

It was upon this socio-economic foundation that political events ignited the explosion.

5. The Political Events

Apart from the Arab and international situation already mentioned, the armed presence of Palestinians in Lebanon aroused a twofold confessional reaction. The Muslims had a sense of having gained protection, and of being able to defy the others; the Christians, meanwhile, felt threatened by the 'Muslim tide'. Indeed, demographic growth, and access to Lebanese and Arab universities encouraged the Christians in their retrenchment. The Cairo accords of 1969 between the Lebanese state and the Palestinian resistance, which granted the Palestinians sole control of the camps and allowed them to acquire heavy weapons, represented a rupture of the confessional balance. In the absence of a powerful state, which the Christian leaders had themselves contributed to undermining, the Christian parties formed militias and trained them to 'protect the sovereignty of the state and the freedom of the Christians, and to demand equality with the Muslims', whom they saw as an undifferentiated mass striving to drive the Christians back to the *millas* system of the Ottoman Empire and to reduce them to *dhimmis*.[5]

5. Second-class, non-Muslim citizens in a Muslim state, living under the protection of Muslims in exchange for their acquiescence.

For their part, the Muslims were convinced that the Christians were going to 'liquidate' the Palestinian resistance, a number of armed clashes having meanwhile erupted.

The incident in the Christian neighbourhood of 'Ain al-Rummaneh on 13 April 1975, when Phalangist and National Liberal militiamen, retaliating for the murder of two of their members, killed twenty-seven Palestinian passengers on a bus returning from a meeting, was the spark that ignited the conflagration. During the night, Dekwaneh, a Maronite suburb, was shelled by mortars dug in at Tel al-Za'tar, the Palestinian camp situated close by.

The fighting was waged according to the policy of 'inflicting the greatest possible damage on the enemy'. The decision of the Front of National Progressive Parties and Forces and of Yasser Arafat to 'eliminate the Phalangists' cut off any possible path of retreat. It was the first time that Arafat had come to an agreement with some Lebanese leaders to exclude another Lebanese party from the political life of the country. It was followed, later, by the participation of the Palestinian leader in most of the 'Islamic summits' assembling the traditional pillars of the Lebanese Muslim community

B. The Vicious Fighting

The war in Lebanon—which has cost more than twenty thousand dead (most of the victims being people not engaged in the fighting), ruined a good part of the national economy, and caused the exodus of tens of thousands of people and the emigration of several hundred thousand others—has been striking in its despicability. It has seen all the horrors of the worst civil wars while lacking their one advantage: that which enables the victor to blame all the horrors on the vanquished.

In analysing the form taken by the fighting, we can take note of the scope of the devastation and glimpse the path to national redemption.

1. The Form of the Fighting

a. *Positional Warfare*
Unlike wars of liberation, and even the majority of civil wars, the

Lebanese civil war was not a mobile war. Two observations are appropriate here.

First, if the Palestinians had wanted to isolate the Phalangist party from the Lebanese masses because of that party's fascist and counter-revolutionary politics, they would have attacked the party's headquarters and armed positions, and not the entirety of the Christian neighbourhoods (peopled by peaceful inhabitants) in which these headquarters were located. These attacks caused the Christians to rally to the Phalangists and their allies for sheer self-protection.

Second, if the Phalangists had wanted to 'restore Lebanese state sovereignty in all of Lebanon's territory', including the Palestinian camps, they would not have attacked the Muslims, causing them to rally around the armed organizations of the resistance and thus removing more than half of Lebanese territory from state control.

The inescapable conclusion. is that the Lebanese war was not waged in pursuit of victory, but rather in order to consolidate the control of the various parties over the regions they 'protected', at the smallest possible cost to themselves. This, moreover, was the *modus vivendi* sanctioned by the Syrian intervention.

b. The Snipers

In all the 'border' regions, in other words, along the fringes of the Muslim and Christian neighbourhoods, snipers posted atop the tallest buildings and covered by artillery fire would shoot at anything that moved in the opposite neighbourhood. After the initial days of the war, the victims were generally poor people, most of them peddlers, who were on the streets because they were hungry. Of course, since a sniper across the way was doing the same thing to your own neighbourhood, terror spread, and the people of the neighbourhoods no longer dared to venture out into the dangerous zones. They were thus at the mercy of the local organizations, which protected them, fed them, and warned them to stay inside.

c. Kidnappings

Even more horrible, if possible, were the confessional kidnappings, which wreaked the greatest devastation among the population. The Lebanese have been so traumatized by the people kidnapped, beaten, mutilated and then murdered, their bodies thrown under bridges or onto garbage heaps—simply because they had the wrong religion listed on their identity cards—that it is difficult to imagine that they will ever get over the automatic nervous twitch that seizes them whenever they find themselves on a route that passes through an area controlled by members of the 'other' religion.

The phenomenon of kidnapping spread like wildfire, and persisted even after the 'return to normality'. Some of the victims were taken as hostages and exchanged for other victims. But the organizations of both clans indulged systematically in the most repugnant acts of this kind, sometimes deliberately to provoke fighting, to induce mass flight, and so on. Here more than anywhere else, the real confessional face of the war was revealed, as militiamen at the Christian barricades sported huge wooden crosses around their necks, while the Muslim militiamen spurred one another to holy war with cries of *Allahu akbar!* even when this bit of folklore was not strictly necessary for the accomplishment of their foul job.

d. Scorched Earth

The combatants departed from the strategy of positional warfare only when 'enemy' corridors or enclaves in 'their' regions were 'liberated'. Like Qarantina, Damour, Jyeh, Dbayeh, the Christian villages of the 'Akkar and the Beqaa.[6] At times like these a scorched-earth policy prevailed. Nothing was to be left, even at the cost of hundreds or thousands of deaths.

2. On the Fringes of the Fighting

a. Theft

Most, if not all, of the organizations on both sides engaged in systematic plunder, more than filling their treasuries, with the chiefs garnering the lion's share of the booty. Poor people also stole, of course, because they had to survive, but that was no more than small change. The organizations also extorted money from shopkeepers, landlords, and neighbourhood inhabitants who displeased them, something that continues even now.

---

6. The list is of Christian and Muslim villages in which indiscriminate massacres were committed by militias of the opposing side, most often against unarmed civilian populations.

b. Immunity for Leaders

Although the political leaders are universally recognized as primarily responsible for the massacre and destruction, they themselves have remained generally undisturbed, except for Chamoun, whose residence at Saadyat was destroyed. Jumblatt, in any case, denied that he had had anything to do with it. These gentlemen are always able to arrive at an understanding when their own interests are at stake. And the people go along, because the leaders have held themselves up as larger than life, and this has been completely accepted by the combatants. Some big capitalists also owe the safety of their person and property to the organizations of the left and the right alike.

c. The Mercenary Spirit

As the months of unemployment caused by the war dragged on, the population became accustomed to being maintained by organizations whose resources come either from abroad, or from various forms of theft. Many people joined the militias for material reasons, and the parties did not bother to provide them with even rudimentary ideological training. No disinterested public action will be possible until these financial resources are exhausted.

d. Fear of the Gunman

The gunman strikes fear into the population on both sides, because he has become a sort of institutionalized outlaw. It is not anarchy that prevails in Lebanon, for there is no absence of authority, but rather a multiplicity of absolute authorities, none of which possesses the slightest legitimacy or is subject to any popular control.

These, of course, are just a few of the war's essential characteristics, and their after-effects will long be felt. But the real—and thoroughly negative—results of this war lie much deeper.

3. De Facto Partition

The war has aggravated confessionalism by rallying the masses even more closely around 'their' confessional protectors. A *de facto* partition has been brought about in which the big winners are the confessional leaders and the system based on religious communities.

The role these latter have played in dealing with refugees is note-worthy. Each community has also produced its own war literature, newspapers distributed daily, reeking from top to bottom with religious fanaticism. The major organizations of both sides have reaped the fruit of their efforts. These, of course, are not the results expected by sincere combatants on both sides: instead of the re-establishment of state sovereignty over all of Lebanese territory, three-quarters of the country is under the *de facto* authority of the Palestinian organizations, and more especially of those organizations that have won Syrian approval; on their side, the Phalangists and their allies control the territories north of Beirut and south of Tripoli, where they impose their own law in a virtually official manner.

Instead of the united Lebanon for which they were supposedly struggling, the Palestinian and 'progressive' organizations have achieved a *de facto* partition to which they contributed with their confessional behaviour.

Finally, the state today is non-existent, parliament ineffective, the army in ruins, the executive paralysed, the judicial system absent. The Lebanese no longer know whether they have any national identity. And although the document announced by the president of the republic on 14 February 1976 acknowledged that Lebanon was 'Arab', and not merely a country 'with an Arab face' (as the National Pact of 1943 had said), this will hardly heal the breach opened by the war as far as the average Lebanese is concerned. In any case, this document sanctioned confessionalism yet again. Except for functionaries below the highest levels, the confessional division of the state posts is maintained, as if competence were irrelevant in the selection of top functionaries.

For all its horrors, the war at least helped to unmask the 'national progressive' left in the eyes of the masses, and thus to strip away slogans and fictions and to uncover the reality underneath. No genuinely patriotic spirit can distinguish between poor masses supposedly progressive because they are Muslim and reactionary because they are Christian. It is intolerable for gangsters and murderers sheltered by the political parties to annihilate democracy and treat the people like servants who owe them even their very lives. It is intolerable for human beings to be killed—in the name of liberty and humanism on the one side, and of progressivism on the other—

simply because they were born to Christian or Muslim parents.

Until a third force arises—one that is not besmirched by the horrors of the fighting—the complex of parties must be abandoned. A new ideological current must take shape, returning to the roots of this courageous people and respecting the popular culture. Muslim or Christian, that culture is in reality Arab. Nonetheless, it must be linked to a genuinely secular state. That, perhaps, may ultimately be Lebanon's contribution to severing the bond between Arabism and Islam.

The Lebanese Communities and Their Little Wars

Magida Salman

Will the election of Amin Gemayel as president of 'all of Lebanon' finally put an end to the ghastly pageant of civil war in that country? Many Lebanese hope so, but their desires are as mangled and bewildering as were their heroes of yesterday – or their martyrs, whose portraits still cover the bullet-ridden walls of Beirut.

Seven years of wars great and small – all of them waged by all camps in the name of victory, with Muslims, Christians, leftists, and rightists ever flashing the *V* sign – have forged myths and reinforced them. Chief among these is the myth of Lebanon 'the way it used to be', that battleground of two rival visions, on the one hand the three *b*'s – brothels, banks, and brawls – on the other the crossroads of civilizations, Switzerland of the Middle East. The old Lebanon, in which pro-Western and Arab nationalist outlooks vied with one another, is now becoming an object of joint nostalgia: the lost paradise that must be regained at any price. Lebanon's population now believes that it faces a choice between a strong state and the anarchic and arbitrary rule of rival armed groups and neighbourhood gangs. The former option seems to be carrying the day, at least for the moment.

This view is shared by the various religious communities. Christians of all sects, Sunnis, Shi'is, and Druze, have suffered the same calamities and identical violent daily tragedies, and each community has drawn its own conclusions. These remain divergent, but they concur in the desire to rebuild an everyday life that approximates normality. By forcing the Palestinian resistance to leave Lebanon, by destroying those buildings that were still standing, Sharon's army has offered the Lebanese an opportunity to weave illusions about a future peace that will not be without its scapegoats: the Palestinian population of the refugee camps.

The Christian community in Lebanon, although heterogeneous in its class structure, has nevertheless always been united in its feeling that it constitutes a threatened minority and in its need to assert its specific identity, which it calls Lebanese. A statement by Bashir Gemayel epitomizes this sentiment: 'We were under attack as Christians, we defended ourselves as Lebanese.' Such is the Christian conception of Lebanese nationalism, intransigent in its opposition to Arab nationalism, which the Christians regard as a clear and present danger menacing their traditions and culture (which, however Arab it might be, is nevertheless non-Muslim). The Christians saw Nasser's Arab nationalism purely as a threat, to integrate Lebanon into a 'rapacious Islamic entity' within which the Christians of Lebanon would enjoy the same unenviable status as the Iraqi Christians or the Egyptian Copts.

The choice confronting the Christian community in Lebanon seemed to be defined in stark terms: Islamization or Westernization. The Christians of Lebanon have long gazed westwards with affection. Their oppression during the Ottoman era (the Porte cleverly playing on Muslim unity in an effort to cement its rule), as well as their economic marginalization (paralleled by that of the Armenians), encouraged them to look in directions in which the sea afforded openings the Ottomans lacked the power to block. To this day the nationalism of the Lebanese Christians is imbued with the heroic memories and romantic literature of the struggle against the 'Turkish oppressor'.

The attitude to France was not so one-sided. Although French competition crushed the Christian silk workshops of the Lebanese mountains, which were unable to meet the challenge of the city of Lyon towards the end of the nineteenth century, the French won the gratitude of the mountain populace by making their future friends the merchants for the silk trade, and soon for other commodities as well.

The defeat of the Ottoman Empire in the First World War and the formal Allied recognition of French hegemony in the post-war order transformed the status of the Lebanese Christians from one of a cautious minority to a majority fiercely defending a new political system and national borders that entailed privileged representation in the ruling institutions of the Lebanese state. Ever since the establishment of the National Pact in the mid-forties, the Christians have viewed the confessional structure of the state as synonymous with its very existence. Whether they were workers (and 45 per cent of the Lebanese working class was Christian, especially Maronite, on the eve of the outbreak of the civil war), rich traders, or petty bourgeois, the Christians saw what they called the 'Lebanese formula' as the only alternative to their absorption into the dominant Arab-Muslim current of the Middle East. Hence the label 'isolationists' slapped on them by the 'Islamo-progressive' forces during the civil war.

This tendency to confound the very existence of any Lebanese state with the confessional partition of the state power was especially deeply rooted among the Maronites, while the Greek Orthodox Christians enjoyed neither such a healthy slice of the pie nor the same history of struggle in the Lebanese mountains. But the dynamic of the civil war itself, although it concentrated political power in the Christian sector in the hands of the largely Maronite Phalangists, paradoxically integrated the adherents of Greek Orthodoxy more closely into the Christian community. The mortars, bombs and bullets slung back and forth indiscriminately between Christian and Muslim neighbourhoods made no distinctions between one sort of church and another, or between one sort of mosque and another. When the feeling of being subjected arbitrarily to sudden death becomes paramount, it is difficult not to come to believe in the forces shooting at the other side from your own neighbourhood, whoever they may be.

Like any minority seeking to preserve its own specific character in the face of a perceived threat, the Christian community combined hatred and contempt for its adversary: Arabist Islam. The ideology that embodied this sentiment saw itself as based on so-called Western values: 'We represent European civilization in this backward and under-developed corner of the world.' 'At least our men don't marry four wives.' But these European pretensions nevertheless remained firmly anchored in the Arab Mediterranean reality of which these same Christians so clearly are part; pure and simple confessionalism, and belief in a highly politicized god and church are themselves characteristic of that reality.

After 1967, the Palestinians, most of them Muslim, were no longer 'only' refugees in Lebanon. They became a political and military force that bolstered the 'Arabist' camp, the exponents of a cause that

was more Arab than Lebanese, a cause that was intermingled with
that of Egypt, Syria, Jordan, and other Arab states.

The Phalangists, representative *par excellence* of Christian Leb-
anism, became the vanguard in the counter-attack against 'this new
reality'. The little wars and armed clashes that erupted sporadically
between Phalangists and Palestinian organizations—rather coyly
known as 'events' and resulting regularly in handfuls of injuries here
and there—heralded the big 'event', the civil war that broke out in
the spring of 1975.

The *Palestino-Muslim* camp was always far more heterogeneous
than the 'Christian camp'. Hence the fluid, vague—and false—app-
elations that were attributed to it: 'Islamo-progressive', 'progressive
forces', or 'nationalist forces'.

Among the components of this camp were the Sunni Muslims,
their allegiance divided among the traditional Muslim leaders (like
Saeb Salam and Rashid Karameh, two former prime ministers), various Nasserist formations, the largest of which was the Murabitun,
and various rival Ba'thist factions. The Lebanese left (Jumblatists,
the Lebanese Communist Party, the Communist Action Organization of Lebanon) joined—or rather, merged with—this component.

The Lebanese Sunnis were as heterogeneous as the Christians in
their class composition, except that the proportion of workers was
even smaller among this Muslim community. Their integration into
the Lebanese economy paralleled that of the Christians and was
similar to it. In the realm of ideology, however, things were completely different. The Sunnis had no phobia against the Syrians,
Egyptians, and other Arabs and could afford to flirt with the idea of
Arab unity. Large photographs of Nasser were proudly displayed in
the streets of West Beirut, along with, less frequently, this or that
Ba'thist leader in the act of praying with some Sunni personality
from Beirut or Tripoli.

But the Sunni elite lacked the political instruments with which the
Maronite leaders were endowed. They had no political party in the
modern sense of the word. The relationship between voters and
leaders thus remained more traditional, resting not only on the
inherited authority transmitted from father to son within the ruling
family, but also on the patriarchal or tribal relationship between
representative and represented.

This element is essential in understanding the proliferation of dozens of armed groups and grouplets and the power acquired by their *qa'ids* in the streets of West Beirut.

Historically, southern Lebanon was by-passed by the anarchic development of the country. An agricultural region dominated by the cultivation of tobacco – in small plantations of peasant families or agricultural workers employed by large landlords – southern Lebanon remained one of the most disadvantaged regions of the country even after the Second World War and the boom of the sixties. Until that decade, the super-exploited peasants of the South never questioned their loyalty to their traditional leaders, the scions of rich families. These families garnered fat profits either by directly appropriating the produce of these peasants or by selling it to the state tobacco monopoly. These profits were never reinvested in the South but were put into commercial transactions and companies headquartered in Beirut. Despite this, the families of notables—Assad, Zain, etc.—remained masters in the South.

The persistent Israeli attacks after 1967, along with the great migration of Shi'i workers to the cities, especially Beirut, where they formed a pool of cheap or perennially unemployed labour huddled together in large families in the periphery of Beirut, eventually transformed the political climate within the Shi'i community and thereby within Lebanese Islam.

From the early seventies onwards, Imam Musa Sadr, religious chief of the Shi'i community, forged his popularity out of this base, first in the South and later in the suburbs of Beirut.

In the best Shi'i tradition, he launched a movement of the *mahrumin*, the 'dispossessed'. It was an essentially populist movement whose vague social demands were married both to religious masochism (self-flagellation ceremonies during the Shi'i holiday of 'Ashurah) and to the more general sentiments of a deprived and neglected community.

This movement, whose slogans and statutes (an assembly around a religious chief) were easily adaptable to the political consciousness of poor peasants and workers freshly crammed into the Beirut suburbs, had little difficulty reducing the left organizations first to secondary competitors and then to enemies within the Shi'i community.

With the civil war, the movement of Musa Sadr (called *Amal*, or

Hope) grew apace in both size and force of persuasion, for the war drastically worsened the conditions of the poor layers of Shi'is, who rapidly lost even their status as workers and peasants, and became instead mere groups of refugees, now fleeing the South as a result of Israeli attacks, now pouring out of their densely populated neighbourhoods in and around Beirut, caught in the fighting between the enemy factions in the civil war.

The example of Naba'a, a neighbourhood adjacent to the Palestinian camp of Tel al-Za'tar, is illustrative. At the start of the war it was an agglomeration of insalubrious buildings and shanties often inhabited by as many as a dozen people each, an enclave in Christian East Beirut, most of whose population were Shi'i workers, with a small minority of poor Christians.

At the beginning of the civil war, the inhabitants of Naba'a supported the various organizations of the Palestinian movement or of the Lebanese left, which had located their central headquarters in this geographically strategic neighbourhood. But the longer the war dragged on, as the bombing and shelling took their mounting toll of lives and a stifling blockade strangled the neighbourhood, the more the enthusiasm of the inhabitants of Naba'a gave way to rancour. The organizations of the 'Islamo-Palestinian left' cared little about the problems faced by the local population in their daily civilian life (housing, food, and so on), and acted exclusively in the military domain. Shi'i communal sentiments were inflamed again, and flared higher when Musa Sadr established a small hospital in the neighbourhood, in sharp contrast to the politico-military organizations, which had spent money only on arms.

Soon afterwards, when Naba'a fell to Phalangist assault, the Shi'i population did not resist; in a battle between rival 'occupation forces', the neighbourhood's inhabitants felt themselves unconcerned.

This involution, the last resort of self-identification, spread and deepened as the Shi'i masses were increasingly transformed into permanent refugees finding no place to house their families except in miserable agglomerations in the proximity of Palestinian camps. Amal, the Shi'i movement, made ever wider use of its arsenal, which turned out to be far from negligible. After 1980, the political and military life of Beirut and the cities of southern Lebanon was dominated by battles between Amal and the Palestinian organizations and between Amal and the Lebanese Communist Party. A new dimension was added to the already intricate amalgam of religious sects, currents, and politico-military organizations in Lebanon.

'With the introduction of arms, a radical change in roles occurs. Weakness becomes strength. The weapons acquire an exaggerated, almost magical, quality: a defence and a shield, the symbol of a new identity. Hence the vanity of the oppressed man displaying his weapons. It is an exhibition of that new existence which has finally put an end to resignation . . . and thus it is that the act of liberation, unless organized and channeled, is transformed into a kind of magical revolt. It is as if liberation itself consisted in the act of bearing arms, which has opened the way to individual liberation . . . The inferiority complex cedes to the superiority complex, the complex of submission to that of omnipotence. The old complex of non-identity, the status of lack of status, gives way to the status of exceptionality. For the oppressed man who has taken up arms, anything is possible, including any excess.'[1]

To sum up the atmosphere that prevailed in the streets of Lebanon during the civil war, it is sufficient simply to observe how this 'psychology of under-development' operated in practice and determined the fate of the Lebanese population. A 'state of exception', not decreed by a dictatorial state but brought about by a multitude of tiny dictatorships, destroyed the life of the country's inhabitants during the civil war, and constituted the only politics the Lebanese actually experienced.

On the one side were the civilians, the victims of both camps, and on the other those who bore arms, the members of the politico-military organizations that enforced their own law. Within just a few months of the outbreak of the civil war, that law had become the survival of the fittest, or of the best armed, a sadistic and arbitrary regime under which the whim of this or that gang, this or that powerful individual, could and often did decide the fate of any person's life and property.

Auto theft, burglaries and robberies of houses, harassment on the street-corners, where the militants of the various politico-military

1. Mustafa Hijazi, *al-Takhalluf al-Ijtima'i: Madkhal ila Sikolojiat al-Insan al-Maqhur* (Social Backwardness: Introduction to the Psychology of the Subjugated Personality), Beirut 1976 (in Arabic).

organizations would establish their barricades and search, pester, insult and sometimes murder passers-by – these things, little by little, came to constitute the bulk of the activities of the members of political organizations, when they were not simply engaging in indiscriminate shelling of the 'enemy' neighbourhoods. On the other hand, these same organizations protected the neighbourhoods in which they were based against eventual murderous attacks by 'the other side'. The result was an agonizing contradiction for the helpless populace. 'The local thief is our protector' was a frequent lament, discreetly voiced, in both Lebanons, Christian and 'Palestino-Muslim'.

In the Christian part of Lebanon, or at least in East Beirut, the Phalangists slaughtered their opposition with sufficient ruthlessness to create a unified order, a state controlled by the dominant Phalangist militia. Such was not the case in West Beirut, Tripoli, Sidon and other cities, where the militias gave rise to dozens of mini-states, often competing with one another for control of even the smallest neighbourhoods. In East Beirut, for example, the Phalangists alone taxed the population, after their victory over the other Christian militias. They were thus able to impose taxes according to some rules, as the Lebanese state had done previously. Although the inhabitants of East Beirut complained about militia-law, they nevertheless felt that a single strong militia was preferable to 'the anarchy that reigns on the other side'. In the West, Muslim Lebanese increasingly came to envy the security that had been imposed on the Christians in the East. There were more and more complaints about the competition between rival militias, the cost of which was paid by the population in fear and human life. The Syrian army itself acted as just another militia along with all the rest, one that used its influence to intimidate the population the better to participate in the multifarious exactions the militias had made their way of life.

It was not long before the old reflexes re-asserted themselves. The most facile outlet for frustration is to blame all the trouble on the Palestinians, who are after all not Lebanese (and the PLO, moreover, flaunted its friendship with the heartily detested Syrian army), even though their behaviour was not a whit different from that of the 'Islamo-progressive' militias.

A double language thus took root in 'Islamo-Palestinian', or 'Islamo-progressive' Lebanon. Hate-filled denunciation of the

Palestinian resistance and the Palestinians themselves was voiced in private, while publicly the press and the militias repeated the immutable slogans: 'Lebanese-Palestinian solidarity', 'Lebanese-Syrian solidarity'. Even Berri, the leader of Amal, declared ceaselessly in the press that his organization stood side by side with the Palestinian Resistance in its struggle against Israel, whereas in reality that organization was waging an equally relentless armed battle against the Palestinians in southern Lebanon and in the neighbourhoods of West Beirut.

The Israeli invasion, with its thousands of victims in the space of a few weeks, with the devastation of cities by bombing and shelling, put an end to the slew of permanent little wars that had come to constitute the daily life of the Lebanese population. For most of that population, the available choices were as pressing as the shock was terrible. On the one hand was the strong state, whoever might stand at the helm, on the other not merely anarchy, but the real possibility of an even more sweeping devastation.

But the peace longed for by the population is fragile. The Israeli and Syrian armies stand head to head, exchanging angry looks and communiqués, threatening to resort to more lethal projectiles. The future of the regions controlled by these two occupying powers is impossible to predict. Confessionalism, further inflamed by the war, is once again rampant in these areas. In the Israeli-dominated region, Druze and Maronites savagely attack one another sporadically but continually. In the Syrian-dominated regions of the north, warfare between Sunni and Shi'i Muslims erupts from week to week. Both occupations have imposed their own law, but neither has brought about order.

Only in Beirut, where the international forces (Italian, French, American, and British) are stationed, has there been a modicum of peace. But even there, it is doubtful whether the return to normality will be able to survive the withdrawal of the foreign troops, for none of the factors that caused the little wars of the Lebanese has been resolved by the civil war or by the subsequent outside intervention, from whatever quarter.

4

Religion

'Criticism of religion', Karl Marx once wrote, 'is the prerequisite of all criticism.' Anti-religious thought, however isolated it has been at various times, nevertheless has millennial roots in the West. In an essay written more than half a century ago, Bertrand Russell, himself one of the prominent exponents of the critical tradition, was able to cite a forebear who lived some two thousand years before him: 'My own view on religion is that of Lucretius. I regard it as a disease born of fear and as a source of untold misery to the human race.' This tradition, half-interred at the time, was rediscovered during the Enlightenment and then extensively elaborated by early-nineteenth-century radical philosophy; it has served, as others besides Marx have noted, as the pivot of rational thought in nearly all spheres of human endeavour.

No such tradition exists in the Middle East, where as far as religion goes, it is still the Middle Ages. This region, which has given the world three monotheistic varieties of the disorder, is even now widely gripped by clericalism and obscurantism. Religious fana-ticism is rife, criticism of religion near to non-existent, and—in a negative confirmation of Marx's observation—criticism itself enfeebled.

In the Arab societies of the region, intellectuals, with few excep-tions, have produced no serious challenge to religion on the ideo-logical plane, and the rulers no codified alternative to a system of civic law grounded on the precepts of the holy book. For decades the left sought generally to avoid the issue, as socialists and radical theorists either claimed that religion is no more than a by-product of the underlying socio-economic structure (and that any struggle against it is therefore a waste of energy or worse), or else denied that the place of Islam in Arab societies differs significantly from that of Christianity in those of Western Europe. More recently, another, more pernicious idea has gained some currency: that whatever is anti-Western is anti-imperialist, and whatever is anti-imperialist is anti-capitalist and therefore progressive and revolutionary. This implicit proposition—based upon the curious assumption that anything that opposes something bad must be good, when logic and bitter experience demonstrate that it can well be worse—has impelled many a European and Middle Eastern socialist to discover in Islam progressive features that they would never dream of detecting in Christianity.

Recent events have demonstrated the utter futility and danger of this illusion. The triumph of obscurantist reaction in Iran—where a popular revolution under religious leadership has given rise to a regime that has long since surpassed its sanguinary predecessor in dementia and repression—and the resurgence of mass movements of Islamic reaction in many parts of the Arab world show that the problem of religion must be confronted as one of the major political, and not merely philosophical, issues in the Arab and Islamic countries.

In certain circles, indulgence of or indifference to Islam has also had a somewhat less novel, but equally peculiar and lamentably widespread pendant in a wholly misplaced admiration for supposedly forward-looking currents within Judaism, which in reality yields nothing to its two Middle Eastern cousins when it comes to obscurantism. The nineteenth-century movement of Jewish enlightenment —humanist, cosmopolitan, and assimilationist—was overtaken by the rise of modern anti-Semitism. The subsequent victory of Zionism, however ostensibly secular, brought with it a reversion to some of the most reactionary, xenophobic, and isolationist strands of medieval Judaism. These proclivities, aggravated more or less steadily since the foundation of the state of Israel, were given fresh impetus by the advent of the Likud government in 1977 and its re-election in 1981. They are increasingly prominent features of Israeli society today.

Khamsin 8 was entirely devoted to the 'Politics of Religion in the Middle East'. All the articles in this section are taken from that attempt to take up what the issue's editorial called 'the sadly neglected twin tasks of confrontation with Islam and Judaism'. The most extensive contribution, written by Israel Shahak, chairman of the Israeli Human Rights League and for many years a tireless campaigner against abuses of democratic rights by the Israeli state, was a merciless critique of medieval Judaism, and in particular of that religion's inhuman attitude to non-Jews. Shahak's analysis, continued in *Khamsin 9*, was accompanied by an appendix recounting the many rabbinical laws directed against non-Jews. A brilliant polemical effort that certainly merits republication in book form, it is unfortunately far too long to have been included in this volume.

The other articles, collected here, treat various aspects of the main theme.

In 'Why the Reversion to Islamic Archaism?', Lafif Lakhdar, a revolutionary of Tunisian origin who was also active in Lebanon, looks at the internal and external forces fuelling the resurgence of what he calls Islamic integralism, a trend embodied not only by Khomeini and his followers, but also by the various branches of the Muslim Brotherhood, a newly invigorated organization in a number of Arab countries, principally Egypt. He examines the historical antecedents and social context of contemporary Islamic revivalism, and concludes with an assessment of the potential of this movement to seize and wield power.

Ehud Ein-Gil, a member of the Socialist Organization in Israel (Matzpen), is the author of 'Religion, Zionism, and Secularism', a discussion of the recent rise of clericalism in Israel and an examination of the relation between the struggle against it and the broader fight against Zionism. Readers may be struck by the similarity of many of the social tenets of Orthodox Judaism to those now being imposed in Iran in the name of Islam.

In 'Iran: Islam and the Struggle for Socialism', Muhammad Ja'far and Azar Tabari, the former an Iraqi member of the *Khamsin* editorial group, the latter an Iranian journalist and *Khamsin* editorial group member, present an analysis of the Islamic revolution in Iran that is remarkable for its prescience. Written at a time when most of the left was singing the praises of the revolutionary anti-imperialist Khomeini, this article not only calls attention to the profoundly un-democratic essence of Islamic political theory, but also seeks to demonstrate that the battle against Islamic fundamentalism, far from being a quixotic and misguided crusade against a supposedly superstructural epiphenomenon, must be the heart of any search for progress in Iran, in much the same way as the fight against Zionism is a *sine qua non* of any real transformation of Israeli society. In 'Orientalism and Orientalism in Reverse', Sadiq Jalal al-'Azm, a Syrian philosopher and author of a famous and fiercely controversial critique of religious thought that caused him serious problems when it was published in Lebanon, deals with a subject closely related to religion. 'Orientalism', a term given great currency by the publication of the book of that name by Edward Said, is the totality of ideological constructions and concepts through which Western academics have viewed the unfamiliar world of 'the Orient' and Islam. Beginning with a critique of Said's methodology, al-'Azm goes on to criticize a converse ideology now prevalent among many Arab academics and left intellectuals who have recently become enamoured of Islam.

At a time when progressive-minded people in many countries seem inclined to forget the important role that opposition to religion has played in shaping rational thought and social progress, the articles in this section, despite the diversity of their subjects and sometimes even of their particular points of view, are ultimately motivated by the sentiment expressed so trenchantly by Russell in his classic essay 'Why I Am Not a Christian': 'A good world needs knowledge, kindliness, and courage; it does not need a regretful hankering after the past or a fettering of the free intelligence by the words uttered long ago by ignorant men.'

Why the Reversion to Islamic Archaism?

Lafif Lakhdar

In order to gain a critical understanding of the persistence of Islamic archaism and all its paraphernalia, one must approach it through the logic of its own history, as well as that of the Arab-Muslim bourgeoisie of the nineteenth and twentieth centuries, which is radically different from the process of European history and from the residual folkloric Christianity of the present-day West.

Islamic Integralism—Not a Reformation

Let me explain: some orientalists, such as the American Richard Michel, see in the activist Islamic movements a potential for reforming Islam. In other words, a way of rationalizing it, thus bringing it closer to Western liberalism. Such writers have clearly succumbed to the comic temptation of analogy and to the lazy facility of repetition. For, if one sets up a parallel between the contemporary Islamic Brotherhoods and the European Reformation, one is making a mockery of concrete history.

Seen historically, the Reformation is an integral part of the making of the modern world, of the birth of nations and their languages out of the ruins of the Holy Roman Empire and its celestial counterpart—the Church. This process led, through a long route of development, to the explosion of the third estate—a fact of decisive importance, without parallel in the modern history of Islam—an explosion that brought forth the French revolution and hence modern nations and classes.

The Islamic movements are located in a completely different historical context. To conflate this context with that of the Reformation is to misunderstand the origins and development of the current movement of Islamic integralism, as well as its historical antecedent—the pan-Islamic movement of the nineteenth century.

Pan-Islamism took form under the political direction of the Ottoman sultan himself and the ideological direction of al-Afghani and 'Abduh. Its aim was to defend the caliphate (the empire) which was slowly but surely breaking up as a result of the combined thrusts of European economic and ideological penetration, and of the nationalist demands of the Balkan peoples, especially the Serbs and the Bulgars, who were struggling for emancipation both from the domination of the Ottoman rulers and from the religious rule of the ecumenical patriarchate who still hankered after the idea of a grand new empire with Greece at its centre. Blinded by their pro-Ottoman prejudices, the believers in pan-Islamism did not realize that times had changed and that the era of modern nation-states had succeeded that of the empires of former days. True to itself, pan-Islamism was keenly opposed to the secular and liberal anti-Ottoman tendency of the Arab Christians—Shibli Shumayyil, the Darwinist, was one of their leading spokesmen—during the last quarter of the nineteenth century. This latter tendency considered the only answer to European penetration and Ottoman despotism to be the complete adoption of the European model of civilization as well as the separation of the Arab provinces from the empire and hence the formation of a modern nation.

Pan-Islamism countered these liberal demands with its famous old rubbish about the need for a just despot modelled on the second caliph, 'Umar, who would impose on his subjects a bovine discipline for fifteen years before guiding them step by step to the age of reason. To the idea of the formation of a secular Arab nation comprising Muslims, Christians, and Jews, pan-Islamism replied with the Muslim nation in the Koranic meaning of the term—that is, a community of believers. They even thought that they could stop the Arab-Muslim provinces of the empire from breaking away by unifying Sunni Islam through the merging of its four rites.

This response to the challenge of European modernism was not only anachronistic: it was also uncertain. The leading spokesman of pan-Islamism, al-Afghani, vacillated from one position to another. This high priest of pan-Islamism sometimes opted for pan-Arabism, which implied the break up of the empire; a staunch pro-Ottoman, at times he advocated the Arabization of the empire, which would mean that the Turks, the empire's dominant element, would be in an inferior position; a militant opponent of socialism, as a theory imported from Europe, at times he predicted the universal victory of socialism; an ideologist of Islamic fundamentalism, at times (probably under the influence of Free-Masonry, of which he was a member) he advocated the merging of the three monotheistic religions in a new synthesis which would be superior to each of them. This idea was openly heretical. His disciple 'Abduh, after having taken part in the 'Urabi uprising (an anti-British and anti-authoritarian revolt in 1881, violently condemned by the sultan) later recanted.

This confusion and incoherence of pan-Islamism are closely linked to the decline of the Arab-Muslim world since the second half of the thirteenth century, and to its having been conquered, for the first time in its history, by bourgeois Europe.

In the last analysis, the followers of pan-Islamism reflected the feelings of the big pro-Ottoman landowners. These landowners owed their position to the first attempt at privatization of the crown dominial estates, which was carried out in the semi-modern, semi-oriental state of Muhammad 'Ali. They were aware of the threat European influence presented to their interests. Besides, British domination was to encourage, at their expense, the growth of a new rural class based on small and medium landowners. It is this very class that constituted the core of the modern Arab bourgeoisie.

The pan-Islamism of the nineteenth century, known as *al-Nahda* (Awakening), is in no way comparable to the Reformation and still less to the Renaissance, which was a return to the pre-Christian values of pagan Graeco-Roman civilization. Even the Counter-Reformation was a progressive movement in comparison with contemporary Muslim integralism. The latter began in 1928, that is after the First World War, which marks the beginning of the decline of the capitalist mode of production, whose crisis since then has been permanent. Henceforth all variants of the bourgeoisie are regressive. Besides, one cannot, without making a fool of oneself, identify the path of the history of the Arab-Islamic world with that of modern Europe. The dynamics are quite different.

An impassioned criticism of the religious illusion; successive

revolutions—commercial, cultural, scientific, philosophic, bourgeois, industrial—and finally the creation of the nation-state; this
sums up the essence of Europe's history since the Renaissance.

The Copernican earthquake, the heresies, the Enlightenment,
1792, 1848, 1871, 1917 were so many mortal blows to religion and to
mystical obscurantism. Priests had already become a species
doomed to extinction, and Christianity is a shadow of its former self
thanks to the anti-Christian currents which the French revolution
brought forth. From the fury of the direct democracy of the revolution, year II to Freud, who demonstrated that the mechanisms and
pulsations of the unconscious owe nothing to a Great Supervisor,
religious indifference bordering on atheism became internalized in
the collective unconscious of the greatest number. Whereas in the
Islamic world the mosque still seeks to dominate everything, in the
West television every evening admirably plays the roles of the
Father, the Son and the Holy Spirit and thus turns church, family,
and soon school into as many anachronisms.[1]

God having been put to death by the bourgeois revolution, and the
Church having become marginalized, the nation-state appears upon
the altar at which all citizens, irrespective of racial and religious
origin, take communion.

Within this profoundly profane Europe, the nation-state imposed
itself through the dual process of assimilation of the bourgeoisies
and of ethnic or religious minority groups, and the marginalization
of national and religious particularisms. It was that outcome of the
bourgeois revolution which cut the umbilical cord linking the
modern bourgeoisie to its medieval ancestors.

Bourgeoisie Without Bourgeois Revolution

In the Arab-Muslim world this process has not taken place, and the
nation-state did not see the light of dawn. The modern Arab state—
an abortion of the project for a state which Napoleon attempted to
implement in Egypt, which was taken over by Muhammad 'Ali, and
which still survives today with a modernistic façade and caliphate
foundations—has not succeeded in rising to the rank of the nation-

1. See my pamphlet 'The Position on Religion', Beirut 1972 (in Arabic).

state. It has remained a confessional state, subject to the following cycle: composition, decomposition, recomposition. It has in the main remained inveterately despotic and denominational. Religion, in this case Islam, plays the role of a catalyst for the collective memory of the *umma*, the Koranic nation, undifferentiated and cemented by divine law. As the bourgeois *patrie* has not been created, the wars that the Arab-Muslim bourgeoisie has been fighting from one decade to the next are not patriotic wars but *jihads*.

For lack of a bourgeois revolution, the Arab state, although bourgeois in its social and anti-proletarian role, has not been able to attain its true development into a self-sufficient modern state that can forgo the crutches of Islam. Its denominational character, since Islam is proclaimed the state religion, has so far prevented it from creating a true national cohesion. This could only be carried out in a non-denominational state that would result from a fusion and re-casting of all the present components of its national bourgeoisie. Since they have not succeeded in this respect, each Arab state is a mosaic of particularisms of all sorts, whose creeds, ethnic loyalties, dialects, and mental outlooks are different and contradictory. Syria, Iraq, and Lebanon are dramatic examples of this. This explains why at times of crisis regional, tribal, ethnic, or confessional bonds often blunt the edge of social interests and the horizontal division of Arab-Islamic society, which is unconsciously experienced as a juxta-position of clannish partisanships (*'asabiyat*) rather than as a society of open class struggle.

The fact that there is still no secular dimension within the Arab state means that the Christians and the Jews, not to mention the free thinkers, are still subject in effect to a status of *dhimmi* (tributary) as they were fourteen centuries ago.

The secularization of the Arab-Muslim state, so bitterly opposed both by the pan-Islamism of the nineteenth century and by present-day Islamic integralism, was never insisted on by any party or Arab-Muslim thinker. True, al-Kawakibi recommended the union of Christian and Muslim Arabs—but within the framework of the sacrosanct Islamic caliphate, whose caliph must be a Qurayshi (Arab from Muhammad's tribe). Similarly, the Arab uprising of 1916 – 19, which was supported by Great Britain, attacked the Ottoman empire only in order to appeal to 'all true Muslims to overthrow the atheist government which had dethroned the sultan and confiscated his property'.[2] Even the Egyptian National Party, which considered itself to be Jacobin, was fiercely anti-secular. They attacked Qasim Amin for having recommended a measure of emancipation for Muslim women within the confines of a slightly re-interpreted Islam. Their leader Mustafa Kamil jumped for joy when a law court annulled the marriage of a Muslim lady with a Coptic journalist. Worse still, the party's paper, *al-Mu'ayyed*, made a concerted attack on the Copts for not having converted to Islam.

The present leaders of the Arab bourgeoisie are in this respect faithful to their predecessors. Qadhafi recently stated that 'Arab nationalism is part of Islam. . . . It is not normal that there be in the Arab homeland an Arab who is not a Muslim. The Christian Arab has no right to belong to the Arab nation, whose religion is not his own.'[3] Just as the fully fledged subject in medieval Europe was a Christian, the true 'citizen' in the Arab world is a Muslim.

Qadhafi says out loud what his Arab-Muslim colleagues whisper to each other. King Faisal told Sadat when the latter came to tell him of his decision (along with Syria) to open hostilities against Israel in 1973: 'It would be catastrophic to declare war together with a Syria governed by the Ba'thists and the 'Alawis [a sect of Shi'i Islam]. To ally with Ba'thists is to risk disaster. But with 'Alawis especially, it would be tantamount to courting a double disaster.'[4] This morbid confessionalism is explained by the conditions that gave rise to the Arab-Muslim bourgeoisie and by its vital need to resort to Islam for its survival. This bourgeoisie emerged not in a revolution but as the result of a lame compromise with its colonialist opposite number; for it was born from agriculture and not from industry. Finally, it is a late arrival on the scene, a class whose birth, after the First World War, coincided with the beginning of the decline of the bourgeoisie on a world scale. In order to remain in command when faced with the challenge of the 'people', it could only rely (apart from the armed forces) on Allah and Islam as the principal mystification of the toiling masses, since it had not succeeded, due to its immense economic backwardness, in setting up the modern mystifications inherent in

2. See the circular of Husain Ibn 'Ali, leader of the revolt, in M. Atlas, *The Great Pan-Arab Revolution*, Damascus 1978 (in Arabic).
3. Interview in the Beirut daily *al-Safir*, 10 August 1980.
4. Recounted by Sadat; see the Cairo daily *al-Ahram*, 4 September 1980.

political and trade-union pluralism. Its incapacity to create a prosperous economy capable of satisfying the quantitative demands of the proletariat left only Islam as an ideological weapon for paralysing social dynamics, blocking the intellect of the masses, maintaining the sub-animal status of women, and mystifying the class struggle. The struggle between the oppressors and the oppressed degenerated—often through the efforts of the political and religious establishments—into a sterile confrontation between Muslims and non-Muslims, Sunnis and Shi'is. In short, Islam, as its etymological meaning indicates, was able to force its subjects into submission.

Being decadent from birth, the Arab bourgeoisie was incapable of creating either its own market or its own national unity. Hence its allegiance to the imperialisms of today and to the Ottoman empire of former times. 'Urabi, in the midst of the war against the British expeditionary force, refused to publish and to refute his excommunication as an *'asiy* (rebel) by the Ottoman sultan – this excommunication was obtained, moreover, thanks to the promises and threats of the British. When the Khedive and the British spread it about in the Egyptian army, the latter became demoralized. The soldiers of the first national Egyptian uprising no longer wished to die as rebels rather than as martyrs bearing the blessing of a Turkish sultan. More than forty years later, Sa'd Zaghlul—the father of secular Egyptian nationalism—refused to support the abolition of the Ottoman empire by the Turks themselves, 'because', he said, 'the multitude is very sensitive to this subject'. Muhammad Farid, leader of the Egyptian National Party, went even further when he wrote, 'The Muslims of Egypt owe it to themselves to link themselves forever to Turkey, which is the capital of the Islamic caliphate, without the slightest consideration for their history in Egypt or elsewhere.' We find in the words of an Egyptian Jacobin the fundamental thesis of the pan-Islamism of al-Afghani: 'The nationality of Muslims is only their religion'.

From Failed Pan-Islamism to Ineffectual Modernism

Although the ideological demarcations between the discourse and the confessional practices of the Arab-Muslim bourgeoisie on the one hand and pan-Islamic fundamentalism on the other are tangled, a new fact did emerge—the defeat of pan-Islamism. In 1919, Islam appeared to be the loser. The 'House of Islam', apart from North Yemen, Afghanistan, and what was to become Saudi Arabia, was totally under European domination. The recipe of the pan-Islamists—an Islam reunified and purified by a return to the sources and thus able to defy the European challenge—turned out to be ineffectual. Its original contradiction, between the need to accede to power and therefore to modernism, and the tendency to regress to a primitive Islam full of taboos, incompatible with the demands of power and modernity, became flagrant. This contradiction in fact expresses the historical impossibility of the realization of this double aim. In the epoch of permanent crisis, it was impossible for the Islamic bourgeoisie to catch up with advanced capitalism; and at a time when the world market was being unified under the dictatorship of mass consumption, it was impracticable to return to a pure and undiluted, austere and inward-looking Islam.

The abolition of the Islamic caliphate by Atatürk in 1924 and the separation of the Arab provinces from Turkey meant that pan-Islamism, whose centre was the Ottoman empire, became meaningless. By setting up, thirty-three years after Jules Ferry, republican schools which were compulsory and non-denominational and opting for the European model of life, Atatürk rehabilitated the tendency of Shibli Shumayyil, the rival of pan-Islamism. Moreover, this was to be the tendency of the new Westernized Arab-Muslim intelligentsia which began to emerge between the two world wars. Traditionalist Islamic discourse was no longer a central theme. Their leading spokesman, Taha Husain, even went so far as to mock the rhetoric of the Koran, which was unanimously considered as the one and only divine miracle authenticating the message of Muhammad. He crossed swords with the traditionalists whose writings were nothing more than nauseating lamentations about the Judeo-Christian 'plot' to undermine Islam. Taha Husain was condemned even by the most enlightened leaders of the Arab bourgeoisie. He and his fellow-thinkers were more representative of their Parisian teachers than of their own feeble-minded bourgeoisie, which did not put up with the slightest criticism.

The intelligentsia of the period between the two world wars was in advance of the bourgeoisie, but behind the times—and failed in its absurd attempt to reconcile fundamentalist authenticity with commercial modernism, the specificity of traditionalism with the uniformization which the world market imposed. In short, they wanted to identify with the bourgeoisie and to be themselves at one and the same time. Drawing their own conclusion from their failure, almost all the modernist intellectuals recanted before the end of the 1940s and tuned into the religious stupidity of the bourgeoisie, which had in the main remained prisoner of the bric-à-brac of 'Abduh's pan-Islamism, but within the confines of an Islam that had definitively broken up.

In the meantime, in Egypt—epicentre of the Arab-Muslim world, and the model for its evolution—the liberal bourgeoisie under the leadership of the Wafd, a bi-denominational and therefore implicitly secular party, also failed in its task of modernizing the economy. The other bourgeoisies came to the same impasse. When the failure of the liberal faction of the bourgeoisie was complete, the statist faction took over: 1952 in Egypt, 1954 in Syria, 1958 in Iraq, and finally the civilian Neo-Destour in Tunisia 1956.

Once in power, the modernist, authoritarian faction of the Arab bourgeoisie, with its belief in a planned economy, appeared to the old-fashioned faction of the Muslim bourgeoisie as 'communist' in Egypt, Syria, and Algeria and as 'Westernized' in Tunisia. All the more so as the pro-Soviet tendencies of the former and the pro-Western tendencies of the latter were obvious. In the Middle East the pan-Arab message checked the influence of pan-Islamism. Some agrarian reforms, while not greatly improving the situation of the fellahin, encroached upon the interest of the old landed bourgeoisie, which in many cases included or had close ties with the clergy.

The Arab state, even under the modernists, remained true to form, hypocritical and bigoted; the speeches of people such as Bourguiba or Nasser were constantly interspersed with as many quotations from the Koran as statistics. Nevertheless, the reform projects were ill-suited to a profoundly traditionalist Islam. The 1962 Charter in Egypt prattled about scientific socialism, as did the Charters of Algeria and Syria in 1964. In Tunisia a code of personal law was introduced in 1957 that was ultra-modern and quite unique in the Muslim world. It forbade polygamy, which is permitted in the Koran. Divorce, reduced to a business transaction, was made symmetric, whereas Islam—the summit of male chauvinism—makes it the sole privilege of the husband. To get an idea of the Muslim clergy's hostility to measures of this type, recall that immediately upon achieving power, the Khomeinist government repealed the restrictions that the previous regime had imposed upon a husband's unilateral right to divorce his wife.

The ultimate in the relinquishing of Islamic dogmas was Bourguiba's abolition of the fast during the month of Ramadan in 1958 in an attempt to deal with the drastic fall in production caused by the fast.

As a result of the economic and legislative measures taken by the modernist bourgeoisie where in power, society began to break up and the family to fall apart. The rapid rise to riches of the new bourgeoisie, legendary for its corruption, favoured the emergence—in societies in which family or community solidarity was still a matter of honour—of a utilitarian outlook bent on money and success. In short, the old form of society was eroded and the traditional economy was destroyed without anything new taking their place. The failure of the modernization of the economy was ubiquitous. To this economic failure, the modernizing bourgeoisie added in 1967 the military defeat by Israel. The occupation of the whole of Jerusalem, the second most sacred place of Islam, afforded the bitterly persecuted Muslim Brotherhoods another unhoped for argument to set the middle classes, the social mainstay of those in power, not only against Israel and the USSR but also against the Arab governments, whose 'lack of faith brought about the whole catastrophe'.[5]

Internal Causes of Islamic Integralism

The old liberal bourgeoisie of landowners and compradors, seriously weakened and discredited by its own failure, could no longer claim to be able to replace the more modern statist bourgeoisie. Only the religious faction, who moreover had the advantage of never having directly exercised power, could do that. All the more so as they were alone in having dared to face those in authority even

5. This is the conclusion of what seems to be the first leaflet of the Muslim Brethren in Egypt, July 1967.

when the latter seemed to be at the height of their glory.

The anguish evoked by the defeat, the permanent crisis of the regimes, which the consequences of the war only deepened, and finally the black sun of melancholy which hardly ever sets in this region, favoured those birds who fly only in the twilight moments of history—the religious pulpiteers. At times when the air is filled with doubts and questions, they come forward to offer the afflicted masses their demagogic recipe: a return to Islamic archaism.

The fact that the Islamic integralists are the only mass opposition party in the Arab world is not due alone to the successive failures of both the liberal and statist factions of the bourgeoisie. There are other reasons, both internal and external, which interact with one another. These deserve a closer look.

Christianity was first modernized to adapt it to the new Europe. Since the Renaissance it has been exposed to implacable criticism (from Copernicus to Freud), not to mention heresies and revolutions. For lack of a powerful industrial Arab-Muslim bourgeoisie with its own intelligentsia, contemporary Islam has remained sheltered from any sort of subversive criticism. However, it is as sensitive to any type of criticism, be it social or scientific, as any other religion, if not more so. For the Koran has its own bit to add to the biblical absurdities of Genesis. The earth is flat; the sun 'goes down in a boiling spring near to a people'; the stars 'of the neighbouring sky' are destined to be 'thrown at demons'; 'seven heavens and as many earths' were created by Allah. The Universe, it is true, is infinitely huge and poor Allah might well be unable to make head or tail of it. But when it comes to man—a minute being—there is less excuse. From among myriad examples: sperm, if we are to believe a verse in the Koran, is not secreted by the testicles but comes from somewhere 'between the loins and the ribs'. Woe betide the Creator who does not even know the anatomy of his own creatures.

Even well-informed Muslims tend not to be aware that Allah, who swore in the Koran 'always to keep his word', did not keep his promise to keep the Koran intact. 'Uthman, the third caliph, when collating the Koran, disregarded the three other versions brought by three distinguished Companions of Muhammad: Ubayy, Ibn Mas'ud and 'Ali, who was to become the fourth caliph. Similarly they are not aware that their Koran was inspired not only by Allah but also by Satan: the 'satanic verses', which for some time permitted the people to worship the idols of the Meccans in order to win them over.

The Arab intellectuals of today shun any criticism of Islam, of the most abominable of its dogmas, and even the translation or publication of books clarifying the genesis of Islam, such as Maxime Rodinson's *Mohammed*. The main explanation for this is the fact that the Arab intelligentsia as a whole has made a compact with the left and right factions of the bourgeoisie—factions which differ from each other as much as Tweedledum and Tweedledee.

In the Arab world, those who think for themselves and are capable of elaborating a criticism of all the sacred or profane mystifications come up against the political and religious censorship of the present Arab state—a censorship that is far worse than that of the caliphate state. The fact is that the best Arab poets and thinkers of the early centuries of Islam would not be able to exist in the present-day Arab world—people like Abu Nuwas, who loved wine and good-looking boys; al-Ma'arri, who was radically anti-religious; or even al-Jahiz, with his free libertine style, who was nevertheless considered one of the leading thinkers of the mu'tazilite school.

As proof, consider the tentacles of a censorship that has not even spared the translations of the works of antiquity and of modern times. In Ovid's *Metamorphoses* the chaos of the beginnings of the world has been transformed into a certain order of Allah. Plato's *Republic* and *Symposium* and the Greek tragedies and comedies are radically purged of any references to homosexuality or remarks that might outrage conventional morality. In the *Divine Comedy*, Muhammad is no longer to be found in the eighth circle of the Inferno. In 1954, 'Abd al-Rahman Badwi collected and translated the articles of the Arab free-thinkers of the Middle Ages, entitling the collection *Atheism and Islam*. The book was rapidly withdrawn from circulation, and nothing more was heard about it. In Syria, since 1971, censorship has been preventing the publication of the translation of Marx's *German Ideology*. My own writings, published in Lebanon before the 1973 war, are forbidden everywhere else. They sometimes manage to get through the *cordon sanitaire* that extends from the Gulf to the Atlantic, thanks to the practice of smuggling, not always for purely commercial aims.

This stupid and totalitarian censorship is part of an unspeakable generalized dictatorship. The Arab bourgeoisie's only means of mitigating the under-development in the techniques for lying in the mass media—its television is still not credible—are strong-arm methods from which the whole of society suffers. There is no legal means of defending oneself. Even the few appearances of democracy left by the European colonizers such as the freedom of the press, the party system, the right to strike are abolished in the name of sacrosanct economic development. While retaining a veneer of Westernization, the *dirigiste* Arab state has retrieved its memory of the caliphate.

In the Maghreb, the masses, given their desire for a Messiah and the demagogy of the nationalist elites, imagined that independence would be a home-coming, a return to their traditional culture and to their community solidarity where 'all Muslims are brothers'. The nationalist elites, once in power, did not, of course, keep their promises. For them independence meant their own independence from the masses. Worse still, the post-colonial state behaved towards the latter with the same cruelty as the colonial state.

In this claustrophobic and decadent Arab society which had no perspective, the most ridiculous mysticisms were able to develop. The context, it is true, was ideal. A profound and generalized falsification of both social and inter-personal relations, the fatalism of Islam which, once internalized, prevents a person from being himself or herself, from thinking and acting as oneself, from seeking the truth of one's own destiny in oneself and not in Allah.

The occupation by Israel of the Arab territories provided the integralists with an unhoped-for pretext: it could be interpreted as a 'just punishment from Allah inflicted on all those who had abandoned his religion'.

The integralist Muslim sects, haloed with their martyrs from 1954 to 1966, especially in Egypt, swarmed clandestinely. Worse still, they became credible. All the more so since they were favoured by the fact that the unspeakable authoritarianism of those in power left practically no means of expression or autonomous organization. Only the mosques were protected from censorship. They became places where the masses whose ranks were broken by despotism received a politico-religious indoctrination.

Then came the October war of 1973 with its parade of intense Islamic propaganda, and the oil boom which enabled Libya and especially Saudi Arabia to distribute their petro-dollars to the integralist groups everywhere in order to undermine left-wing extremists, or pro-Soviet groups as in Syria. Even at the time when the modernist statist bourgeois faction was still credible, Saudi Arabia was used as the prototype by repressed or persecuted Islamic archaism; and its emergence following the October war on the ruins of Nasser's Egypt as the leader of the Arab world gave the Brotherhoods of Sunni Islam not only more subsidies, but the model of an Islam true to itself. The propaganda pounded out by Western media —depicting Saudi Arabia as the new giant with the power of life and death over Western civilization—stimulated, in old and young alike, the nostalgic desire for the return of Islam to its former strength.

External Causes

These are the *internal* causes favouring a massive return to Islam. There are also external causes: the decline of the West, and its attempt to take advantage of the Islamic movements.

The decline of the West has become obvious. Its death throes are shaking the economic, ethical, and aesthetic order; its traditional ideologies—'socialist' as well as liberal—are dead. In short, it no longer presents a feasible project for civilization, even for itself. The Arab-Muslim intelligentsia, which had formerly earned its daily bread by circulating the latest cultural fashions of this same Western civilization, is now thrown back on its own resources and outdated values. As though by some magic power, it has begun to rediscover the long-forgotten virtues of the celebrated Return to the Source advocated by the pan-Islamism of a bygone age. Thus Zaki Najib Mahmud, grown grey in the service of American positivism, realizes at the end of his life that he had 'considerably under-estimated' *al-turath*, the Arab-Islamic heritage, which—if we are to believe him— is capable after all of rejuvenating Arab society! Others in turn have suddenly discovered, more than two generations after the Dadaists, the bankruptcy of eighteenth-century rationalism, which had promised to usher in the reign of reason in everyday life—a belated discovery of a bankruptcy which was already clearly visible in the debris of the First World Butchery. Yet others have discovered that the alcoholism, drug addiction and youth vandalism rampant in the West are all due to the decline of religious feelings, and they would like to protect their own society from these evils. In short, the fact that the Arab-Muslim intelligentsia as a whole, which only yesterday was looking to the West, is now withdrawing into itself is grist to the mill of Islamic integralism.

The monotheistic religions arose from the ashes of ancient civilizations. The present return to religious archaism (which, in varying degrees, is taking place all over the world) is nourished by the putrescence of 'our' civilization, which constantly reminds the human species of death and makes the apocalypse a daily occurrence. Within one generation it has led to two world carnages resulting in twenty and fifty million deaths and several hundred million wounded and permanently shocked. There is now talk of a third world war. Two great powers, the USA and the USSR, have at their disposal sufficient nuclear arms to destroy our planet five times over. In the industrialized societies people are dying of obesity. In the Third World, fifty million human beings—of whom fifteen million are children—die from malnutrition every year. That is, as many people die of malnutrition every year as died in the Second World War.

The West encourages the return to Islamic archaism not only by its own decline, but even more by its intrigues. Both Europeans and Americans have long been forced to seek the help of Islam in the suppression of embryonic social struggles in Muslim countries and in opposing their Soviet rival. Moreover, the latter used to try to exploit Nasser's pan-Arabism against the West.

M. Copeland, the former chief of the CIA in the Middle East, revealed in his book *The Game of Nations* that as from the 1950s the CIA began to encourage the Muslim Brotherhood to counteract communist influence in Egypt. This trend has become more pronounced since then.

We hear the same tune from Giscard d'Estaing, who confided to members of his cabinet before taking the plane for the Gulf in March 1980: 'To combat communism we have to oppose it with another ideology. In the West, we have nothing. This is why we must support Islam.'[6] Brzezinski, the chief adviser to the White House, discovers

6. 'The President in the Land of 1001 Wells', in *Le Canard Enchaîné*, 8 March 1980.

still other virtues in religious wars: 'The religious troubles in the Middle East could arouse a common desire to find a definitive settlement between the Arabs and Israel.'[7] It is therefore clear that the coming to power of Khomeinism in Iran has in no way altered the West's determination to manipulate militant Islam. Future Islamic governments would be, especially at the outset, difficult clients, but clients all the same.

Restructuring the Arab World

The West's need to ally with Islam is considerably more compelling than the brevity of the declarations would lead us to believe. As in Latin America, the American bourgeoisie attempts to democratize as far as possible outdated dictatorships of the Iranian type within its sphere of influence in the Islamic world. In fact, the traditionalist caste-like dictatorships, the clannish patriarchal type of government—as in Saudi Arabia, the Emirates in the Gulf, or elsewhere—which forbid any change in power, are incompatible with two major requirements: that of the new international division of labour and that of the remodelling of the map of the Arab-Muslim world.

The restructuring of the saturated world market, demanded by the new reorganization of the international division of labour undertaken by the multinationals, requires in turn a restructuring of the political powers in the regions concerned, so that they can play their role there. The leading technology on which the development of the highly profitable economic sectors of the future depend, such as computers or micro-electronics, will be the monopoly of the West, with the USA in the lead; the outdated or polluting industries (steel, naval construction), specialization in certain types of agriculture and some sub-contracted industries, will be the lot of the Third World. The possessors of the manna, in the form of petro-dollars, will have to play the role of international bankers financing the projects evolved by Western experts for the 'development' of certain underdeveloped countries. The implementation of this new international division of labour is dependent in the Arab-Muslim world on the remodelling of its map.

7. Declaration reproduced in the Tunisian newspaper *al-Sabah*, 6 February 1980.

The balance of power in this area between the Ottomans, British, and Russians, which was upset by the consequences of the First World War, was restored by a new balance between British and French. These two divided between them the spoils of the defeated Ottoman Empire. In their turn, the consequences of the Second World War meant the wane of British and French imperialism and the rise of American and Russian imperialism. In 1920 there was the Treaty of Sèvres and in 1945 there was Yalta. But after the departure of the British and the French and their replacement by the Americans and the Russians there was no proper agreement to ratify the new *de facto* balance of power. The Arab-Muslim world has remained a shady area open to all rivalries. The intensification of the world crisis now demands a new imperialist distribution of the energy market (the USSR needs 18 per cent of the Middle East oil), access to raw materials and spheres of influence. In short, a new Yalta, or world settlement, is required for oil, since the alternative is open bargaining or open confrontation.

All the states, apart from Israel, and perhaps Egypt, will probably have to change their frontiers, their populations, their names, and, naturally, their patrons.

The map that will emerge from this new Yalta will probably be an outcome of the break-up of the present states into denominational mini-states, which may then be regrouped into federations or confederations. The keystone of this attempt to politically re-structure the Arab-Muslim area will be the rise of the new middle classes. Local technocracies have considerably developed due to the export of oil and the spread of education. Their ambition is to participate in public affairs, hitherto monopolized by the tribal-dynastic castes. This participation, which implies a degree of modernization of the states in question, is (if we are to believe the specialists of the multinationals and their computers) going to prevent both autonomous popular movements and possible pro-Soviet *coups d'état*, even in Saudi Arabia. But how can this be achieved? In Brzezinski's own words, by the manipulation of the 'existing forces' with the aim of changing the out-dated socio-economic *status quo*, before Moscow does so to its advantage.

Henceforth, it would be preferable not to risk military *coups d'état* except in cases of extreme emergency. True, armies have for decades been the agents of change which the West has manipulated as it desired; but the situation has now changed. Thirty years ago, given the widespread weakness of all the social classes, they were the only organized force capable of disciplining the toiling masses, who were too turbulent at the time. Then they failed in their task of modernizing the economy. Worse still: a series of *coups d'état*— beginning with Egypt, then in Syria, Algeria, Libya, and finally Ethiopia—had started off in Washington and ended up in Moscow.

When the tactic of the *coup d'état* had been exhausted, the West thought it had found a replacement in the religious movements. These movements were the mouthpiece of the urban and rural middle classes, and of the mystified sub-proletariat which crowded into the poverty belts surrounding the luxuriant capitals. It is possible that the idea was not to give over all power to the clergy but preferably to manipulate the religious and secular opposition as a whole to clear the way for the technocrats. Once the battle was won, the clergy would return to their flocks and would busy themselves with the management of their estates. (However, the example of Iran is not too encouraging.) In short, the idea was to replace the ana-chronisms by modernist, liberal formations with a religious outlook or backing. *Modernist* means: capable of setting up an economy enmeshed, by the very constraints of the laws of the market, with that of the West. It also implies the ability to maintain an army efficiently equipped and trained, but closely linked to the Western system of defence. There is also the need to look after the interests of the multinationals whose guardians they are to be. *Liberal* means: capable of exploiting to the utmost parliamentary mystification and political and trade-unionist pluralism in order to enlarge and consol-idate the social basis of the regime. *Religious outlook or backing* means: the re-forging of the good old alliance between the sword and the Koran in order to check any rebirth of radical social movements, and if possible to destabilize the Muslim republics in the USSR. Translated into Koranic terms, this is what Carter wanted to see imp-lemented in this area—'friendly governments, Islamic and liberal, who respect human rights'.

Given the explosive contradictions at work, the economic situation approaching bankruptcy almost everywhere, there is nothing to ensure that the will of the Master of the White House be done. Neither the crowned monarchy nor the jackbooted republic was able to extricate this part of the world from its chronic, general crisis. Will the turbanned republic be able to do so?

Nothing is less likely. The Islamic movements, given their composite social nature and especially their lack of an even remotely credible programme, are not capable of coming to power, or of remaining there for any length of time.

The Muslim Brotherhood

The double failure of the first rising of the modern Egyptian bourgeoisie in 1919, which achieved neither independence nor a constitutional government; Atatürk's abolition of the Islamic caliphate in 1923; the rise of fascism in Italy, which impressed the majority of the average traditionalist Muslim intelligentsia; the rise of Stalinism in the USSR, which attracted the attention of the left-wing Christian intellectuals, who were also fascinated by the impotent cult of power; finally the grimness of the inter-war period, dominated by the general feeling of defeat of Western civilization, with its basis in the cult of science and of reason—all these created an environment that favoured the irruption of the irrational into contemporary history.

In this setting, the Fraternity of Muslim Brethren was founded in Egypt in 1928, only a few months before the outbreak of the crisis of 1929, which was to lead to the Second World War. Their organizational model was based both on esoteric Muslim sects of the Middle Ages and on modern fascism. Article 2 of their statutes states that members must undertake 'to submit to iron discipline and to carry out the orders of their superiors'. Their charismatic 'Supreme Guide' is, like a caliph, beyond all questioning. From their founding, the Brethren chose to collaborate with the regime in power. Thus they immediately came to terms with the 'iron hand' government of Muhammad Mahmud, then with that of the dictator Isma'il Sidqi, and even with the Suez Canal Company; the latter contributed £500 to their funds, in order to encourage them to dampen the ardour of the youth of the secular Wafd party, which at that time had broken with the British. (The Brethren were the only Egyptian group to have a newspaper.)

In fact, their nostalgic appeals for the restoration of the Golden

Age of Islam, the crossed swords and the Koran which served them as emblems, symbolizing to perfection the morbid ideal of the practice of death, attracted to their cause a whole layer of the frustrated petty-bourgeois youth, who were horribly repressed, prey to all sorts of fears, and hostile to any pleasurable activity. In short, the palace and the British used the Brethren as an anaesthetic.

During the Second World War, despite their sympathy for the Axis, the Brethren supported the Allies, apparently for tactical reasons. In practice they were able to use the mosques for their propaganda and to establish themselves especially in the schools and in the countryside.

As a result of their truly Machiavellian tactics, the organization of the Brethren became, in less than thirteen years, the most formidable mass party. In 1941, the Brethren allied with the Sa'dists, the party in power, which was close to the palace. As soon as the latter was ousted from the harem, they had not the slightest hesitation in joining forces with its rival and successor, the Wafd. When the Wafd was in turn eliminated from office, they allied once again with the same Sa'dists who, it is true, allowed them to set up a para-military organization, *al-Jawwala*, with some twenty thousand members. Later they allied with the National Committee of Students and Workers, spear-headed by the Communists. Not longer after, they opposed the Committee by supporting the government of the famous Isma'il Sidqi, leader of the Sa'dists. But just before the elections, the latter broke his alliance with the Brotherhood, which by that time numbered half a million members and sympathizers. In December 1948, suspecting that the Brotherhood wished to take power, al-Naqrashi, the head of the government, outlawed the movement. Their response was immediate. Al-Naqrashi was assassinated by a medical student, a member of the movement. For a whole year, the authorities manoeuvred Hasan al-Banna', the Supreme Guide of the Brethren, from one compromise to another, until he disowned his own followers by publicly declaring that 'they are not brethren and even less Muslims'. He was finally killed in 1949. His successor, the magistrate Hasan al-Hudaibi, allied the Brotherhood once again with the palace, and was even solemnly received by King Faruq, who stated in his presence and with his agreement: 'Since the British will soon leave Egypt, our only enemy now is communism'. But when Faruq was ousted by Nasser in 1952, the Brethren supported the latter with the same fervour. However, the honeymoon did not last long. When Nasser decided to limit individual landed property holdings to 200 acres, the Brethren suggested the figure of 500 and also demanded that the new government undertake to re-Islamize society and the state. In 1954 they attempted to assassinate the president. Their Brotherhood was disbanded. In 1959, it was clandestinely re-formed, and once again decapitated in 1965. Sadat, himself a former member of the Brotherhood, allowed them to reappear in 1972 and to publish a journal, *al-Da'wa* (the Sermon). Similarly, the Muslim International founded by al-Banna' in the 1930s was reconstituted in Cairo. Through it, Egypt, amongst others, gave aid to the armed vanguard, the Mujahidin, who are at present fighting the Syrian regime.

In the writings of the Brethren, any social programme is conspicuous by its absence. Al-Banna' justified his refusal to outline a programme by his desire to 'avoid the possibility of a great schism between the various Muslim rites and confessions'. When one fine day the leaders of the para-military organization of the Brotherhood informed him that they were in a position to take power, he challenged them to submit to him within a week an Islamic radio programme for the first week of the *coup d'état*—a task they were incapable of fulfilling.

After the death of the leader, it fell to Muhammad al-Ghazali, an ideologist of the Brotherhood, to risk undertaking this project. In his book *Islam and the Economic Orders* he devotes a whole chapter to the 'intermediate economic order' of Islam. After dismissing 'that Jew Marx' in a few words, he reveals to us the secret of the Islamic economic order, 'alone capable of saving humanity'. 'It is the economic order', he writes, 'that was implemented in fascist Italy, in Nazi Germany, and which is still in force in Britain, thanks to state control of the big firms and to the state holding over 50 per cent of the shares in these firms'.[8] Clearly, 'the Islamic economy' is simply state control and militarization of the economy, as practised since the First World War. Rather more subtly, Sayyid Qutb, another of the Brotherhood's thinkers, does not have faith in any programme. In 1964, one year before his execution by Nasser, he published his swan-song,

8. *Islam and the Economic Order*, Beirut (in Arabic), pp. 62 – 63.

whose title sounds like a call for the re-Islamization by the sword of an apostate society: *The Jahiliya of the 20th Century (Jahiliyat al-qarn al-'ishrin)*. The *Jahiliya*, the period of pre-Islamic paganism, is usually depicted as 'inadmissibly permissive', full of *joie de vivre* and with no ethic other than love, wine, and hunting. And Qutb says: 'Give us power and you shall see; we shall obliterate all trace of this paganism.'

In other countries, other Islamic organizations proved equally incapable of elaborating a programme for their Islamic state. In 1972, when the government of the United Arab Emirates invited Hasan al-Turabi, the Supreme Guide of the Brethren in the Sudan, to write an Islamic constitution, his reply was at first negative: 'This is a difficult task', he said. But they would not take no for an answer, and with the help of petro-dollars he managed to do it. This was the constitution that allowed Shaikh Zaid Ibn Sultan to be the absolute boss of Abu Dhabi.

Even the Syrian Muslim Brethren have not been able to overthrow a hard-pressed minority regime with which they had been openly at war, despite massive aid from Jordan, Saudi Arabia, and elsewhere —mainly because they are incapable of producing a programme likely to attract the other forces hostile to the regime.

In my opinion, this is an open revelation of the historic impossibility of the implementation for any length of time of an Islamic society in a world which commodity production and its consequences have unified and predisposed to an alternative order, in which the return to religion has no place.

Return to What?

Given their inability to address the downtrodden masses with a programme that makes any sense, the integralists—consummate demagogues that they are—have opted for the facile slogan of return to primitive Islam, the Islam of the four *Rashidun*, the 'rightly guided' early caliphs, who supposedly differed from all their successors in their strict respect for the Koran and their adherence to the procedure of consulting the communal council of believers. Al-Afghani even speaks of a return to the era of the libertine caliph, Harun al-

Rashid, when Islam—more than in any other period—played the role of a mere state ideology. It is therefore a question of a return to the imperial power of Islam, but not to the Islam that respects its dogmas.

It will be obvious that the Koran, the trans-historical constitution of the Islamic *umma*, has never been entirely respected, even by the first four caliphs. Muhammad never hesitated to delete verses which the evolution of his sermons, or the demands of his alliances, had rendered anachronistic. Thus the well-known Meccan verse in favour of the *mustaz'afin* (the downtrodden) was replaced by another favouring those with property: 'We have, said Allah, favoured some and not others as far as riches are concerned.' Muhammad, however, had a water-tight alibi—did he not claim to be in touch with Allah himself, whose acts are inscrutable?

The period of the first four caliphs was in no way the Golden Age that contemporary legend depicts. There were cruel struggles for power. Of the four 'rightly guided' caliphs, only Abu Bakr died a natural death—and *his* caliphate was exceptionally short. The three others were assassinated: 'Umar by a Persian slave; 'Uthman at the hands of one of Abu Bakr's own sons, 'Abd al-Rahman; and 'Ali by Muslims just as pious as himself. Less than thirty-seven years after the founding by Muhammad of the first Arab-Muslim state at Medina, the Community of Believers, whom he had always instructed to remain united in the faith and in the law, split into two groups, which were mortal enemies.

Since the caliphate of Mu'awiya, the fifth caliph, and the consolidation of the conquering Arab-Muslims as a ruling class, the Koran has been continually trampled underfoot by the caliphs of Islam, who merely used it as a sort of philosophy of history, a state ideology, to justify the redistribution of power and goods.

The Shi'ites do not demand a return to the times of the first four caliphs. They describe Abu Bakr, 'Umar, and 'Uthman as 'usurpers'. Indeed, 'Ali was reluctant to swear allegiance to them, and disapproved of their rule. And if 'Uthman defeated him in the bid for power, it was effectively because he refused to follow the example of Abu Bakr and 'Umar. The insurgents who assassinated 'Uthman, moreover, were in league with him.

Iran

A return to 'Ali's caliphate—from first to last a period of open civil war—would mean a return to one of the most troubled times of the whole history of Islam. In this respect, Iran has succeeded.

Some Islamic ideologists consider that in Khomeini's Iran, Islam has gone beyond the confines of Wahhabi reformism, with its pan-Islamism and its creed of the *jihad*, and has entered upon its ultimate evolution: the revolutionary stage. Intellectually incapable of understanding their own period, they do not realize that Khomeinism, in a period when the revolution can only be social, contains absolutely no project that is in any way progressive.

On the contrary, in Iran Islam can congratulate itself on having caught up, five centuries later, with the Europe of the Inquisition. Recently, Bani Sadr, the head of state, wondered in his *Inqilab Islami*: 'Is it true that an Inquisition-like tribunal has been set up in the university?'. But the Holy Inquisition was set up throughout the country at the outset, under the crosier of that blood-thirsty psychopath Ayatollah Khalkhali.

This inquisition is not the work of the Islamic Republican Party alone, but of all those in power. They are incapable of dealing with the crisis, and can only resort to appeals for austerity and the practice of violent repression. The Iranian working class lost more than seventy thousand members in the struggle to get rid of the Shah. Their only reward is a medieval religious dictatorship, plus the horrors of inflation (70 per cent), of unemployment (4 million), and the humiliation of public whipping for the simple act of drinking beer, or because a woman bathed on a beach reserved for men. The two million drug addicts, mainly located in South Tehran, were given six months to kick the habit—otherwise they would be executed.

This cult of death may well fascinate a large number of middle-class youths, who are the victims of emotional blocks and are frightened of freedom and libertarian ways. It is, however, no solution to the real problems shaking the very foundations of Iranian society.

A person such as Khomeini, who suffers from historical sclerosis, who in his book *Islamic Government* deals with such serious problems as the buggery of a poor donkey by a poor Muslim, and who is incapable of creating an Iranian bourgeoisie, can only return to the

American fold or fall under Soviet influence. 'We are less independent today', admits Bani Sadr, 'than we were under the Shah. Our
budget depends on the credit of foreign banks. Our dependence on
arms and foreign military experts is quite simply tragic.'[9] Has Bani
Sadr, the spiritual son of the Imam, finally grasped that in a world
unified by the violence of the laws of the market Iran cannot be
independent, whether the Imam, present or absent, likes it or not?
Has he understood that the Koran cannot be applied in one area of
capital importance: the banking system? Before the Shah left, this
Islamic economist calmly promised those who wanted to listen that
he would abolish the banking system, 'as it is incompatible with the
prohibition of usury in the Koran'. Has he now realized that this
abolition requires the fulfilment of nineteen conditions which would
take nineteen years? Obviously, the logic of capital is stronger than
all the prohibitions of all the religions.

The middle classes, who at first idolized Khomeini in the belief
that they had found in him the universal miracle cure, now turn away
from him to await the *coup d'état*. The sub-proletariat, who served
him as cannon fodder, now suffer more than ever with the repression
of Khalkhali. The proletariat is engaged in a permanent struggle in
the work-places to counter the intervention of the Islamic committees, and stop specific strikes only to return to their permanent go-
slow.

Contrary to what Islamic propaganda claims, and many Western
leftists believe, today's Iran does not represent the reinvigoration of
Islam but its swan-song, except that it lacks any beauty.

*   *   *

The fallacy of a new Islam, which many people have fallen for, is
now beginning to be dispelled. The awakening of the 'ordinary
people' could be fatal for it. In fact, the 'ordinary people', although
contaminated by the plague of Koranic fatalism, are everywhere
dissatisfied by this over-abstract Allah—too distant and too impene-
trable to play a role in their daily life. This is why the ordinary
Muslim, both in Africa and in Asia, is so fond of totemic and pagan
cults under the façade of Islam. He reveres fetishes, amulets,

9. The Beirut daily *al-Anwar*, 24 September 1980.

marabouts, and tombs which help him to deal with the suffering of everyday life, to cure ills and to foretell the future. This humble Muslim, once the first surprise and the enthusiasm is over, appears as unwilling for and even resistant to a literal application of Koranic barbarity, which condemns him to asceticism, flagellation, and stoning. In a moment of frankness, Hasan al-Banna' admitted in 1947 to the members of his Brotherhood that the first obstacle they would meet on the path to the re-Islamization of secular Muslim society, in his opinion, would be the hostility of the people. 'I must tell you', he said, 'that your preaching is still a closed book to the majority. The day when they discover it and realize what it aims for they will resist violently and oppose you tenaciously.' He added, 'You will first have to confront the ignorance of ordinary people concerning the truth of Islam.'[10] In fact, for the people Islam is more of a refuge than a set of deadly dogmas—take for example the public transgression this year of the fast of Ramadan in countries such as Egypt and Iran where Islamic discourse dominates.

The return to Islamic archaism is part of the process of totalitarian uniformization of all aspects of cultural consumption. Outside the confines of the dominant model—that of Islam for the Muslim and of Christianity for the Christian, that of Judaism for the Jew and that of the media for all—thinking is forbidden. There is no room left for free and critical reflection. The arbitrary in Khomeini's Iran encroaches even on the freedom of choice in clothing for women and in choice of food for all.

Under the rule of a mercantile civilization, which impoverishes more each day and is in its own way bigoted, any creation becomes necessarily heretical. When Khomeinist moralism becomes the norm, any reflection or 'abnormal' act can only be punished.

Apart from its exemplary punishments, Islamic archaism has nothing new to offer. It appears to me to be part of the process of the break-up of the state in a world which is becoming ungovernable. If the Islamic movements were to take power following the failure and the expected fall of Khomeinism, they could only profoundly destabilize the Islamic world, which is already smitten with crisis, terrorism, and open or masked civil war. It is, however, obvious that

10. *Sayings of the Martyr Hasan al-Banna*, pamphlet published by 'Ibad al-Rahman (the Lebanese Brethren), Beirut 1960 (in Arabic).

Islamic archaism cannot come to power, or remain in power in an acceptable manner. Its force is already spent before it begins.

'After the death of God', says Nietzsche, 'the most difficult thing to overcome is his shadow.'

His sinister shadow is this stupid and stupefying society, which produces and reproduces religion and spectacle; this society of exploitation, of radical alienation, of emotional plague, of loneliness, of insecurity, of degeneration, of generalized passivity, of representations that represent nothing but themselves, of waste and malnutrition, of fear and war. If religion is the sigh of the oppressed creature, it will cease to exist when that creature is no longer oppressed but has become the creator of his own daily history.

Religion, Zionism, and Secularism

Ehud Ein-Gil

When man's life lay for all to see foully grovelling upon the ground, crushed beneath the weight of Religion, which displayed her head in the regions of heaven, threatening mortals from on high with horrible aspect, a man of Greece was the first that dared to uplift mortal eyes against her, the first to make stand against her; for neither fables of the gods could quell him, nor the thunderbolts, nor heaven with menacing roar, nay all the more they goaded the eager courage of his soul, so that he should desire, first of all men, to shatter the confining bars of nature's gates. Therefore the lively power of his mind prevailed, and forth he marched far beyond the flaming walls of the heavens, as he traversed the immeasurable universe in thought and imagination; whence victorious he returns bearing his prize, the knowledge what can come into being, what can not, in a word, how each thing has its powers defined and its deep-set boundary mark. Wherefore Religion is now in her turn cast down and trampled underfoot, whilst we by the victory are exalted high as heaven.

One thing I fear in this matter, that in this your apprenticeship to philosophy you may perhaps see impiety, and the entering on a path of crime; whereas on the contrary too often it is that very Religion which has brought forth criminal and impious deeds.

LUCRETIUS, *DE RERUM NATURA*

India is supposed to be a religious country above everything else, and Hindu and Moslem and Sikh and others take pride in their faiths and testify to their truth by breaking heads. The spectacle of what is called religion, or at any rate organized religion, in India and else-where has filled me with horror, and I have frequently condemned it and wished to make a clean sweep of it. Almost always it seems to stand for blind belief and reaction, dogma and bigotry, superstition and exploitation, and the preservation of vested interests. And yet I knew well that there was something else in it, something which supplied a deep inner craving of human beings. How else could it have been the tremendous power it has been and brought peace and comfort to innumerable tortured souls? Was that peace merely the shelter of blind belief and absence of questioning, the calm that comes from being safe in harbour, protected from the storms of the open sea, or was it something more? In some cases certainly it was something more. . . .

A Roman Catholic friend sent me in prison many books on Catholicism and Papal Encyclicals and I read them with interest. Studying them, I realized the hold it had on such large numbers of people. It offered, as Islam and popular Hinduism offer, a safe anchorage from doubt and mental conflict, an assurance of a future life which will make up for the deficiencies of this life.

I am afraid it is impossible for me to seek harbourage in this way. I prefer the open sea, with all its storms and tempests. Nor am I greatly interested in the after life, in what happens after death. I find the problems of this life sufficiently absorbing to fill my mind. The traditional Chinese outlook, fundamentally ethical and yet irreligious or tinged with religious scepticism, has an appeal for me, though in its application to life I may not agree. It is the Tao, the path to be followed and the way of life that interests me: how to understand life, not to reject it but to accept it, to conform to it and to improve it. But the usual religious outlook does not concern itself with this world. It seems to me to be the enemy of clear thought, for it is based not only on the acceptance without demur of certain fixed and unalterable theories and dogmas, but also on sentiment and emotion and passion. It is far removed from what I consider spirituality and things of the spirit, and it deliberately or unconsciously shuts its eyes to reality lest reality may not fit in with preconceived notions. It is narrow and intolerant of other opinions and ideas; it is self-centred and egotistic, and it often allows itself to be exploited by self-seekers and opportunists.

This does not mean that men of religion have not been and are not still often of the highest moral and spiritual type. But it does mean that the religious outlook does not help, and even hinders, the moral and spiritual progress of a people, if morality and spirituality are to be judged by this world's standards, and not by the hereafter. Usually religion becomes an asocial quest for God or the Absolute, and the religious man is concerned far more with his own salvation than with the good of society. The mystic tries to rid himself of self, and in the process usually becomes obsessed with it. Moral standards have no relation to social needs, but are based on a highly metaphysical doctrine of sin. And organized religion invariably becomes a vested interest and thus inevitably a reactionary force opposing change and progress.

J. NEHRU, *AUTOBIOGRAPHY*

The success of the 'Islamic revolution' in Iran and its effects on many Muslims in the neighbouring countries have focused the world's attention on this religious phenomenon, as though it were an exceptional revival, peculiar to Islam, of medieval ideas in the last quarter of the twentieth century. The facts, of course, are quite different. Religious revival has been registered during the last few years in various parts of the world. Outstanding examples are the mass welcome of the Pope in the United States (the 'first world'), Poland (the 'second world'), and Mexico (the 'third world'); the growth of various religious and mystical sects, mostly of Asian origin, in the West, where they have attracted many young people; the strengthened hold of Catholicism in Latin America, following the spread of the 'revolutionary priests' movement; and the 'repentance' of Israeli Jews who 'go back' to orthodox Judaism.

Each instance of this religious revival has its own social causes, specific to its own place and time. Nevertheless, since capitalism has embraced the world of the twentieth century and has formed it into one entity, this religious revival, with its various specific causes, has a common social background.

This assertion might seem far-fetched, were it not for the fact that the same 'psychological' or 'psycho-social' terms are used everywhere to explain the religious revival. 'Frustration', 'alienation', 'helplessness', 'a dead-end feeling'—do these words describe the emotions of an Iranian peasant towards the penetration of modern capitalism and its cultural values into his country, or the feelings of an American youth in the face of the economic (but also ideological) crisis that has hit modern industrial society, or the sentiments of a

Polish worker confronted with a rigid bureaucratic regime and the ever-felt presence of the Soviet Union behind it? These words in fact provide some explanation, however superficial, for the feelings of people under all three regimes, in all three parts of today's world.

At the root of the religious revival is the ideological crisis of our time. For about a hundred years, the feelings of frustration and alienation had an outlet: there was hope for change, there was faith that despite many retreats the world was moving forwards, to a better future. There was less reason for feelings of dead-end helplessness. And in the absence of these, there was no impetus for searches for a religious alternative. The way out, the hope, the alternative were seen as bound up with the forward motion of the wheels of history; 'one more thrust forwards' was needed in order to allow the achievements of science and technology to be used for the benefit of the whole of society, in order to overthrow capitalism and establish the socialist society for which so many yearned. It was those whose class interests were threatened by that advance who tried to find refuge in religion, or used it as 'opium for the masses' in order to blunt the latter's desire for change. Even where socialism seemed far off, as in the Third World, hopes were still pinned on advance, industrialization, modernization.

But despite various successes, the experience of the last hundred years has generally been a bitter one. The thrust forwards has given birth not to socialism but to a series of oppressive bureaucratic regimes, which are far from providing a credible alternative to capitalism not only in the industrialized countries but now also in the countries of the Third World. The same thrust forwards also gave rise, albeit indirectly, to fascist regimes, which were put up by capitalism as one more line of defence against the forces of social revolution. At the same time, it has become clear that under capitalism the countries of the Third World cannot make great and significant advances.

As the road of 'progress' appeared to be a blind alley, alternatives began to be sought in the past. Hence the search for 'roots'; hence the opposition to modern technology (for instance, irrational horror of computers or robots); hence also the fear of catastrophe (atomic war, pollution of the environment, population explosion, star wars, test-tube babies). These fears have also penetrated into circles of the revolutionary left, inducing an atmosphere of disenchantment with progress and encouraging the growth of various reactionary and mystical ideas. (By the way, a similar phenomenon also occurred in Bolshevik circles after the failure of the 1905 Russian revolution, when some members of the left faction of the party started to 'search for God'.)

In these circumstances, it is not surprising that the last few years have been a time of religious revival.

Religious Revival in Israel

Israel, like South Africa, is an unusual state inasmuch as its social structure includes features of developed industrial capitalism alongside colonial-style features of a settler state. This peculiar structure has led the Jewish religious revival in Israel to take a specific path.

The phenomenon of 'return to religion' in Israel (known in Hebrew as *hazarah bitshuvah*—'repentance') is in fact not one but two quite distinct phenomena, although religious circles are trying, rather successfully, to blur the differences between the two.

The first kind of 'return to religion' is a reaction to the existential problems generic to all developed capitalist societies, combined with the dead-end feeling engendered by the loss of faith in meaningful social change. To this is also added, of course, a specific ingredient: the existential problem of the Jews as a minority in the Arab East. But while it is difficult to disentangle the generic factors from the specific ones, I believe that the former predominate, as far as this first kind of 'return to religion' is concerned.

It is perhaps symbolic that the first famous 'repentant' of this kind in the recent wave of conversions came from the circles of Matzpen and landed, of all places, in the camp of Neturei Karta, the most conservative and hence the least modern sect of Judaism. (It is important to point out that, contrary to other Jewish religious sects and groups, Neturei Karta has remained uncompromisingly hostile to Zionism.) The dozens who have followed him are no different in motivation from those young Israeli Jews (or, for that matter, young people in the West generally) who have been driven by alienation and hopelessness to seek a guru and join various religious or mystic sects. Such conversions constitute a rejection of modern life and society and of their values, and imply—at least in principle—withdrawal from social and political activity.

The second current of 'repentants' in Israel is driven by quite different motives and is composed of people seeking other things altogether. This current consists mainly of ostensibly secular-minded Jews who, due to the ideological malaise of Zionism and the shedding of its last democratic veils in recent years, have found themselves unable to justify their presence in Palestine. The only valid justification—based on the democratic right of every person to live where he or she likes—is unacceptable to them because it also implies the right of the Palestinian refugees to be repatriated. The only way open to such people, so long as they remain Zionists, is to seek legitimation in the 'ancient sources', in the Jewish religious interpretation of history.

This current includes people who begin to practise some—but definitely not all—of the precepts of Judaism, as well as many ostensibly secular-minded people who for reasons of convenience continue to ignore all religious precepts, but are willing to allow the clericalists to run wild as they please, because they are the bearers of the 'legitimation' and 'justification' for the Jewish presence in Palestine.

Since the first-mentioned current is similar in nature to well-known phenomena in the Western world, and since it is mainly made up of individuals genuinely searching for a solution to their existential problems, I shall not discuss it any further. The second current, on the contrary, is specific to Israel and is overtly political; I shall therefore deal with it in some detail.

The Alliance Between 'Secular' and 'Religious' Zionists

From its very beginning, Zionism was marked by an alliance between 'secular' and 'religious' elements. Claiming to be a 'national movement', Zionism always regarded the preservation of Jewish 'national unity' as a supreme value; and it was always the religious members of the movement who drew the 'red line' beyond which they would prefer to cause a split. Thus the tradition whereby the secular Zionists always make concessions to the religious Zionists when the latter threaten to cause a split is as old as the movement itself. The religious Zionists have always kept the initiative in the movement on matters involving religion.

In addition to the ideological importance of religion as the ultimate source of legitimation for Zionism, the religious Zionists also rendered the whole movement an invaluable service of a more directly political kind. Up to the Second World War, Zionism was a minority movement among world Jewry, opposed not only by Jewish democrats, socialists, and communists, but also by large sections of Orthodox Judaism. The latter condemned Zionism as a heresy against the doctrines of Judaism and particularly against the belief in divine (rather than political) messianic salvation. In the Zionist struggle against this type of religious opposition, religious Zionists played a key role, which goes a long way towards explaining the readiness with which 'secular' Zionists capitulated to their dictates.

The history of the Zionist project in the period immediately following the First World War bears out the importance for Zionism of the collaboration of religious Jews. At that time, Orthodox anti-Zionists were in the majority among the Jewish inhabitants of Palestine. This Orthodox anti-Zionist camp had a spokesman of great stature: Jacob de Haan, a well-known Dutch poet who became a religious Zionist and immigrated to Palestine, where he underwent another conversion and joined the religious anti-Zionist camp. The Zionist leaders' fears of this camp were particularly great because it had a real chance of winning a majority in the elected representative body of the Jewish community in Palestine. The Zionists rightly feared that such an outcome would irreparably damage their chances of maintaining the massive support of the British authorities in Britain and Palestine. The religious argumentation of anti-Zionist Judaism was so effective that the Zionists decided to gag it by force. In 1924, a group of assassins (which included Rachel Yana'it, wife of Yitzhak Ben-Zvi, who was later to become the second president of Israel) murdered Jacob de Haan. These facts were kept secret for decades, and have been published only recently, when most of the protagonists of the affair were no longer alive.

If the Zionists were ready to go so far as to liquidate a spokesman of their religious opponents, they were clearly also ready to go very far in making concessions to their religious allies.

But the main role of religious Zionism was ideological. Religious tradition provided the only legitimation for the Zionist colonization of Palestine. Zionism could not afford to alienate its religious adherents, because in their absence it would lose the ideological justification for the Zionist project in Palestine.

Religion was thus used as a tool by the 'secular' leaders of Zionism. Following the Second World War, during which the Nazis (aided by the acquiescence, and in some cases the actual collaboration, of the Zionist leaders) exterminated millions of Jews, most of whom were anti-Zionist, the majority of Jewish religious leaders harnessed themselves to the Zionist cart. This only served to reinforce Zionism's religious connection, especially in view of the fact that the organized power of Jewish communities in the United States and elsewhere is for the most part concentrated in the hands of rabbis and religious leaders. Israeli Zionist activists and emissaries, including those who regard themselves as atheists, often proudly describe how, on their visit to a Jewish community in Latin America or Eastern Europe, they go to a synagogue to pray. This is invariably described as a 'deeply moving experience'.

At first religion was merely used, in some cases very cynically, by leaders who were non-believers. This is well illustrated by the mission of the 'socialist' Zionist activist Yavni'eli, who was sent to Yemen in 1910 to recruit Yemeni Jews as a cheap labour force, fit to compete with the cheap labour of the Palestinian Arabs and thus serve Zionism in its struggle for 'Jewish labour'. In order to persuade Yemen's Jews to leave their homeland and go to Palestine, Yavni'eli presented himself to them as a herald of the Messiah and declared that the day of salvation had arrived. (For further details see R. Shapiro, 'Zionism and Its Oriental Subjects', *Khamsin 5*, p. 23ff of this volume.)

But in time the attitude of many Zionists to religion became gradually less cynical: they were undergoing a process of self-conversion. A tool used for many years begins to arouse genuine feelings of attachment in its user and becomes a sort of fetish. This is what happened to the 'secular' Zionist leaders; they developed a liking for religion, which had served them as a useful tool for so long. They came to feel that they could not live without it, and even those—still a majority—who are not inclined to practise it personally are nevertheless well-disposed towards those who not only preach it but also wish to impose it on others. Hence the great willingness to allocate lavish public financial support to religious bodies and institutions in today's Israel, where pressing social needs are cast aside because of 'lack of funds'.

The Shifting Status Quo

With the creation of Israel as a 'Jewish State', which grants special privileges to 'Jews' according to the Law of Return, there was an immediate need to define who would be entitled to these privileges—in other words, who is a Jew. As the leaders of religious Zionism threatened that if their demands were not met 'the nation would be split', the religious definition of 'Jew' was adopted. In order to prevent a split, it was decided not to enact a constitution (in which the status of religion in Israel would have had to be defined explicitly) but to subject the citizens of Israel to the jurisdiction of religious institutions—those religious institutions, that is, which are recognized by the state—in all matters of personal law. Thus civil marriage and divorce are not allowed in Israel. Under the same threat of a 'split', the 'secular' Zionists also capitulated to religious dictate in the matter of burial; Israel allows religious burial only, and the 'unity of the nation' is preserved beyond the grave.

Political realities led 'secular' Zionism to an alliance with only one current within the Jewish religion—Orthodox Judaism. This was not because all Orthodox Jews (as opposed to members of the Conservative and Reformed synagogues) were ardent Zionists. On the contrary, some of the most determined opponents of Zionism, including Neturei Karta, belong to the Orthodox camp. But other currents of Judaism were more inclined to seek the integration of Jews in their respective countries as one tolerant and tolerated religious community among many, in tolerant pluralistic societies. For this reason, Orthodox Judaism was the only Jewish religious current to have any real presence in Palestine. (For the sake of clarity it must be pointed out that this current includes both the Sephardi and the Ashkenazi Rabbinates, the anti-Zionist Neturei Karta, the Agudat Israel Party, which had opposed Zionism at first but later accepted it, the National Religious Party, NRP, which is supported by the majority of religious Zionists, as well as the Gush Emunim militants.)

Thus it was the presence in Palestine of Orthodox Judaism, and the absence of other currents, that determined to which religious camp the Zionist movement was to capitulate, as well as the terms of this capitulation. For, despite all the differences and mutual hatred between the various Orthodox groups, they are all united in their adamant opposition to the two other main currents of Judaism. The Reformists and Conservatives are virtually barred from gaining a foothold in Israel; in fact, in some ways they suffer worse discrimination than some non-Jewish religious denominations. They receive no government grants, their rabbis are not empowered to officiate in marriages or to grant divorce, and conversions performed by them are generally not recognized. For example, a person converted to Judaism by the Reformist rabbi Alexander Shindler, leader of the Jewish establishment in the USA, may be refused recognition as a 'Jew' (and hence refused Israeli citizenship under the Law of Return) by the Israeli Ministry of the Interior, which is traditionally a domain of the NRP. The Ministry of Religions, as well as the Religious Councils financed jointly by the government and local authorities, who pay the salaries of a host of Orthodox rabbis (and indeed of many religious officials of recognized non-Jewish denominations), do not employ Reformist or Conservative rabbis.

This systematic discrimination, which gives the lie to the Zionist claim that Israel allows freedom of worship and religious equality to all, is practised and accepted by both main Zionist party blocs, the Likud and the Labour Alignment. Thus, for example, in March 1980 the chairman of the Labour Party, Shim'on Peres, helped the Likud government to pass a new Chief Rabbinate Law, which confirms the exclusion of Reformed and Conservative Judaism from the list of religious denominations recognized in Israel. And this is the same Shim'on Peres who had promised the leaders of these two communities in the USA that when the Labour Party returned to office it would grant equality to all Jewish religious currents.

The Jewish population in Israel is subjected—by virtue of the state's laws—to the grip of the Orthodox clericalists, who impose their code in many spheres of life. Public transport does not operate on Saturdays; cinemas and theatres are closed on Friday nights; during the Passover week bread is not sold; on Yom Kippur the whole country is virtually closed down. Religious studies increasingly encroach upon the syllabus of state schools, and religion dominates personal and family law: the laws concerning marriage, divorce, and burial.

Their experience in turning the Jewish religion into a tool of Zionism led the Zionist leaders to try to make use of other religions as well. Without being consulted, the non-Jewish citizens of Israel were subjected to 'their own' religious establishments. Thus Israel is one of the few remaining countries in which Catholics cannot obtain a divorce (since civil divorce does not exist), and where a man and a woman who may both be atheists but who were born to parents of different religions cannot marry each other.

The state of Israel does not recognize its Palestinian Arab citizens as a national minority, but merely as members of various religious denominations. (Despite this, most Israeli Jews, who resent the fact that the PLO regards *them* merely as a religious community, have never considered demanding that their own government recognize the Palestinians in Israel as a national minority.) The state has bestowed its recognition of Muslim religious officials (which entails payment of a monthly salary as state employees) in a selective manner. In this way virtually the whole Muslim religious establishment has been turned into an instrument used by the authorities for controlling and containing the Palestinian population.

These officially established religious leaders have been a prime target of attacks by all kinds of religious 'reformers' and fundamentalists, who denounce them for 'falsifying Islam' and 'collaborating with the Jews'. Attacks of this kind have recently acquired momentum because, following the victory of the Iranian 'Islamic revolution', circles close to the Muslim Brethren have gained influence among the Palestinians inside Israel. The struggle of these circles is directed primarily against their rivals within the Palestinian community—the Communists and nationalists on the one hand and the officially established religious leaders on the other. Thanks to their struggle against the former, these fundamentalist Islamic circles do not, for the moment, bear the full brunt of the Zionist repressive machine.

The state of Israel 'transformed' its Palestinian citizens from a national minority into a collection of confessional groups; at the same time, the Druze confessional group was 'transformed' into a so-called nationality. In the early 1950s the government made a pact with certain Druze clerics, recognized them as leaders of their community and granted the community itself recognition as a 'nationality'. As part of this deal, young Druze men, unlike other young Arab men, are conscripted into the army. (As a concession to Druze religious sensitivities, young Druze women are exempted.) Is it therefore surprising that among the heads of the Druze Initiative Committee—which struggles against the old Druze leadership, against conscription and for the recognition of the Druze as an inseparable part of the Palestinian Arab people—there is also a religious leader, Shaikh Farhud Farhud?

Since May 1977, when the Likud came to power and Zebulun Hammer, member of the NRP and supporter of Gush Emunim, became minister of education, the penetration of religion into the education system has accelerated. School textbooks have been re-edited: new chapters on Jewish religious subjects were added, and at the instruction of the new minister every picture or illustration showing men or boys was removed if among the figures there was none wearing a skull-cap (that is, a religious Jew); such pictures and illustrations were replaced by new ones, showing boys or men in skull-caps and girls or women in 'modest' dress (long sleeves, low hem-lines). In addition to this hidden brainwashing, there is also open, but no less subtle, brainwashing. School-children are taken on organized tours of synagogues 'in order to acquaint them with their Jewish heritage'. Religious studies (Bible and Talmud) take up a bigger part of the syllabus. In the history syllabus, the share of Jewish history has been increased at the expense of the history of other peoples. There is a definite policy to appoint religious teachers to teach these and other subjects.

All this has been taking place in the so-called *secular* state schools. In Israel, unlike some Western countries, religious studies are provided by the state. In addition to the network of religious state schools, there is an 'autonomous' school system, also financed by the state but run by the Agudat Israel Party, for which the ordinary religious state schools are not strict enough. But the clericalists are not satisfied with these two systems of religious schools and—with the approval of the 'secular' politicians of both the Labour Alignment and the Likud—have made considerable inroads into the so-called secular state schools.

This religious coercion in the educational system meets with hardly any resistance on the part of the non-religious public. Parents put up with the increasing penetration of religious preaching into the schools, just as most Israelis put up with religious coercion in other spheres of life. Many parents even react by saying, 'What is so bad about this? It is good for the kids to be aware of their roots.'

This attitude of acquiescence, or at best indifference, towards religious coercion derives from the same cause as the second current of Israeli 'repentants' mentioned in the beginning of this article.

A Political Religious Revival

The international isolation of Israel following the 1967 war, the diplomatic successes of the Palestinian national movement (which have undermined pro-Zionist ideology around the world) and the economic, social, and ideological crisis of Israeli society have led many Israelis to feel dissatisfied with the ideological justification of Zionism which they had hitherto taken for granted. Even the kibbutzim—strongholds of allegedly secular and socialist Zionism, a version of Zionism that used to be justified as 'egalitarian'—have lost confidence in those old 'values'.

In any case, it is a fact that the Zionist aspiration to 'return to the land of the forefathers' has always had to be legitimated by an appeal to 'the sources'—that is, to the Jewish religion; it is a fact that using the term 'historic rights' as a secular substitute for 'divine promise' has solved nothing, for the channel through which the modern Jew is supposed to have acquired these 'historic rights' is the continuity of Jewish existence over the centuries, which was a religious existence; it is a fact that Zionism from its very beginning was not (as some secular Zionists try to argue) a progressive movement of 'rebellion against religion' but, on the contrary, a reaction *against* secular trends towards the integration of Jews into the society in which they were living—individual integration by assimilation, or political integration through participation in democratic or socialist movements. All these facts constantly undermine the repeated attempts of secular Zionists to sever the organic connection of Zionism with religion. For Zionism and the Jewish religion are tied to each other ideologically as well as in practice. If Zionism were to lose its last ideological line of defence, which is provided by religion, then its true nature would be exposed even to its own adherents—its nature as a colonizing, xenophobic, and racist movement.

In order to counter Arab arguments, the Zionists can no longer be satisfied with their old excuses. In the present world-wide climate of religious revival, the Zionists feel secure in putting forward religious arguments. Moreover, without religious gloss the basic concepts of Zionist ideology and practice—'the Chosen People', 'the Divine Promise', 'hatred of the Gentiles', Jewish colonization and expropriation of non-Jews—are clearly revealed as extreme racism. In putting a religious gloss on these concepts, in presenting them as an integral part of Judaism, the Zionists are in effect attempting to purify an abomination by an appeal to the presumed ethical values of religion. In this connection the Zionists can use their favourite weapon of emotional blackmail: anyone who rejects the fundamental principles of Zionism and attacks its basic concepts, which are justified by means of religion, is represented as attacking the principles of Judaism, and anyone attacking Judaism is branded as an anti-Semite. Once this trick is seen to work, it is repeated again and again, until it no longer fools anyone, except those who use it.

What is strange is that religious arguments are used not only by the annexationists. Once the latter had put forward their religious justification, their opponents too—'moderate' Zionists, including such people as the anti-clericalist member of Knesset, Shulamit Aloni—were not far behind with quotations from the Old Testament and from the writings of various rabbis, intended to prove that there is religious sanction for withdrawal from the occupied territories (or for abortions, or for the right of illegitimate children to marry, and so on). In this way the debate comes full circle: everyone uses religious arguments, political controversy gradually turns into theological disputation; and religion celebrates.

Is it therefore surprising that it is Gush Emunim that has become the spearhead of annexationism, rather than the Movement for Greater Eretz Israel, which had been established much earlier and attempted to justify annexation with 'secular' arguments? Is it surprising that virtually all the 'secular' annexationists have joined the bandwagon of Gush Emunim and have willingly capitulated to all its religious demands? Is it surprising, too, that the opponents of Gush Emunim within the Zionist camp have a feeling of inferiority in their ideological debate with it, in view of the combination of 'pioneering energy' and 'total faith' with which the members of the Gush are possessed?

No, there is nothing surprising in all this, just as it should surprise no one that many kibbutzim have in recent years built synagogues for the use of their members, that they have set up well-attended circles for the study of the Old Testament, Talmud, and cabbala, and that this lively religious activity encompasses not only the 'founding fathers' but also their children and descendants. These people are not themselves religious fanatics. In the Zionist camp religious fanatics are a numerically insignificant minority, but their activities are supported by a much larger minority of believers, and legitimated by the vast majority of the Jewish public in Israel. The motives for this support and legitimation are for the most part not merely religious but clearly political. And, as I pointed out earlier, those who have used religion as a tool for so long grow attached to it and fetishize it into what eventually becomes a kind of religious faith.

The Secular Struggle

From the foregoing it should be clear why, despite the growing clericalization of many spheres of life in Israel, the secular or anti-clerical struggle has scored no significant success. The small steps that the 'secular' Zionist parties were pressurized into taking against clericalist opposition, such as the legalization of abortion for social reasons, were short-lived. The League Against Religious Coercion, which in its heyday in the 1960s managed to mobilize several thousand to street demonstrations, flickered out and disintegrated following the capitulation of the political parties that had supported it—particularly Mapam—to their interest in getting a share of political power through an accommodation with the clericalists. But the League was not a secularist movement. It campaigned only against religious coercion, and in doing so was supported by some religious people who were disgusted by the way in which both religious and 'secular' leaders were making use of religion. Even so, the League did not escape being accused by the clericalists of trying to 'divide the people'. (In this connection it is worth pointing out that the clericalists, who so often accuse others of 'divisiveness' are in fact themselves divisive in the worst sense: it is they who press for discrimination between the 'priestly tribe'—which includes every Cohen, Katz, Kaplan, etc.— and other Jews, between Sephardim and Ashkenazim, men and women, 'bastards'—Jews born of 'impure' or incestuous union, who are barred from marrying—and 'proper' Jews.)

The separation of religion from Zionism—which is the true meaning of the aim of would-be secular Zionists—would seriously undermine the Zionist ideological edifice, and for this reason any struggle for this aim, insofar as it remains tied to Zionist ideology, is doomed to failure. For this reason, too, it is difficult to find 'secular' Zionists who are prepared to wage a determined and consistent struggle for this aim.

One of the biggest mistakes made by most Israeli anti-clericalist campaigners was to assume that the majority of Israeli Jews are secularists, who perceive the clericalists' *diktat* as an oppressive imposition and are ready to rebel against it. Thinking that they represented a 'silent secular majority', those anti-clericalist campaigners made far-reaching statements and demands that had no basis in reality. Their tactics were founded on the illusion that broad masses could be easily mobilized for the struggle, and when it became clear that the masses would not respond to the clarion call of their self-appointed 'leadership', the latter soon sank into despair.

The Israeli Secularist Movement, founded in early 1977, still suffers from some of the weaknesses that had led to the defeat of previous anti-clericalist struggles. But in defining itself as *secularist*, and thus emphasizing a positive value in contraposition to religion, the Movement has acquired strength to persevere despite its small numbers (after three years in existence, it only had about three hundred members), as well as the patience required for making a thorough assessment of the situation. In the 13th issue (July 1979) of the movement's paper, *Mabba' Hofshi* (Free Expression), there is the text of a lecture, entitled 'Theological Politics', delivered by Gershon Weiler during a night of discussion held by the Movement in Kibbutz Ga'aton. This is how he assesses the position of secularism in Israel:

'All these matters we are talking about, it must be clear to us, do not interest about sixty per cent of the people of this country. About forty per cent understand what we are saying, and of these about thirty per cent are firmly against us. We are left with ten per cent who both understand and agree with us, and of these ten, nine do not go with us because they have other considerations, economic interests, interests of peace and war. We remain one per cent. Our struggle, the struggle of the one per cent—let us be clear about what is happening in this country—is over the remaining nine per cent.'

And later he says: 'As far as educating the people is concerned, what must be destroyed . . . is the consciousness of elitism, of the Chosen People. And I say this deliberately in kibbutzim, in this kibbutz, because I was surprised to discover that one of the processes that seems to be taking place in the kibbutzim is that people are falling for this elitism of the Chosen People in various forms, and I remonstrate against this.

'The normalization of the Jewish people has two meanings. One meaning is accepted by everybody. Yes, they say, the Jewish people has become normalized; there is now a Jewish postal service, a Jewish army, Jewish roads, and so on. This administrative technical part is acceptable to everyone. But there is also another aspect, the secularization of life; and this is rejected as I said by ninety per cent, including those who do not understand and those who are against it. They oppose secularization and normalization in the sense of giving life a secular meaning.'

Although Gershon Weiler is a professor of philosophy, he has managed to grasp the true relation of forces in the struggle between clericalists and secularists. One can hardly expect more than that from him, because, being a 'teacher of ideas', he likes to be listened to rather than to listen. That is why he is capable of blurting out this rubbish about 'Jewish postal services' and 'Jewish roads', things which do not exist. Gershon Weiler does not call himself a Zionist, and is not particularly interested in world Jewry. But neither does he grasp the complexity of the connection between Zionism and religion. He is therefore obsessed by one issue, on which he bombards the press with letters and on which he speaks whenever he gets the chance: the exemption from military service of Jewish women who declare themselves to be religious.

In his battle for 'freedom' and 'equality', Weiler does not struggle for a uniform criterion for exemption on conscientious grounds which would be applicable to all—men and women, religious and non-religious, Arabs and Jews—but would like religious Jewish women to be *compelled* to do military service. He is not alone in this, and on several occasions the leadership of the Secularist Movement has allowed itself to be carried away into making statements that smack of anti-religious coercion. And on these occasions many of the Movement's Zionist members were surprised to discover that it is precisely the anti-Zionist socialists of Matzpen who, within the movement, insist on consistent support for the principle of religious freedom.

What are members of Matzpen doing in the Secularist Movement? The answer is that the Movement's aims are formulated in sufficiently broad and general terms to allow for a very wide spectrum of views.

Nevertheless, no political party has dared openly to support these aims. The 'secular' Zionist parties are afraid of antagonizing some of their own members who are religious, and the religious parties, who are their potential coalition partners. And the Communist Party (RAKAH) has also preferred to keep well away from the Movement; because RAKAH too is flirting with certain religious circles—in this case Palestinian Arab, whether they are Muslim, Christian, or Druze.

Although the Israeli Secularist Movement is by no means anti-Zionist, and only a small minority of its members are anti-Zionists, it cannot help but run foul of the nexus between Zionism and the Jewish religion. The majority of the movement's members try in vain to unravel this Gordian knot with their bare hands, but from time to time they are forced to cast a fleeting glance in the direction of Alexander's sword.

In April 1980 the Movement held its annual general meeting, attended by some seventy members. The resolutions proposed at that meeting, as well as the amendments finally adopted, illustrate the clash of views within the movement, as well as the occasional fleeting glance. In some cases, the 'compromise' finally adopted is so far-reaching that some of those who voted for it would probably not do so on second thought.

One of the proposed resolutions said: 'The Meeting states that the Movement has come into existence in order to wage political-ideological war for a secular state, and is therefore open to all who support this idea . . . '. After several amendments, the following final text won a decisive majority: 'The Meeting states that the Movement has come into existence in order to wage an ideological war for a secularist world-view and for a secular, free, and democratic state, and is therefore open to all who support this idea.' One amendment was inserted to emphasize the positive secularist content of the Movement's struggle, as distinct from mere anti-clericalism. The second amendment was opposed at first because of its similarity to the PLO formula of 'secular democratic state', and for this reason the word 'free' was added to distinguish one formulation from the other.

If the PLO were serious about its slogan of a 'secular' state, it would have been able to embarrass most members of the Secularist Movement by calling for collaboration between the two organizations. But in reality the PLO is proposing not a secular state but a tri-religious (Muslim, Christian, and Jewish) state, in which Islam would enjoy a measure of hegemony (witness the message of Arafat to Khomeini, in which the Palestinian revolution was described as part of the Islamic revolution). In the state proposed by the PLO the citizens would be classified as belonging to this or that *religious* community—which is not fundamentally different from the existing situation in Israel.

In contrast to the above radical resolution, which was adopted, another proposed resolution said that 'the Israeli Secularist Movement will call for recognition of humanist secularism as one of the four currents which exist within the Jewish people'. This was an expression of the strange attempt to invent something called 'secular Judaism'. Since the term 'Judaism' denotes a particular religion, namely the Jewish religion, 'secular Judaism' is a piece of Orwellian Newspeak. The source of this confusion is the fact that—because Zionist ideology postulates the unity of world Jewry as a supposedly 'national' entity—most Israeli Jews are utterly mystified regarding the distinction between Judaism as a religion and the Israeli-Jewish people as a real national entity. In the event, the members of the Secularist Movement displayed sufficient political maturity to defeat this proposed resolution by an overwhelming majority. But those who are emotionally attached to 'Jewishness' nevertheless succeeded in smuggling it into the Movement through the back door, by pushing through a 'compromise' resolution: 'The Movement regards humanistic secularism as part of the spiritual heritage of the Jewish people.'

Someone even proposed a resolution saying that 'the Movement condemns the phenomenon of Jewish emigration from Israel, and will combat it to the best of its ability'. Although the majority in the meeting were Zionists, they protested strongly against this attempt to drag in 'matters that have nothing to do with the secularist cause'. This was the crudest attempt to harness the Secularist Movement to the interests of Zionism; and it was defeated. It does not follow that the Movement's Zionist members realize that secularism and Zionism are incompatible; but many of them clearly sense that secularism cannot go all the way with Zionism.

Another resolution, adopted unanimously, also points to the direction in which the Movement may be going: 'Faced with the waves of Jewish and Muslim fanatic religious revival and "repentance", the Secularist Movement calls upon all Israel's inhabitants, regardless of their origin, to join the Movement and to struggle together and in equality against those on either side who incite human beings against each other in the name of a god who supposedly prefers his own believers who "carry out his commands", and for the enactment of a secular constitution in the spirit of the Movement's principles.'

I have no doubt that the political contradiction between Zionism and secularism is the basic reason for the power of religion and its influence on the minds of most Israeli Jews; it is also one reason why the Secularist Movement cannot become a mass movement. But despite its present confinement to the margin of Israeli society, the quest of the Movement may make a considerable contribution to the ideological struggle against religion and may also help to shatter the widespread myth about the 'secular' nature of the state of Israel.

April 1980

Iran:
Islam and the
Struggle for Socialism

Muhammad Ja'far and Azar Tabari

This article is based in part on a talk given at a Khamsin *public forum in February 1980. An earlier and briefer version of it appeared in* Issues, *May 1980. The present article has since been expanded and new sections have been added.*

Almost two years have elapsed since the fall of the shah and the establishment of the Islamic regime in Iran. Whereas before and shortly after the February 1979 overthrow of the monarchy in Iran events in that country were given prominent, and often exuberant, coverage in the pages of the left press, they have since been demoted to occasional references to this or that new repressive move by the regime. More frequently, old rhetorical cliches against US imperialism and other non-problematic targets are paraded.

It is no exaggeration to say that none of the expectations, predictions, and prognoses of left circles, whether inside or outside Iran, has been confirmed by the passage of time. The speed with which a highly repressive and deeply reactionary regime has emerged, in the wake of colossal mass mobilizations involving millions, has left many in political shock and disillusionment.

There are lessons, however, that have to be drawn, particularly for revolutionaries from Muslim societies; for it is clear that an Islamic 'alternative' has succeeded in gaining mass political allegiance in Iran. The repercussions are not limited to that country alone. Signs of Shi'ite revivalism are evident in Iraq and other Arab countries. A new growth of pan-Islamism seems likely. To avoid impressionistic generalizations and hasty conclusions, a thorough critical balance-sheet of Iranian events from a revolutionary socialist viewpoint is long overdue.

1. WHAT REALLY HAPPENED IN IRAN?

The key to understanding the events of the past two years in Iran is the character of the mass movement. At its height, the struggle against the shah engulfed the overwhelming majority of the urban population in street demonstrations involving the most enormous mass mobilizations since the Chinese revolution. The very breadth of the movement, and the fact that it was fighting one of the world's most repressive and powerful dictatorships, presented a picture too alluring to be marred by any unpleasant observations about its goals or leadership. The apparent ability of the Islamic clergy to dominate events was dismissed as incidental. It was often simply denied that the Islamic hierarchy genuinely commanded mass allegiance. Alternatively, those who were unable to convince themselves that Islam was secondary or irrelevant, fastened their gaze in another direction. Perhaps the mullahs did stand in the forefront of the movement, but if so, it was primarily because of their intransigent opposition to the shah. The implication was that masses of people could not possibly be drawn into action around a mystical or backward-looking programme. Or if they were temporarily so moved, their consciousness would automatically undergo a progressive evolution as the struggle unfolded.

In fact, there is no reason, logical or sociological, why the oppressed cannot be mobilized in a sustained fight for reactionary objectives. Indeed, history is sadly laden with such instances. Moreover, far from being an empty abstraction, a political system based on Islamic precepts is inherently retrograde, regardless of the forces opposing its establishment. A reactionary struggle is not rendered progressive simply because its opponents are themselves reactionary.

Despite its mass character, the anti-shah movement was not undifferentiated. Its politically coherent core was made up of the traditional urban petty bourgeoisie, organized through the many mosques and various religious societies. The political and social programme behind which these masses mobilized was embodied in the concept of 'Islamic government'. The Shi'ite clerical hierarchy, the theological student body, and many young enthusiasts finding the embodiment of their social ideals in Islam provided the ideologues and political leaders with whose aid the traditional petty bourgeoisie was able to draw the rest of the urban population in its wake.

In its upper range, this traditional petty bourgeoisie overlapped, sociologically and politically, with sections of the traditional traders of the bazaar and with a certain portion of the bourgeoisie that had remained unconnected to the state apparatus that had burgeoned around the Pahlavi court and its entourage since the late 1950s. This section of the bourgeoisie lacked access to one of the crucial mechanisms of 'primitive accumulation': state handouts and subsidies. Since state agencies dominated most investment opportunities, this sector was deprived of outlets by its lack of access to top state functionaries.

The political representatives of these layers were the remnants of the National Front, headed by Sanjabi, and the Freedom Movement, headed by Bazargan. Since the days of Mosaddeq in the late 1940s and early 1950s, the National Front had lost much of its social base and most of its political influence. Part of the former was integrated into the growing modern bourgeoisie, finding its place in the new state apparatus and taking full advantage of a booming economy. Another significant part had declared its disillusionment with the National Front by breaking away in the early 1960s and founding the Freedom Movement, an attempt to amalgamate Iranian nationalism and Islam and thus to mend relations with the more traditional religious currents.

In its lower reaches, the traditional urban petty bourgeoisie shaded into the multi-million masses of urban poor: pauperized artisans and shopkeepers and uprooted peasant migrants. The already appalling living conditions of the urban poor became unbearable as the Iranian economy sank into crisis in 1975 – 76. By the time of the Amouzgar cabinet (1976) unemployment was approaching one million and the official inflation rate stood near 30 per cent. Rising unemployment and inflation made everyday life precarious and inculcated in the urban poor a desperation that would later find expression in militancy. Their traditional fatalism and longing hopes for a better life were fused in the promised paradise of social justice offered by the clergy under the banner of Islam. The absence of any unemployment benefits or other welfare and social services gave the clergy the unique opportunity to disburse part of their traditional charity funds (*zakât*) in order to lend some material force to their promises.

The major battalions of the working class entered the fight in the last few months before February 1979. Deprived of any independent political or organizational experience as a class, disillusioned by the failure of both 'socialism' (as embodied for them by Stalinism internationally and the Tudeh Party nationally) and bourgeois nationalism, and impatient with the parliamentarism of the National Front, the working class let itself be drawn behind the petty-bourgeoisie. The Islamic ideologues used the calamities of 'communism' and the collapse of nationalism as evidence of the inevitability of the rise of Islam: Cambodia and Egypt became their favourite talking points. The Mujahedeen's reinterpretation of *Jame'a Tawhidi* (unitarian society) as the classless society was an instance of the ideological aberrations through which the working class was enticed by the utopias of the petty-bourgeois masses.

The Revolt Against History

The impact of capitalist development in Iran over the past two decades threatened the very existence of the traditional urban middle class. Innumerable independent small producers and distributors were driven into bankruptcy by factory production of traditional consumer goods and the emergence of large-scale distribution networks. Others barely survived by intensifying family labour and reducing their living standards. Still others, who enjoyed some increased prosperity because of the relative expansion of the internal market, nevertheless resented the striking widening of differentials in income and living standards. They were also hit in 1975 – 77 when the shah reacted to worsening economic difficulties by making further inroads on small-scale production. Bank credits were restricted, import controls relaxed, and import tariffs lowered. Campaigns against 'over-pricing' hit this layer hardest.

It thus became a matter of life and death to resist the regime. The dissatisfied bazaari merchants provided the funds, the desperate urban poor the militants and combativity, the clergy and *tullab* (the theological student body) the organizing cadre. Shi'ite Islam offered the ideal ideological adhesive. Thus the revolt of the urban petty bourgeoisie against the pitiless realities of capitalism took shape.

But it was a revolt against the present and the future, to reconquer a mythical past that had never really existed. In a sense it was a 'revolt against history', as 'Ali Shari'ati had called Shi'ism.

The ideological origins of Shi'ite Islam itself provided the starting point. Islam generally was suited to become the ideology of a society based on commerce and petty commodity production; but Shi'ism *in particular* prided itself on being the 'idealist essence' of Islam. It arose as a revolt against the institutionalization of an Islamic state structure, to which it counterposed primitive semi-tribal patriarchal custom. Its inevitable defeat drove it increasingly into obscure mystification in the name of preserving the purity of Islam.

This endowed Shi'ite Islam with a rich historical tradition of protest and martyrdom. In Iran, the many Shi'ite sects had provided the organizational and ideological medium for repeated urban and rural revolts. Since it lacked any coherent vision and was inherently contradictory (fighting the *existing* governmental authority, but also denying the authority of *any* government in the absence of the Twelfth Imam), it usually led those protest movements to martyrdom rather than salvation. Its one famous success, the Sarbedaran revolt (mid fourteenth century in western Khorasan), was short-lived. And Shi'ite authorities deny that the Safavid period (sixteenth century) represented a true Shi'ite experience, since the Safavids, once in power, abandoned Shi'ism and became corrupt earthly rulers. In mid-nineteenth-century Iran the clergy again provided the cadre and ideology for revolt. That experience, however, was quite different from the present one, as we shall see.

A combination of current economic, social, and political factors *has now given Shi'ite Islam a unique and wholly unprecedented opportunity to actualize its programme.* Not only have political and social factors made it a plausible alternative to wide sectors of the population, but probably for the first time in the turbulent history of Shi'ism economic conditions are exceptionally favourable to its project. Never before has an autarkic national economy been as *potentially viable* in Iran as it is today. The country has sufficient natural resources to provide for domestic consumption, particularly once Khomeini's austere standards are imposed on the mass of the population. What it lacks in resources, it can simply buy with oil revenues. No other contemporary social formation is so well placed to adhere to the motto 'small is beautiful'. In the long run, of course, trends towards class differentiation and capital accumulation will compel the Iranian economy to open up once again. But in the short run economic autarky will permit the most reactionary policies.

Moreover, the traditional political-ideological contradiction of Shi'ism has been resolved through the concepts developed in recent years by Shari'ati and Khomeini. Shari'ati has emphasized that the task of government is properly the province of an elite that understands Shi'ism and thus deserves to lead the rest of the community. Khomeini's essay *Velayat-e Faghih* (first published in 1971, and often referred to as *Islamic Government*) develops the same notion of clerical political responsibility more systematically, explicitly designating the clergy as the governing elite.

The 'Nation' in the Wake of the Petty Bourgeoisie

(We have put *nation* between quotation marks because Iran is in fact a multi-national state.)

It is undeniable that other forces and social classes that backed the revolt of the urban petty bourgeoisie did not share its 'historical vision'. Sectors of the bourgeoisie and the bazaari supporters of the Islamic Republic hoped for a 'rationalization' of capitalism and 'democratization' of the dictatorship. They yearned for access to state power and a larger, 'more just' share of the internal market and its investment opportunities. In backing the clergy and Khomeini, their political representatives, the National Front and the Freedom Movement, were reviving their traditional alliance with the Shi'ite clergy. The top echelon of the clergy, always closely linked to the merchants of the bazaar, provided the natural ligature of the alliance.

Attention has sometimes been drawn to a similar alliance of bourgeois nationalists and the clergy during the 1905 – 11 Constitutional Revolution. The contrasts, however, are more striking than the analogies. The bourgeois nationalists had the upper hand in the constitutional movement, barely tolerating their clerical allies. Seventy years later the opposite balance obtains, the clergy dominating its bourgeois allies. In the constitutional movement the clergy attempted to formulate religious justification for what were then *new concepts* of parliamentary democracy. Clerics laboured to demonstrate that all Western constitutions were 'actually' derived from the Islamic *shari'a* (legal code), which meant that democracy was 'Islamic'. Seventy years later, the bourgeois nationalists of the Freedom Movement and the National Front were striving to weave a democratic cloak for Islamic theocracy, trying to show that Islam is the most democratic system. In the constitutional revolution, it was the bourgeois nationalists who enjoyed mass support for their concepts of political democracy and constitutional reform; they succeeded in out-manoeuvring the clergy, and introduced a constitution that declared that 'the national government is derived from the people'. Seventy years on, the popular imagination, disappointed by the bourgeois nationalists, disenchanted by what they knew as 'socialism', and repelled by the record of the Tudeh Party, was gripped by the clergy. Betrayed by earthly doctrines, the masses put their trust in heavenly promises. With this support, the clergy was now in a position to take its revenge against its secular allies. Khomeini's 'experts' have drafted a constitution that declares that the Islamic Republic is based 'on belief in God, and on the principle that government and *tashri'* (legislation) belong to God, and on the willingness to accept submission to His orders'. It was now the clergy's turn to out-manoeuvre the bourgeois nationalists by establishing its theocratic state.

It is quite evident that nearly all components of the mass upsurge against the shah's dictatorship supported the idea of the Islamic Republic (as indicated by the overwhelming vote in the referendum of 30-31 March 1979). But, except for the bastions of the traditional urban petty bourgeosie, this support is merely a result of their false identification of their own demands and aspirations with the programme of an Islamic Republic.

The public-sector employees and the working class, whose prolonged general strike halted the very functioning of the shah's regime, were fighting for improved social conditions and democratic rights, such as freedom of press and association, freedom of trade-unions, and the right to strike. But given the overwhelming political hegemony of the clergy in the anti-shah movement, these progressive struggles and tendencies could have come to fruition *only if they had broken from the clergy and come forward as an independent pole of attraction*. Once the clergy captured state power through the events of February 1979, the clergy, now wielding the weapon of the state, became an immediate and mortal threat to any advance of the class struggle.

The reason for this lies in the very nature of 'Islamic government'. Islam is not simply a system of religious thought and practices regulating the mystical relation of man to 'his god'. It is above all a body of social, economic, and political precepts on whose basis the Islamic community is to be governed in its earthly existence. The particularly reactionary and dangerous character of the clergy's hegemony does not arise primarily from its *particular* social and economic *policies*, although these are reactionary enough, ranging from oppressive laws against women to reactionary populist-sounding schemes, like trying to eliminate unemployment by granting each unemployed person a small amount of capital to set up a small workshop, or granting each homeless family land and construction materials to build its own hovel. Rather, the most menacing feature of the clergy's rule stems from its *concept of government*, as formulated in the many writings on the subject by Khomeini and others, and as implemented since February 1979. Government, the clerics maintain, is properly the business of the direct representatives of God on earth. The task of ruling is reserved for the spokesmen of God, and in the last instance for the supreme *faghih* (the person most knowledgeable in Islamic law), final arbiter of what is good for the Islamic community economically, politically, morally, and socially. The scope of control extends even to the most trivial details of everyday life.

Khomeini himself has put it thus: 'Islamic government is the government of the laws of God over people. This is the main difference between Islamic government and constitutional monarchies or republics. That is, in the latter types of government the king or the representatives of the people engage in the act of legislation, while in Islam the legislative power, the act of *tashri'*, belongs solely to God. The holy Islamic *shari'a* is the only legislative power. No one else has the right to legislate. No law other than the divine decree can be implemented. For this reason, in the Islamic government instead of a legislative assembly . . . one has only a planning assembly that arranges the work of different ministries according to Islamic laws.

'The body of Islamic law, as collected in the Koran and the *sunna*, is accepted and obeyed by the Muslims. This acceptance and agreement makes the task of government easy. . . . The Islamic government is a government of law, the governing belongs to God, and the law is the law and order of God. Islamic law, that is, the divine decree, has absolute authority over everyone and over the Islamic government.'

He then concludes, quite logically, that under the Islamic government those who are knowledgeable in Islamic law and who are just must rule. Hence: 'If the rulers are to follow Islam, they must follow the *faghihs* about the laws and decrees. Under such circumstances, it is clear that the *faghihs* are really ruling. Therefore the act of government must formally belong to the *faghihs* and not to those who due to their ignorance of the law must follow the *faghihs*. . . .

'These characteristics of knowledge in law and justice are present in many of our contemporary *faghihs*. If they get together, they would be able to form a just government throughout the world.

'If a suitable person who has these two characteristics arises and forms a government . . . obedience to him is obligatory upon all people.'

Such a government of 'just *faghihs*' would enact all the Islamic laws, 'would implement all the *hads* and *qasas* [Islamic punishments], . . . would collect all the *khoms, zakât*, the charities, the *jizya*, and *kharaj* [Islamic taxes] and would decide how to spend it for the benefit of Muslims. . . .

'These just *faghihs* must become the rulers, must implement the laws, and establish the Islamic social order.' (All quotations are from the essay *Velayat-e Faghih*.)

Independent thought and action have no place whatever in such a system of government. Mass activity is encouraged only when it unfolds under the control of the *faghihs* or in their support; it is ruthlessly crushed the moment it steps beyond such limits. Complete conformity is the rule. This is only logical in a system whose final authority rests beyond human judgement. What is most dangerous in this project, and distinguishes it from others, is that it is based on the complete negation of all popular sovereignty; the rulers are not accountable to the ruled *even in theory*.

The nefarious effects of this project on the consciousness of the workers and urban and rural poor should not be underestimated. The consolidation of Khomeini's authority, backed by his success in ousting the shah, has increasingly meant surrender by the masses of all their confidence and independence in favour of trust in God and obedience to his Imam. Since February 1979, important struggles and strikes in factories and in the army have been stifled not through armed force or the threat of force, but at the order of the Imam.

After February 1979: Problems of Power Based on Conformism

Efforts to implement this political project have been at the centre of events in Iran since February 1979. On each major issue the clergy has set itself in opposition to progressive change, the exigencies of Islamic government contradicting those of social progress. Consequently, mass participation in efforts to recast Iranian society implicitly threatens the Islamic project, unless directly controlled by clerics or their agents. The success of the clergy's political rule therefore hinges on its ability to check or suppress all the independent struggles that had arisen with the crisis and collapse of the shah's regime: the struggles of the nationalities for self-determination; the fight for democratic rights; the struggle of women for equality; and finally, some primarily economic struggles of workers and peasants.

These latter have been contained quite easily. In and of themselves, the struggles of workers for higher wages and better working conditions, of the unemployed for jobs, and of the peasants for land pose no particular challenge to the political project of the clergy. On the other hand, the struggle for independent workers' and peasant organizations had been led into the blind alley of corporatist Islamic councils, with the obliging cooperation of the confused left and the theoretical elaborations of the Mujahedeen. Two years after the collapse of the Pahlavi dictatorship, *no independent workers' movement exists in Iran.*

Inevitably, conflict on the issue of women's rights followed the seizure of power by the clergy. Islam upholds unambiguously reactionary and oppressive codes and laws for women. Any move towards implementing them was bound to meet strenuous opposition from those women who had hoped that the overthrow of the shah's regime would open a new era of the flowering of their rights. Despite the vicissitudes of women's struggles during the past two years, this remains one of the major 'problem' areas for the clergy. It also offers one of the key challenges and hopes for revolutionary socialists. (These issues are discussed in greater detail in 'Enigma of the Veiled Iranian Woman', *Feminist Review* no. 5, 1980.) For the first time in the history of Iran, the nature of the political regime makes quite likely the emergence of a women's movement similar to the suffragist movements of late-nineteenth and early-twentieth-century Europe. Issues of legal and political equality will tend to come to the fore of women's struggles.

The collapse of the highly centralized Pahlavi state naturally set in motion a fresh round of battles for national self-determination all over Iran, a patchwork of nationalities and ethnic groupings. The modern state was born of the bloody suppression of national struggles and has indulged in continual acts of repression to forestall any new uprisings. Any endeavour by oppressed nationalities to determine their own fate, in particular to erect their own political structures, had to clash with the clergy's project of instituting a centralized theocracy. That the majority of these nationalities and ethnic minorities are Sunnis aggravated the issue. Since February 1979, there have been intermittent clashes between Khomeini's supporters and the forces for local autonomy or self-government in Gonbad, Khuzistan, Kurdistan, Baluchistan, and Azarbaijan. Despite the vicious, chauvinist campaign launched against the Kurds in August 1979, Khomeini's forces did not succeed in defeating them. In the other regions the relationship of forces has been more favourable to the regime. The single greatest obstacle to the consolidation of clerical rule has remained the struggle of the oppressed nationalities, especially the Kurds.

The collapse of the shah's dictatorship temporarily ended a twenty-five-year period of suppression of all democratic rights. The flood of newspapers and books, the gatherings and meetings that proliferated in workshops, universities, and schools, and the formation of political parties and other associations, including the many grass-roots committees, all reflected the popular thirst for democracy.

Contrary to a common misconception on the left, the numerous committees that sprang up throughout the country during the first few months of 1979 were in no way soviet-type formations. Most of the neighbourhood committees were set up through the local mosques, directly under the clergy's control. Other committees, set up at work-places, colleges, and secondary schools, often began as strike committees and nearly always remained concerned with local issues, or with coordination of mobilizations against the shah's regime (in support of the journalists' strike against censorship, for example). Some of these committees were taken over by Khomeini's supporters after February 1979 and quickly lost all independence. Where they remained genuinely independent bodies elected by workers, employees, or students, they devoted themselves exclusively to local issues of this or that factory, office, or school. At no time did these bodies begin to act (or conceive of themselves) as organs of a new power. Primarily they reflected a genuine desire for grass-roots democracy that remained limited to local issues. Exactly for this reason, the new rulers found it relatively easy gradually to transform these bodies into corporatist *consultative* councils. The highest degree of political development occurred in the south, amongst oil workers, whose council issued a statement calling for a workers' representative to be placed on the Revolutionary Council, since 'workers had played such a significant role in the downfall of the shah'. Even this modest proposal, however, was never followed up by the workers.

But the very existence of such independent committees, the outpouring of newspapers and books, the formation of parties and organizations, and the exercise of freedom of speech and assembly inevitably threatened the establishment and consolidation of the government of God on earth. In the first months after it came to power, Khomeini's regime set out systematically to stamp out this threat.

The August Attacks

There were two periods in this process, separated from each other by the August 1979 attacks against the press, the left, and Kurdistan. In the early period, the regime was not capable of launching an all-out assault, nor was such drastic action necessary.

Despite the attempts of the leading factions around Bazargan and Khomeini to effect a smooth transition of power that would preserve all the main military and repressive instruments of the state intact, the bulk of the Iranian army collapsed and SAVAK premises were taken over and often burnt down during the February 1979 days. Several months of confronting mass street demonstrations had severely undermined the morale of the soldiers, leading to widespread desertion and indiscipline. The execution of many leading figures of the army and SAVAK (advocated and implemented by Khomeini's supporters over Bazargan's objections) further sapped army morale, especially among the officers. What remained of the army was an ineffective body whose soldiers were temporarily more concerned with experiments in rank-and-file democracy than with drills and other army exercises. The reconstruction of the army, or the construction of new repressive instruments such as the Islamic militias, the Pasdaran, required time.

Meanwhile, political preparations were under way to demoralize and demobilize those sectors of the mass movement that were not politically shaped and organizationally dominated by the clergy. Months of careful preparation preceded the August 1979 crackdown, the regime testing the balance of forces as it went along. (The move against certain newspapers in June 1979, though unsuccessful, was one example.)

The leitmotif of Khomeini's policy during the pre-August period was the elimination of any popular participation in directing the affairs of the country *independent of the clergy*. Independent committees were often dissolved; non-conformist elements were demoralized and driven out of those that remained. The foundation for later political developments was laid by the referendum on the Islamic Republic. The oft-promised constituent assembly was postponed several times. Had such a body been convened earlier, an even more solid and genuine majority for Khomeini's supporters might have been returned. But early elections would have run against the long-term political goals of establishing a 'chosen' (as opposed to an *elected*) government. It would have strengthened that element in mass consciousness that favoured free and democratic elections and an elective system of government. Elections had first to be reduced from a positive action of a determinative character to an act of consultation or mere ratification. The majority of the population (and not just the solid bastions of the urban petty bourgeoisie) had to be either demoralized and reduced to political apathy and inactivity or convinced that only 'Islamic experts' are fit to govern. Concepts of political democracy were deemed 'Western', 'corrupt', and defunct. After all, wasn't the whole system of imperialist exploitation based on bourgeois democracy? So the argument went. Primitive populism was declared superior.

For months hesitant discontent was held in check by constant harping on themes such as 'the threat of counter-revolution', 'the danger of restoration', 'the impending imperialist and Zionist intervention'. Meanwhile, the imposition of Islamic codes began to drive home the message that this was going to be a genuinely Islamic government. The left was most obliging to the clergy on the former themes, and kept silent on the latter. Some may have shared the prudish and cruel codes of behaviour the clergy was imposing. Others dismissed them as irrelevant details of no real concern to the working masses. When the clergy began executing prostitutes, for example, not a single voice was raised in defence of the victims. By allowing the all-embracing imposition of Islamic codes without challenge, the left effectively cooperated in preparing the rope for its own strangulation.

Revenge against the past became the overriding theme of everyday life. This was not simply intended to divert popular attention from more 'mundane' problems of today and tomorrow, nor was it merely a means of fostering an atmosphere of generalized fear, terror, and uncertainty. It was, in addition, part of the revival of Islamic tradition and values, among which was the importance of revenge and punishment, as opposed to what Muslims have often considered the passive Christian tradition of forgiveness. The most important Islamic tradition to be revived, however, was the Friday prayers. Every major city and town in Iran today has a Friday Imam appointed by Khomeini, who unfailingly conveys the latest political message in his Friday *khotba* (the sermon preceding the actual prayer).

Once the regime felt strong enough, it scrapped the constituent assembly in favour of a farcical 'Assembly of Experts'. The absence of any organized resistance to these 'elections' apparently convinced Khomeini that the time was ripe to rid himself of potential critics and irritants to his rule. He understood the meaning of the large rate of abstention—less than half the electorate participated in the vote—much better than the left. Far from indicating an active boycott or rising dissent, it reflected the fact that disillusionment with the Islamic Republic was generating a mood of apathy and demoralization. Most of the electorate felt that their votes were either futile or unnecessary. Those dissatisfied with the prevailing state of affairs were already feeling impotent, and some of the supporters of the Islamic regime felt secure enough not to bother with registering their support.

In the aftermath of the election of the Assembly of Experts, a wave of protest by certain groups, including some of the clergy around Shari'atmadari, expressed belated grievances against the electoral practices, thereby signalling a potential threat to Khomeini's project. Feeble though these protests were, they were intolerable in a political system that demands total submission and conformity. The continued strength of the Kurdish movement also loomed as a danger to a centralized theocracy. It was time to put an end to the independent press, the left, and the Kurds, each of which, in varying ways, constituted an obstacle to the clergy's project.

The campaign was launched with a speech by Khomeini on the occasion of the Day of Jerusalem, in which he said that it had been a mistake not to have acted in a sufficiently revolutionary manner after the seizure of power:

'When we broke down the corrupt regime, and destroyed this very corrupt dam, had we acted in a revolutionary manner from the beginning, had we closed down this hired press, these corrupt magazines, these corrupt papers, had we put their editors on trial, had we banned all these corrupt parties and punished their leaders, had we erected scaffolds for hanging in all major squares, and had we chopped off all the corrupters and the corrupted, we would not have had these troubles today. I beg forgiveness from the almighty God and my dear people.... Had we been revolutionary, we would not have allowed them to express their existence, we would have banned all parties, we would have banned all fronts, we would have formed only one party, the party of the *mustaz'afeen* [the oppressed]. I ask for repentance for my mistake, and I declare to these corrupt layers all over Iran, that if they do not sit in their place, we will deal with them in a revolutionary manner ... like our master 'Ali, ... who would pull his sword against the *mustakbereen* [the oppressors] and the conspirators, and who it is said beheaded 700 in one day of the Jews of Bani Qarantia, who were like the Israelis and maybe these Israelis are their descendants.... These conspirators are in the same category as the *kuffar* [heathen], these conspirators in Kurdistan and elsewhere are in the ranks of the infidels, they should be dealt with harshly.... The Prosecutor of the Revolution must close down all magazines that are against the popular will, and are conspirators; he must invite all their writers to court and put them on trial. He is obligated to call upon those who engage in conspiracies and call themselves parties, put the leaders of these parties on trial ... those layers of the army who disobey [in failing to suppress the corrupters and the conspirators] must know that I will deal with them in a revolutionary manner.... I demand of all layers of the population, of all intellectuals and of all parties and groups, whose number unfortunately now exceeds two hundred, that they follow the popular path, the path of Islam . . . otherwise they will become the victims of their own wrongdoing.... Other nations must learn from our movement,... the people of Afghanistan must learn from Iran.... We hope that the unity of the world of Muslims will solve the problems of Islam, the problems of Palestine, and those of Afghanistan.'

The following day all independent newspapers were banned, headquarters of dissident groups were ransacked, and the military campaign against Kurdistan was launched. This latter proved unsuccessful in defeating the Kurds, but the press was silenced and the left marginalized. Today no paper is legal that dares to oppose Khomeini and the Islamic Republic. Those papers that have gained temporary legalization have paid a heavy political price: capitulation to Khomeini.

The events around the US embassy take-over, the holding of hostages, and the demand for the return of the shah accelerated theocratic consolidation and exacerbated the confusion and capitulation of the left.

Just prior to the siege in November 1979, the Iranian situation was marked by increasing anti-government ferment—among the Kurds; in the universities, where issues of freedom of political debate had again been raised; among women, some of whom were beginning to organize against the new marriage and divorce laws, which repeal the small gains that had been made under the shah; among the workers, where there was a modest rise in economic struggles.

The embassy siege, far from impelling these struggles forward, acted as a brake on them, simultaneously diverting attention from the real issues facing Iran and serving as an occasion for typical obscurantist calls for 'national unity', overlaid with the Islamic cast that renders this time-honoured reactionary appeal even more retrogressive. Khomeini was now in a position to blame all economic shortages on American sabotage; a huge propaganda campaign for the restriction of consumption was launched. All dissidents could now be branded as agents of US imperialism and suffer the wrath of the masses accordingly. Khomeini has used the occasion to implement what he had failed to achieve before: a massive mobilization of youth into armed militias under the total control of the clergy and their henchmen and a reintroduction of discipline into the army.

The effects of the events on mass consciousness have been hardly less lamentable. The complete diversion of the population's attention from real problems and enemies at home further set back the process of differentiation between Khomeini and his mass base and intensified the obscurantism and mystification that have marked the Iranian upheaval from the outset.

The US embassy occupation and the mobilizations around it provided the regime with a favourable political climate for holding a referendum on the new constitution. This was followed by the presidential and parliamentary elections in early 1980. Once the elections were over, fresh attacks against the left and the nationalities ensued.

New assaults against the Kurdish people began early in April 1980. Within two weeks these had developed into a full-scale civil war. The Iranian air force joined the army and the Islamic militias in mop-up operations against whole villages and towns.

A new offensive against all dissidents was already under way with the attacks against the Mujahedeen headquarters during March 1980. By early April 'followers of the line of the Imam' were regularly attacking left headquarters on university campuses. Bani-Sadr personally moved in, legitimating these attacks by giving on 18 April a three-day ultimatum to all left groups to evacuate their university headquarters. These were the last public sanctuaries of the left, since their other headquarters had been shut down in August 1979. In the ensuing days, Islamic thugs ransacked the left headquarters, causing thousands of casualties. Hundreds were arrested. Several executions followed. Bonfires were made of all leftist literature on the campuses.

2. WHAT PROSPECTS FOR SOCIALISM IN IRAN?

In discussing the future development of the class struggle in Iran, two questions have to be clearly distinguished. First, there is the question of an assessment of the present balance of forces in the country and the likely tendencies of their development. Second, one must begin to develop a revolutionary programme for socialism in Iran.

The Relationship of Forces in Iran Today

Notwithstanding the jubilation of the left in Iran and abroad over the issue of the US embassy takeover, the present political situation in Iran is not at all favourable for the struggle for socialism, as is shown by a cursory look at the state of affairs two years after the overthrow of the monarchy.

The general trend of struggles independent of the clergy and its political programme has been on the decline, except in Kurdistan. The other nationalities and ethnic minorities have been unable to sustain any resistance since the attacks against the Arabs in Khuzistan in early summer 1979 and those against the Baluchis in autumn 1979. New attacks against the Turkomans were launched in spring 1980. Twelve leaders were found beheaded and a new climate against 'losing an inch of our national land' was created in anticipation of fresh attacks against the Turkomans and the Kurds, followed by a full-scale war against them.

The struggle of women for equal rights, which saw a modest revival in early autumn, was subsequently overshadowed by the embassy events and the presidential and parliamentary elections. But even the autumn 1979 mobilizations were much smaller than those of March 1979 against the compulsory veil. On that occasion nearly twenty thousand women demonstrated, on only one day's notice, against Khomeini's edict on the veil. The autumn protests primarily comprised women from the far left and barely numbered in the thousands. The strict imposition of 'Islamic modesty' on women in the summer of 1980 evoked very limited and totally disorganized resistance.

Censorship over the national media is in full force; the judiciary has been delivered from the clutches of SAVAK only to fall under the cloak of the clergy; no independent working-class organizations have emerged; the living conditions of the working class and the urban poor have deteriorated and are likely to continue doing so.

What is most disconcerting of all, however, is the political polarization that has emerged in the country. The bourgeois nationalist wing of the ruling alliance has been eliminated from the scene for all practical purposes. The majority of those who had supported Bazargan and his government in the first half of 1979 have now become his open enemies. Although this does reflect the impotence of this political current in dealing with the social problems facing the country, the celebration of much of the left in Iran is worse than misplaced. Far from signifying a leftward shift in the mood of the masses away from bourgeois liberalism, this polarization has further strengthened the hegemony of the clergy and the appeal of its Islamic government as the only possible alternative. The growth of the left, on the other hand, has been minimal in this polarization.

Moreover, under deteriorating economic conditions coupled with a government repressive apparatus that remains weak, and in the absence of any avenues of progressive political struggles, there has been a rise of workers' economic struggles around unemployment, wages, hours, and conditions of work. This has made daily life increasingly intolerable for the petty bourgeoisie and the bazaaris. They are clamouring for 'law and order', pressing for a rapid reinforcement of the central government. For the moment, they seem to have given their support, with Khomeini's blessing, to Bani-Sadr. To stay in power (and to save his own neck) he has to succeed in satisfying the demands for order. If he fails, there are other candidates for the job. The Partisans of God (Hezb-o Allahis) have been quietly organizing and have grown considerably. The concerted attacks against Mujahedeen headquarters all over the country gave an indication of their forces.

Regardless of the exact short-term balance of forces between different ruling factions, it must be emphasized that the period ahead for revolutionary socialists will be one of prolonged patient political education. Unless there is a victorious upsurge towards socialist democracy in the Soviet Union or a victorious socialist revolution in one of the imperialist countries (thereby giving rise to a new attractive image of socialism on a world scale), the majority of Iranians, in Persian-speaking areas in particular, have set themselves to experiment with their 'neither Western, nor Eastern, but Islamic' model. Within this overall context, we can project the future of other political tendencies, as well as the tasks and programme of revolutionary socialism.

For reasons already pointed out above, bourgeois nationalist currents of various shades, the National Front and the Freedom Movement, have no real future. The National Front, already in demise, has suffered further losses of its political figureheads and social base. It has been reduced to commemorating its past, rather than projecting the image of a new future. The only significant initiative it has shown has been to celebrate Mosaddeq's birthday and to commemorate the anniversary of his death. Over the summer 1980 period, in the aftermath of the uncovering of a coup plot, there was a systematic campaign to implicate the National Front in the plans. Its headquarters have been taken over by the Pasdaran, and it can no longer even publish a paper.

The more radical offshoot of the National Front, the National Democratic Front, gained a certain momentum for a few months by organizing opposition to the clergy on a secular and democratic basis, but it has not recovered from the physical attacks against its last demonstration in defence of freedom of the press in August 1979.

The Freedom Movement, originally a breakaway from the National Front in the early 1960s, had set itself the task of governing the state on behalf of the clergy, whom they thought should remain in the mosques to provide 'spiritual' leadership. With the clergy now in command of the state, there is very little room left for the Freedom Movement. In any case, it is quite unlikely that the masses, once they begin to break with Khomeini, would look towards political currents whose bankruptcy has been transparent for so many decades and who have no coherent alternative.

The major groups on the secular left have a very small popular base, especially amongst the workers and the urban poor. They are stronger amongst students, white-collar workers, and state employees. All these groups—the Tudeh Party, Fedaeen, Paykar—have also politically capitulated to the clergy in various degrees. The Fedaeen and Paykar in particular are also politically very confused and heterogeneous organizations. It is difficult to see how they could offer an attractive alternative to forces breaking away from clerical rule.

Within the Islamic framework there are many tendencies. Here is where a reshaping of the political map may take place in the coming years. These political currents range from the left reformism of the Mujahedeen, through different shades and factions within the clergy and political personalities related to them, all the way through to extreme right fascistic groupings such as the Hezb-o Allahis. The Mujahedeen have a substantial base in the working class and are influential in many of the workers' councils. They are the current most likely to grow in the coming years as an Islamic workerist tendency. On many vital issues they have held progressive positions and at times supported the struggles of women, nationalities, and workers; nevertheless as long as they remain within an Islamic ideological framework they are bound to end up on the side of reaction when vital questions are posed (for instance, their silence on the attacks against the Kurds, and their acceptance of Khomeini's orders to evacuate their central headquarters). They have made their political trademark the question of the Islamic councils (*shoras*), advocating a governmental system based on them. These councils, however, as long as the Mujahedeen accept Khomeini's doctrine of vesting power and authority in the supreme *faghih*, will remain essentially consultative bodies which lend themselves to becoming vehicles for a populist corporatist base of support for the Islamic regime.

Bani-Sadr, around whom a whole layer of intellectuals and state-functionaries has now coalesced, can be broadly characterized as a serious Islamic thinker who is interested in laying the economic foundations for an Islamic republic. His relatively more 'rational' attempts to put the economy in order have come into direct conflict with the programme of the clergy to take control of the state machinery (through their majority bloc in the Majlis) and to base all decisions on precepts derived from the Koran and the *shari'a*.

The two major factions of the clergy are the Islamic Republican Party, headed by Beheshti, and those around Kho'ini-ha. One could say that the basic difference between the two is that the former tries to come to grips with post-power problems, trying to make the adjustments and alliances that would stabilize the situation. Kho'ini-ha, on the other hand, wants to remain faithful to pre-power visions of a purist and fundamentalist Islamic social order. The 'students following the line of the Imam' who occupied the US embassy are aligned with this faction.

The Hezb-o Allahis (Partisans of God, called thus because of their motto: *Only one party, the party of Allah; only one leader, Ruh-o Allah* [Khomeini's first name]) is a fascistic grouping. It is still small but growing rapidly. It enjoys the support of a number of well-known clerics (notably Hojjat-o al-Islam Ghaffari) as well as certain bazaaris. It recruits its thugs primarily from the mass of the declassed urban population.

Towards a Revolutionary Marxist Programme for Iran

Much of the Iranian far left's propaganda and activity has focused around workers' economic struggles. However, the economic demands, measured by their actual impact on the course of the class struggle, are of secondary importance today. On the other hand, demands related to the nature of the political structure are central and cannot be reduced, as has often been done by the left, to secondary points concerning separation of religion and state and the abolition of all privileges for the Shi'ite or any other religion.

The specific character of the political system in Iran today, the fact that it is a theocratic Islamic government, shapes all political questions in Iran and must therefore form the central axis of a revolutionary socialist programme.

This question cannot be posed simply in terms of secularization (separation of religion from the state), because of the specificities of Islam as a social and political system. As any Muslim would readily point out, *Islam cannot be 'separated from the state', precisely because it is above all else a total governmental social programme.* This point cannot be over-emphasized. By turning to Islam, the Iranian masses have not become more *religious*, but more *political—* in a very particular and reactionary way. They have turned to Islam as a vision of a future that they mistakenly identify with a betterment of their lives. Like any other political programme that is objectively in conflict with the interests of the toilers and the oppressed, but for political and historical reasons has succeeded in becoming the expression of their rebellion and the focus of their hope, Islam has to be taken up and challenged at every level. Moreover, this challenge is more immediately posed in the case of Islam than in any other political formation. The growth of social democracy, for example, indicates an elementary but essential growth of working-class organization. The very power of social democracy rests on the organization of workers as a class. The recent growth of sentiments for a labour party in Brazil, for example, is a very positive development. Revolutionary socialists welcome it and along with other working-class militants fight for it (and for their programme) even though, in the given balance of forces between revolutionaries and reformists, it may very well lead to the emergence of a reformist party. Islam, however, is based on the absolute and complete negation of all independent thought or action. It is a deeply anti-democratic view of the world. Its growth, therefore, far from representing any partial step forward for the oppressed, signifies their subordination to the clergy, who remain—in theory and not only in practice—beyond the accountability of the masses. Its social and economic policies, moreover, are such that they in turn increase the material dependence of the oppressed on religious institutions, rather than encouraging any form of self-organization (for example, the disbursement of charities as a means of 'social equalization'). This means that one cannot deal with Islam as a social and political system without challenging and fighting it all the way down the line. One is almost tempted to counterpose a full socialist programme to the programme of an Islamic society. This, of course, is necessary at the level of the general presentation of revolutionary socialist propaganda. But it, too, would be inadequate. To focus simply and solely on general anti-capitalist and anti-imperialist demands in Iran today is pointless. Power is in the hands of the clergy and the fact that there is a bourgeois government and that the mode of production is capitalist is almost irrelevant to the issues of the day and therefore to immediate political tasks.

To elucidate this point we will draw an analogy. Israel is a modern bourgeois social formation based on the capitalist mode of production. The struggle between capital and labour is fundamental and must be integrated into the programme of action of Israeli revolutionaries. In this sense, Israel is similar to other capitalist countries. But there is a very important sense in which Israel is *different* from West European countries, for example. Israel is also an exclusively Jewish Zionist state. It is a settler state based on the expropriation and expulsion of its former Palestinian inhabitants. These features of the Israeli state pervade all aspects of life in that country. They affect state institutions, laws, culture; and they enter in one form or another as formative ingredients of the consciousness of every citizen of Israel. To arrive at a revolutionary socialist consciousness in Israel, that is, for the Israeli working class to become convinced of the necessity to overthrow the *bourgeois* state, it is necessary to break with *Zionism*. Left Zionists, for example, who consider themselves socialists and are often very well versed in Marxism, are in fact the purest Zionists of all, and they were after all the real pioneers of the modern Israeli state.

Anti-Zionist demands, therefore, must form the central axis of a revolutionary programme in Israel. The problem for Israeli revolutionaries is to win the masses away from Zionism towards socialism; and the chain of demands leading up to that constitutes the specific form that a revolutionary transitional programme takes amongst the Jewish masses in Israel. In other words, anti-Zionist demands are not some nice additional touch added to distinguish revolutionary socialists from other currents in the workers' movement. The most militant and explosive struggles of the Jewish masses in Israel will be contained, derailed, and defeated (with arguments such as the threat to the security of the Jewish state, etc.), unless in the process of struggle the masses begin to break with Zionism.

Similar observations apply in the case of Iran today. Of course, the Islamic state is different from the example of Israel in the sense that clerical rule is not based on specific material economic privileges of the clergy itself. It is above all a distinct *political* system.

An *Islamic* political system is distinguished from all others in that it is *inherently* anti-democratic. In a system based on laws that are not subject to human intervention, questioning and blasphemy, dissent and heresy become identical. No significant Muslim political theorist has ever produced a theory of democracy—*of popular rule* —and no Muslim state has ever yet rested on political democracy. An Islamic regime insists on *forced implementation* of what the clergy considers to be in the interest of the Islamic community, based on the Koran, the *shari'a*, and so on. This is known as the principle of *al-amr bi al-ma'ruf wa al-nahy 'an al-munkar* (command the good and forbid the bad). Moreover, this body of 'the good and the bad' comprises a whole range of retrogressive laws, social norms, and reactionary economic policies. One cannot deal with this phenomenon by tinkering with this or that economic policy, and reacting instinctively, empirically, and on a day-to-day basis to this or that attack on women, the nationalities, the left, etc. One cannot sit back and repeat banalities about capitalism and imperialism, and be content with general anti-capitalist anti-imperialist demands. The specific transitional programme for socialist revolution in Iran must start from the specific political character of the state.

The establishment of an Islamic theocratic state is the central fact of what happened in Iran in February 1979. This regime is *historically* more retrogressive than even the shah's regime. Unfortunately and tragically, the overthrow of the shah's dictatorship has not resulted in any gains for the struggle for socialism. Even the partial improvement of conditions for struggle—purely as a result of the collapse of the dictatorial apparatus and completely unrelated to the nature of the current regime itself—has been more than rolled back by the consolidation of the Islamic regime. Furthermore, the new regime has turned back, and will continue to turn back, the most minimal and partial advance made in such matters as family laws, the legal system, the criminal code. The Islamic constitution of Khomeini, promulgated by the Assembly of Experts, is more backward than its 1906 predecessor.

Once the Islamic regime is politically and militarily stabilized, the implementation of its economic policies will also set back the forces of production in Iran for a considerable period of time. Unlike nationalist regimes—Nasser in Egypt, Perón in Argentina, Ben-Bella in Algeria—which arose in the period after the Second World War and which brought about partial and limited economic reforms (land reform, partial industrialization), the Khomeini regime has had and will continue to have a destructive and retrogressive effect on the forces of production. In fact, from a 'socio-economic' viewpoint, the shah, and not Khomeini, was Iran's equivalent to Egypt's Nasser. It was the so-called 'white revolution' that accelerated the partial, uneven, limited, *and yet real* development of capitalism in Iran.

The standard of living under Khomeini's regime has steadily dropped and it will continue to do so. The dependence on oil revenues will grow as factories and industrial production grind to a halt. At the same time, the production of oil has dropped to less than one-fifth of what it was under the shah. The regime is incapable of running the factories without the capitalists who have fled the country. The cumulative effect of all this, in the absence of any alternative, will generate further apathy and demoralization.

Khomeini's regime is also having a very pernicious effect on the general level of culture in Iran. Islamic monolithism of thought is undermining the development of all individuality of thought, nonconformism, and independence. The traditional oppressive Middle Eastern family structure is given new strength in forcing children and youth into Islamic patterns of behaviour. Religious intolerance has already led to attacks against Christians, Jews, Baha'is, and even

Sunni Muslims. Revolting and inhumane concepts, like the glorification of 'martyrdom', violence and vengeance, are rampant in Iran today. The effect that all this will have on the future of the Iranian masses, on their thinkers, poets, writers, artists, and musicians, cannot easily be measured today. Nevertheless, it is frighteningly real, and a very bitter price is being exacted by the clergy in this sphere alone.

To conclude: a revolutionary socialist programme for Iran today must include as its central plank hostility to this theocratic Islamic regime and to the very idea of an Islamic republic. Every struggle and every demand must be linked up in the press and agitation of revolutionary socialists with the urgency of undermining in every possible way the abomination that has come to power in Iran. Breaking individuals and currents or sections of the masses from the hold of Islam as a social and political system is the only way in which a revolutionary vanguard will emerge that is capable, willing, and effective in struggle against the regime. *The break with Islam, therefore, takes on a transitional character in Iran today, in a similar sense to a break with Zionism in Israel.* It is no longer possible to act as a revolutionary militant in Iran without having arrived at a state of total hostility to the very concept of the 'Islamic revolution' and the Islamic republic. Strikes led and organized against the regime or against capitalists, but on a left workerist Islamic basis, are doomed to failure in the long run, just as purely economic strikes in Israel have always failed to challenge the hold of the ruling class, because they did not challenge Zionism, which is the central divide in that country. Are you for or against the rule of the clergy—this is the most central political divide that will arise in Iranian society. Given the nature of the Islamic government, based on the intolerant theological concept of 'command the good and forbid the bad', the struggle for political democracy and individual liberties will become the most central issue of the class struggle.

The demands and slogans that will arise in Iran will cover a whole range of issues from the most general governmental ones (the struggle for a genuinely popular democratic republic; the convening of a *sovereign* constituent assembly; demands related to making all governmental offices elective and recallable; abolition of the *faghih*'s post and the so-called Council of Islamic Guardians;

democratization of all election laws; abolition of all restrictions on governmental jobs based on religion; the sovereignty of the legislative, executive, and judicial organs vis-à-vis the clergy) down to the most specific policies regarding the judicial system (complete secularization of the judiciary and the laws, establishment of an elective jury system, rights of defence and appeal, abolition of execution, flogging, and all such punishments, reinstating the right of women to hold judiciary posts including the post of judge, abolition of the special courts for the clergy). One will have to fight also for a whole range of democratic rights (freedom of expression, the press, association, etc.), artistic and cultural freedoms (lifting the ban on music and dance, ending the censorship of movies and theatres, and lifting state control over the mass media, in particular over the radio and television, ending the strangulation of the universities, etc.). Socialists must also intransigently demand an end to all infringements of individual liberties and state intervention in matters of personal life.

As argued above, amongst all the social questions, the national question and women's rights have been and will continue to be the most explosive ones. The struggle of oppressed nationalities for self-determination will remain the major obstacle to the consolidation of power by the clergy.

Given the nature of Islamic laws regarding women, we shall also witness a rise in the struggle of women for equal rights over the next period. It remains the responsibility of revolutionary socialists to take an active initiative in this field.

It is within this general political framework and such a set of priorities of tasks and demands, focusing as they do on the centrality of the question of the Islamic state, that all other points will find their proper place as part of a comprehensive programme for revolutionaries in Iran in the wake of the February 1979 'Islamic revolution'.

Orientalism and Orientalism in Reverse

Sadiq Jalal al-'Azm

1. ORIENTALISM

In his sharply debated book,[1] Edward Said introduces us to the subject of 'Orientalism' through a broadly historical perspective that situates Europe's interest in the Orient within the context of the general historical expansion of modern bourgeois Europe beyond its traditional confines and at the expense of the rest of the world in the form of its subjugation, pillage, and exploitation. In this sense Orientalism may be seen as a complex phenomenon deriving from the overall historical trend of modern European expansion and involving: a set of progressively expanding institutions, a created and cumulative body of theory and practice, a suitable ideological superstructure with an apparatus of complicated assumptions, beliefs, images, literary productions, and rationalizations (not to mention the underlying foundation of commercial, economic and strategic vital interests). I shall call this phenomenon *Institutional Orientalism*.

Edward Said also deals with Orientalism in the more restricted sense of a developing tradition of disciplined learning whose main function is to 'scientifically research' the Orient. Naturally, this *Cultural-Academic Orientalism* makes all the usual pious claims about its 'disinterested pursuit of the truth' about the Orient, and its efforts to apply impartial scientific methods and value-free techniques in studying the peoples, cultures, religions, and languages of the Orient. The bulk of Said's book, not unexpectedly, is devoted to Cultural-Academic Orientalism in an attempt to expose the ties that bind it to Institutional Orientalism.

1. *Orientalism*, New York and London 1978.

In this way, Said deflates the self-righteous claims of Cultural-Academic Orientalism to such traits as scholarly independence, scientific detachment, and political objectivity. It should be made clear, however, that the author never seeks to belittle the genuine scholarly achievements, scientific discoveries, and creative contributions made by Orientalists and Orientalism over the years, particularly at the technical level of accomplishment.[2] His main concern is to convey the message that the overall image of the Orient constructed by Cultural-Academic Orientalism, from the viewpoint of its own technical achievements and scientific contributions to the field, is shot through with racist assumptions, barely camouflaged mercenary interests, reductionist explanations, and anti-human prejudices. It can easily be shown that this image, when properly scrutinized, can hardly be the product of genuinely objective scientific investigation and detached scholarly discipline.

Critique of Orientalism

One of the most vicious aspects of this image, as carefully pointed out by Said, is the deep-rooted belief—shared by Cultural-Academic and Institutional Orientalism—that there is a fundamental ontological difference between the essential natures of the Orient and Occident, to the decisive advantage of the latter. Western societies, cultures, languages, and mentalities are supposed to be essentially and inherently superior to the Eastern ones. In Edward Said's words, 'the essence of Orientalism is the ineradicable distinction between Western superiority and Oriental inferiority.'[3] According to this reading of Said's initial thesis, Orientalism (in both its institutional and cultural-academic forms) can hardly be said to have existed, as a structured phenomenon and organized movement, prior to the rise, consolidation, and expansion of modern bourgeois Europe. Accordingly, the author at one point dates the rise of Academic Orientalism with the European Renaissance.[4] But unfortunately, the stylist and polemicist in Edward Said very often runs away with the systematic thinker. As a result, he does not

2. Said recounts the achievements of Academic Orientalism on p. 96.
3. *Orientalism*, p. 42.
4. Ibid., p. 50.

consistently adhere to the above approach either in dating the phenomenon of Orientalism or in interpreting its historical origins and
ascent.

We thus find Said, in an act of retrospective historical projection,
tracing the origins of Orientalism all the way back to Homer,
Aeschylus, Euripides, and Dante.[5] In other words, Orientalism is not
really a thoroughly modern phenomenon, as we thought earlier, but
is the natural product of an ancient and almost irresistible European
bent of mind to misrepresent the realities of other cultures, peoples,
and their languages, in favour of Occidental self-affirmation,
domination, and ascendency. Here the author seems to be saying
that the 'European mind', from Homer to Karl Marx and H.A.R.
Gibb, is inherently inclined to distort all human realities other than
its own—for the sake of its own aggrandizement.

It seems to me that this manner of construing the origins of Orientalism simply lends strength to the essentialistic categories of
'Orient' and 'Occident', representing the ineradicable distinction
between East and West, which Said's book is ostensibly set on
demolishing. Similarly, it lends the ontological distinction of Europe
versus Asia, so characteristic of Orientalism, the kind of credibility
and respectability normally associated with continuity, persistence,
pervasiveness, and distant historical roots. This sort of credibility
and respectability is, of course, misplaced and undeserved. For
Orientalism, like so many other characteristically modern European
phenomena and movements (notably nationalism), is a genuinely
recent creation—the product of modern European history—seeking
to acquire legitimacy, credibility, and support by claiming ancient
roots and classical origins for itself. Certainly Homer, Euripides,
Dante, St. Thomas, and all the other authorities that one may care to
mention held the more or less standard distorted views prevalent in
their milieux about other cultures and peoples. However, it is equally
certain that the two forms of Orientalism built their relatively
modern repertoires of systematic conventional wisdom by calling
upon the views and biases of such prestigious figures as well as by
drawing on ancient myth, legend, imagery, folklore, and plain
prejudice. Although much of this is well documented (directly and
indirectly) in Said's book, his work nevertheless remains dominated

5. Ibid., pp. 56, 62, 68.

by a unilinear conception of 'Orientalism' as somehow flowing straight from Homer to Grunebaum. Furthermore, this unilinear, almost essentialistic, presentation of the origins and development of Orientalism renders a great disservice to the vital concerns of Said's book, namely, preparing the ground for approaching the difficult question of 'how one can study other cultures and peoples from a libertarian, or nonrepressive and nonmanipulative, perspective,'[6] and for eliminating, in the name of a common humanity, both 'Orient' and 'Occident' as ontological categories and classificatory concepts bearing the marks of racial superiority and inferiority. It seems to me that as a logical consequence of Said's tendency to view the origins and development of Orientalism in terms of such unilinear constancy, the task of combating and transcending its essentialistic categories, in the name of this common humanity, is made all the more difficult.

Another important result of this approach bears on Said's interpretation of the supposed relationship between Cultural-Academic Orientalism as representation and disciplined learning on the one hand, and Institutional Orientalism as expansionary movement and socio-economic force on the other. In other words, when Said leans heavily on his unilinear conception of 'Orientalism', he produces a picture which says that this cultural apparatus known as 'Orientalism' is the real source of the West's political interest in the Orient, that it is the real source of modern Institutional Orientalism. Thus, for him, European and, later, American political interest in the Orient was really created by the sort of Western cultural tradition known as Orientalism.[7] Furthermore, according to one of his renderings, Orientalism is a distribution of the awareness that the world is made up of two unequal halves—Orient and Occident—into aesthetic, scholarly, economic, sociological, historical, and philosophical texts. This awareness not only created a whole series of Occidental 'interests' (political, economic, strategic) in the Orient, but also helped to maintain them.[8] Hence, for Said the relationship between Academic Orientalism as a cultural apparatus and Institutional Orientalism as economic interest and political force is seen in terms of a *'preposterous* transition' from 'a merely textual

6. Ibid., p. 24.
7. Ibid., p. 12.
8. Ibid.

apprehension, formulation or definition of the Orient to the putting of all this into practice in the Orient.'[9] According to this interpretation, Said's phrase 'Orientalism overrode the Orient'[10] can only mean that the Institutional Orientalism that invaded and subjugated the East was really the legitimate offspring and product of that other kind of Orientalism, so intrinsic, it seems, to the minds, texts, aesthetics, representations, lore, and imagery of Westerners as far back as Homer, Aeschylus, and Euripides! To understand the subjugation of the East in modern times, Said keeps referring us back to earlier times, when the Orient was no more than an awareness, a word, a representation, a piece of learning to the Occident:[11] 'What we must reckon with is a large and slow process of appropriation by which Europe, or the European awareness of the Orient, transformed itself from being textual and contemplative into being administrative, economic, and even military.'[12]

Edward Said therefore sees the 'Suez Canal idea' as 'the logical conclusion of Orientalist thought and effort'[13] much more than as the result of Franco-British imperial interests and rivalries (although he does not ignore the latter).

One cannot escape the impression that for Said the emergence of such observers, administrators, and invaders of the Orient as Napoleon, Cromer, and Balfour was somehow made inevitable by 'Orientalism', and that the political orientations, careers, and ambitions of these figures are better understood by reference to d'Herbelot and Dante than to more immediately relevant and mundane interests. Accordingly, it is hardly surprising to see Said, when touching on the role of the European powers in deciding the history of the Near Orient in the early twentieth century, select for prominent notice the 'peculiar epistemological framework through which the Powers saw the Orient',[14] which was built by the long tradition of Orientalism. He then affirms that the powers acted on the Orient as they did because of that peculiar epistemological framework. Presumably, had the long tradition of Cultural-Academic Orientalism fashioned

9. Ibid., p. 96.
10. Ibid.
11. Ibid., pp. 202 – 03.
12. Ibid., p. 210.
13. Ibid., p. 91.
14. Ibid., p. 221.

a less peculiar, more sympathetic and truthful epistemological framework, then the powers would have acted more charitably and viewed the Orient in a more favourable light!

Raw Reality and its Representations

When Said thinks and writes along these lines, it is hard to escape the strong impression that for him representations, images, words, metaphors, idioms, styles, universes of discourse, political ambiances, cultural sensitivities, highly mediated pieces of knowledge, extremely rarefied truths are, if not the very stuff of reality, then certainly much more important and informative substitutes for raw reality itself. If Academic Orientalism transmutes the reality of the Orient into the stuff of texts (as he says on page 86), then it would seem that Said sublimates the earthly realities of the Occident's interaction with the Orient into the ethereal stuff of the spirit. One detects, therefore, a strong and unwarranted general anti-scientific bias in his book. This comes out most clearly in his constant inveighing against Cultural-Academic Orientalism for having categorized, classified, tabulated, codified, indexed, schematized, reduced, dissected the Orient (and hence for having distorted its reality and disfigured its particular mode of being), as if such operations were somehow evil in themselves and unfit for the proper understanding of human societies, cultures, languages, and so on.

Yet Said himself readily admits that it is impossible for a culture, be it Eastern or Western or South American, to grasp much about the reality of another, alien culture without resort to categorization, classification, schematization, and reduction—with the necessarily accompanying distortions and misrepresentations. If, as Said insists, the unfamiliar, exotic, and alien is always apprehended, domesticated, assimilated, and represented in terms of the already familiar, then such distortions and misrepresentations become inevitable. For Said: '...cultures have always been inclined to impose complete transformations on other cultures, receiving these other cultures not as they are but as, for the benefit of the receiver, they ought to be.'[15]

15. Ibid., p. 67.

He even finds 'nothing especially controversial or reprehensible' about the domestication of an exotic and alien culture in the terms of reference of another culture, because 'such domestications of the exotic take place between all cultures, certainly between all men.'[16] In fact, Said elevates this to a general principle that emanates from 'the nature of the human mind' and invariably governs the dynamics of the reception of one culture by another. Thus, 'all cultures impose corrections upon raw reality, changing it from free-floating objects into units of knowledge', because 'it is perfectly natural for the human mind to resist the assault on it of untreated strangeness'.[17]

In fact, at one point Said goes so far as to deny entirely the possibility of attaining 'objective truth' about other cultures, especially if they seem exotic, alien, and strange. The only means for approaching and receiving them are those of reduction, representation, and schematization, with all the attending distortions and falsifications that such operations imply and impose. According to Said: '... the real issue is whether indeed there can be a true representation of anything, or whether any and all representations, because they *are* representations, are embedded first in the language and then in the culture, institutions, and political ambience of the representer. If the latter alternative is the correct one (as I believe it is), then we must be prepared to accept the fact that a representation is *eo ipso* implicated, intertwined, embedded, interwoven with a great many other things besides the "truth", which is itself a representation.'[18]

If, as the author keeps repeating (by way of censure and castigation), the Orient studied by Orientalism is no more than an image and a representation in the mind and culture of the Occident (the representer in this case), then it is also true that the Occident is thereby behaving perfectly naturally and in accordance with the general rule—as stated by Said himself—governing the dynamics of the reception of one culture by another. Accordingly, in trying to deal (via its Orientalism) with the raw reality of the Orient, the Occident does what all cultures do under the circumstances, namely:

1) domesticate the alien and represent it through its own familiar terms and frames of reference;

16. Ibid., p. 60.
17. Ibid., p. 67.
18. Ibid., p. 272.

2) impose on the Orient those 'complete transformations' which Edward Said says cultures are prone to effect on each other so as to receive the strange, not as it is but as it ought to be, for the benefit of the receiver;

3) impose upon the raw reality of the Orient the necessary corrections needed to change it 'from free-floating objects into units of knowledge'; and

4) follow the natural bent of the human mind in resisting 'the assault on it of untreated strangeness'.

The Representation of Islam by the West

One of the examples given by Said is of particular interest: 'The reception of Islam in the West is a perfect case in point, and has been admirably studied by Norman Daniel. One constraint acting upon Christian thinkers who tried to understand Islam was an analogical one; since Christ is the basis of Christian faith, it was assumed—quite incorrectly—that Mohammed was to Islam as Christ was to Christianity. Hence the polemic name "Mohammedanism" given to Islam, and the automatic epithet "imposter" applied to Mohammed. Out of such and many other misconceptions "there formed a circle which was never broken by imaginative exteriorization ... The Christian concept of Islam was integral and self-sufficient"; Islam became an image—the word is Daniel's but it seems to me to have remarkable implications for Orientalism in general—whose function was not so much to represent Islam in itself as to represent it for the medieval Christian.'[19]

The significance of the above argument lies in the fact that Said nowhere carries it to its logical conclusion in the light of what he had stated to be generally true about the reductive dynamics of the reception of one culture by another. As he knows very well, the reception of Christianity by Islam in the East differs little from the account given above. To make this point I shall present the gist of the same passage with a few appropriate alterations:

'One constraint acting upon Muslim thinkers who tried to understand Christianity was an analogical one; since Mohammed was no

19. Ibid., p. 60.

more than the Messenger of God it was assumed—quite incorrectly —that Christ was to Christianity as Mohammed was to Islam, namely, a plain Messenger of God or ordinary prophet. Hence the polemics against His incarnation, sonship, divinity, crucifixion, resurrection, and the automatic epithet of "forgers" applied to the first guardians of the Holy Scriptures. Out of such and many other conceptions "there formed a circle which was never broken by imaginative exteriorization ... the Muslim concept of Christianity was integral and self-sufficient." Christianity became an image —the word is Daniel's but it seems to me to have remarkable implications for how one culture receives another in general—whose function was not so much to represent Christianity in itself as to represent it for the medieval Muslim.'

In the light of these critical remarks it should become clear: (a) why Said deals so harshly with Marx's attempts to understand and interpret Oriental societies; (b) why he deals so much more kindly with the Macdonald-Gibb view of Islam; and (c) why he deals so charitably and sympathetically with the mystico-theosophical extrapolations bred by Massignon's brand of Orientalism.

Said criticizes and exposes the falsity of the sort of declarative assertions made by the Macdonald-Gibb variety of Orientalism about Islam and the Muslims. He attacks them for being abstract, metaphysical, and untrue. Here is a sample of such assertions.

1. 'It is plain, I think, and admitted that the conception of the Unseen is much more immediate and real to the Oriental than to the Western peoples.'

2. 'The essential difference in the Oriental mind is not credulity as to unseen things, but inability to construe a system as to seen things.'

3. 'The difference in the Oriental is not essentially religiosity, but the lack of the sense of law.[20] For him, there is no immovable order of nature.'

4. 'It is evident that anything is possible to the Oriental. The supernatural is so near that it may touch him at any moment.'

5. 'Until recently, the ordinary Muslim citizen and cultivator had no political interests or functions, and no literature of easy access except religious literature, had no festivals and no communal life except in connection with religion, saw little or nothing of the outside

20. In other words, a natural order governed by invariable laws.

world except through religious glasses. *To him, in consequence, religion meant everything.*'[21]

The trouble with such affirmations does not lie in their mere falsity, abstractness, and metaphysical character. Certainly, neither Macdonald nor Gibb were simple victims when making these declarations of the 'epistemological framework' built by the traditions of Orientalism, as Said seems to suggest. In fact, one can argue convincingly that in a certain very significant sense:

1. It is true that in general the Unseen is much more immediate and real to the common citizens of Cairo and Damascus than it is to the present inhabitants of New York and Paris.

2. It is true that religion 'means everything' to the life of Moroccan peasants in a way that must remain incomprehensible to present-day American farmers.

3. It is true that the idea of an independent inviolable lawful order of nature is in many respects much more real, concrete, and firmly established to the minds of the students of Moscow University than it is to the minds of the students of al-Azhar University (or any other university in the Muslim world for that matter).

What Said fails to bring out is the fact that the affirmations of the Macdonald-Gibb brand of Orientalism are really declarative only in a very narrow sense. They masquerade as fully and genuinely declarative statements of permanent fact only to conceal a set of broad directives and instructions on how Occidentals should go about dealing with and handling the Orient and the Orientals, here and now. These directives are necessarily of a general nature and hence require a variety of 'operational definitions' to turn them into useful practical steps taken by such a varied lot as Western missionaries, teachers, administrators, businessmen, army officers, diplomats, intelligence experts, politicians, policy-makers. For example, such people are guided by these implicit directives and instructions to allow for and take advantage of the fact that religious beliefs, tribal loyalties, theological explanations, and so on still play a much more decisive role in the life of contemporary Oriental societies than they do in modern Western ones.

The very limitation of the declarative scope of the Macdonald-Gibb type of affirmations betrays not only their practical function

21. *Orientalism*, pp. 276 – 79 (emphasis added by Said).

and immediate relevance to actual situations, but also the profoundly ahistorical frame of mind and thought out of which they emanate. They pretend that the Unseen was always (and always will be) more immediate and real to the Orientals than to the Western peoples past, present, and future. Similarly, they pretend that the idea of an independent lawful order of nature was always and will for ever be more real, concrete, and firmly established to the Occidental's mind and life than it could ever be in the consciousness of Oriental human beings. The simple historical fact that at one time, say before the break-up of Christendom, the Unseen was as immediate and real to Occidentals, is not permitted to disturb the Olympian serenity of the Macdonald-Gibb pseudo-declaratives.

If one could speak of the hero of a book like *Orientalism*, then Massignon emerges as the preferred candidate for the role. This towering French Orientalist is praised for having surpassed all others in the almost impossible task of genuinely and sympathetically understanding Oriental Muslim culture, religion, and mentality. Due to his profound humanism and compassion, Massignon, we are told, accomplished the feat of identifying with the 'vital forces' informing Eastern culture and of grasping its 'spiritual dimension' as no one else in the West before or since.[22]

But in the final analysis, is not Massignon's presumed identification with the 'vital forces' and 'spiritual dimension' of Eastern culture simply a personalized, idealized and reiterated version of the classical Orientalist representation of an Orient 'overvalued for its pantheism, spirituality, longevity and primitivity',[23] a representation Said has debunked so masterfully? Furthermore, we may infer from the discussion of the meaning and importance of Massignon's work that he nowhere abandoned the cardinal assumption (and original sin, according to Said) of all Orientalism, namely the insistence on the essentialistic separation of the world into two halves: an Orient and an Occident, each with its inherently different nature and traits. It is evident, then, that with Massignon, as with the work of any other Orientalist attacked by Said, Orient and Occident remain fundamental ontological categories and classificatory schemes, with all their attendant implications and applications.

22. Ibid., pp. 265 – 70.
23. Ibid., p. 150.

We learn from Said's book that Massignon's Orient is completely consonant with the world of the Seven Sleepers and the Abrahamanic prayers;[24] that his 'repeated efforts to understand and report on the Palestine conflict, for all their profound humanism, never really got past the quarrel between Isaac and Ishmael';[25] that for him the essence of the difference between East and West is between modernity and ancient tradition;[26] that in his view the Islamic Orient is always spiritual, Semitic, tribalistic, radically monotheistic and not Aryan;[27] that he was widely sought after as an expert on Islamic matters by colonial administrators;[28] and that he was of the conviction that it was France's obligation to associate itself with the Muslims' desire to defend their traditional culture, the rule of their dynastic life, and the patrimony of believers.[29]

Now, how can the most acute and versatile contemporary critic of Orientalism offer such high praise to an Orientalist who obviously subscribes to the entire apparatus of Orientalism's discredited dogmas?

Karl Marx and the Orient

The picture Said presents of Marx's attitude to the East runs more or less as follows.[30] Through his analyses of British rule in India, Marx arrived at 'the notion of an Asiatic economic system' (the famous Asiatic mode of production) which acted as the solid foundation for a sort of political rule known as 'Oriental despotism'. At first, the violent destruction and transformation of India's traditional social organization appalled Marx and shocked him as a human being and thinker. His humanity was moved, and sympathy engaged, by the human miseries and suffering attendant upon such a process of transformation. At this stage of his development, Marx still identified with downtrodden Asia and sensed some fellowship with its wretched masses. But then Marx fell under the sway of Orientalist

24. Ibid., p. 267.
25. Ibid., p. 270.
26. Ibid., p. 269.
27. Ibid., p. 271.
28. Ibid., p. 210.
29. Ibid., p. 271.
30. Ibid., pp. 153 – 56.

learning, and the picture quickly changed. The labels of Orientalism, its vocabulary, abstractions, and definitions came to dominate his mind and emotions.

According to Said, Marx—who initially recognized the individuality of Asia—became the captive of that formidable censor created by the vocabulary, learning, and lore of Orientalism. He cites what supposedly happened to Marx's thought as an instance of how a 'non-Orientalist's human engagements are dissolved [and] then usurped by Orientalist generalizations'. The initial sympathy and gush of sentiment experienced by Marx disappeared as he encountered the unshakeable definitions built up by Orientalist science and supported by the Oriental lore that was supposed to be appropriate to it. Briefly, the case of Marx shows how 'an experience was dislodged by a dictionary definition'.[31]

This is how Said sees the metamorphosis that led Marx to the view (highly objectionable to Said) that Britain was making possible a real social revolution in India, acting as the unconscious tool of history in bringing about that revolution. In this instance, Britain is viewed by Marx as acting simultaneously as an agency of destruction and regeneration in Asia. Said unambiguously traces this mature view of Marx to Orientalism's pseudo-learning and fancies about the East, especially in its nineteenth-century messianic and romantic variety. For him, Marx is no exception to all the Europeans who dealt with the East in terms of Orientalism's basic category of the inequality between East and West. Furthermore, he declares flatly that Marx's economic analyses of Asia are perfectly suited to a standard Orientalist undertaking.

I think that this account of Marx's views and analyses of highly complex historical processes and situations is a travesty. Undoubtedly, like any other creative genius, Marx was greatly influenced by the lexicographical learning, dictionary definitions, abstractions, representations, generalizations, and linguistic norms prevalent in his time and milieu. But only Said's excessive fascination with the verbal, textual, and linguistic could lead him to portray Marx's mind as somehow usurped (against his better judgement and nobler sentiments) by the vocabulary, lexicography, and dictionary definitions

31. Ibid., p. 155.

of the Orientalist tradition in the West! Said stands at times on the verge of regression into belief in the magical efficacy of words.

Marx's manner of analysing British rule in India in terms of an unconscious tool of history—which is making possible a real social revolution by destroying the old India and laying the foundations of a new order—cannot under any circumstances be ascribed to the usurpation of Marx's mind by conventional Orientalist verbiage. Marx's explanation (regardless of whether one agrees or disagrees with it) testifies to his theoretical consistency in general, and to his keen realism in analysing specific historical situations. This is evident from the fact that Marx always tended to explain historical processes in terms of social agencies, economic struggles, political movements, and great personalities that simultaneously played the role of destroyers and creators. He often cast these as 'unconscious tools' of a history unfolding in stages, and sometimes in inscrutable and unpredictable ways. There is nothing specific to either Asia or the Orient in Marx's theoretical interpretations of the past, present, and future. On this score, his sources are thoroughly 'European' in reference and owe nothing to Orientalist learning. One only need recall those vivid passages in the *Communist Manifesto* in which Marx portrays the modern European bourgeoisie in the double role of destroyer and creator: destroyer of the old inherited Europe, maker of its liberal present, and usher of its proletarian future. Like the European capitalist class, British rule in India was its own gravedigger. There is nothing particularly 'Orientalistic' about this explanation. Furthermore, Marx's call for revolution in Asia is more realistic and promising historically than any noble sentiments he could have lavished on necessarily vanishing socio-economic formations.

I shall cite another example related neither to Orientalism nor to Asia or the realm of politics: how Marx described the dual role of usurer's capital in the destruction of 'small-peasant and small-burgher-production' and in the making of modern industrial Europe.[32]

On the one hand:

'[T]his usurer's capital impoverishes the mode of production, paralyses the productive forces instead of developing them. . . . It

32. *Capital* Volume 3, chapter 36.

does not alter the mode of production, but attaches itself firmly to it like a parasite and makes it wretched. It sucks out its blood, enervates it and compels reproduction to proceed under ever more pitiable conditions. Hence the popular hatred against usurers.'

On the other hand:

'Usury, in contradistinction to consuming wealth, is historically important, inasmuch as it is in itself a process generating capital. . . . Usury is a powerful lever in developing the pre-conditions for industrial capital in so far as it plays the following double role, first, building up, in general, an independent money wealth alongside that of the merchant, and, secondly, appropriating the conditions of labour, that is, ruining the owners of the old conditions of labour.'

Said's accusation that Marx subscribed to the basic Orientalist idea of the superiority of the West over the East seems plausible only because of the ambiguity underlying his own discussion of this matter. That nineteenth-century Europe was superior to Asia and much of the rest of the world in terms of productive capacities, social organization, historical ascendency, military might, and scientific and technological development is indisputable as a contingent historical fact. Orientalism, with its ahistorical bourgeois bent of mind, did its best to eternalize this mutable fact, to turn it into a permanent reality past, present, and future. Hence Orientalism's essentialistic ontology of East and West. Marx, like anyone else, knew of the superiority of modern Europe over the Orient. But to accuse a radically historicist thinker such as Marx of turning this contingent fact into a necessary reality for all time is simply absurd. The fact that he used terms related to or derived from the Orientalist tradition does not make him a partisan of the essentialistic ontology of East and West any more than his constant use of such pejorative epithets as 'nigger' and 'Jew' (to describe foes, class enemies, despised persons, and so on) could turn him into a systematic racist and anti-Semite. No doubt, the typical messianic romantic vision was an essential part of Marx's historicism. But Said errs greatly in attributing this vision to the later influence of Orientalism. For the messianic and romantic aspect of Marx's interpretation of human history was with him from the beginning, and it encompassed the West long before he extended it to the East.

Orientalism and Dependence

I would like to end this section of my critique by drawing attention to a rather curious and enigmatic passage that occurs towards the end of Said's book, right after his sharp critique of the contemporary Area Study Programmes that have come to replace the traditional departments and disciplines of Orientalism in Western universities, particularly in the United States. Said makes the following observation and judgement: 'The Arab World today is an intellectual, political, and cultural satellite of the United States. This is not in itself something to be lamented; the specific form of the satellite relationship, however, is.'[33]

If I understand this passage correctly, Said finds the intellectual, political, and cultural dependence of the Arab world on the United States quite acceptable; what he deplores is only the manner in which this dependence manifests itself at present. There are basically two standpoints from which we can view this position. The first emanates from a 'soft' and liberal interpretation of the meaning and implications of dependence, while the second flows from a 'hard' and genuinely radical understanding of the nature and consequences of this relationship.

According to the 'soft' interpretation, Said seems to be simply taking note of the well-known fact of the superiority and supremacy of the United States over its satellites, and hoping that, given greater American comprehension and appreciation of the realities of the Arab world, the lamentable aspects of the satellite relationship can be ameliorated. Such a development would greatly enhance the chances of greater political maturity, cultural independence, and intellectual originality in the Arab world. In other words, the objective is not for the Arab world to shake off its dependence altogether, but to alter and improve its circumstances, terms, and *modus operandi*, in the direction of a more genuinely equal and balanced relationship. As a result, Said blames the United States—and not the satellite—for an unsatisfactory and deplorable condition relating to 'the specific form of the satellite relationship'. More precisely, he blames the American Middle East experts who advise the policy-makers, because neither of these two have succeeded in

33. *Orientalism*, p. 322.

freeing themselves from the system of ideological fictions created by Orientalism. He even warns these experts and their masters that unless they look at the Arab world more realistically and try to understand it without the abstractions and fanciful constructions of Orientalism, America's investment in the Middle East will lack any solid foundation. He says:

'The system of ideological fictions I have been calling Orientalism has serious implications not only because it is intellectually discreditable. For the United States today is heavily invested in the Middle East, more heavily than anywhere else on earth: the Middle East experts who advise policymakers are imbued with Orientalism almost to a person. Most of this investment, appropriately enough, is built on foundations of sand, since the experts instruct policy on the basis of such marketable abstractions as political elites, modernization, and stability, most of which are simply the old Orientalist stereotypes dressed up in policy jargon, and most of which have been completely inadequate to describe what took place recently in Lebanon or earlier in the Palestinian popular resistance to Israel.'[34]

All in all, Said's position here departs little from the conventional wisdom of the liberal establishments of the West in general and of the United States in particular.

The 'hard' and radical interpretation of the meaning and consequences of dependence has been developed and widely publicized by such scholars and social thinkers as Paul Baran, Andre Gunder Frank, Pierre Jalée, Claude Julien, Samir Amin, and Arghiri Emmanuel. According to their account, dependence is structurally incapable of generating any sort of ties save those of the intensified exploitation, pillage, and subjugation of the satellite by the centre.

According to this view, Said's vague thoughts on the subject can only foster additional illusions concerning the nature of the satellite relationship and generate dangerously false expectations about its possible implications and actual applications. The essence of the illusion lies in Said's perilous assumption that the lamentable aspects and manifestations of the satellite relationship can be satisfactorily reformed and improved to the ultimate benefit of both the Arab world and the heavy American investment in the Middle East. For

34. Ibid. p. 321.

the radical view of dependence holds that the satellite relationship leads to the further development of the already profound underdevelopment of the satellite itself. Hence its inevitable conclusion that salvation for the Arab world will remain an unattainable goal until the relationship of dependence is definitively and unambiguously smashed. From this also derives its inevitable criticism of Said for ending his book on a distinctly classical Orientalist note:

1) by not finding the satellite relationship between East (the Middle East) and West (America) lamentable as such;

2) by giving good advice to American policy-makers and their Middle East experts on how to strengthen the basis of their investment in the area and on how to ameliorate the conditions of 'the specific satellite relationship', by ridding themselves of misleading Orientalist fictions and illusions;

3) by forgetting that should American experts and their masters heed his advice, the Orient will find an even more formidable enemy in American imperialism than it already has.

2. ORIENTALISM IN REVERSE

One of the most salient and interesting accomplishments of Said's book is its laying bare of Orientalism's persistent belief that there is a radical ontological difference between the natures of the Orient and the Occident—that is, between the essential natures of Eastern and Western societies, cultures, and peoples. This alleged ontological difference immediately entails an epistemological one which holds that the sort of conceptual instruments, scientific categories, sociological concepts, political descriptions, and ideological distinctions employed to understand and deal with Western societies remain, in principle, irrelevant and inapplicable to Eastern ones. This epistemological assumption is epitomized in H.A.R. Gibb's statement that applying 'the psychology and mechanics of Western political institutions to Asian or Arab situations is pure Walt Disney.'[35] It is also shown in Bernard Lewis' declared belief that 'recourse to the language of left-wing and right-wing, progressive and conservative, and the rest of the Western terminology . . . in

35. Ibid., p. 107.

explaining Muslim political phenomena is about as accurate and as enlightening as an account of a cricket match by a baseball correspondent.'[36] In other words, the vast and readily discernible differences between Islamic societies and cultures on the one hand and European ones on the other, are neither a matter of complex processes in the historical evolution of humanity nor a matter of empirical facts to be acknowledged and dealt with accordingly. There are, in addition to all that, emanations from a certain enduring Oriental (or Islamic) cultural, psychic, or racial essence, as the case may be, bearing identifiable fundamental and unchanging attributes. This ahistorical, anti-human, and even anti-historical 'Orientalist' doctrine I shall call *Ontological Orientalism*.

Obviously, Ontological Orientalism is thoroughly ideological and metaphysical in the most pejorative senses of these terms. Furthermore, in his book Said spared no effort to expose this fact.

Ontological Orientalism is the foundation of the image created by modern Europe of the Orient. As Said has shown, this image affords more genuine and instructive revelations about certain European states of affairs, particularly about expansionary projects and imperial designs, than it does about its supposed object. But nonetheless, this image has left its profound imprint on the Orient's modern and contemporary consciousness of itself. Hence Said's important warning to the subjects and victims of Orientalism against the dangers and temptations of applying the readily available structures, styles, and ontological biases of Orientalism to themselves and others.

I would like to contend that such applications not only have taken place but are continuing on a fairly wide scale. Furthermore, to fall in the temptations against which Said has warned engenders what may be called *Orientalism in Reverse*.

In what follows, I shall discuss this contention in terms of a specific instance of this reversed Orientalism, namely *Ontological Orientalism in Reverse*.

To explain, I shall refer to two instances: the first drawn from the well-known phenomenon of secular Arab nationalism, the second from the recent movement of Islamic revival.

---

36. Ibid., p. 318.

Arab Nationalism and Orientalism in Reverse

About two years ago, a prominent man of thought and politics in Syria published a series of articles in which he proposed to study certain 'basic' words in the Arabic language as a means to attaining 'genuine knowledge' of some of the essential characteristics of the primordial 'Arab mentality' underlying those words.[37] Upon noting that the word for 'man' in Arabic (*insân*) suggests 'companionship', 'sociability', 'friendliness', and 'familiarity' (*anisa, uns, anîs*, etc), he triumphantly concluded that the implicit view held by the 'primordial Arab mind' says that man has a natural tendency to live with other men, or, as he himself explained, 'the primordial Arab mind innately possesses the philosophical idea that man is by nature a social being.' Then our author made the following telling comparison:

'The philosophy of Hobbes is based on his famous saying that "every man is a wolf unto other men", while, on the contrary, the inner philosophy implicit in the word *insân* preaches that "every man is a brother unto other men".'

I submit that this piece of so-called analysis and comparison contains, in a highly condensed form, the entire apparatus of metaphysical abstractions and ideological mystifications so characteristic of Ontological Orientalism and so deftly and justly denounced in Said's book. The only new element is the fact that the Orientalist essentialistic ontology has been reversed to favour one specific people of the Orient.

It should be evident that one of the significant features of Ontological Orientalism in Reverse is the typical Orientalist obsession with language, texts, philology, and allied subjects. It simply imitates the great Orientalist masters—a poor imitation at that —when it seeks to unravel the secrets of the primordial Arab 'mind', 'psyche', or 'character' in and through words. In other words, it has obediently and uncritically adopted what Said pejoratively called the Orientalists' 'textual'[38] attitude to reality. In the above instance of

---

37. Georges Saddikni, 'Man, Reason, and Synonyms', *al-Ma'rifa*, Damascus, October 1978, pp. 7–17. Mr Saddikni was until very recently a member of the National (Pan-Arab) Command of the Ba'th Party and head of its Bureau for Cultural Affairs. He was Syria's minister of information for many years.

38. *Orientalism*, p. 92.

so-called analysis and comparison, one can easily see the Panglos-
sian and even quixotic character of the attempt to capture something
about such a complex historical phenomenon as the cultural, mental, and psychic life of the Arabs, past and present, by literally applying what has been learned from Orientalist books and philological
analyses.

This reversed Orientalism sins doubly because it tries to capture
the essence of the 'Arab mind' by learning how to analyse Arabic
words and texts from the words and texts of the master Orientalists.
Like a platonic work of art, its textual attitude becomes twice
removed from the original reality.

Thus Orientalism in Reverse presents us with variations on Renan's racist theme as derived from his philological analyses and linguistic speculations. But the novel element is the conclusion of Orientalism in Reverse that comparative philological and linguistic studies
prove the ontological superiority of the Oriental mind (the 'Arab
mind' in this case) over the Occidental one. For, have we not shown
that the sublime idea of the 'brotherhood of man' is innate and original to the 'primordial Arab mind,' while Hobbes's base idea of 'the
war of all against all' is innate and original to the 'primordial European mind'?

In classical Orientalist fashion, the essence of the 'Arab mind' is
explored by an Arab thinker through language only and in hermetic
seclusion from such unwelcome intrusions as socio-economic infra-
structures, politics, historical change, class conflicts, revolutions,
and so on. This primordial Arab 'mind', 'psyche', or 'essence' is
supposed to reveal its potency, genius, and distinguishing characteristics through the flux of historical events and the accidents of time,
without either history or time ever biting into its intrinsic nature.
Conversely, the series of events, circumstances, and accidents form-
ing the history of such a people as the Arabs can never be genuinely
understood from this point of view, without reduction, through a
series of mediations and steps, to the primary manifestations of the
original unchanging nature of the Arab 'mind', 'psyche', or 'essence'.

Here I shall cite another example. Said points out correctly that:
'The exaggerated value heaped upon Arabic as a language permits
the Orientalist to make the language equivalent to mind, society,
history, and nature. For the Orientalist the language *speaks* the Arab
Oriental, not vice versa.'[39]

Orientalism in Reverse follows suit—not only faithfully but also more recklessly and crudely. Thus, another Syrian author wrote the following remarks on the unique status of the Arabic language and the wonders it reveals about the 'primitivity' of the Arab and his language:

'After having studied the vocal characteristics of every letter of the Arabic language, I proceeded to apply their emotional and sensory connotations to the meanings of the words starting with those letters, or at times ending with them, by means of statistical tables drawn from the dictionaries of the Arabic language. After carefully examining the marvellous results yielded by this study, it appeared to me that the originality of the Arabic language transcends the limits of human potentialities. I thought then that no logical and reasonable explanation of this miracle of a language can be supplied except in terms of the category of the primitivity of the Arab and his language.'[40]

The crucial conclusion of this line of reasoning runs as follows: 'Thus, Arabic letters become transformed from mere vocal containers filled with human sensations and emotions to the quintessence of the Arab, of his *'asabiya*, spirit, and even of the constituents of his nationality.'[41]

In perfect Renanian fashion this notion of the primitivity of the Arab and his language is made to define a primary human type with its inimitable essentialistic traits out of which more specific forms of behaviour necessarily flow. This is very explicitly and roughly—hence candidly and honestly—stated by still another Syrian ideologue in the following manner: 'The essence of the Arab nation enjoys certain absolute and essential characteristics which are: theism, spiritualism, idealism, humanism, and civilization-ism.'[42]

Not unexpectedly, it follows that this absolute essence of the Arab nation is also the implicit bearer of a civilizing mission affecting the whole world. Given the decline of the West at the end of the

39. Ibid., p. 321.
40. Hasan Abbas, 'The Arabic Letters and the Six Senses', *al-Ma'rifa*, Damascus, October 1978, pp. 140–41.
41. Ibid., p. 143.
42. Isma'il 'Arafi, *Qital al-'Arab al-Qawmi*, published by the Ministry of Culture and National Guidance, Damascus 1977, p. 70.

twentieth century, the Orient is supposed to rise under the leadership of the Arab nation and under the banner of its *mission civilisatrice* to guide humanity out of the state of decadence to which Western leadership has brought it. For, the 'Western essence' produced such unmistakable signs of decadence as: 'mechanism, Darwinism, Freudianism, Marxism, Malthusianism, secularism, realism, positivism, existentialism, phenomenalism, pragmatism, Machiavellianism, liberalism, and imperialism', all of which are worldly doctrines manifesting 'a purely materialist essence.'[43]

In contrast, 'the human universe' (that is, humanity, the world, life, civilization) is today awaiting its appointed encounter with 'the nation bearing that mission and chosen to lead it out of its impasse'. Furthermore: 'No matter how tragic the condition of the Arab nation may be at present, there is not a shred of doubt that this nation alone is the promised and awaited one, because it alone acquired perfectly, ages ago, all the ideal constituents, characteristics, and features of a nation. Accordingly, it has come to possess, in a uniquely deep-rooted manner, all the various ideal human traits, excellences, and virtues which render it capable and deserving of carrying out the lofty mission for which it was chosen.'[44]

I turn now to the second instance illustrating what I have defined as Ontological Orientalism in Reverse.

Islamic Revivalism and Orientalism in Reverse

Under the impact of the Iranian revolutionary process, a revisionist Arab line of political thought has surfaced. Its prominent protagonists are drawn, in the main, from the ranks of the left: former radicals, ex-Communists, unorthodox Marxists, and disillusioned nationalists of one sort or another. This nebulous political line found an enthusiastic response among a number of distinguished Arab intellectuals and writers, such as the poet Adonis, the progressive thinker Anwar Abdel Malek, and the young and talented Lebanese critic Ilias Khoury. I would add also that its partisans proved themselves quite prolific, utilizing various forums in

43. Ibid., p. 145.
44. Ibid., pp. 147 – 48.

Lebanon and Western Europe to make their views, analyses, and ideas known to the reading public. Their central thesis may be summarized as follows: The national salvation so eagerly sought by the Arabs since the Napoleonic occupation of Egypt is to be found neither in secular nationalism (be it radical, conservative, or liberal) nor in revolutionary communism, socialism, or what have you, but in a return to the authenticity of what they call 'popular political Islam'. For purposes of distinctness I shall refer to this approach as the *Islamanic trend*.

I do not wish to dispute the above thesis of the Islamanics in this presentation. Instead, I would like to point out that the analyses, beliefs, and ideas produced by the Islamanic trend in defence of its central thesis simply reproduce the whole discredited apparatus of classical Orientalist doctrine concerning the difference between East and West, Islam and Europe. This reiteration occurs at both the ontological and epistemological levels, only reversed to favour Islam and the East in its implicit and explicit value judgements.

A prominent feature in the political literature produced by the Islamanic trend is its insistence on replacing the familiar opposition of national liberation against imperialist domination by the more reactionary opposition of East against West.[45] In the West, the historical process may be moved by economic interests, class struggles, and socio-political forces. But in the East the 'prime mover' of history is Islam, according to a recent declaration by Adonis.[46]

Adonis explains himself by openly admitting that in studying Arab society and its internal struggles, 'I have attributed primacy to the ideological-religious factor because in Arab society, which is built completely on the basis of religion, the modes and means of production did not develop in a manner leading to the rise of class consciousness. The religious factor remains its prime mover. Consequently, its movement cannot be explained by means of such categories as class, class consciousness, economics, let alone economism. This means that the struggle within Arab society has been in the main of an ideological-religious nature.'[47]

45. Anwar Abdel Malek recently emphasized his conviction that the main feature of our time is the continuing 'civilizational confrontation between the Orient and the Occident'. (*Arab Studies Quarterly*, vol. 1, no. 3, summer 1979, p. 180.)

46. 'Islam and Political Islam', *al-Nahar al-'Arabi al-Duwali*, Paris (in Arabic), 22 January 1979, p. 64. Republished in *Mawaqif*, Beirut, no. 34, winter 1979, pp. 149 – 60.

47. *Mawaqif*, no. 34, winter 1979, p. 155.

Adonis' sweeping conclusion is, naturally enough, to 'do away with class struggle, oil, and economics,'[48] in order to arrive at a proper understanding of Oriental (Muslim, Arab, Iranian) social dynamics.

In other words: ideas, beliefs, philosophical systems, and ideological superstructures are sufficient to explain the 'laws of motion' of Oriental societies and cultures. Thus, an enthusiastic Islamanic announced that 'the Iranian revolution reveals to us with the greatest emphasis . . . that the laws of evolution, struggle, and unity in our countries and the Orient are other than and different from those of Europe and the West.'[49] A third Islamanic assured us that 'all this permits Khomeini to translate his simple Islamic ideas into a socio-political earthquake which the most perfect and sophisticated theoretical/philosophical systems failed to detonate.'[50] Accordingly, the latest advice of the Islamanics to the Arab left is to rearrange their priorities in such a way as to stand them on their head: 'to give ultimate importance to the cultural and ideological factors which move the masses and to proceed to reformulate scientific, economic, and social truths on this basis'.[51]

According to an Orientalist such as H.A.R. Gibb (and others), this stable, unique, self-identical Islamic totality regulates the detailed workings of all human, cultural, social, and economic phenomena subsumed under it. Furthermore, its coherence, placidity, and inner strength are primarily imperilled by such foreign intrusions as class struggles, economic interests, secular nationalist movements, democratic ideas, 'Westernized' intellectuals, Communist parties, and so on. So, it is hardly surprising to see Adonis doing two things:

First, opposing 'nationalism, secularism, socialism, Marxism, communism, and capitalism'[52] à la Gibb *et al.*, on account of the Western source of these ideas and their corrosive influence on the inner structures of Islam, which keep it Oriental.[53]

Second, interpreting the Iranian revolution in terms of a simple

48. Ibid., p. 152.
49. Walid Nuwayhid, *al-Safir*, Beirut daily, 19 December 1979, editorial page.
50. Suhail Kash, *al-Safir*, 3 January 1979.
51. Sa'd Mehio, *al-Safir*, 20 January 1979.
52. *Mawaqif*, no. 34, winter 1979, pp. 147–48.
53. *Orientalism*, p. 263.

emphatic formula: 'Islam is simply Islam', 'regardless and in spite of politics, the class struggle, oil and economics.' Here, Adonis is presenting as ultimate wisdom the barren tautology of Ontological Orientalism, so well brought out in Said's critique: 'The Orient is the Orient', 'Islam is Islam'; and, following the illustrious footsteps of such Ontological Orientalists as Renan, Macdonald, Von Grunebaum, and Bernard Lewis, Adonis and the other Islamanics imagine that they can comprehend its essence in isolation from the economics, sociology, oil, and politics of the Islamic peoples. As a result they are anxious to secure Islam's Orientalist ontological status not only as the 'prime mover' of Islamic history, but also as the alpha and omega of the 'Islamic Orient'. In the Islamic world nothing really counts save Islam.

It is noteworthy that the favourite metaphor of the Islamanics is derived from the basically fixed, unprogressive, uninnovative cyclic movement of the oceans. Islam, they say, is once again in high tide after the low ebb of past generations and even centuries. I submit that this Islamanic view of Islam is in essence, and in the light of its logical consequences, no different from the metaphysical preachings of Ontological Orientalism. In other words, Islam is paraded before us in much the same way as H.A.R. Gibb saw it, as a monolithic unique Oriental totality ineradicably distinct in its essential nature from Europe, the West, and the rest of humanity.

Thus, in classical Orientalist fashion (reversed, however), Adonis affirms condescendingly that the peculiar characteristic of the Western essence is 'technologism and not originality'. He then proceeds to enumerate the major features distinguishing Western thought on account of that inherent trait. According to him these are: system, order, method, and symmetry. On the other hand, 'the peculiarity of the Orient', for him, 'lies in originality' and this is why its nature cannot be captured except through 'the prophetic, the visionary, the magical, the miraculous, the infinite, the inner, the beyond, the fanciful, the ecstatic', and so on.[54]

Accordingly, it should come as no surprise if the revolutionary struggles and sacrifices of the Iranian people amount, in the eyes of the Islamanics, to no more than either 'a return of Islam' (the high tide metaphor) or to a manifestation of the innate Islamic opposition

54. *Mawaqif*, no. 36, winter 1980, pp. 150–53.

to non-Islamic peoples and influences (the East-West contradiction), as Bernard Lewis would have us believe.[55] Similarly, the
Islamanics would seem to be in full accord with Morroe Berger's
conclusion that 'for modern Islam neither capitalism nor socialism is
an adequate rubric.'[56] But why? The reason, as pointed out by Said,
is that according to Ontological Orientalism (both in its reversed and
original versions) it really makes no sense to talk about classical,
medieval, or modern Islam; because Islam is always Islam. Islam can
withdraw, return, be in low ebb or high tide, but not much more than
that. And since so-called 'Modern Islam', according to Ontological
Orientalism Reversed, is really no more than a reasserted version of
the old Islam, Adonis finds no embarrassment in advising the Iranian revolution about its present and future problems in the following
archaic and theological jargon:

'It is self-evident that the politics of prophecy laid the foundations
for a new life and a new order. It is also self-evident that the politics
of the *imâmate* or *wilâya* is correct guidance by the politics of
prophecy, or rather it is the same as the politics of prophecy by
inspiration and without full identification. For, every *imâmate* or
wilâya belongs to a particular age, and every age has its particular
problems. Thus, the importance of the politics of the *imâmate* and
even its legitimacy lie in the extent to which it is capable of *ijtihâd* to
comprehend the change of modes and the newly arising realities
under the correct guidance of the politics of prophecy.'[57]

Similarly, is it not this kind of conservative 'Orientalistic' logic
which underlies the recent Iranian debate on whether the 'Islamic
republic' may be described as democratic? The official Islamic line,
which prevailed, argued that 'Islam' cannot accept any additional
qualifiers, since it can only be Islam. In other terms, just as it makes
no sense to speak about classical, medieval, or modern Islam—
since Islam is always Islam—similarly, it makes no sense to talk
about an Islamic republic being democratic, since the Islamic
republic is always Islamic and cannot be anything else. Hence
Khomeini's statement in one of his many interviews about the
Islamic republic: 'The term *Islam* needs no adjective, such as

55. *Orientalism*, p. 107.
56. Ibid., p. 108.
57. *Al-Nahar al-'Arabi al-Duwali*, 26 February 1979, p. 24. See also *Mawaqif*, no.
34, p. 158.

democratic, to be attributed to it. . . . The term *Islam* is perfect, and having to put another word right next to it is, indeed, a source of sorrow.'[58]

Ontological Orientalism in Reverse is, in the end, no less reactionary, mystifying, ahistorical, and anti-human than Ontological Orientalism proper.

Beirut, Autumn 1980

---

58. *Al-Safir*, 10 October 1979.

5

A Dialogue

Said Hammami was born in Jaffa in 1941. His father, Adil, was a member of the city council and of the Istiqlaal (Independence) Party. In 1948, when war broke out, many Palestinian supporters of the Hashemite family fled eastward to Jordan, while backers of the mufti of Jerusalem, who was then in an alliance with the Egyptian regime, tended to go south, towards Gaza. The Hammamis, however, decided to stay in Jaffa.

But the Haganah (the Israeli armed forces) soon began deporting Arabs from the city. The Hammami family—mother, father, five daughters, and seven sons—were placed on a lorry, along with what possessions they could muster, and driven south. At a crossroads, they were ordered off the lorry and directed toward Gaza. Their possessions remained behind. Said Hammami spent the early years of his exile in Gaza, but later managed to make his way to Lebanon, where he became active in the Palestinian resistance movement. In the early 1970s, he became the official representative in London of the Palestine Liberation Organization (PLO).

Hammami took a keen interest in the political groupings in Britain, and in particular in those that concerned themselves with the Middle East and the Arab-Israeli conflict. He became aware of the activities of a group of anti-Zionist Israelis living in Britain and several other European countries, as they participated in a number of movements together. Some personal contacts were established.

After the October war of 1973, an intense factional struggle erupted within the Palestinian movement over the prospects of what came to be called 'the peaceful solution'. Discussion of closely related matters arose alongside this debate. What is the nature of the Israeli Jewish population? Do they constitute a collection of coreligionists, an ethnic group, a nationality? What rights should they have, if any, in a 'liberated' Palestine? Could anti-Zionist Israeli Jews play any part in the fight against Zionism? Was any cooperation between Israeli Jews and Palestinian Arabs possible, and if so, on what basis?

In 1975, the Socialist Organization in Israel, publishers of the journal *Matzpen*, approached Said Hammami with the proposal that he grant them an interview dealing with some of these questions, to be published in Hebrew in Israel. The interviewer would be Moshé Machover, a member of Matzpen, a founder of *Khamsin* and member of its editorial group, and one of Israel's most active anti-Zionists abroad, who had established friendly personal relations with Hammami in London. Hammami agreed to this request; subsequently, at his suggestion, the interview was transformed into a dialogue, with a more active participation by Machover.

The final text of this dialogue was translated into Hebrew and published by Matzpen in Israel, where it achieved some notoriety. It was also published, in a French translation, in *Khamsin 3*, under the title 'Vivre Ensemble'.

There had, of course, been previous written exchanges of views between Palestinian organizations and Israelis—but these were conducted at long range, so to speak, the participants merely writing articles discussing one another's positions. On the other hand, there had been informal, personal contacts between Israelis and Arabs. But this was the first time that an official representative of the Palestinian movement had agreed, in his official capacity, to engage in a face-to-face exchange of views with an Israeli in a format designed from the outset to produce a discussion intended for publication— and publication in Israel at that. For that reason alone, the dialogue is of historical interest. But its sequel lends it a special poignancy.

Whatever may be said about Hammami's political views on particular points, with which one may agree or not, there is no denying the non-sectarianism of his attitude to the Israeli Jewish population: he recognizes that they constitute a nationality just as much as the Palestinian Arabs, and that they, too, are entitled to national rights in Palestine. To hear a Palestinian spokesman say this was not necessarily congenial to fanatics on both sides. To the Zionist leaders, Said Hammami was just another 'terrorist', an epithet they freely apply to any Arab who fails to grasp the majesty of the Zionist endeavour. To chauvinists in the Arab camp, he was a traitor simply because he saw the Israelis as a people too, and considered some of them potential partners in a struggle against injustice.

In February 1978, Said Hammami was murdered in London. The assassins were never captured, and no organization claimed responsibility for the act. But it was widely assumed at the time that those responsible were members of the Palestinian group led by Abu Nidal, which had split away from the PLO.

Although the conjunctural situation has changed since this dialogue took place, the deeper issues raised in it are as pressing as ever. In that sense, it has lost none of its significance.

To Live Together

Moshé Machover and Said Hammami

Moshé.   If you don't mind, Said, I'll start with questions about the long-term aim of the PLO, the unitary democratic secular state. The first question is very simple. In Yasser Arafat's speech in the UN, and in your article about Palestinian strategy, you say that the Jews now living in Israel are welcome to stay, provided they live together as equals with the Palestinian Arabs. On the other hand, there is that well-known paragraph 6 of the Palestinian Covenant. How do these things square with each other?

Said.   You are right in saying that it is a long-term solution; it cannot be anything but a long-term solution; it cannot happen to-morrow. In paragraph 6 we say that all Jews who were living in Palestine before the Zionist aggression are Palestinians. When did Zionist aggression start? This is not said in the Covenant. If we consider that Zionist aggression started in 1917, then it is true that Jews who were living in Palestine then are Palestinians. Even if we consider that Zionist aggression started in 1947, then again, it is true that Jews then living in Palestine were Palestinians. There was then no state of Israel.

The Convenant was drawn up in 1964 and it was then considered a major step forward in the Palestinians' understanding of the Jewish community in Palestine, in the Middle East, in Israel. Before 1948, the reactionary leadership—the mufti and the rest—considered that only those Jews who had always lived in Palestine (in old Jerusalem, some in Tiberias, and so on) were Palestinians. The rest had no right to be there and they had to go back. In 1964, Shuqairi and the Covenant said that all Jews who came before the aggression are Palestinians. It was a step forward because the Covenant didn't speak of the Jews as a religious group opposing us as a religious group. It was no longer a question of holy war.

The Covenant was the only authorized Palestinian charter until 1970. In 1970, in the political programme, the Palestine National Council decided that all Jews living in Israel could be citizens of the democratic state for which we struggle.

M.   *So the formulation of the 1970 programme supersedes that of Paragraph 6 of the Covenant?*

S.   Yes, of course. I read in the Zionist propaganda that we say that only those Jews who were there before the aggression will be allowed to stay. This is untrue. The Covenant made a statement of fact that only the Jews who were there before Zionist aggression were Palestinians. Now, what about the Jews who came after that? The reply is in the political programme of 1970, which became known last year after Yasser Arafat's speech to the UN, when he said, 'When we think of the Palestine of the future, we have in mind all the Jews living there who wish to live in harmony and peace with us.'

M.   *In your article about Palestinian strategy and also in some other recent articles by people of the PLO, you talk about the Israeli Jews as a people, not as a religious group. In the past, Palestinian spokespeople have always called the Israeli Jews a religious community. This is implicit, for example, in the formula 'democratic secular state in which Muslims, Jews, and Christians can live together'. This often-repeated formula refers to the 'Jews' exactly as it does to the 'Christians' and 'Muslims', in other words, as a religious community. From our point of view, this is a mistake. First of all, the majority of Israeli Jews are not religious and consider themselves not as part of a religious group but as part of a national group. Second, from an objective point of view as well, the Jewish community in Israel possesses a national character, since it has all the usual national characteristics, in particular a language of its own. We reject, of course, the Zionist claim that all the Jews of the world constitute a people. But we do think that the Jews of Israel surely constitute a nationality. It is true that this nationality was artificially created through the Zionist colonization and that this process occurred at the expense of the Palestinian Arab people. But just as a hill created by a bulldozer rather than by natural processes is none the less a hill, so a people created artificially is none the less a people, and this fact cannot be ignored. The question then becomes, How will the national character of the Israeli Jewish people find expression, and what will its status be, in the unitary democratic state? There is also another side to this question, concerning the Palestinian Arabs: they have a national character of their own too; they are a people. How do you envisage the way in which these two national entities will find expression in a common unitary state?*

S.   Well, as you said, I believe, and all progressive Palestinians believe, that the Israeli Jews now living in Palestine constitute a people, a new people, a people that has been created in the fifty years of conflict, but specifically from the mid-forties or so. There is an Israeli working class, there are Israeli progressive organizations. Now, the fact is that there are two peoples: the Palestinian Arab people and the Israeli Jewish people. These two peoples have a just claim to Palestine. I believe that we belong to Palestine, that the country is ours. I also believe that every genuine Israeli Jew, especially those who were born there and have lived there for years and years, believe that they come from this country, that it is their country. I don't blame them for what Herut have done. I don't blame them for what the Zionist reactionary and terrorist organizations did to my country. I don't even blame the present Israeli generation for what their fathers did to me personally, expelling me from my country. But they should also know that we exist as a people and have a just claim to that country. Not a single progressive Palestinian can say to an Israeli Jew, 'You don't have a right to this country.' But not a single Israeli Jew can say to a Palestinian Arab, 'I have more right to this country than you.' We probably have a bit more right to Palestine than the Israeli Jews. The fact is that we both exist as peoples. The question is: Is conflict the only relation possible between these two peoples?

My reply is: Definitely not. This conflict started as a result of the policies and ambitions of the agents of imperialism. On both sides. The reactionary Zionists and reactionary Arabs. The question is now how to bring peace between these two sides, the Palestinian Arabs and the Israeli Jews. They both believe that they belong to one country, so the simple answer is, let them both live in it. How can two peoples with different languages and cultures live together? In a secular state, in a democratic state, in a non-sectarian state, or perhaps in a binational state. But they both must live in the same country. Probably as a first step—and I believe that it is a necessary step, an inevitable step, whether we or they like it or not—Palestine should be partitioned between the two peoples.

I say as a first step, and only as a first step, because it is ridiculous to think of such a tiny area divided permanently into two states. You stand at the mountain of al-Salt and you can see the whole country from Baisan to Wadi 'Araba. You can motor from this side of Palestine to the other in half a day. Apart from the Negev desert, Palestine is a very small country. In the long run, it cannot be divided into two viable independent states. But for the sake of peace between the two peoples, there must be two states as a first step, and from that first step I think the solution will be in the hands of the progressive forces on the two sides.

M. But supposing now that we have managed to unify these two states—I'm talking now about the future. How would the distinct national characters of these two peoples find expression within this unified and common state? I ask this question because the formula repeated so often by PLO spokesmen—'a democratic secular state in which Muslims, Christians, and Jews can live together'—has been rejected by many Israelis who have the best intentions. They would say, more or less: 'The Palestinian Arabs are waging a war of national liberation, and consider themselves as constituting a national community. But on the other hand, they speak of us as only a religious community. It thus seems that they deny the national existence of the Israeli Jews and do not intend to permit this existence in the future.' Recently, you have explicitly spoken of the Israeli Jews as a people. I would like to ask you, Said, whether within this future unified state that you envisage, there will remain national institutions through which the distinct national cultures, different languages, and so on will be expressed?

S. Yes. It is in our political programme. There will be freedom of expression, freedom of faith, there won't be any racial discrimination, no national discrimination, and all people will have the right to form their own political and *national* organizations. I remember in 1971, during the discussion of this first paragraph of our political programme, there was a two-day-long argument about the word 'national'. Do we accept that the Israeli Jews are a nation and have the right to establish their own national organization in the future Palestine? We did accept this.

You remember, you and I used to discuss this point, and I used to ask you how an anti-Zionist would define the people now living in Israel. I remember you once used the expression 'Hebrew-speaking community'. And in fact I used this term for some time. Through our continuing discussion of this point, you and I can now call that community the Israeli Jewish people.

As I have said, the Palestinian programme has accepted the idea that within the future unified Palestine, the Israeli Jews will have the right to their own national organization. They have the right to keep their language, their traditions, their faith, their culture. Once we agree that it must be a democratic state, it must be a real democracy, not the kind of so-called democracy that gives privileges to some people while others are under-privileged.

M.   And of course, on the other hand, one cannot require from the Palestinian Arabs that they sever their contacts and connections with the rest of the Arab world.

S.   Of course. I'm well aware of the fact that the majority of Israeli Jews are afraid of becoming a minority among the Arabs. But there is a fact that all Israelis should know: that Palestine is in the Middle East, in that part of the Middle East that is called the Arab homeland. They, like all the non-Arab minorities who live in the Arab homeland, must have the right to self-determination, self-determination which should not contradict the interest of the greater majority of the people. The Hebrew-speaking community of the present Israel, of the Palestine of the future, must grasp the fact that they are living in the Middle East, not in Europe. They are part of the Arab world. The term 'the Arab world' is not one that I invented. It has been known as such for centuries. The Israeli Jews are a Middle Eastern people. I know that this is a fact that arrogantly reactionary Zionists in particular cannot digest, do not want to face. But if Israel is to have any chance of survival, if the Israeli people is to have any chance of being accepted by the neighbouring Arabs, they must understand this fact and behave in accordance with it.

I, as a progressive, the PLO, as a progressive organization, believe that the Israeli Jews, like the Kurds, like all the non-Arab nationalities living in the Arab homeland, have the right to keep their language, to have their own political and trade-union organizations, to keep their culture, to maintain their religion, and to realize all their traditions, to study their history, and even to maintain their relations with non-Arab people outside the Arab world. In the same way, I believe that the Kurds of Iraq must have the right to keep their relations with the Kurds of Turkey and the Kurds of Russia...

M.   *I think that the right to form separate trade unions for each nationality ought to be excluded from that list. Trade unions are, or anyway should be, class organizations, and should be organized on a supra-national basis.*

You mention the Kurds. Their unhappy existence is often used to show that it is impossible for different peoples to live together. Here are the Kurds in Iraq, and they are being suppressed, and their right to self-determination is not respected. Also, more recently, the events in Lebanon are used by a lot of Zionists to show that living together in a pluralist society does not work.

S.   As for the Kurds, it is very simple. There was a statement by the Central Council of the PLO that supported the Kurdish national movement but at the same time condemned the collaboration of the reactionary elements in the Kurdish leadership with the shah of Iran. We were the first Arab power that warned the Kurdish people that by aligning with a reactionary regime like that of the shah of Iran they would destroy the interest of the whole people of Kurdistan. I can say this with pride: we, the Palestinians, with our experience, came to the conclusion from the beginning of the Kurdish uprising, and we said that if the Kurdish people are ever to have a good future in Kurdistan, their national liberation movement should align itself with the national liberation movement of the Arab people and not with the shah of Iran. We support the right of the Kurds to self-determination. Now about Lebanon. Lebanon is not a secular state at all....

M.   But it was a state composed of different communities having some arrangement to live together. And it does not seem to work.

S.   Yes, It did not work for two reasons. First because it was not secular, and second because it was not socialist.

It could not be a secular state when the president must be a Maronite, the prime minister must be a Sunni Muslim, the leader of the Parliament must be a Shi'i Muslim, the commander of the army must be a Maronite, the chief of staff must be a Druze. This is not a secular state. I think the roots of the latest bloodshed lie in the National Pact of Lebanon, in the so-called gentleman's agreement between the heads of the religious groups. These people were not really religious; it was only class interest. This leads to the second point. It was not a socialist state. What Lebanon has seen lately was inevitable. In a society like this, where the rich got very much richer, especially in the past five years, and the poor got very much poorer, also especially in the past five years, it was very much to be expected. But to say that it was a conflict between Christians and Muslims and Druze is not true. The leader of the Phalangists, the right-wing Maronite Kata'ib, is Pierre Gemayel, and he is a Maronite. All right. But the vice-chairman, Kazem Khalil, is a Shi'i Muslim from the south, from Tyre. The leader of the left-wing, so-called Muslim alliance, is not a Muslim. He is a Druze, Kemal Jumblatt. Another leader of this alliance, Nicola Shaawi, is a Christian, and a third, George Hawi, is a Communist. To say that it is Muslims against Christians is as wrong as it is misleading. From the papers you might think it is between Christians and Muslims, but if you lived there for just five weeks, you would say, 'My god, there must be a civil war one day in this country.' If you see all these great buildings, the shopping areas in Beirut, all the luxury of the West, and then you drive for just five minutes, and you see the slums—and these are Lebanese people! In Lebanon, the number of proper Lebanese people living in camps is double the number of Palestinian refugees living in camps.

M.   Let us now take up a problem relating to the short term. I want to ask you about the demand of the PLO to establish an independent Palestinian authority in the areas from which Israel is compelled to withdraw. Since this is a transitional stage towards the establishment of a unitary state in Palestine, and since, as you say in your document, you hope that the future stage can be achieved by peaceful means, how do you estimate the reality of this demand now, two years after the October war? How realistic do you estimate it to be? It is known that the USSR supports this demand. What about the Americans? Do they support it? Do you know of any steps they have made to indicate support for such a settlement?

S. This should be known very well. When we demand the establishment of a Palestinian state in the West Bank and Gaza, those parts of Palestine from which Israel should withdraw, it is not a conciliatory step, it is a realistic step. Whether there is a peaceful settlement or not, there is a fact we should be aware of: that there is an Israeli Jewish people, and there is a fact they should be aware of: that there is a Palestinian Arab people. And in order to bring these two peoples together to live in one state, there must be, as a first step, two states. The Russians did not support this in the beginning. Now we are very happy to see that the USSR understands us better, and lately *Pravda* has written that they believe that the legitimate rights of the people of Palestine are the central issue of the conflict, and that there won't be peace in the Middle East so long as there is Zionism. This is a very big change in the USSR.

So far, the Americans say that they will not talk to the Palestinians if the Palestinians do not recognize the state of Israel as an independent state and guarantee its future security, integrity, and independence. We never tried to contact the Americans. They tried to contact us indirectly and they wanted some private secret talks. We said no. If you want to talk to us, you talk to us openly. If we do something, we are not ashamed of it, so why do it secretly? No secret talks, no secret deals! And so long as we continue to struggle, I believe that there will come a day, probably soon, when the Americans realize that if they, for their own reasons, want to avoid war, then they will have to speak to us. I can see this day coming.

M. Everyone knows that there are factions within the Palestinian movement, known by the name 'Rejection Front', that oppose this demand for a Palestinian state on any territories that Israel is forced to evacuate. George Habash's Popular Front is part of that faction, as is the group of Ahmed Jibril. On our side of the border as well, some people echo the same rejection. Abroad, some far-left Israelis, as individuals not really representing any group, are opposed to the principle of self-determination in any event—not only in the case of the Israeli Jews or the Palestinian Arabs, but for any people. Also in Israel, there is a Trotskyist group, which split from Matzpen about four years ago and became the Israeli branch of the Trotskyist Fourth International. (This group is sometimes confused with Matzpen, because they sometimes use the same name, although their political line is different.) These Trotskyists, although they accept the principle of self-determination in general, oppose this immediate demand for a Palestinian state.

These advocates of the 'Rejection Front' sometimes claim that the creation of a Palestinian state in any territories Israel is forced to evacuate is no more than one element of an entire arrangement for pax americana, *an objective of American imperialism in the Middle East. What is more, in their eyes, this demand for a Palestinian state has no meaning outside the context of an imperialist settlement. In raising the demand for such a state, they therefore argue, the PLO is making itself an accomplice of American imperialism. Arguments like this have been made on both sides of the border. What have you got to say to this?*

S.   Some of those who say this are American agents who want to sell this idea to the people: that nothing can ever happen without an American OK. So that if a Palestinian state comes into existence, it would be just because the Americans approve it. If there is no state, it is because the Americans don't want it. The idea is that the Americans are like God. If they withdraw from South-East Asia, it is because they had a deal with Russia. This would mean that peoples should go to sleep and do nothing; it is the super-powers who do everything. It is very dangerous, and I always suspect those who preach this idea.

The other sort of people who talk this way are anarchists or ignorant people who don't know what a people's struggle is. Anyone going to the Middle East, to any Palestinian refugee camp, in Lebanon, seeing the people, how they train, how they behave, their morale, and tries to remember how things were, say, ten years ago, can realize the change. This change took place as the result of a long and bloody struggle. If you and I can see this, the Americans can see it. If our demand to establish a Palestinian state is ever ful-filled—and I hope it will be, soon—it will be the result of the bloody struggle of the Palestinian people. To those who say that this will be just a part of *pax americana*, I say this: imperialism, especially American imperialism, has never given a people a homeland or any-thing good. I know of imperialism giving people napalm, death, des-troyed cities, destroyed countries, bloodshed. But they don't give them states. If American imperialism is to become a charity organiz-ation giving the Palestinians a state and giving the South-East Asian people independence, then we will have to change our mind about imperialism. To put it briefly, those who believe that if the Palestinians liberate any part of their country and establish an indep-endent state on it, then it will be part of an American deal, those people should go and see the Palestinian fighters who have been fighting for it for ten years. If this does not convince them, then nothing will.

M.   I also believe—and I think that this is the opinion of the majority of the comrades of Matzpen—that there is no chance of the Americans offering the Palestinian people the slightest independent state on a silver platter, so to speak. The reason flows from the nature of relations between the United States and Israel, and from the fact that the Zionist leadership is opposed in principle to the crea-tion of a Palestinian state.

Today, since the October war of 1973, Israel is no longer the exclu-sive ally of the United States in this part of the world; but it is still the closest and most reliable of Washington's allies. The United States now also has allies among the Arab states. But the relations between the United States and the Arab countries have always been based on exploitation, and that is still the case. Therefore, even if the regime of a given Arab state is at present prepared to collaborate with the United States, there will always exist in this country significant social and historical forces that threaten to shift state policy in an anti-imperialist direction. For Israel, the situation is different. This state is not economically exploited, but subsidized by imperialism. Hence, so long as imperialism remains dominant in the region and is in a position to control Israel, this country will remain a sure ally. The Americans are prepared to exert pressure on the Israeli government and to impose concessions on it here and there, but I think that this pressure will not be so great as to compel the Zionist leadership of Israel to make concessions on what is, for it, a question of principle.

I therefore think that opposition to the creation of any independent Palestinian state is a question of principle for the Zionist leadership. The reason for this rejection is not that they fear such a state militarily, in the short term. The problem is more fundamental. The entire legitimacy of the existence of Israel as a Zionist state has never been based on the right of self-determination of the Jews who live there, but on the so-called historic right of the Jews of the entire world to Palestine. From that starting point, to acknowledge that another people exists in Palestine who can legitimately lay claim to this country would amount to undermining the legitimacy and self-justification of Zionism.

It seems to me clear that for the immense majority of the Zionist leadership—whether in the government or in the right opposition—this is an absolute principle. And given the importance of Israel for American interests in the region, I surmise that the United States will be in no hurry to compel Israel to make any concession on this point, on which the Zionist regime will remain intransigent. Consequently, I also conclude that a Palestinian state is not something that the Americans will hurry to offer the Palestinian people; such a state can arise only from struggle. By the sound of what you just said, I gather that this is your opinion too.

S.   Yes, of course, and it may be a long struggle, and certainly bloody. It is a demand: that is the correct word. We demand the establishment of a Palestinian society, a Palestinian authority, a Palestinian state on any part of Palestine that we can liberate. Once this is established, there will be a new atmosphere, a new situation, that might require a new strategy.

I find that the rejectionists confuse the slogan, the demand, and the aim. Our slogan is 'Revolution until victory!'. Our demand is the establishment of an independent Palestinian state in any part of Palestine that is liberated. And our aim is the establishment of one united, secular, non-sectarian Palestine in which *all* the Israeli Jews and *all* the Palestinian Arabs can live democratically, according to 'one man, one vote'. We should not mix up these three things, or else we shall be misled into the realm of the Arabian Nights, of Alladin.

Because of what has happened in the Middle East during the past two years, the number of people who believe that this Palestinian state will be established as a result of *pax americana* is becoming very small, and these days I see hardly any of them around.

M.   Some further questions connected with this demand for a Palestinian authority, a Palestinian state. The first is this: I can see how the establishment of such an authority will give some satisfaction to those people now living under Israeli occupation. But what about the Palestinian refugees of 1948, those living in Jordan on the East Bank, in Lebanon, and other places? How will this relate to their *problem? We members of Matzpen, along with other progressive groups and organizations within Israel, struggle for the right of the Palestinian people to create its own state, as a part of its right to self-determination. But at the same time, we think that the creation of a Palestinian state in the West Bank and Gaza would* directly *satisfy the needs of only that part of the Palestinian people which lives in the occupied territory. In our view, for those who live outside Palestine, other demands must be added. In fact, isn't there a danger, as some people say, that if a Palestinian authority is established, then some of the Arab governments will try to expel the Palestinians living in their countries, so that rather than helping these people, the establishment of such a state may be detrimental to them?*

S.   Nothing could be worse than the *present* life of the refugees of 1948. The establishment of a Palestinian state cannot make things worse. Things will be much worse if such a state is *not* established. Some people say that the Arab states will expel the Palestinian refugees to this newly established state. Well, the Arab states won't have to expel them; *we* will *ask* them all to come and live in their own country, in their own Palestine. There is something about us, the Palestinian people, that everyone should understand; it is not that I come from Jaffa or Acre or Nablus or Jerusalem. I come from *Palestine.* I am a Palestinian. And this state will be a part of Palestine and it is going to be called the Democratic State of Palestine. We believe in a democratic state over all of Palestine, and if we take one inch we will call it the Democratic State of Palestine, and it will be a democratic state. And as I said in my paper, I would like to see this state welcome any Jew who wants to come and live with us without discrimination. We shall have our own law of return, but it will not be a racist, reactionary law of return. It is going to be a democratic progressive law, and we want as many Palestinians as possible to come and live in their country. I can't see any logic in the argument of those who say that the establishment of such a state will endanger the interests of the 1948 refugees.

M.   But what about their right to return to the other side of the border? The part that will be in Israel, within the pre-1967 borders? Ever since the formation of Matzpen, about five years before the 1967 war, we have fought for the right of the refugees of 1948 to return to their homes. We believe that this demand is equally just today, and we fight for it, while at the same time supporting the right of the Palestinian people to create an independent state.

S.   Yes, their right must be maintained. I believe that in principle everyone should have the right to live and work anywhere. This is in the Human and Civil Rights Charter of the United Nations. But let us take an example. In 1948, seventy thousand people were expelled from Jaffa and became refugees. I was one of them, and I was physically expelled. I remember it very well, in great detail. My father, my mother, all my family, we remember it in detail. Now, if we bring these seventy thousand people to Jaffa tomorrow, and I am one of them, I am sure that the next day there will be a civil war. We will come to a town called Jaffa that will be very new to us; we will find people living in our homes; we don't speak their language, and they don't speak ours. We have different cultures, and this background of violence cannot be a very good step towards coexistence.
    . So I say, let us have a state. This would draw the poison out of the hatred. This would relax the exaggerated alarm of the Israeli Jews; this would reduce the tension among the Palestinians. And then give it time: ten, fifteen years. In ten or fifteen years, the Israeli Jews will find out what nice people we are—and I really believe in this. They will realize that we are not monsters, but people like them; that there are many things that make us friendly, many things that make us happy, that there are many things that we would die for: first freedom, and we have been dying for freedom for the last ten years. We want them to know this. But what is more important than all this is

that the progressive organizations among the Palestinians and the Israelis will have a much better atmosphere for struggling, for a dialogue.

Today, with this alarming slogan that the 'enemy is at the gates', progressive Israelis cannot speak freely to progressive Palestinians, and vice versa. Not because we, the PLO, do not want to speak to progressive Israelis. But even when we want to speak to them, we have to go to Europe. We can't go to Israel and we can't invite them to any Arab country. If we have our own state, we can invite them to our capital, they can come and talk to us there. And this will, of course, disarm all those right-wing chauvinists in the Zionist movement in Israel, and it will also disarm or weaken the already weak position of the right-wing chauvinists among us. This is another reason why I believe that a Palestinian state must be a necessary first step. We, the PLO, know very well—and this is in our documents—that in all our meetings we issue greetings to all the progressive elements in Israeli society. Why can't we invite them to our meetings? Simply because our meetings are held outside Palestinian territory. It is not our territory, we are guests there. If we had a state, it would make dialogue much easier, and it would make it easier for them to struggle against Zionism.

M.   I would like to mention another portion of the Palestinian people: those living in Israel within the pre-1967 borders. Some members of Matzpen are members of this community, and many Arab workers, students, and peasants in Israel read our publications. In other words, we know the problems of this community close up. We support—and we have always supported—their double struggle: against discrimination and the negation of their individual rights, and against the negation of their national rights as members of the Palestinian Arab people. The members of this community, about half a million strong, are Israelis in the legal sense. But from a national point of view, and in the light of their own consciousness, they are part of the Palestinian Arab people. It does not seem that the creation of a Palestinian state in the territories Israel is compelled to withdraw from would directly improve their lot. What about their right to self-determination?

*S.   We are very much concerned with what happens to the

Palestinians living in Israel, but we believe that the immediate problem facing us is not them. Their problem is a big one, but the biggest problem is that of the refugees and the people living under occupation in the West Bank and Gaza, because there is a Palestinian society that the Zionists are trying to destroy. If that society were destroyed, it would be the greatest setback to the Palestinians. I personally think that if we establish a Palestinian state on part of Palestine, we should say: Because we believe in the reunification of Palestine, anyone with Israeli citizenship can also have Palestinian citizenship. And I hope that this will be reciprocated. Of course, the Zionist authorities of Israel will say, 'No, we want an exclusive Jewish state.' But this would be an objective and realistic demand for progressive people in Israel to raise. And without the immediate danger of war, the atmosphere for struggling for this demand will be better.

The Palestinian people in Israel were once called 'Israeli Arabs'. When we began struggling, they became Palestinian again. The Israeli authorities realized that they were no longer Israeli Arabs, but that they now define themselves as Palestinians. I think that their identification as Palestinian will become stronger when there is a Palestinian state. As I have already said, there will be a new atmosphere in the Middle East: you won't be in danger of being called up to the army at any moment; I, living in a camp, won't be in danger of being bombed by napalm at any moment. For the Palestinians inside Israel, this will be a major step forward for consolidating their national identity.

The problem of the Palestinians in Israel is one more reason why I think that a Palestinian state is just a first step. It should be followed by further steps, to consolidate peace. It is only a first step because it is not going to solve all the problems. But—and I will never tire of repeating this again and again—it will create a new atmosphere of understanding.

The establishment of such a state will also be a major retreat for Zionism. I, as a Palestinian, whose entity was ignored, who was never accepted as a Palestinian, I know what it would mean to the Zionist authorities to recognize the existence of the Palestinian people, and our right to have our own state in Palestine. For Zionism, to recognize us would be a great retreat. We hope that by struggle we will gain such recognition. By struggle only. To go back to what we were talking about before, about the rejectionists, they should realize what it is for a Zionist, especially members of the Israeli cabinet, to recognize us as a people, and to acknowledge our right to have a state. To many of them this would mean the end of Israel. In fact, I know that it is not going to be the end of Israel. The state of Israel will probably continue to exist for four or five decades after the establishment of a Palestinian state. But it might be the beginning of the end of Zionism. The beginning of the de-Zionization of the state of Israel.

M.   I now have a delicate question. You have spoken of the Israeli Jews as a national entity. You did so both in this discussion and in your article, which, I should mention, we have published in Israel, in Hebrew. Is this just your personal opinion or is it the opinion of part of the PLO, or the whole PLO? Are these things also said in Arabic?

S.   I wrote this paper about Palestinian strategy while I was an official representative of the PLO. That was about ten months ago— and so far I am still an official representative. I signed this paper 'Said Hammami, PLO representative'. If you represent an organization, then what you say should represent the organization. However, I am not a civil servant. We are not a bureaucratic organization with ambassadors and civil servants who just echo what is said in head-quarters. I am also a member of the Palestine National Council (PNC), I am also a member of Fatah, and what I said in that paper had enough support within the PLO and Fatah to keep me in my position. If it did not have the support of a substantial majority, I could not have remained a PLO representative.

It is true that it is not the official position of the PLO. The rejectionists' policy is also not the official position of the PLO. But the difference is that the rejectionists have never had an official PLO representative expressing their views, while there are many PLO representatives who speak the way I do. I have the support of the majority of the Palestinians, the Democratic Front supports me, the great majority of Fatah supports me. I am very proud to say that when Chairman Arafat was asked about my paper, he said, 'I read it and I think it is full of logic, full of logical proposals.' He was also asked whether this was official PLO policy. He said, 'It is not, but it is full of logic.' What he meant is clear. In the next meeting of the Palestine National Council, I shall present my paper and propose it for official endorsement by the PNC, and I hope it will be endorsed.

M.   I have another difficult question. Let me first make it clear that we in Matzpen thoroughly denounce the cruel actions of the Israeli army, very often against civilians, including women and children—indiscriminate bombing of civilian populations and of refugee camps, for instance. Having said this, I would like to ask what you think of such actions as the one carried out in Ma'alot, and similar incidents, in which the victims were civilians, especially children? I am not asking about the legitimacy of armed struggle, which is another issue. I am asking about the specific choice of civilian targets, especially children.

S.   Like you, I denounce the killing of civilians, especially children, women, and old people, whatever the circumstances. But I also believe that the Christian-like attitude of standing up to condemn terrorism and then sitting down with a clear conscience is as facile as it is futile. It means nothing. Without finding the roots of the conflict you cannot put an end to it. Terrorism is just a symptom of the real disease, which is aggression, which is Zionism, which is the destruction of Palestinian society, which is the creation of a state in the Middle East on the ruins of Palestinian society. If we do not start from this point, we will get nowhere. There is a conflict, there is a war, between us and the Israeli establishment; and in the course of this war many crimes have been committed. It is ironic to hear some Zionists talking about the Palestinians as terrorists, because terrorism was brought to the Middle East by the Zionists. Take a man like Yalin-Mor—a terrorist. My friend Abdullah al-Hourani told me that during a conference in Paris, Yalin-Mor stood up and said: 'I am a terrorist, and I killed civilians. I bombed, I burned, I shelled civilian targets, and I know very well that without terrorism there would not have been a state of Israel. You, the Palestinians, are now engaged in terrorism; it could be justified, but I want to tell you that politically it is not doing you any good, because it pushes the Israeli public into the arms of the establishment.'

Many of the leaders of this present Israeli establishment are ex-terrorists, aren't they? Perhaps all of them are: Allon and Rabin were in the Palmach, Begin was the leader of the Irgun, and so on. Under British law they were all terrorists. As for Ma'alot, the real criminal was Dayan, who misled the Israeli cabinet about the intentions of the Palestinians from the Democratic Front. He then gave the troops an order to start shooting, and the children were killed in the cross-fire. I don't want this to be understood as if I am justifying terrorism. I cannot accept terrorism, not only for moral but also for political reasons. Because I am a progressive Palestinian, and I believe that if you kill Israelis indiscriminately, you are playing into the hands of the Zionist establishment. Our enemy is Zionism, not all the Israelis. But I want to say that if the Israeli public does not realize that in this state of conflict any one of their children might be killed, exactly as any one of the Palestinian children might be killed by the Israeli air force, if they don't realize this and also grasp that this killing can be stopped only by a peaceful solution—then terrorism will go on, and I am afraid that it might become worse.

M.   To conclude, I would like to raise another point. We in Matzpen have never regarded ourselves as working for a separate and isolated revolution inside Israel, but as part of the revolutionary forces of the entire region, of the whole Arab East. Our aim is the creation of a socialist union of the entire Arab East, a union in which all the non-Arab nationalities living in the region can participate, on a basis of equality and respect for their rights. For us, our support to all the just struggles of the region—and most particularly to the fight being waged by the Palestinian Arab people for their national and social liberation—is a matter not merely of abstract solidarity, but of close participation. In this respect, I would like to ask: what can the progressive and anti-chauvinist forces on both sides do? In particular, what can be done in a co-ordinated way, towards a common goal?

S.   Well, we don't give lessons. I think the progressive organizations in Israel should themselves say what they can do. We can't tell them. They know their society better than we do. We don't believe in giving lessons or in taking them. But once we and they agree on basic and fundamental facts, we and they can be sure that we are going in the right direction. I think that they have a very great role to play. It takes a lot of courage for any Israeli Jew to stand up in

Israel and say: 'Look, fellow Israelis, you have got to withdraw, you have got to negotiate with the Palestinians, they must have their own state, and the state must be a first step towards the reunification of Israel-Palestine, of the whole country.'

What can we do together? Well, they can help us in educating our masses and we can help them to educate their masses. We need to know more about Israeli society, and they need to know more about Palestinian society. We need to know more facts about the Israeli working class, about the future potential of that society, and they need to know similar facts about us. If it was not a crime under Israeli law, we would invite progressive anti-Zionist Israelis to come and participate with us in the PNC. We believe that the PLO, as an organization struggling for a united secular Palestine, should itself be a reflection in miniature of that envisaged society, and that is why we would invite all progressive anti-Zionist elements in Israel to come and participate in planning our policy. This might sound a bit optimistic. It is. But first we need to know more about each other. We need a continuous dialogue. Then we can cooperate in publicizing their literature among our masses, and they can publicize our literature among their masses. A lot can be done together, but first we need a common understanding.

M.   Thank you very much, Said. I hope that our discussion today may contribute to this understanding and this dialogue.